GOSPEL THEATER

THE GOSPEL PLAYERS' SCRIPT BOOK

The Four Gospels, the Acts of the Apostles, & 13 other Bible chapters in character parts

Edited by Sister Mary Rose Reddy, DMML

GOSPEL THEATER

Daughters of Mary, Mother of Healing Love
279 Cartier St.
Manchester, NH 03102
www.motherofhealinglove.org
1st edition 2026
Revised with catechetical correlations and
additional Scripture chapters added 2026.

The Crucial Path LLC
Aster Rd
Sycamore, IL
www.thecrucialpath.com
info@thecrucialpath.com
www.gospeltheater.org
Print ISBN: 978-1-967865-09-3
Digital ISBN: 978-1-967865-10-9
Cover Image: Lee Fredrickson

The Purchase of this book includes A license to use the material as follows:
Gospel Theater: The Gospel Players' Script Book is a unique resource that presents the entire unabridged four Gospels, the Acts of the Apostles, and 13 other salvation history chapters of the Bible in character parts. The Scripture translation is the Ignatius Revised Standard Version, Second Catholic Edition (RSV-2CE). A license to perform each play is included with the purchase of this book.

Bishop's Recommendation

You are invited to deepen your knowledge and understanding of the Sacred Scriptures by using *Gospel Theater* to enter personally into the drama and life changing words of the *Holy Gospels* and the *Acts of the Apostles*. I recommend this book to families, OCIA, Bible study groups, youth groups, faith formation classes, and people of all ages. May God bless all who make use of this book and may the Holy Spirit use it to draw souls ever more deeply into the "words of eternal life" given by Jesus Christ, the Bridegroom, to His Bride, the Church!

—Most Rev. Peter A. Libasci, D.D.
Bishop of Manchester

Endorsement

Gospel Theater is a masterful blend of catechetical depth and spiritual resonance. Sr Mary Rose Reddy offers educators and parents a transformative resource rooted in fidelity to Sacred Scripture and animated by pastoral sensitivity. By dramatizing Gospel passages using the exact words of Scripture—never paraphrased—this work invites a direct, unfiltered encounter with Christ. The result is not only pedagogically rich but spiritually healing.

Drawing from the charism of the Daughters of Mary, Mother of Healing Love, this book is more than a teaching tool—it is a catechesis of the heart, stirring imaginations and opening pathways to understanding, formation, and healing.

Gospel Theater deserves a place in the libraries of all families and Catholic educators. It is a gift to the Church: crafted with clarity, conviction, and reverent love for the Word of God.

—Dr Gerard O'Shea
Professor of Religious Education, University of Notre Dame, Australia

Dedication

Gospel Theater is dedicated to the Most Holy Trinity through St. Joseph and Our Lady of Champion. On October 7, 2025, the feast of Our Lady of the Holy Rosary, Brian Truckenbrod and Sister Mary Rose Reddy, DMML, dedicated the whole work and future fruit of *Gospel Theater* to Our Blessed Mother at her Shrine in Champion, Wisconsin, USA.

On October 9, 1859, Our Blessed Mother appeared to Belgian immigrant Adele Brice in what is now Champion, Wisconsin, with this request:

> "Gather the children in this wild country and teach them what they should know for salvation. Teach them, their catechism, how to sign themselves with the sign of the Cross, and how to approach the sacraments; that is what I wish you to do. Go and fear nothing, I will help you."[1]

May Our Heavenly Father, through the Gift of His Divine Word and Holy Spirit use *Gospel Theater* to deepen our understanding of the catechism, how to approach the sacraments, and what we should know for salvation.

May our Lady of Champion, who miraculously stopped the Peshtigo fire at the border of her shrine on October 8, 1871, draw the Fire of her Spouse the Holy Spirit into the hearts of all who use this book. May He consume all the destructive fires of sin in our hearts, allowing our hearts to burn within us while Jesus speaks to us on the Way and explains to us the Scriptures *(cf. Lk 24:32).*

---

1. *Our Story* The National Shrine of Our Lady of Champion, February 14, 2026, https://championshrine.org/our-story/.

Acknowledgements

The primary acknowledgement for *Gospel Theater* and all its derivative books goes to Jesus Christ, present in the Most Blessed Sacrament. It is He, Who over the course of months and years has inspired the step by step refinement of *Gospel Theater* until it has become an instrument for bringing people of all ages into relationship with Himself, the Living Word of God.

Once when I was in His Eucharistic Presence I asked Jesus, "Why, with so many cateehetical programs, are we failing to keep people in the Catholic faith? It seemed to me that He replied, "It would be as if St. Andrew, instead of bringing to me the boy who had five loaves and two fishes, had said to himself, 'I have to find a way to feed these five thousand men with these five loaves of bread.'" I understood from this that just as St. Andrew brought that boy with his limited resources to Jesus Christ, so we as catechists need to bring all the people entrusted to us with all their (and our) limited resources to Him—Who is the Living Word of God. Then we will marvel to see Him feed the multitudes!

Additionally I acknowledge our Blessed Mother, St. Joseph, St. Peter, St. Mary Magdalene, St. Philomena, St. Padre Pio, St. Therese, St. Agatha, Servant of God Father John A. Hardon, SJ (d. 2000), all the Holy Angels, and particularly my Guardian Angel for their support and guidance. Without the influence of Servant of God Father John A. Hardon, SJ, the idea of correlating the 130 Scripture Chapters of *Gospel Theater* to cited paragraphs in the *Catechism of the Catholic Church* would most likely not have occurred to me. In the early 1980s Fr. Hardon came often to Baltic, CT to the Sisters of Charity of Our Lady, Mother of the Church *(which was the community to which I belonged before we formed the Daughters of Mary, Mother of Healing Love in 2003)*. Fr. Hardon taught us the faith with extreme clarity and he urged us to memorize Scripture *(advising either the Confraternity or the Jerusalem Bible translation)*. He warned that if we did not do this then our faith would "be at the mercy of the translators." Because I took Fr. Hardon's advice to memorize Scripture seriously I developed a great love for accurate, complete translations of Sacred Scripture and their intrinsic power for communicating the new wine of the Holy Spirit to our thirsty souls.

2. cf. Jn 6:1–13.

Special acknowledgement is due to my friend, Brian Truckenbrod —whose support and guidance in this project has been inestimable! Special thanks are also owed to: Bishop Peter A. Libasci, Fr. Paul Gousse, Msgr. Marc Montminy, Fr. Moe LaRochelle, David Thibault, Dr. Gerard O'Shea, Sr. Mary Michael Fox, OP, Lee Fredrickson, John Jelinek, the Jacobo family, Julie Johnson, Lori Smith, Marilyn Yorke, the Sisters of Charity of Our Lady, Mother of the Church, and my beloved community—the Daughters of Mary, Mother of Healing Love!

I also need to acknowledge St. John Paul II, Pope Benedict XVI and all those who worked on the *Catechism of the Catholic Church*—particularly on the Index of Scripture citations. I wish to thank Dr. Scott Hahn and all the other scholars for their work producing *The Ignatius Catholic Study Bible* and published by Ignatius Press and National Council of Churches. And I acknowledge the inventors of Microsoft Excel—since I could not have completed the correlations to the *Catechism of the Catholic Church* without the help of that program.

Key to CCC themes for Table of Contents

The following correlation charts enable readers to connect the 130 Scripture chapters that are in Gospel Theater to cited themes in the *Catechism of the Catholic Church* (CCC).

Keep in mind, though, that since Sacred Scripture is the Infinite Word of God, there are no limits to the number of cross references that could be made between the teachings of the Church and the God breathed words of Sacred Scripture;—but these are listed because they are the ones the Church has chosen to cite in the *Catechism of the Catholic Church.*

CCC Themes Citations Key

PLG–Prologue (CCC 1–25)
Q–Quest
Q1–Man's Capacity for God (CCC 26–49)
Q2–God Comes to Meet Man (CCC 50–141)
Q3–Man's Response to God (CCC 142–197)

F1–1st Article Creed: I believe in God, the Father almighty, Creator of heaven and earth, (CCC 198–421)
F2–2nd Article Creed: And in Jesus Christ, his only Son, our Lord, (CCC 422–455)
F3–3rd Article Creed: Who was conceived by the Holy Spirit, born of the Virgin Mary, (CCC 456–570)
F4–4th Article Creed: Suffered under Pontius Pilate, was crucified, died and was buried; (CCC 571–630)
F5–5th Article Creed: He descended into hell; on the third day he rose again from the dead; (CCC 631–658)
F6–6th Article Creed: He ascended into heaven, and is seated at the right hand of God the Father almighty; (CCC 659–667)
F7–7th Article Creed: From there he will come to judge the living and the dead. (CCC 668–682)
F8–8th Article Creed: I believe in the Holy Spirit, (CCC 683–747)
F9–9th Article Creed: The holy Catholic Church, the communion of saints, (CCC 748–975)
F10–10th Article Creed: The forgiveness of sins, (CCC 976–987)
F11–11th Article Creed: The resurrection of the body, (CCC 988–1019)
F12–12th Article Creed: And life everlasting. Amen. (CCC 1020–1065)

LT–Celebration Christian Mystery—Liturgy (CCC 1066–1212)

S1–1st Sacrament: Baptism (CCC 1213–1284)

S2–2nd Sacrament: Confirmation (CCC 1285–1321)
S3–3rd Sacrament: Holy Eucharist (CCC 1322–1419)
S4–4th Sacrament: Reconciliation (CCC 1420–1498)
S5–5th Sacrament: Anointing of the Sick (CCC 1499–1532)
S6–6th: Sacrament: Holy Orders (CCC 1533–1600)
S7–7th Sacrament: Matrimony (CCC 1601–1666)

STL–Sacramentals (CCC 1667–1690)

LC–Life in Christ (CCC 1691–2083)

C1–1st Commandment: I am the Lord your God. You shall not have other gods besides me. (CCC 2083–2141)
C2–2nd Commandment: You shall not take the name of the Lord, your God, in vain. (CCC 2142–2167)
C3–3rd Commandment: Remember to keep holy the Lord's day. (CCC 2168–2196)
C4–4th Commandment: Honor your father and your mother. (CCC 2197–2257)
C5–5th Commandment: You shall not kill. (CCC 2258–2330)
C6–6th Commandment: You shall not commit adultery. (CCC 2331–2400)
C7–7th Commandment: You shall not steal. (CCC 2401–2463)
C8–8th Commandment: You shall not bear false witness against your neighbor. (CCC 2464–2513)
C9–9th Commandment: You shall not covet your neighbor's wife. (CCC 2514–2533)
C10–10th Commandment: You shall not covet your neighbor's goods. (CCC 2534–2557)

P–Christian Prayer (CCC 2558–2776)

P1–1st Petition of Lord's Prayer: Our Father, Who art in heaven, Hallowed be Thy Name. (CCC 2777–2815)
P2–2nd Petition of Lord's Prayer: Thy Kingdom come. (CCC 2816–2821)
P3–3rd Petition of Lord's Prayer: Thy Will be done, on earth as it is in Heaven. (CCC 2822–2827)
P4–4th Petition of Lord's Prayer: Give us this day our daily bread. (CCC 2828–2837)
P5–5th Petition of Lord's Prayer: And forgive us our trespasses, as we forgive those who trespass against us. (CCC 2838–2845)
P6–6th Petition of Lord's Prayer: And lead us not into temptation, (CCC 2846–2849)
P7–7th Petition of Lord's Prayer: But deliver us from evil. Amen. (CCC 2850–2865)

Table of Contents

Old Testament Salvation History Chapters

The Gospel of St. Matthew

The Gospel of St. Mark

The Gospel of St. Luke

The Gospel of St. John

The Acts of the Apostles

~ The Arrest of Stephen (Acts 6:8–15) 374

Revelation 11 and 12

Introduction

Calling Upon God the Holy Spirit

The Holy Spirit is the primary Author of Sacred Scripture.[3] During their forty years of wandering in the desert, the Israelites were led by a pillar of cloud during the day which turned to a pillar of fire during the night.[4] Since the Heart of Christ was opened on Calvary and the Father poured out the Holy Spirit on Pentecost, the People of God have been led by God's own Holy Spirit.

Before entering into "all the treasures of wisdom and knowledge"[5] that are hid in Christ, the Incarnate Word of God, it is essential to call upon the Holy Spirit. Here is one traditional prayer to Him:

Prayer to the Holy Spirit

Come, Holy Spirit, fill the hearts of your faithful
and kindle in them the fire of your love.

Send forth your Spirit and they shall be created,
and you shall renew the face of the earth.

Let us pray.

O God, who have taught the hearts of the faithful
by the light of the Holy Spirit,
grant that in the same Spirit we may be truly wise
and ever rejoice in his consolation.

Through Christ our Lord. Amen.

---

3. *Catechism of the Catholic Church*, 2nd ed. (Vatican City: Libreria Editrice Vaticana, 1997), § 105, February 14, 2026, https://www.vatican.va/archive/ENG0015/_INDEX.HTM.

4. Ex 13:21–22.

5. Col 2:3.

Asking the Intercession of the Saints and Angels

Each of us has been created male or female in the image of God —Who is Three Persons. For this reason we are created to be in relation and we find our personal identity through self-gift to other persons.[6] The human persons who have fully realized the power of self-gift are the saints. The angelic persons who have fully realized this truth are the holy angels—one of whom has been personally assigned to each one of us as a guardian angel.[7] Just as you wouldn't decide to build your own plane if you had to fly across the ocean, so you shouldn't assume that you can easily find your way home to God without the help of these trailblazers.

The two primary saints whom Jesus gave to us as spiritual parents, as He was dying on the Cross, are Mary, His Mother and her husband Joseph.[8] As St. John Paul II explains this:

> We see that at the beginning of the New Testament, as at the beginning of the Old, there is a married couple. But whereas Adam and Eve were the source of evil which was unleashed on the world, Joseph and Mary are the summit from which holiness spreads all over the earth.[9]

Let's always remember to ask the help of our spiritual parents, all the holy saints and angels, and especially our guardian angels! They are more certain highway guides to eternal joy than the most refined GPS systems are for the highways of the earth. An ideal way to begin a *Gospel Theater* session is by meditating on one of the twenty Mysteries of the Holy Rosary. See *Suggested Scriptures for the Rosary Mysteries* at the end of this book.

---

6. Second Vatican Council, *Pastoral Constitution on the Church in the Modern World (Gaudium et Spes)*, December 7, 1965, no. 24, accessed February 14, 2026, https://www.vatican.va/archive/hist_councils/ii_vatican_council/documents/vat-ii_const_19651207_gaudium-et-spes_en.html.
7. Matt. 18:10.
8. Cf. John 19:26–27.
9. John Paul II, *Redemptoris Custos: Apostolic Exhortation on the Person and Mission of Saint Joseph in the Life of Christ and of the Church*, August 15, 1989, sec. 7, https://www.vatican.va/content/john-paul-ii/en/apost_exhortations/documents/hf_jp-ii_exh_15081989_redemptoris-custos.html.

The Power of Gospel Theater

"All scripture is inspired by God and profitable for teaching,..." *(2 Tm 3:16).*

Gospel Theater is for families, Bible study groups, OCIA, classes, and all those who desire to dive more deeply into the Infinite Treasury of the Word of God.

Allow the Power of the Holy Spirit to perfect you in unity[10] as you ***read the Sacred Scriptures together in character parts*** and delve into related paragraphs from the *Catechism of the Catholic Church*[11] (CCC) and the *Ignatius Catholic Study Bible.*

Gospel Theater includes, ***in character parts,*** these 130 RSV–2CE chapters of Sacred Scripture:

1. Genesis Chapters 1, 2, 3, 22, and 45
2. Exodus Chapters 3 and 14
3. Deuteronomy Chapters 5 and 6
4. 2 Samuel Chapter 7
5. Matthew Chapters 1–28
6. Mark Chapters 1–16
7. Luke Chapters 1–24
8. John Chapters 1–21
9. Acts of the Apostles Chapters 1–28
10. Revelation Chapters 11, 12, and 22

The 586 subsection ttitles of *Gospel Theater*'s 130 Scripture chapters correspond with the subheading titles, chapters and verses of the *Ignatius Catholic Study Bible.* This precise correspondence with the *Ignatius Catholic Study Bible* is intended to encourage *Gospel Theater* readers to access this beautiful resource with its insightful footnotes and commentaries—particularly as they relate to the subsections of the Sacred Scriptures that are being read together in character parts.

---

10. cf. Jn 17:23.
11. *Catechism of the Catholic Church*, 2nd ed. (Vatican City: Libreria Editrice Vaticana, 1997), § 1234, accessed February 23, 2026, https://www.vatican.va/archive/ENG0015/_INDEX.HTM.

Study CCC Themes using *Gospel Theater*

All the major themes in the CCC's 2865 paragraphs can be studied using *Gospel Theater*.

The subsection titles in *Gospel Theater* include *(in addition to the same wording as the Ignatius Catholc Study Bible subtitles)* theme codes followed by dashes indicating specific CCC paragraph numbers where Scripture verses within that subsection have been cited.

The 586 Scripture subsections in *Gospel Theater* have been correlated by 45 theme codes to 702 specific CCC paragraphs which cite verses within those subsections.

Gospel Theater is limited to just two citations of the CCC in those Scripture subsections containing more than two; but a star preceding the subheading indicates that there are more CCC citations than the two listed. Beneficial research includes finding the other CCC citations for the starred subheadings by referring to the *Catechism of the Catholic Church* Index of Citations Sacred Scripture (available online or at the back of the large editions of the *Catechism*).[12] If the subsection has been cited in the CCC, the specific *Catechism* paragraph and cited Sripture verses for up to two of these citations are indicated in both the Table of Contents and within the text itself.

When using the various scripts, you will notice occasional script adaptations for teaching purposes. Sometimes speaking roles are given to people not actually speaking in the given text, but who are being quoted. This helps students to better grasp the connection between various people and events in the Bible.

***Gospel Theater* readers can find Scripture subsections related to any CCC theme by using the following theme code chart.**

How to Read the Theme Code Chart

The 45 theme codes which have been assigned to cover the 2865 paragraphs of the CCC are in bold font. Following them in regular font are specific CCC paragraphs numbers and the specific Scripture verses which they cite.

For example, here is one of the themes and its entries:

F10.–The forgiveness of sins; CCC 976–987

F10–976; Jn 20:22–23
F10–977; Mk 16:15–16
F10–981; Lk 24:47
F10–982; Mt 18:21–22

F10 is the theme code for the tenth article of the Apostles' Creed which is "The forgiveness of sins." This theme is discussed in CCC paragraphs 976–987.

1. F10–976; Jn 20:22–23—means that the theme "The Forgiveness of sins," is cited in CCC paragraph 976 in reference to Jn 20:22–23.

2. F10–977; Mk 16:15–16—means that the theme "The Forgiveness of sins," is cited in CCC paragraph 977 in reference to Mk 16:15–16.

3. F10–981; Lk 24:47—means that the theme "The Forgiveness of sins," is cited in CCC paragraph 981 in reference to Lk 24:47.

4. F10–982; Mt 18:21–22—means that the theme "The Forgiveness of sins," is cited in CCC paragraph 982 in reference to Mt 18:21–2

Readers desiring to study the theme of forgiveness of sins can first pray to the Holy Spirit for enlightenment, then read in character parts the Scripture subsections which include the CCC cited verses.

Afterwards they can read the CCC cited paragraphs (and also consult footnotes in the *Ignatius Catholic Study Bible* relating to those Scriptures). Prayer and discussion can follow relating to insights they have received into the theme of the forgiveness of sins.

CCC Theme Codes with paragraph numbers and cited Scripture verses

PLG.–Prologue; CCC 1–25
- PLG–2; Mk 16:20
- PLG–3; Acts 2:42
- PLG–14; Mt 10:32

PF1.–Man's Capacity for God; CCC 26–49
- PF1–28; Acts 17:26–28
- PF1–29; Mt 13:22
- PF1–32; Acts 14:17

PF2.–God Comes to Meet Man; CCC 50–141
- PF2–57; Acts 17:26–28
- PF2–58; Jn 11:52
- PF2–58; Lk 21:24
- PF2–70; Gen 3:14–19
- PF2–74; Jn 14:6
- PF2–87; Lk 10:16
- PF2–89; Jn 8:31–32
- PF2–91; Jn 16:13

PF3.–Man's Response to God; CCC 142–197
- PF3–64; Lk 1:38
- PF3–129; Mk 12:28–34
- PF3–151; Mk 1:11
- PF3–151; Mk 9:7
- PF3–153; Mt 16:17, 18–19
- PF3–161; Mt 10:22
- PF3–161; Mt 24:12, 13
- PF3–162; Lk 17:3–4
- PF3–162; Lk 22:32

F1.–I believe in God, the Father almighty, Creator of heaven and earth; CCC 198–421
- F1–202; Mk 12:35–37
- F1–205; Ex 3:5, 6
- F1–208; Lk 5:8
- F1–226; Mt 16:24
- F1–238; 2 Sm 7:14
- F1–241; Jn 1:1
- F1–243; Jn 14:26
- F1–268; Gen 1:1, 2
- F1–308; Jn 15:5
- F1–312; Gen 45:8
- F1–330; Lk 20:36, 39
- F1–332; Gen 22:8, 11
- F1–333; Mk 1:12–13
- F1–333; Mt 2:19
- F1–333; Mt 26:53
- F1–334; Acts 10:3–8
- F1–334; Acts 12:6–11
- F1–334; Acts 27:23–25
- F1–334; Acts 8:26–29, 37
- F1–342; Mt 12:12
- F1–363; Mt 26:36–44
- F1–368; Dt 6:5
- F1–368; Lk 8:13–15
- F1–369; Gen 2:7
- F1–385; Lk 11:20, 21–22
- F1–391; Jn 8:44
- F1–391; Rev 12:9
- F1–394; Mt 4:1–11

F2.–And in Jesus Christ, his only Son, our Lord; CCC 422–455
- F2–441; 2 Sm 7:14
- F2–422; Lk 1:68
- F2–422; Mk 1:1
- F2–422; Mk 1:11
- F2–432; Acts 4:12
- F2–434; Acts 16:16–18, 33
- F2–434; Acts 19:13–16
- F2–436; Acts 4:26–28
- F2–436; Lk 4:16–22
- F2–437; Jn 10:36
- F2–437; Mt 1:16
- F2–438; Acts 10:38

F2–439; Jn 4:25–26, 34
F2–439; Jn 6:15
F2–439; Mt 15:22
F2–439; Mt 20:30
F2–439; Mt 21:1–11
F2–439; Mt 21:13, 15–16
F2–439; Mt 22:41–46
F2–439; Mt 9:27
F2–440; Jn 6:62–63
F2–440; Mt 20:28
F2–442; Acts 9:20
F2–442; Acts 9:3–18, 20
F2–442; Jn 20:31
F2–443; Lk 11:5–13
F2–443; Lk 22:70
F2–443; Mk 14:57–58
F2–443; Mt 21:33–43
F2–443; Mt 24:36, 44
F2–443; Mt 26:64–66
F2–444; Mt 17:5, 10–13
F2–446; Ex 3:14
F2–447; Mt 22:41–46
F2–448; Mt 14:30
F2–448; Mt 15:22
F2–448; Mt 8:2, 4
F2–450; Acts 5:29
F2–450; Mk 12:17
F2–450; Rev 11:15
F2–453; Acts 28:20
F2–453; Lk 7:18–23
F2–454; Acts 8:26–29, 37

F3.-Who was conceived by the Holy Spirit, born of the Virgin Mary; CCC 456-570

F3–459; Mk 9:7
F3–472; Jn 11:28, 34
F3–472; Mk 6:38
F3–472; Mk 8:27
F3–473; Mk 14:36
F3–474; Mk 10:32–34
F3–474; Mk 14:12–25
F3–474; Mk 14:26–30
F3–474; Mk 9:31–32
F3–486; Jn 2:11
F3–486; Lk 2:8–20
F3–486; Mt 2:1–12
F3–495; Mt 13:55
F3–497; Mt 1:18–25
F3–500; Mk 3:31–35
F3–500; Mk 6:5
F3–500; Mt 13:55
F3–500; Mt 28:1
F3–501; Rev 12:17
F3–504; Jn 3:34
F3–512; Acts 1:1–2, 3
F3–514; Jn 20:31
F3–515; Jn 21:22, 24
F3–515; Lk 2:6–7
F3–515; Mk 1:1
F3–517; Mt 8:17
F3–523; Jn 1:29
F3–523; Jn 3:29
F3–523; Lk 1:17
F3–523; Lk 16:18
F3–523; Mk 6:17–29
F3–523; Mt 11:13–14
F3–523; Mt 3:7–12
F3–525; Lk 2:6–7
F3–525; Lk 2:8–20
F3–526; Mt 18:3–4
F3–527; Lk 2:21
F3–528; Mt 2:1–12
F3–529; Lk 2:22–39
F3–530; Mt 2:13–18
F3–532; Lk 22:42
F3–534; Lk 2:41–52
F3–535; Lk 3:23
F3–535; Mt 21:28–32
F3–535; Mt 3:13–17
F3–538; Mk 1:12–13
F3–540; Mt 16:21–23
F3–544; Lk 9:58
F3–544; Mk 2:23–27
F3–544; Mt 21:18, 22

F4–588; Lk 7:36–50
F4–589; Jn 5:18
F4–589; Mt 9:13
F4–590; Mt 12:36–37
F4–590; Mt 12:41–42
F4–591; Lk 23:34
F4–591; Mk 3:4,5
F4–591; Mt 26:64–66
F4–595; Acts 15:5, 10
F4–595; Acts 21:20, 23–24
F4–595; Acts 6:6, 7
F4–596; Jn 18:31
F4–596; Jn 9:16
F4–596; Lk 23:19
F4–596; Lk 23:2
F4–597; Acts 7:52
F4–597; Mk 15:11
F4–597; Mt 27:25
F4–600; Acts 4:26–28
F4–601; Acts 26:22–23
F4–601; Acts 7:52
F4–601; Mt 20:28
F4–603; Jn 8:29
F4–603; Mk 15:34
F4–605; Mt 18:14
F4–607; Jn 18:4–6, 11
F4–607; Jn 19:28
F4–607; Mt 16:21–23
F4–608; Jn 1:36, 43
F4–608; Lk 3:21
F4–609; Mt 26:53
F4–610; Lk 22:19
F4–610; Mt 26:17–29
F4–613; Jn 1:19
F4–618; Mt 16:24
F4–619; Jn 18:4–6, 11
F4–624; Jn 19:42

F5.–He descended into hell; on the third day he rose again from the dead; CCC 631–658

F5–632; Acts 3:15
F5–633; Mt 27:51, 52–53
F5–635; Acts 3:15
F5–639; Acts 9:3–18, 20
F5–640; Jn 11:41–42, 44
F5–640; Jn 20:1, 2
F5–640; Mt 28:11–15
F5–641; Jn 19:42
F5–641; Lk 24:1
F5–641; Mk 16:1
F5–643; Mk 16:11
F5–645; Jn 20:17
F5–645; Jn 20:26
F5–645; Jn 21:4
F5–645; Mk 16:12
F5–647; Acts 13:31, 33
F5–649; Mk 9:9–31

F6.–He ascended into heaven, and is seated at the right hand of God the Father almighty; CCC 659–667

F6–659; Acts 1:1–2, 3
F6–659; Acts 1:9
F6–659; Acts 2:33
F6–659; Acts 7:56, 60
F6–659; Jn 20:26
F6–659; Jn 21:4
F6–659; Lk 24:51
F6–659; Mk 16:12
F6–661; Jn 16:28

F7.–From there he will come to judge the living and the dead; CCC 668–682

F7–670; Mk 16:20
F7–671; Lk 21:27
F7–672; Mk 13:33–37
F7–672; Mt 25:1–13
F7–673; Mt 24:36, 44
F7–674; Lk 21:24
F7–674; Mt 23:37, 39
F7–675; Lk 21:12
F7–675; Mt 24:12, 13
F7–678; Lk 12:1–3
F7–678; Mk 12:38–40

F7–678; Mt 11:20–24
F7–678; Mt 12:41–42
F7–678; Mt 3:7–12
F7–678; Mt 7:1–5
F7–679; Jn 12:48, 49
F7–679; Mt 12:32
F7–722; Lk 1:46–55

F8.–I believe in the Holy Spirit; CCC 683–747

F8–690; Jn 3:34
F8–692; Jn 14:26
F8–694; Jn 19:34
F8–695; Lk 8:46
F8–696; Acts 2:1–4
F8–696; Lk 1:17
F8–697; Acts 1:9
F8–697; Lk 21:27
F8–699; Acts 13:3
F8–699; Acts 14:3
F8–699; Acts 19:5–6
F8–699; Acts 5:12
F8–699; Mk 6:5
F8–700; Lk 11:20, 21–22
F8–703; Gen 1:1, 2
F8–703; Gen 2:7
F8–712; Jn 12:37, 41
F8–713; Mt 12:18–21
F8–717; Lk 1:68
F8–718; Mt 17:5, 10–13
F8–719; Jn 15:26
F8–719; Mt 11:13–14
F8–726; Acts 1:14
F8–728; Jn 3:5–8
F8–728; Jn 6:62–63
F8–728; Jn 7:37–39
F8–730; Lk 23:46

F9.–The holy Catholic Church, the communion of saints; CCC 748–975

F9–751; Acts 19:39
F9–755; Mt 21:33–43
F9–756; Mt 21:42
F9–764; Jn 10:1–21
F9–764; Lk 12:32
F9–764; Mt 12:49
F9–764; Mt 26:31
F9–765; Lk 10:1–2
F9–782; Mt 5:13–16
F9–787; Lk 10:17–20
F9–787; Lk 22:27, 28–30
F9–787; Mk 1:16–20
F9–787; Mk 3:13–19
F9–787; Mt 13:10–17
F9–788; Acts 2:33
F9–796; Jn 3:29
F9–796; Mk 2:19
F9–796; Mt 22:1–14
F9–796; Mt 25:1–13
F9–798; Acts 20:32, 36
F9–827; Mt 13:24–30
F9–849; Mt 28:19–20
F9–858; Lk 10:16
F9–858; Mt 10:40
F9–859; Jn 15:5
F9–859; Jn 5:30
F9–878; Jn 1:36, 43
F9–878; Jn 1:43
F9–878; Jn 21:22, 24
F9–878; Mt 4:19, 21
F9–881; Mt 16:17, 18–19
F9–952; Acts 4:32
F9–952; Lk 16:13

F10.–The forgiveness of sins; CCC 976–987

F10–976; Jn 20:22–23
F10–977; Mk 16:15–16
F10–981; Lk 24:47
F10–982; Mt 18:21–22

F11.–The resurrection of the body; CCC 988–1019

F11–1001; Jn 11:24
F11–1011; Lk 23:46

F11-993; Acts 23:6
F11-993; Jn 11:24
F11-993; Mk 12:27
F11-994; Jn 11
F11-994; Jn 2:19-22
F11-994; Lk 7:11-17
F11-994; Mk 5:21-42

F12.-And life everlasting. Amen; CCC 1020-1065

F12-1023; Rev 22:1, 4
F12-1033; Mt 25:31-46
F12-1034; Mk 9:43-48
F12-1034; Mt 13:44-45, 50
F12-1036; Mt 7:13-14
F12-1039; Jn 12:48, 49
F12-1063; Jn 5:19, 24
F12-1063; Mt 6:16-18

LT.-Celebration Christian Mystery-Liturgy; CCC 1066-1212

LT-1083; Lk 10:21-23
LT-1116; Lk 5:17
LT-1116; Lk 6:19
LT-1116; Lk 8:46
LT-1117; Mt 13:52
LT-1120; Lk 24:47
LT-1137; Rev 22:1, 4
LT-1138; Rev 12
LT-1147; Acts 14:17
LT-1151; Jn 9:6
LT-1151; Lk 22:7-20
LT-1151; Lk 9:31
LT-1151; Mk 7:32-36
LT-1151; Mk 8:22-25

S1.-Baptism; CCC 1213-1284

S1-1223; Mk 16:15-16
S1-1223; Mt 28:19-20
S1-1225; Jn 19:34
S1-1225; Lk 12:50
S1-1225; Mk 10:43-45
S1-1226; Acts 10:48
S1-1226; Acts 16:15
S1-1226; Acts 8:12-13, 20
S1-1244; Mk 10:14
S1-1252; Acts 16:15
S1-1252; Acts 16:16-18, 33
S1-1252; Acts 18:8
S1-1261; Mk 10:14

S2.-Confirmation; CCC 1285-1321

S2-1286; Lk 4:16-22
S2-1286; Mt 3:13-17
S2-1287; Acts 2:1-4
S2-1287; Jn 3:5-8
S2-1287; Jn 7:37-39
S2-1287; Lk 12:10
S2-1288; Acts 19:5-6
S2-1289; Acts 10:38
S2-1310; Acts 1:14

S3.-Holy Eucharist; CCC 1322-1419

S3-1328; Lk 22:19
S3-1329; Acts 2:42
S3-1329; Acts 20:7
S3-1329; Lk 24:13-35
S3-1329; Mk 8:19
S3-1329; Mk 8:6
S3-1329; Mt 14:13-21
S3-1329; Mt 15:32-39
S3-1335; Jn 2:11
S3-1335; Mk 14:25
S3-1335; Mt 14:13-21
S3-1335; Mt 15:32-39
S3-1339; Lk 22:7-20
S3-1339; Mk 14:12-25
S3-1339; Mt 26:17-29
S3-1342; Acts 2:46
S3-1343; Acts 20:7
S3-1347; Lk 24:13-35
S3-1365; Mt 26:28
S3-1386; Mt 8:8, 10
S3-1403; Mk 14:25
S3-1403; Rev 22:20
S3-1406; Jn 6:26-58

S4.–Reconciliation; CCC 1420–1498
S4–1423; Mk 1:15
S4–1427; Mk 1:15
S4–1428; Jn 12:32
S4–1429; Jn 21:15–17
S4–1429; Lk 22:61
S4–1430; Mt 6:16–18
S4–1433; Jn 15:26
S4–1435; Lk 9:23
S4–1443; Lk 15
S4–1443; Lk 19:1–10
S4–1444; Mt 18:18
S4–1460; Lk 3:8, 11
S4–1470; Jn 5:19, 24
S4–1484; Mk 2:17
S4–1485; Jn 20:22–23

S5.–Anointing of the Sick; CCC 1499–1532
S5–1502; Mk 2:5–12
S5–1503; Lk 7:11–17
S5–1503; Mk 2:17
S5–1503; Mk 2:5–12
S5–1503; Mt 4:24
S5–1504; Jn 9:6
S5–1504; Mk 1:41
S5–1504; Mk 3:10
S5–1504; Mk 6:56
S5–1504; Mk 7:32–36
S5–1504; Mk 8:22–25
S5–1504; Mk 9:23
S5–1505; Jn 1:29
S5–1505; Mt 8:17
S5–1506; Mk 6:7, 12–13
S5–1506; Mt 10:37, 38
S5–1507; Acts 14:3
S5–1507; Acts 4:12
S5–1507; Acts 9:34
S5–1509; Mt 10:8
S5–1514; Lk 6:19
S5–1524; Jn 13:1

S6.–Holy Orders; CCC 1533–1600
S6–1551; Jn 21:15–17
S6–1551; Mk 10:43–45
S6–1562; Jn 10:36
S6–1570; Lk 22:27, 28–30
S6–1577; Lk 6:12–16

S7.–Matrimony; CCC 1601–1666
S7–1618; Lk 14:26, 33
S7–1618; Mk 10:28–31
S7–1619; Mk 12:27
S7–1620; Mt 19:1–12
S7–1639; Mk 10:9
S7–1655; Acts 11:14
S7–1655; Acts 18:8

STL–Sacramentals; CCC 1667–1690
STL–1669; Lk 6:28, 36
STL–1673; Mk 1:21, 25–26
STL–1673; Mk 3:13–19
STL–1673; Mk 6:7, 12–13

LC–Life in Christ; CCC 1691–2083
LC–2058; Dt 5:22
LC–1720; Mt 4:17
LC–1753; Mt 6:2–4
LC–1794; Acts 24:16–17
LC–1821; Mt 10:22
LC–1821; Mt 7:21
LC–1824; Mt 22:37–40
LC–1825; Mk 9:37
LC–1846; Lk 15
LC–1859; Lk 16:19–31
LC–1864; Lk 12:10
LC–1864; Mt 12:32
LC–1880; Lk 19:11–27
LC–1889; Lk 17:19–31
LC–1933; Mt 5:43–44
LC–1936; Lk 19:11–27

LC–1936; Mt 25:14–30
LC–1967; Mt 5:17–19
LC–1968; Mt 15:18–19
LC–1969; Mt 6:9–13
LC–1989; Mt 4:17
LC–2005; Mt 7:15, 20
LC–2054; Mt 5:21–22
LC–2055; Mt 22:37–40
LC–2056; Dt 5:22
LC–2083; Lk 10:25–37

C1.–I am the Lord your God. You shall not have other gods besides me; CCC 2084–2141

C1–2096; Dt 6:13
C1–2100; Mt 9:13
C1–2102; Acts 18:18
C1–2102; Acts 21:20, 23–24
C1–2111; Mt 23:9, 16–22
C1–2113; Mt 6:24
C1–2121; Acts 8:12–13, 20
C1–2121; Mt 10:8
C1–2122; Lk 10:1–2
C1–2133; Dt 6:5

C2.–You shall not take the name of the Lord, your God, in vain; CCC 2142–2167

C2–2145; Mt 10:32
C2–2150; Dt 6:13
C2–2158; Jn 10:1–21

C3.–Remember to keep holy the Lord's day; CCC 2168–2196

C3–2173; Jn 9:16
C3–2173; Mk 1:21, 25–26
C3–2173; Mk 3:4,5
C3–2173; Mt 12:5
C3–2174; Jn 20:1, 2
C3–2174; Lk 24:1
C3–2174; Mk 16:1
C3–2174; Mt 28:1
C3–2195; Jn 13:34

C4.–Honor your father and your mother; CCC 2197–2257

C4–2218; Mk 7:8,10–12
C4–2232; Mt 10:37, 38
C4–2233; Mt 12:49
C4–2242; Acts 5:29
C4–2242; Mt 22:21
C4–2257; Mt 5:21–22

C5.–You shall not kill; CCC 2258–2330

C5–2285; Mt 18:6
C5–2285; Mt 7:15, 20
C5–2330; Dt 5:17, 21
C5–2330; Mt 5:27–28
C5–2330; Mt 5:8,9

C6.–You shall not commit adultery; CCC 2331–2400

C6–2364; Mk 10:9
C6–2364; Mt 19:1–12
C6–2367; Mt 23:9, 16–22
C6–2380; Mt 5:27–28
C6–2380; Mt 5:31–32
C6–2382; Lk 16:18
C6–2382; Mt 5:31–32

C7.–You shall not steal; CCC 2401–2463

C7–2427; Gen 3:14–19
C7–2153; Mt 5:37
C7–2412; Lk 19:1–10
C7–2424; Lk 16:13
C7–2443; Mt 11:5
C7–2443; Mt 5:42
C7–2444; Lk 6:20–22
C7–2444; Mk 12:41–44
C7–2444; Mt 8:20
C7–2447; Lk 3:8, 11
C7–2447; Lk 39–54
C7–2447; Mt 6:2–4
C7–2449; Jn 12:8
C7–2463; Lk 17:19–31

C8.–You shall not bear false witness against your neighbor; CCC 2464–2513

C8–2465; 2 Sm 7:18–29
C8–2466; Jn 14:6
C8–2466; Jn 16:13
C8–2466; Jn 8:12
C8–2466; Jn 8:31–32
C8–2466; Mt 5:37
C8–2471; Acts 24:16–17
C8–2471; Jn 18:37

C9.–You shall not covet your neighbor's wife; CCC 2514–2533

C9–2517; Mt 15:18–19
C9–2518; Mt 5:8,9
C9–2533; Dt 5:17, 21
C9–2533; Mt 6:21

C10.–You shall not covet your neighbor's goods; CCC 2534–2557

C10–2544; Lk 14:26, 33
C10–2544; Lk 21:4
C10–2544; Mk 8:31–33
C10–2546; Lk 6:20–22
C10–2547; Mt 6:25–34
C10–2551; Mt 6:21

P.–Christian Prayer; CCC 2558–2776

P–2579; 2 Sm 7:18–29
P–2561; Jn 19:28
P–2572; Gen 22:8, 11
P–2573; Lk 18:1–8
P–2600; Lk 3:21
P–2600; Lk 6:12–16
P–2600; Lk 9:18–20
P–2602; Lk 5:16
P–2602; Mk 1:35
P–2602; Mk 6:46
P–2603; Lk 10:21–23
P–2603; Mt 11:25–27
P–2604; Jn 11:41–42, 44
P–2605; Lk 23:34
P–2605; Mk 15:34
P–2606; Acts 13:31, 33
P–2609; Mt 7:13–14
P–2609; Mt 7:7–11
P–2610; Mk 11:25
P–2610; Mk 9:23
P–2610; Mt 21:18, 22
P–2610; Mt 8:26
P–2610; Mt 8:8, 10
P–2611; Mt 7:21
P–2611; Mt 9:38
P–2612; Lk 21:34–36
P–2612; Mk 13
P–2613; Lk 11:5–13
P–2613; Lk 18:1–8
P–2613; Lk 18:9–14
P–2615; Jn 16:24
P–2616; Mk 1:41
P–2616; Mk 10:46–52
P–2616; Mk 7:29
P–2616; Mt 9:27
P–2619; Lk 1:46–55
P–2632; Acts 13:3
P–2632; Acts 6:6, 7
P–2635; Acts 7:56, 60
P–2636; Acts 12:5
P–2636; Acts 20:32, 36
P–2636; Acts 21:5
P–2640; Acts 3:1, 9
P–2660; Lk 13:20–21
P–2667; Mk 10:46–52
P–2701; Mk 14:36
P–2707; Mk 4:11, 15–19
P–2707; Mk 4:4–7
P–2712; Lk 7:36–50
P–2728; Mk 10:28–31
P–2731; Jn 12:24
P–2731; Lk 8:6
P–2743; Lk 8:24
P–2759; Lk 11:1
P–2759; Mt 6:9–13

LP1.-Our Father, Who art in heaven, Hallowed be Thy Name; CCC 2777-2815

LP1-2777; Ex 3:5, 6
LP1-2779; Mt 11:25-27
LP1-2780; Jn 1:1
LP1-2785; Mt 18:3-4
LP1-2790; Acts 4:32
LP1-2793; Jn 11:52
LP1-2795; Jn 12:32
LP1-2795; Jn 16:28
LP1-2795; Jn 20:17
LP1-2804; Lk 12:50
LP1-2810; Ex 3:14
LP1-2812; Mt 1:18-25
LP1-2815; Jn 16:24
LP1-2815; Jn 17:11

LP2.-Thy Kingdom come; CCC 2816-2821

LP2-2821; Mt 5:13-16
LP2-2821; Mt 6:24

LP3.-Thy Will be done, on earth as it is in Heaven; CCC 2822-2827

LP3-2822; Jn 13:34
LP3-2822; Lk 10:25-37
LP3-2822; Mt 18:14
LP3-2824; Jn 4:25-26, 34
LP3-2824; Jn 5:30
LP3-2824; Jn 8:29
LP3-2824; Lk 22:42

LP4.-Give us this day our daily bread; CCC 2828-2837

LP4-2830; Mt 6:25-34
LP4-2831; Lk 16:19-31
LP4-2831; Mt 25:31-46
LP4-2835; Jn 6:26-58

LP5.-And forgive us our trespasses, as we forgive those who trespass against us.; CCC 2838-2845

LP5-2839; Lk 15:11-32
LP5-2839; Lk 18:9-14
LP5-2839; Mt 26:28
LP5-2841; Mk 11:25
LP5-2842; Lk 6:28, 36
LP5-2843; Jn 13:1
LP5-2843; Mt 18:23-35
LP5-2844; Mt 5:43-44
LP5-2845; Lk 11:1
LP5-2845; Lk 17:3-4
LP5-2845; Mt 18:21-22

LP6.-And lead us not into temptation; CCC 2846-2849

LP6-2847; Lk 8:13-15
LP6-2849; Jn 17:11
LP6-2849; Lk 12:35-40
LP6-2849; Mk 13:23
LP6-2849; Mk 13:33-37
LP6-2849; Mk 13:9
LP6-2849; Mt 26:36-44
LP6-2849; Mt 4:1-11

LP7.-But deliver us from evil. Amen; CCC 2850-2854

LP7-2852; Jn 8:44
LP7-2852; Rev 12:9
LP7-2853; Rev 12:17
LP7-2853; Rev 22:20

DOX.-The Final Doxology; CCC 2855-2865

DOX-2855; Lk 4:5-6
DOX-2856; Lk 1:38

Deciphering Subheading Codes

Here are four possible appearances of subheading codes:

	~ The Sound Eye (Mt 6:22–23)
	* The Birth of Jesus of Jesus Christ (Mt 1:18–25); F3–497; LP1–2812
	A Tree and Its Fruit (Mt 12:33–37); F4–590
	Jesus Heals Many at Peter's House (Mt 8:14–17); F3–517; S5–1505

~ indicates there are no *Catechism of the Catholic Church* (CCC) citations for that subheading;

* indicates that this Scripture subsection has been cited in the CCC; more than the two times indicated.

No symbol preceding indicates there is one CCC citation (as indicated in the third example) or two CCC citations (as indicated in the fourth example).

FOR EXAMPLE:

*** The Birth of Jesus of Jesus Christ (Mt 1:18–25); F3–497; LP1–2812**

* Indicates the *Catechism of the Catholic Church* (CCC) cites this subsection more than the 2 times shown.

The Birth of Jesus of Jesus Christ (Mt 1:18–25) is the title of the *Ignatius Catholic Study Bible* subheading with chapter and verses.

F3–497 indicates that the CCC has cited this subsection in paragraph 497 under the theme of the third article of the Apostles' Creed.

LP1–2812 indicates that the CCC has cited this subsection in paragraph 2812 under the theme of the first petition of the Lord's Prayer.

Old Testament Salvation History Chapters

Genesis Chapter 1

* Six Days of Creation and the Sabbath (Gn 1:1–Gn 2:3); F1–268; F8–703

Genesis Author: In the beginning God created the heavens and the earth. The earth was without form and void, and darkness was upon the face of the deep; and the Spirit of God was moving over the face of the waters. And God said,

God: Let there be light;

Genesis Author: and there was light. And God saw that the light was good; and God separated the light from the darkness. God called the light Day, and the darkness he called Night. And there was evening and there was morning, one day. And God said,

God: Let there be a firmament in the midst of the waters, and let it separate the waters from the waters.

Genesis Author: And God made the firmament and separated the waters which were under the firmament from the waters which were above the firmament. And it was so. And God called the firmament Heaven. And there was evening and there was morning, a second day. And God said,

God: Let the waters under the heavens be gathered together into one place, and let the dry land appear.

Genesis Author: And it was so. God called the dry land Earth, and the waters that were gathered together he called Seas. And God saw that it was good. And God said,

God: Let the earth put forth vegetation, plants yielding seed, and fruit trees bearing fruit in which is their seed, each according to its kind, upon the earth.

Genesis Author: And it was so. The earth brought forth vegetation, plants yielding seed according to their own kinds, and trees bearing fruit in which is their seed, each according to its kind. And God saw that it was good. And there was evening and there was morning, a third day. And God said,

God: Let there be lights in the firmament of the heavens to separate the day from the night; and let them be for signs and for seasons and for days and years, and let them be lights in the firmament of the heavens to give light upon the earth.

Genesis Author: And it was so. And God made the two great lights, the greater light to rule the day, and the lesser light to rule the night; he made the stars also. And God set them in the firmament of the heavens to give light upon the earth, to rule over the day and over the night, and to separate the light from the darkness. And God saw that it was good. And there was evening and there was morning, a fourth day. And God said,

God: Let the waters bring forth swarms of living creatures, and let birds fly above the earth across the firmament of the heavens.

Genesis Author: So God created the great sea monsters and every living creature that moves, with which the waters swarm, according to their kinds, and every winged bird according to its kind. And God saw that it was good. And God blessed them, saying,

God: Be fruitful and multiply and fill the waters in the seas, and let birds multiply on the earth.

Genesis Author: And there was evening and there was morning, a fifth day. And God said,

God: Let the earth bring forth living creatures according to their kinds: cattle and creeping things and beasts of the earth according to their kinds.

Genesis Author: And it was so. And God made the beasts of the earth according to their kinds and the cattle according to their kinds, and everything that creeps upon the ground according to its kind. And God saw that it was good. Then God said,

God: Let us make man in our image, after our likeness; and let them have dominion over the fish of the sea, and over the birds of the air, and over the cattle, and over all the earth, and over every creeping thing that creeps upon the earth.

Genesis Author: So God created man in his own image, in the image of God he created him; male and female he created them. And God blessed them, and God said to them,

God: Be fruitful and multiply, and fill the earth and subdue it; and have dominion over the fish of the sea and over the birds of the air and over every living thing that moves upon the earth.

Genesis Author: And God said,

God: Behold, I have given you every plant yielding seed which is upon the face of all the earth, and every tree with seed in its fruit; you shall have them for food. And to every beast of the earth, and to every bird of the air, and to everything that creeps on the earth, everything that has the breath of life, I have given every green plant for food.

Genesis Author: And it was so. And God saw everything that he had made, and behold, it was very good. And there was evening and there was morning, a sixth day.

Genesis Chapter 2

Genesis Author: Thus the heavens and the earth were finished, and all the host of them. And on the seventh day God finished his work which he had done, and he rested on the seventh day from all his work which he had done.

So God blessed the seventh day and hallowed it, because on it God rested from all his work which he had done in creation.

* Another Account of Creation (Gn 2:4–25); F1–369; F8–703

These are the generations of the heavens and the earth when they were created. In the day that the Lord God made the earth and the heavens, when no plant of the field was yet in the earth and no herb of the field had yet sprung up—for the Lord God had not caused it to rain upon the earth, and there was no man to till the ground; but a mist went up from the earth and watered the whole face of the ground—

Genesis Author: Then the Lord God formed man of dust from the ground, and breathed into his nostrils the breath of life; and man became a living soul. And the Lord God planted a garden in Eden, in the east; and there he put the man whom he had formed.

And out of the ground the Lord God made to grow every tree that is pleasant to the sight and good for food, the tree of life also in the midst of the garden, and the tree of the knowledge of good and evil.

A river flowed out of Eden to water the garden, and there it divided and became four rivers.

The name of the first is Pishon; it is the one which flows around the whole land of Havilah, where there is gold; and the gold of that land is good; bdellium and onyx stone are there.

The name of the second river is Gihon; it is the one which flows around the whole land of Cush.

And the name of the third river is Tigris, which flows east of Assyria.

And the fourth river is the Euphrates. The Lord God took the man and put him in the garden of Eden to till it and keep it. And the Lord God commanded the man, saying,

God: You may freely eat of every tree of the garden; but of the tree of the knowledge of good and evil you shall not eat, for in the day that you eat of it you shall die.

Genesis Author: Then the Lord God said,

God: It is not good that the man should be alone; I will make him a helper fit for him.

Genesis Author: So out of the ground the Lord God formed every beast of the field and every bird of the air, and brought them to the man to see what he would call them; and whatever the man called every living creature, that was its name. The man gave names to all cattle, and to the birds of the air, and to every beast of the field; but for the man there was not found a helper fit for him. So the Lord GOD caused a deep sleep to fall upon the man, and while he slept took one of his ribs and closed up its place with flesh; and the rib which the Lord GOD had taken from the man he made into a woman and brought her to the man. Then the man said,

Adam: This at last is bone of my bones and flesh of my flesh; she shall be called Woman, because she was taken out of Man. Therefore a man leaves his father and his mother and cleaves to his wife, and they become one flesh.

Genesis Author: And the man and his wife were both naked, and were not ashamed.

Genesis Chapter 3

* The Fall of Man (Gn 3:1–24); PF2–70; C7–2427

Genesis Author: Now the serpent was more subtle than any other wild creature that the Lord GOD had made. He said to the woman,

Serpent: Did God say, "You shall not eat of any tree of the garden"?

Genesis Author: And the woman said to the serpent,

Eve: We may eat of the fruit of the trees of the garden; but God said, "You shall not eat of the fruit of the tree which is in the midst of the garden, neither shall you touch it, lest you die."

Genesis Author: But the serpent said to the woman,

Serpent: You will not die. For God knows that when you eat of it your eyes will be opened, and you will be like God, knowing good and evil.

Genesis Author: So when the woman saw that the tree was good for food, and that it was a delight to the eyes, and that the tree was to be desired to make one wise, she took of its fruit and ate; and she also gave some to her husband, and he ate.

Then the eyes of both were opened, and they knew that they were naked; and they sewed fig leaves together and made themselves aprons.

And they heard the sound of the Lord GOD walking in the garden in the cool of the day, and the man and his wife hid themselves from the presence of the Lord GOD among the trees of the garden.

But the Lord GOD called to the man, and said to him,

God: Where are you?

Genesis Author: And he said,

Adam: I heard the sound of you in the garden, and I was afraid, because I was naked; and I hid myself.

Genesis Author: He said,

God: Who told you that you were naked? Have you eaten of the tree of which I commanded you not to eat?

Genesis Author: The man said,

Adam: The woman whom you gave to be with me, she gave me fruit of the tree, and I ate.

Genesis Author: Then the Lord GOD said to the woman,

God: What is this that you have done?

Genesis Author: The woman said,

Eve: The serpent beguiled me, and I ate.

Genesis Author: The Lord GOD said to the serpent,

God: Because you have done this, cursed are you above all cattle, and above all wild animals; upon your belly you shall go, and dust you shall eat all the days of your life. I will put enmity between you and the woman, and between your seed and her seed; he shall bruise your head, and you shall bruise his heel.

Genesis Author: To the woman he said,

God: I will greatly multiply your pain in childbearing; in pain you shall bring forth children, yet your desire shall be for your husband, and he shall rule over you.

Genesis Author: And to Adam he said,

God: Because you have listened to the voice of your wife, and have eaten of the tree of which I commanded you, "You shall not eat of it," cursed is the ground because of you; in toil you shall eat of it all the days of your life; thorns and thistles it shall bring forth to you; and you shall eat the plants of the field. In the sweat of your face you shall eat bread till you return to the ground, for out of it you were taken; you are dust, and to dust you shall return.

Genesis Author: The man called his wife's name Eve, because she was the mother of all living. And the Lord God made for Adam and for his wife garments of skins, and clothed them. Then the Lord God said,

God: Behold, the man has become like one of us, knowing good and evil; and now, lest he put forth his hand and take also of the tree of life, and eat, and live forever—

Genesis Author: therefore the Lord God sent him forth from the garden of Eden, to till the ground from which he was taken. He drove out the man; and at the east of the garden of Eden he placed the cherubim, and a flaming sword which turned every way, to guard the way to the tree of life.

Genesis Chapter 22

* God Tests Abraham (Gn 22:1–19); P–2572; F1–332

Genesis Author: After these things God tested Abraham, and said to him,

Lord God: Abraham!

Genesis Author: And he said,

Abraham: Here am I.

Genesis Author: He said,

Lord God: Take your son, your only son Isaac, whom you love, and go to the land of Moriah, and offer him there as a burnt offering upon one of the mountains of which I shall tell you.

Genesis Author: So Abraham rose early in the morning, saddled his ass, and took two of his young men with him, and his son Isaac; and he cut the wood for the burnt offering, and arose and went to the place of which God had told him. On the third day Abraham lifted up his eyes and saw the place afar off. Then Abraham said to his young men,

Abraham: Stay here with the ass; I and the lad will go yonder and worship, and come again to you.

Genesis Author: And Abraham took the wood of the burnt offering, and laid it on Isaac his son; and he took in his hand the fire and the knife. So they went both of them together. And Isaac said to his father Abraham,

Isaac: My father!

Genesis Author: And he said,

Abraham: Here am I, my son.

Genesis Author: He said,

Isaac: Behold, the fire and the wood; but where is the lamb for a burnt offering?

Genesis Author: Abraham said,

Abraham: God will provide himself the lamb for a burnt offering, my son.

Genesis Author: So they went both of them together. When they came to the place of which God had told him, Abraham built an altar there, and laid the wood in order, and bound Isaac his son, and laid him on the altar, upon the wood. Then Abraham put forth his hand, and took the knife to slay his son. But the angel of the Lord called to him from heaven, and said,

Angel of the Lord: Abraham, Abraham!

Genesis Author: And he said,

Abraham: Here am I.

Genesis Author: He said

Lord God: Do not lay your hand on the lad or do anything to him; for now I know that you fear God, seeing you have not withheld your son, your only son, from me.

Genesis Author: And Abraham lifted up his eyes and looked, and behold, behind him was a ram, caught in a thicket by his horns; and Abraham went and took the ram, and offered it up as a burnt offering instead of his son. So Abraham called the name of that place The Lord will provide; as it is said to this day, "On the mount of the Lord it shall be provided." And the angel of the Lord called to Abraham a second time from heaven, and said,

Lord God: By myself I have sworn, says the Lord, because you have done this, and have not withheld your son, your only son, I will indeed bless you, and I will multiply your descendants as the stars of heaven and as the sand which is on the seashore. And your descendants shall possess the gate of their enemies, and by your descendants shall all the nations of the earth bless themselves, because you have obeyed my voice.

Genesis Author: So Abraham returned to his young men, and they arose and went together to Beer–sheba; and Abraham dwelt at Beer-sheba.

~The Children of Nahor (Gn 22:20–24)

Genesis Author: Now after these things it was told Abraham,

Person: Behold, Milcah also has borne children to your brother Nahor: Uz the first-born, Buz his brother, Kemuel the father of Aram, Chesed, Hazo, Pildash, Jidlaph, and Bethuel.

Genesis Author: Bethuel became the father of Rebekah. These eight Milcah bore to Nahor, Abraham's brother. Moreover, his concubine, whose name was Reumah, bore Tebah, Gaham, Tahash, and Maacah.

Genesis Chapter 45

Joseph Makes Himself Known to His Brothers (Gn 45:1–28); F1–312

Genesis Author: Then Joseph could not control himself before all those who stood by him; and he cried,

Joseph: Make everyone go out from me.

Genesis Author: So no one stayed with him when Joseph made himself known to his brothers. And he wept aloud, so that the Egyptians heard it, and the household of Pharaoh heard it. And Joseph said to his brothers,

Joseph: I am Joseph; is my father still alive?

Genesis Author: But his brothers could not answer him, for they were dismayed at his presence. So Joseph said to his brothers,

Joseph: Come near to me, I pray you.

Genesis Author: And they came near. And he said,

Joseph: I am your brother, Joseph, whom you sold into Egypt. And now do not be distressed, or angry with yourselves, because you sold me here; for God sent me before you to preserve life. For the famine has been in the land these two years; and there are yet five years in which there will be neither plowing nor harvest. And God sent me before you to preserve for you a remnant on earth, and to keep alive for you many survivors. So it was not you who sent me here, but God; and he has made me a father to Pharaoh, and lord of all his house and ruler over all the land of Egypt.

Make haste and go up to my father and say to him, "Thus says your son Joseph, God has made me lord of all Egypt; come down to me, do not tarry; you shall dwell in the land of Goshen, and you shall be near me, you and your children and your children's children, and your flocks, your herds, and all that you have; and there I will provide for you, for there are yet five years of famine to come; lest you and your household, and all that you have, come to poverty."

And now your eyes see, and the eyes of my brother Benjamin see, that it is my mouth that speaks to you. You must tell my father of all my splendor in Egypt, and of all that you have seen. Make haste and bring my father down here.

Genesis Author: Then he fell upon his brother Benjamin's neck and wept; and Benjamin wept upon his neck. And he kissed all his brothers and wept upon them; and after that his brothers talked with him. When the report was heard in Pharaoh's house, "Joseph's brothers have come," it pleased Pharaoh and his servants well. And Pharaoh said to Joseph,

Pharaoh: Say to your brothers, "Do this: load your beasts and go back to the land of Canaan; and take your father and your households, and come to me, and I will give you the best of the land of Egypt, and you shall eat the fat of the land." Command them also, "Do this: take wagons from the land of Egypt for your little ones and for your wives, and bring your father, and come. Give no thought to your goods, for the best of all the land of Egypt is yours."

Genesis Author: The sons of Israel did so; and Joseph gave them wagons, according to the command of Pharaoh, and gave them provisions for the journey. To each and all of them he gave festal garments; but to Benjamin he gave three hundred shekels of silver and five festal garments. To his father he sent as follows: ten asses loaded with the good things of Egypt, and ten she-asses loaded with grain, bread, and provision for his father on the journey. Then he sent his brothers away, and as they departed, he said to them,

Joseph: Do not quarrel on the way.

Genesis Author: So they went up out of Egypt, and came to the land of Canaan to their father Jacob. And they told him,

Brothers of Joseph: Joseph is still alive, and he is ruler over all the land of Egypt.

Genesis Author: And his heart fainted, for he did not believe them. But when they told him all the words of Joseph, which he had said to them, and when he saw the wagons which Joseph had sent to carry him, the spirit of their father Jacob revived; and Israel said,

Jacob: It is enough; Joseph my son is still alive; I will go and see him before I die.

Exodus Chapter 3

* Moses and the Burning Bush (Ex 3:1–12); LP1–2777; F1–205

Exodus Author: Now Moses was keeping the flock of his father-in-law, Jethro, the priest of Midian; and he led his flock to the west side of the wilderness, and came to Horeb, the mountain of God. And the angel of the LORD appeared to him in a flame of fire out of the midst of a bush; and he looked, and behold, the bush was burning, yet it was not consumed. And Moses said,

Moses: I will turn aside and see this great sight, why the bush is not burnt.

Exodus Author: When the LORD saw that he turned aside to see, God called to him out of the bush,

Lord GOD: Moses, Moses!

Exodus Author: And he said,

Moses: Here am I.

Exodus Author: Then he said,

Lord GOD: Do not come near; put off your shoes from your feet, for the place on which you are standing is holy ground.

Exodus Author: And he said,

Lord GOD: I am the God of your father, the God of Abraham, the God of Isaac, and the God of Jacob.

Exodus Author: And Moses hid his face, for he was afraid to look at God. Then the LORD said,

Lord GOD: I have seen the affliction of my people who are in Egypt, and have heard their cry because of their taskmasters; I know their sufferings, and I have come down to deliver them out of the hand of the Egyptians, and to bring them up out of that land to a good and broad land, a land flowing with milk and honey, to the place of the Canaanites, the Hittites, the Amorites, the Perizzites, the Hivites, and the Jebusites. And now, behold, the cry of the people of Israel has come to me, and I have seen the oppression with which the Egyptians oppress them. Come, I will send you to Pharaoh that you may bring forth my people, the sons of Israel, out of Egypt.

Exodus Author: But Moses said to God,

Moses: Who am I that I should go to Pharaoh, and bring the sons of Israel out of Egypt?

Exodus Author: He said,

Lord God: But I will be with you; and this shall be the sign for you, that I have sent you: when you have brought forth the people out of Egypt, you shall serve God upon this mountain.

* God Reveals His Name (Ex 3:13–22); F2–446; LP1–2810

Exodus Author: Then Moses said to God,

Moses: If I come to the people of Israel and say to them, "The God of your fathers has sent me to you," and they ask me, "What is his name?" what shall I say to them?

Exodus Author: God said to Moses,

Lord God: I AM WHO AM.

Exodus Author: And he said,

Lord God: Say this to the people of Israel, "I AM has sent me to you."

Exodus Author: God also said to Moses,

Lord God: Say this to the people of Israel, "The Lord the God of your fathers, the God of Abraham, the God of Isaac, and the God of Jacob, has sent me to you: this is my name for ever, and thus I am to be remembered throughout all generations."

Go and gather the elders of Israel together, and say to them, "The Lord, the God of your fathers, the God of Abraham, of Isaac, and of Jacob, has appeared to me, saying, 'I have observed you and what has been done to you in Egypt; and I promise that I will bring you up out of the affliction of Egypt, to the land of the Canaanites, the Hittites, the Amorites, the

Perizzites, the Hivites, and the Jebusites, a land flowing with milk and honey. And they will hearken to your voice; and you and the elders of Israel shall go to the king of Egypt and say to him, "The LORD, the God of the Hebrews, has met with us; and now, we pray you, let us go a three days' journey into the wilderness, that we may sacrifice to the LORD our God." '

I know that the king of Egypt will not let you go unless compelled by a mighty hand. So I will stretch out my hand and smite Egypt with all the wonders which I will do in it; after that he will let you go.

And I will give this people favor in the sight of the Egyptians; and when you go, you shall not go empty, but each woman shall ask of her neighbor, and of her who sojourns in her house, jewelry of silver and of gold, and clothing, and you shall put them on your sons and on your daughters; thus you shall despoil the Egyptians.

Exodus Chapter 14

~ Crossing the Red Sea (Ex 14:1–25)

Exodus Author: Then the LORD said to Moses,

Lord GOD: Tell the people of Israel to turn back and encamp in front of Pihahiroth, between Migdol and the sea, in front of Baal-zephon; you shall encamp over against it, by the sea. For Pharaoh will say of the people of Israel,

Pharaoh: They are entangled in the land; the wilderness has shut them in.

Lord GOD: And I will harden Pharaoh's heart, and he will pursue them and I will get glory over Pharaoh and all his host; and the Egyptians shall know that I am the LORD.

Exodus Author: And they did so. When the king of Egypt was told that the people had fled, the mind of Pharaoh and his servants was changed toward the people, and they said,

Egyptians: What is this we have done, that we have let Israel go from serving us?

Exodus Author: So he made ready his chariot and took his army with him, and took six hundred picked chariots and all the other chariots of Egypt with officers over all of them. And the LORD hardened the heart of Pharaoh king of Egypt and he pursued the people of Israel as they went forth defiantly. The Egyptians pursued them, all Pharaoh's horses and chariots and his horsemen and his army, and overtook them encamped at the sea, by Pihahiroth, in front of Baal-zephon.

When Pharaoh drew near, the people of Israel lifted up their eyes, and behold, the Egyptians were marching after them; and they were in great fear. And the people of Israel cried out to the LORD; and they said to Moses,

Israelites: Is it because there are no graves in Egypt that you have taken us away to die in the wilderness? What have you done to us, in bringing us out of Egypt? Is not this what we said to you in Egypt, "Let us alone and let us serve the Egyptians"? For it would have been better for us to serve the Egyptians than to die in the wilderness.

Exodus Author: And Moses said to the people,

Moses: Fear not, stand firm, and see the salvation of the LORD, which he will work for you today; for the Egyptians whom you see today, you shall never see again. The LORD will fight for you, and you have only to be still.

Exodus Author: The LORD said to Moses,

Lord GOD: Why do you cry to me? Tell the people of Israel to go forward. Lift up your rod, and stretch out your hand over the sea and divide it, that the people of Israel may go on dry ground through the sea. And I will harden the hearts of the Egyptians so that they shall go in after them, and I will get glory over Pharaoh and all his host, his chariots, and his horsemen. And the Egyptians shall know that I am the LORD, when I have gotten glory over Pharaoh, his chariots, and his horsemen.

Exodus Author: Then the angel of God who went before the host of Israel moved and went behind them; and the pillar of cloud moved from before them and stood behind them, coming between the host of Egypt and the host of Israel. And there was the cloud and the darkness; and the night passed without one coming near the other all night.

Then Moses stretched out his hand over the sea; and the LORD drove the sea back by a strong east wind all night, and made the sea dry land, and the waters were divided. And the people of Israel went into the midst of the sea on dry ground, the waters being a wall to them on their right hand and on their left.

The Egyptians pursued, and went in after them into the midst of the sea, all Pharaoh's horses, his chariots, and his horsemen.

And in the morning watch the LORD in the pillar of fire and of cloud looked down upon the host of the Egyptians, and discomfited the host of the Egyptians, clogging their chariot wheels so that they drove heavily; and the Egyptians said,

Egyptians: Let us flee from before Israel; for the LORD fights for them against the Egyptians.

~ The Egyptians Drown in the Sea (Ex 14:26–31)

Exodus Author: Then the LORD said to Moses,

Lord GOD: Stretch out your hand over the sea, that the water may come back upon the Egyptians, upon their chariots, and upon their horsemen.

Exodus Author: So Moses stretched forth his hand over the sea, and the sea returned to its usual flow when the morning appeared; and the Egyptians fled into it, and the LORD routed the Egyptians in the midst of the sea.

The waters returned and covered the chariots and the horsemen and all the host of Pharaoh that had followed them into the sea; not so much as one of them remained.

But the people of Israel walked on dry ground through the sea, the waters being a wall to them on their right hand and on their left. Thus the LORD saved Israel that day from the hand of the Egyptians; and Israel saw the Egyptians dead upon the seashore.

And Israel saw the great work which the LORD did against the Egyptians, and the people feared the LORD; and they believed in the LORD and in his servant Moses.

Deuteronomy Chapter 5

* The Ten Commandments (Dt 5:1–21); C5–2330; C9–2533

Deuteronomy Author: And Moses summoned all Israel, and said to them,

Moses: Hear, O Israel, the statutes and the ordinances which I speak in your hearing this day, and you shall learn them and be careful to do them. The LORD our God made a covenant with us in Horeb. Not with our fathers did the LORD make this covenant, but with us, who are all of us here alive this day. The LORD spoke with you face to face at the mountain, out of the midst of the fire, while I stood between the LORD and you at that time, to declare to you the word of the LORD; for you were afraid because of the fire, and you did not go up into the mountain. He said:

Lord GOD: I am the LORD your God, who brought you out of the land of Egypt, out of the house of bondage.

You shall have no other gods before me.

You shall not make for yourself a graven image, or any likeness of anything that is in heaven above, or that is on the earth beneath, or that is in the water under the earth; you shall not bow down to them or serve them; for I the LORD your God am a jealous God, visiting the iniquity of the fathers upon the children to the third and fourth generation of those who hate me, but showing steadfast love to thousands of those who love me and keep my commandments.

You shall not take the name of the LORD your God in vain: for the LORD will not hold him guiltless who takes his name in vain.

Observe the sabbath day, to keep it holy, as the LORD your God commanded you. Six days you shall labor, and do all your work; but the seventh day is a sabbath to the LORD your God; in it you shall not do any work, you, or your son, or your daughter, or your manservant, or your maidservant, or your ox, or your donkey, or any of your cattle, or the sojourner who is within your gates, that your manservant and your maidservant may rest as well as you.

You shall remember that you were a servant in the land of Egypt, and the LORD your God brought you out thence with a mighty hand and an outstretched arm; therefore the LORD your God commanded you to keep the sabbath day.

Honor your father and your mother, as the LORD your God commanded you; that your days may be prolonged, and that it may go well with you, in the land which the LORD your God gives you.

You shall not kill.

Neither shall you commit adultery.

Neither shall you steal.

Neither shall you bear false witness against your neighbor.

Neither shall you covet your neighbor's wife; and you shall not desire your neighbor's house, his field, or his manservant, or his maidservant, his ox, or his ass, or anything that is your neighbor's.

Moses the Mediator of God's Will (Dt 5:22–33); LC–2056; L–2058

Moses: These words the LORD spoke to all your assembly at the mountain out of the midst of the fire, the cloud, and the thick darkness, with a loud voice; and he added no more. And he wrote them upon two tables of stone, and gave them to me. And when you heard the voice out of the midst of the darkness, while the mountain was burning with fire, you came near to me, all the heads of your tribes, and your elders; and you said,

Israelites: Behold, the LORD our God has shown us his glory and greatness, and we have heard his voice out of the midst of the fire; we have this day seen God speak with man and man still live. Now therefore why should we die? For this great fire will consume us; if we hear the voice of the LORD our God anymore, we shall die. For who is there of all flesh, that has heard the voice of the living God speaking out of the midst of fire, as we have, and has still lived? Go near, and hear all that the LORD our God will say; and speak to us all that the LORD our God will speak to you; and we will hear and do it.

Moses: And the LORD heard your words, when you spoke to me; and the LORD said to me,

Lord GOD: I have heard the words of this people, which they have spoken to you; they have rightly said all that they have spoken. Oh that they had such a mind as this always, to fear me and to keep all my commandments, that it might go well with them and with their children forever! Go and say to them, "Return to your tents." But you, stand here by me, and I will tell you all the commandment and the statutes and the ordinances which you shall teach them, that they may do them in the land which I give them to possess.

Moses: You shall be careful to do therefore as the LORD your God has commanded you; you shall not turn aside to the right hand or to the left. You shall walk in all the way which the LORD your God has commanded you, that you may live, and that it may go well with you, and that you may live long in the land which you shall possess.

Deuteronomy Chapter 6

* The Great Commandment (Dt 6:1–9); F1–368; C1–2133

Moses: Now this is the commandment, the statutes and the ordinances which the LORD your God commanded me to teach you, that you may do them in the land to which you are going over, to possess it; that you may fear the LORD your God, you and your son and your son's son, by keeping all his statutes and his commandments, which I command you, all the days of your life; and that your days may be prolonged.

Hear therefore, O Israel, and be careful to do them; that it may go well with you, and that you may multiply greatly, as the LORD, the God of your fathers, has promised you, in a land flowing with milk and honey.

Hear, O Israel: The LORD our God is one LORD; and you shall love the LORD your God with all your heart, and with all your soul, and with all your might.

And these words which I command you this day shall be upon your heart; and you shall teach them diligently to your children, and shall talk of them when you sit in your house, and when you walk by the way, and when you lie down, and when you rise.

And you shall bind them as a sign upon your hand, and they shall be as frontlets between your eyes.

And you shall write them on the doorposts of your house and on your gates.

Caution Against Disobedience (Dt 6:10–25); C1–2096; C2–2150

Moses: And when the LORD your God brings you into the land which he swore to your fathers, to Abraham, to Isaac, and to Jacob, to give you, with great and goodly cities, which you did not build, and houses full of all good things, which you did not fill, and cisterns hewn out, which you did not hew, and vineyards and olive trees, which you did not plant, and when you eat and are full, then take heed lest you forget the LORD, who brought you out of the land of Egypt, out of the house of bondage.

You shall fear the Lord your God; you shall serve him, and swear by his name.

You shall not go after other gods, of the gods of the peoples who are round about you; for the Lord your God in the midst of you is a jealous God; lest the anger of the Lord your God be kindled against you, and he destroy you from off the face of the earth.

You shall not put the Lord your God to the test, as you tested him at Massah.

You shall diligently keep the commandments of the Lord your God, and his testimonies, and his statutes, which he has commanded you.

And you shall do what is right and good in the sight of the Lord, that it may go well with you, and that you may go in and take possession of the good land which the Lord swore to give to your fathers by thrusting out all your enemies from before you, as the Lord has promised.

When your son asks you in time to come,

Son: What is the meaning of the testimonies and the statutes and the ordinances which the Lord our God has commanded you?

Moses: Then you shall say to your son,

Father: We were Pharaoh's slaves in Egypt; and the Lord brought us out of Egypt with a mighty hand; and the Lord showed signs and wonders, great and grievous, against Egypt and against Pharaoh and all his household, before our eyes; and he brought us out from there, that he might bring us in and give us the land which he swore to give to our fathers. And the Lord commanded us to do all these statutes, to fear the Lord our God, for our good always, that he might preserve us alive, as at this day. And it will be righteousness for us, if we are careful to do all this commandment before the Lord our God, as he has commanded us.

2 Samuel Chapter 7

* God's Promise to David (2 Sm 7:1–17); F1–238; F2–441

Samuel: Now when the king dwelt in his house, and the LORD had given him rest from all his enemies round about, the king said to Nathan the prophet,

David: See now, I dwell in a house of cedar, but the ark of God dwells in a tent.

Samuel: And Nathan said to the king,

Nathan: Go, do all that is in your heart; for the LORD is with you.

Samuel: But that same night the word of the LORD came to Nathan,

Lord God: Go and tell my servant David, "Thus says the LORD: Would you build me a house to dwell in? I have not dwelt in a house since the day I brought up the people of Israel from Egypt to this day, but I have been moving about in a tent for my dwelling.

"In all places where I have moved with all the people of Israel, did I speak a word with any of the judges of Israel, whom I commanded to shepherd my people Israel, saying, 'Why have you not built me a house of cedar?'"

Now therefore thus you shall say to my servant David,

"Thus says the LORD of hosts, I took you from the pasture, from following the sheep, that you should be prince over my people Israel; and I have been with you wherever you went, and have cut off all your enemies from before you; and I will make for you a great name, like the name of the great ones of the earth.

"And I will appoint a place for my people Israel, and will plant them, that they may dwell in their own place, and be disturbed no more; and violent men shall afflict them no more, as formerly, from the time that I appointed judges over my people Israel; and I will give you rest from all your enemies.

"Moreover the Lord declares to you that the Lord will make you a house. When your days are fulfilled and you lie down with your fathers, I will raise up your offspring after you, who shall come forth from your body, and I will establish his kingdom.

"He shall build a house for my name, and I will establish the throne of his kingdom forever. I will be his father, and he shall be my son. When he commits iniquity, I will chasten him with the rod of men, with the stripes of the sons of men; but I will not take my steadfast love from him, as I took it from Saul, whom I put away from before you.

"And your house and your kingdom shall be made sure for ever before me; your throne shall be established forever."

* David's Prayer (2 Sm 7:18–29); P–2579; C8–2465

Samuel: In accordance with all these words, and in accordance with all this vision, Nathan spoke to David. Then King David went in and sat before the Lord, and said,

David: Who am I, O Lord God, and what is my house, that you have brought me thus far? And yet this was a small thing in your eyes, O Lord God; you have spoken also of your servant's house for a great while to come, and have shown me future generations, O Lord God! And what more can David say to you? For you know your servant, O Lord God! Because of your promise, and according to your own heart, you have wrought all this greatness, to make your servant know it.

Therefore you are great, O Lord God; for there is none like you, and there is no God besides you, according to all that we have heard with our ears. What other nation on earth is like your people Israel, whom God went to redeem to be his people, making himself a name, and doing for them great and terrible things, by driving out before his people a nation and its gods? And you established for yourself your people Israel to be your people for ever; and you, O Lord, became their God.

And now, O Lord God, confirm for ever the word which you have spoken concerning your servant and concerning his house, and do as you have spoken; and your name will be magnified for ever, saying, 'The Lord of hosts is God over Israel,' and the house of your servant David will be established before you. For you, O Lord of hosts, the God of Israel, have made this revelation to your servant, saying, 'I will build you a house'; therefore your servant has found courage to pray this prayer to you.

And now, O Lord God, you are God, and your words are true, and you have promised this good thing to your servant; now therefore may it please you to bless the house of your servant, that it may continue for ever before you; for you, O Lord God, have spoken, and with your blessing shall the house of your servant be blessed for ever.

THE GOSPEL OF ST. MATTHEW

Matthew Chapter 1

The Genealogy of Jesus Christ (Mt 1:1–17); F2–437

St. Matthew: The book of the genealogy of Jesus Christ, the son of David, the son of Abraham. Abraham was the father of Isaac, and Isaac the father of Jacob, and Jacob the father of Judah and his brothers, and Judah the father of Perez and Zerah by Tamar, and Perez the father of Hezron, and Hezron the father of Ram, and Ram the father of Amminadab, and Amminadab the father of Nahshon, and Nahshon the father of Salmon, and Salmon the father of Boaz by Rahab, and Boaz the father of Obed by Ruth, and Obed the father of Jesse, and Jesse the father of David the king. And David was the father of Solomon by the wife of Uriah, and Solomon the father of Rehoboam, and Rehoboam the father of Abijah, and Abijah the father of Asa, and Asa the father of Jehoshaphat, and Jehoshaphat the father of Joram, and Joram the father of Uzziah, and Uzziah the father of Jotham, and Jotham the father of Ahaz, and Ahaz the father of Hezekiah, and Hezekiah the father of Manasseh, and Manasseh the father of Amos, and Amos the father of Josiah, and Josiah the father of Jechoniah and his brothers, at the time of the deportation to Babylon.

St. Matthew 2: And after the deportation to Babylon: Jechoniah was the father of Shealtiel, and Shealtiel the father of Zerubbabel, and Zerubbabel the father of Abiud, and Abiud the father of Eliakim, and Eliakim the father of Azor, and Azor the father of Zadok, and Zadok the father of Achim, and Achim the father of Eliud, and Eliud the father of Eleazar, and Eleazar the father of Matthan, and Matthan the father of Jacob, and Jacob the father of Joseph the husband of Mary, of whom Jesus was born, who is called Christ.

St. Matthew 3: So all the generations from Abraham to David were fourteen generations, and from David to the deportation to Babylon fourteen generations, and from the deportation to Babylon to the Christ fourteen generations.

* The Birth of Jesus Christ (Mt 1:18–25); F3–497; LP1–2812

St. Matthew: Now the birth of Jesus Christ took place in this way. When his mother Mary had been betrothed to Joseph, before they came together she was found to be with child of the Holy Spirit; and her husband Joseph, being a just man and unwilling to put her to shame, resolved to send her away quietly. But as he considered this, behold, an angel of the Lord appeared to him in a dream, saying,

Angel: Joseph, son of David, do not fear to take Mary your wife, for that which is conceived in her is of the Holy Spirit; she will bear a son, and you shall call his name Jesus, for he will save his people from their sins.

St. Matthew: All this took place to fulfil what the Lord had spoken by the prophet:

Isaiah: Behold, a virgin shall conceive and bear a son, and his name shall be called Emmanuel (which means, God with us).

St. Matthew: When Joseph woke from sleep, he did as the angel of the Lord commanded him; he took his wife, but knew her not until she had borne a son; and he called his name Jesus.

Matthew Chapter 2

* The Visit of the Wise Men (Mt 2:1–12); F3–486; F3–528

St. Matthew: Now when Jesus was born in Bethlehem of Judea in the days of Herod the king, behold, Wise Men from the East came to Jerusalem, saying,

Wise Men: Where is he who has been born king of the Jews? For we have seen his star in the East, and have come to worship him.

St. Matthew: When Herod the king heard this, he was troubled, and all Jerusalem with him; and assembling all the chief priests and scribes of the people, he inquired of them where the Christ was to be born. They told him,

Chief Priests and Scribes: In Bethlehem of Judea; for so it is written by the prophet:

Micah: And you, O Bethlehem, in the land of Judah, are by no means least among the rulers of Judah; for from you shall come a ruler who will govern my people Israel.

St. Matthew: Then Herod summoned the wise men secretly and ascertained from them what time the star appeared; and he sent them to Bethlehem, saying,

Herod: Go and search diligently for the child, and when you have found him bring me word, that I too may come and worship him.

St. Matthew: When they had heard the king they went their way; and lo, the star which they had seen in the East went before them, till it came to rest over the place where the child was. When they saw the star, they rejoiced exceedingly with great joy; and going into the house they saw the child with Mary his mother, and they fell down and worshipped him. Then, opening their treasures, they offered him gifts, gold and frankincense and myrrh.

The Escape to Egypt (Mt 2:13–18) F3–530

St. Matthew: And being warned in a dream not to return to Herod, they departed to their own country by another way. Now when they had departed, behold, an angel of the Lord appeared to Joseph in a dream and said,

Angel: Rise, take the child and his mother, and flee to Egypt, and remain there till I tell you; for Herod is about to search for the child, to destroy him.

St. Matthew: And he rose and took the child and his mother by night, and departed to Egypt, and remained there until the death of Herod. This was to fulfil what the Lord had spoken by the prophet,

Prophet: Out of Egypt have I called my son.

St. Matthew: Then Herod, when he saw that he had been tricked by the wise men, was in a furious rage, and he sent and killed all the male children in Bethlehem and in all that region who were two years old or under, according to the time which he had ascertained from the wise men. Then was fulfilled what was spoken by the prophet Jeremiah:

Jeremiah: A voice was heard in Ramah, wailing and loud lamentation, Rachel weeping for her children; she refused to be consoled, because they were no more.

The Return from Egypt (Mt 2:19–23); F1–333

St. Matthew: But when Herod died, behold, an angel of the Lord appeared in a dream to Joseph in Egypt, saying,

Angel: Rise, take the child and his mother, and go to the land of Israel, for those who sought the child's life are dead.

St. Matthew: And he rose and took the child and his mother, and went to the land of Israel. But when he heard that Archelaus reigned over Judea in place of his father Herod, he was afraid to go there, and being warned in a dream he withdrew to the district of Galilee. And he went and dwelt in a city called Nazareth, that what was spoken by the prophets might be fulfilled,

Prophets: He shall be called a Nazarene.

Matthew Chapter 3

* The Preaching of John the Baptist (Mt 3:1–12); F7–678; F3–523

St. Matthew: In those days came John the Baptist, preaching in the wilderness of Judea,

John the Baptist: Repent, for the kingdom of heaven is at hand.

St. Matthew: For this is he who was spoken of by the prophet Isaiah when he said,

Isaiah: The voice of one crying in the wilderness: Prepare the way of the Lord, make his paths straight.

St. Matthew: Now John wore a garment of camel's hair, and a leather belt around his waist; and his food was locusts and wild honey. Then went out to him Jerusalem and all Judea and all the region about the Jordan, and they were baptized by him in the river Jordan, confessing their sins. But when he saw many of the Pharisees and Sadducees coming for baptism, he said to them,

John the Baptist: You brood of vipers! Who warned you to flee from the wrath to come?

Bear fruit that befits repentance, and do not presume to say to yourselves, "We have Abraham as our father"; for I tell you, God is able from these stones to raise up children to Abraham.

Even now the axe is laid to the root of the trees; every tree therefore that does not bear good fruit is cut down and thrown into the fire.

I baptize you with water for repentance, but he who is coming after me is mightier than I, whose sandals I am not worthy to carry; he will baptize you with the Holy Spirit and with fire.

His winnowing fork is in his hand, and he will clear his threshing floor and gather his wheat into the granary, but the chaff he will burn with unquenchable fire.

* The Baptism of Jesus (Mt 3:13–17); F3–535; S2–1286

St. Matthew: Then Jesus came from Galilee to the Jordan to John, to be baptized by him. John would have prevented him, saying,

John the Baptist: I need to be baptized by you, and do you come to me?

St. Matthew: But Jesus answered him,

Jesus: Let it be so now; for thus it is fitting for us to fulfill all righteousness.

St. Matthew: Then he consented. And when Jesus was baptized, he went up immediately from the water, and behold, the heavens were opened and he saw the Spirit of God descending like a dove, and alighting on him; and lo, a voice from heaven, saying,

God the Father: This is my beloved Son, with whom I am well pleased.

Matthew Chapter 4

* The Temptation of Jesus (Mt 4:1–11); F1–394; LP6–2849

St. Matthew: Then Jesus was led up by the Spirit into the wilderness to be tempted by the devil. And he fasted forty days and forty nights, and afterward he was hungry. And the tempter came and said to him,

Devil: If you are the Son of God, command these stones to become loaves of bread.

St. Matthew: But he answered,

Jesus: It is written, "Man shall not live by bread alone, but by every word that proceeds from the mouth of God."

St. Matthew: Then the devil took him to the holy city, and set him on the pinnacle of the temple, and said to him,

Devil: If you are the Son of God, throw yourself down; for it is written, "He will give his angels charge of you," and "On their hands they will bear you up, lest you strike your foot against a stone."

St. Matthew: Jesus said to him,

Jesus: Again it is written, "You shall not tempt the Lord your God."

St. Matthew: Again, the devil took him to a very high mountain, and showed him all the kingdoms of the world and the glory of them; and he said to him,

Devil: All these I will give you, if you will fall down and worship me.

St. Matthew: Then Jesus said to him,

Jesus: Begone, Satan! For it is written, "You shall worship the Lord your God and him only shall you serve."

St. Matthew: Then the devil left him, and behold, angels came and ministered to him.

* Jesus Begins Preaching in Galilee (Mt 4:12–17); LC–1720; LC–1989

St. Matthew: Now when he heard that John had been arrested, he withdrew into Galilee; and leaving Nazareth he went and dwelt in Capernaum by the sea, in the territory of Zebulun and Naphtali, that what was spoken by the prophet Isaiah might be fulfilled:

Isaiah: The land of Zebulun and the land of Naphtali, toward the sea, across the Jordan, Galilee of the Gentiles—the people who sat in darkness have seen a great light, and for those who sat in the region and shadow of death light has dawned.

St. Matthew: From that time Jesus began to preach, saying,

Jesus: Repent, for the kingdom of heaven is at hand.

Jesus Calls the First Disciples (Mt 4:18–22); F9–878

St. Matthew: As he walked by the Sea of Galilee, he saw two brothers, Simon who is called Peter and Andrew his brother, casting a net into the sea; for they were fishermen. And he said to them,

Jesus: Follow me, and I will make you fishers of men.

St. Matthew: Immediately they left their nets and followed him.

And going on from there he saw two other brothers, James the son of Zebedee and John his brother, in the boat with Zebedee their father, mending their nets, and he called them. Immediately they left the boat and their father, and followed him.

Jesus Ministers to Crowds of People (Mt 4:23–25); S5–1503

St. Matthew: And he went about all Galilee, teaching in their synagogues and preaching the gospel of the kingdom and healing every disease and every infirmity among the people.

So his fame spread throughout all Syria, and they brought him all the sick, those afflicted with various diseases and pains, demoniacs, epileptics, and paralytics, and he healed them.

And great crowds followed him from Galilee and the Decapolis and Jerusalem and Judea and from beyond the Jordan.

Matthew Chapter 5

* The Beatitudes (Mt 5:1–12); C9–2518; C5–2330

St. Matthew: Seeing the crowds, he went up on the mountain, and when he sat down his disciples came to him. And he opened his mouth and taught them, saying:

Jesus: Blessed are the poor in spirit, for theirs is the kingdom of heaven.

Blessed are those who mourn, for they shall be comforted.

Blessed are the meek, for they shall inherit the earth.

Blessed are those who hunger and thirst for righteousness, for they shall be satisfied.

Blessed are the merciful, for they shall obtain mercy.

Blessed are the pure in heart, for they shall see God.

Blessed are the peacemakers, for they shall be called sons of God.

Blessed are those who are persecuted for righteousness' sake, for theirs is the kingdom of heaven.

Blessed are you when men revile you and persecute you and utter all kinds of evil against you falsely on my account. Rejoice and be glad, for your reward is great in heaven, for so men persecuted the prophets who were before you.

* Salt and Light (Mt 5:13–16); F9–782; LP2–2821

Jesus 2: You are the salt of the earth; but if salt has lost its taste, how shall its saltiness be restored? It is no longer good for anything except to be thrown out and trodden underfoot by men.

You are the light of the world. A city set on a hill cannot be hid. Nor do men light a lamp and put it under a bushel, but on a stand, and it gives light to all in the house.

Let your light so shine before men, that they may see your good works and give glory to your Father who is in heaven.

* The Fulfillment of the Law and the Prophets (Mt 5:17–20); F4–577; LC–1967

Jesus 3: Think not that I have come to abolish the law and the prophets; I have come not to abolish them but to fulfill them.

For truly, I say to you, till heaven and earth pass away, not an iota, not a dot, will pass from the law until all is accomplished.

Whoever then relaxes one of the least of these commandments and teaches men so, shall be called least in the kingdom of heaven; but he who does them and teaches them shall be called great in the kingdom of heaven.

For I tell you, unless your righteousness exceeds that of the scribes and Pharisees, you will never enter the kingdom of heaven.

* Concerning Anger (Mt 5:21–26); LC–2054; C4–2257

Jesus 3: You have heard that it was said to the men of old,

Moses: You shall not kill; and whoever kills shall be liable to judgment.*

Jesus 3: But I say to you that everyone who is angry with his brother shall be liable to judgment; whoever insults his brother shall be liable to the council, and whoever says, “You fool!” shall be liable to the hell of fire.

So if you are offering your gift at the altar, and there remember that your brother has something against you, leave your gift there before the altar and go; first be reconciled to your brother, and then come and offer your gift.

Make friends quickly with your accuser, while you are going with him to court, lest your accuser hand you over to the judge, and the judge to the guard, and you be put in prison; truly, I say to you, you will never get out till you have paid the last penny.

* Concerning Adultery (Mt 5:27–30); C5–2330; C6–2380

Jesus 4: You have heard that it was said,

Moses: You shall not commit adultery.

Jesus 4: But I say to you that everyone who looks at a woman lustfully has already committed adultery with her in his heart. If your right eye causes you to sin, pluck it out and throw it away; it is better that you lose one of your members than that your whole body be thrown into hell. And if your right hand causes you to sin, cut it off and throw it away; it is better that you lose one of your members than that your whole body go into hell.

Concerning Divorce (Mt 5:31–32); C6–2382; C6–2380

Jesus 5: It was also said,

Moses: Whoever divorces his wife, let him give her a certificate of divorce.

Jesus 5: But I say to you that everyone who divorces his wife, except on the ground of unchastity, makes her an adulteress; and whoever marries a divorced woman commits adultery.

* Concerning Swearing Oaths (Mt 5:33–37); C7–2153; C8–2466

Jesus 6: Again you have heard that it was said to the men of old,

Moses: You shall not swear falsely, but shall perform to the Lord what you have sworn.

Jesus 6: But I say to you, Do not swear at all, either by heaven, for it is the throne of God, or by the earth, for it is his footstool, or by Jerusalem, for it is the city of the great King. And do not swear by your head, for you cannot make one hair white or black.

Let what you say be simply "Yes" or "No"; anything more than this comes from the Evil One.

Concerning Retaliation (Mt 5:38–42); C7–2443

Jesus 7: You have heard that it was said,

Moses: An eye for an eye and a tooth for a tooth.

Jesus 7: But I say to you, Do not resist one who is evil. But if any one strikes you on the right cheek, turn to him the other also; and if any one would sue you and take your coat, let him have your cloak as well; and if any one forces you to go one mile, go with him two miles. Give to him who begs from you, and do not refuse him who would borrow from you.

* Love for Enemies (Mt 5:43–48); LC–1933; LP5–2844

Jesus 8: You have heard that it was said,

Moses: You shall love your neighbor and hate your enemy.

Jesus 8: But I say to you, Love your enemies and pray for those who persecute you, so that you may be sons of your Father who is in heaven; for he makes his sun rise on the evil and on the good, and sends rain on the just and on the unjust. For if you love those who love you, what reward have you? Do not even the tax collectors do the same? And if you salute only your brethren, what more are you doing than others? Do not even the Gentiles do the same? You, therefore, must be perfect, as your heavenly Father is perfect.

Matthew Chapter 6

* Concerning Almsgiving (Mt 6:1–4); LC–1753; C7–2447

Jesus: Beware of practicing your piety before men in order to be seen by them; for then you will have no reward from your Father who is in heaven.

Thus, when you give alms, sound no trumpet before you, as the hypocrites do in the synagogues and in the streets, that they may be praised by men. Truly, I say to you, they have received their reward. But when you give alms, do not let your left hand know what your right hand is doing, so that your alms may be in secret; and your Father who sees in secret will reward you.

* Concerning Prayer (Mt 6:5–15); LC–1969; P–2759

Jesus 2: And when you pray, you must not be like the hypocrites; for they love to stand and pray in the synagogues and at the street corners, that they may be seen by men. Truly, I say to you, they have received their reward. But when you pray, go into your room and shut the door and pray to your Father who is in secret; and your Father who sees in secret will reward you.

And in praying do not heap up empty phrases as the Gentiles do; for they think that they will be heard for their many words. Do not be like them, for your Father knows what you need before you ask him.

Jesus 3: Pray then like this:

Our Father who art in heaven,
Hallowed be Thy name.
Thy kingdom come.
Thy will be done, on earth as it is in heaven.
Give us this day our daily bread;
And forgive us our trespasses, as we forgive those who trespass against us;
And lead us not into temptation,
But deliver us from evil.

For if you forgive men their trespasses, your heavenly Father also will forgive you; but if you do not forgive men their trespasses, neither will your Father forgive your trespasses.

* Concerning Fasting (Mt 6:16–18); S4–1430; F12–1063

Jesus 4: And when you fast, do not look dismal, like the hypocrites, for they disfigure their faces that their fasting may be seen by men. Truly, I say to you, they have received their reward. But when you fast, anoint your head and wash your face, that your fasting may not be seen by men but by your Father who is in secret; and your Father who sees in secret will reward you.

* Concerning Treasures (Mt 6:19–21); C9–2533; C10–2551

Jesus 5: Do not lay up for yourselves treasures on earth, where moth and rust consume and where thieves break in and steal, but lay up for yourselves treasures in heaven, where neither moth nor rust consumes and where thieves do not break in and steal. For where your treasure is, there will your heart be also.

~ The Sound Eye (Mt 6:22–23)

Jesus 6: The eye is the lamp of the body. So, if your eye is sound, your whole body will be full of light; but if your eye is not sound, your whole body will be full of darkness. If then the light in you is darkness, how great is the darkness!

* Serving Two Masters (Mt 6:24); C1–2113; LP2–2821

Jesus 7: No one can serve two masters; for either he will hate the one and love the other, or he will be devoted to the one and despise the other. You cannot serve God and mammon.

* Do Not Be Anxious (Mt 6:25–34); C10–2547; LP4–2830

Jesus 8: Therefore I tell you, do not be anxious about your life, what you shall eat or what you shall drink, nor about your body, what you shall put on. Is not life more than food, and the body more than clothing?

Look at the birds of the air: they neither sow nor reap nor gather into barns, and yet your heavenly Father feeds them. Are you not of more value than they? And which of you by being anxious can add one cubit to his span of life?

And why are you anxious about clothing? Consider the lilies of the field, how they grow; they neither toil nor spin; yet I tell you, even Solomon in all his glory was not arrayed like one of these.

Jesus 9: But if God so clothes the grass of the field, which today is alive and tomorrow is thrown into the oven, will he not much more clothe you, O men of little faith?

Therefore do not be anxious, saying, "What shall we eat?" or "What shall we drink?" or "What shall we wear?" For the Gentiles seek all these things; and your heavenly Father knows that you need them all.

But seek first his kingdom and his righteousness, and all these things shall be yours as well.

Therefore do not be anxious about tomorrow, for tomorrow will be anxious for itself. Let the day's own trouble be sufficient for the day.

Matthew Chapter 7

Judging Others (Mt 7:1–5); F7–678

Jesus: Judge not, that you be not judged. For with the judgment you pronounce you will be judged, and the measure you give will be the measure you get. Why do you see the speck that is in your brother's eye, but do not notice the log that is in your own eye? Or how can you say to your brother,

Person 1: Let me take the speck out of your eye,

Jesus: when there is the log in your own eye? You hypocrite, first take the log out of your own eye, and then you will see clearly to take the speck out of your brother's eye.

~ Profaning the Holy (Mt 7:6)

Jesus 2: Do not give dogs what is holy; and do not throw your pearls before swine, lest they trample them underfoot and turn to attack you.

* Ask, Seek, Knock (Mt 7:7–12); P–2609

Jesus 3: Ask, and it will be given you; seek, and you will find; knock, and it will be opened to you. For everyone who asks receives, and he who seeks finds, and to him who knocks it will be opened.

Jesus 4: Or what man of you, if his son asks him for bread, will give him a stone? Or if he asks for a fish, will give him a serpent? If you then, who are evil, know how to give good gifts to your children, how much more will your Father who is in heaven give good things to those who ask him!

Jesus 5: So whatever you wish that men would do to you, do so to them; for this is the law and the prophets.

* The Narrow Gate (Mt 7:13–14); F12–1036; P–2609

Jesus 6: Enter by the narrow gate; for the gate is wide and the way is easy, that leads to destruction, and those who enter by it are many. For the gate is narrow and the way is hard, that leads to life, and those who find it are few.

False Prophets (Mt 7:15–20); C5–2285; LC–2005

Jesus 7: Beware of false prophets, who come to you in sheep's clothing but inwardly are ravenous wolves. You will know them by their fruits. Are grapes gathered from thorns, or figs from thistles?

Jesus 8: So, every sound tree bears good fruit, but the bad tree bears evil fruit. A sound tree cannot bear evil fruit, nor can a bad tree bear good fruit. Every tree that does not bear good fruit is cut down and thrown into the fire.

Thus you will know them by their fruits.

* Concerning Self-Deception (Mt 7:21–23); LC–1821; P–2611

Jesus 9: Not everyone who says to me,

Person 2: Lord, Lord,

Jesus 9: shall enter the kingdom of heaven, but he who does the will of my Father who is in heaven. On that day many will say to me,

Many: Lord, Lord, did we not prophesy in your name, and cast out demons in your name, and do many mighty works in your name?

Jesus 9: And then will I declare to them, "I never knew you; depart from me, you evildoers."

Hearers and Doers (Mt 7:24–28); F4–581

Jesus 9: Everyone then who hears these words of mine and does them will be like a wise man who built his house upon the rock; and the rain fell, and the floods came, and the winds blew and beat upon that house, but it did not fall, because it had been founded on the rock.

And everyone who hears these words of mine and does not do them will be like a foolish man who built his house upon the sand; and the rain fell, and the floods came, and the winds blew and beat against that house, and it fell; and great was the fall of it.

St. Matthew: And when Jesus finished these sayings, the crowds were astonished at his teaching, for he taught them as one who had authority, and not as their scribes.

Matthew Chapter 8

Jesus Cleanses a Leper (Mt 8:1–4); F2–448; F4–585

St. Matthew: When he came down from the mountain, great crowds followed him; and behold, a leper came to him and knelt before him, saying,

Leper: Lord, if you will, you can make me clean.

St. Matthew: And he stretched out his hand and touched him, saying,

Jesus: I will; be clean.

St. Matthew: And immediately his leprosy was cleansed. And Jesus said to him,

Jesus: See that you say nothing to any one; but go, show yourself to the priest, and offer the gift that Moses commanded, for a proof to the people.

* Jesus Heals a Centurion's Servant (Mt 8:5–13); S3–1386; P–2610

St. Matthew: As he entered Capernaum, a centurion came forward to him, beseeching him and saying,

Centurion: Lord, my servant is lying paralyzed at home, in terrible distress.

St. Matthew: And he said to him,

Jesus: I will come and heal him.

St. Matthew: But the centurion answered him,

Centurion: Lord, I am not worthy to have you come under my roof; but only say the word, and my servant will be healed. For I am a man under authority, with soldiers under me; and I say to one, "Go," and he goes, and to another, "Come," and he comes, and to my slave, "Do this," and he does it.

St. Matthew: When Jesus heard him, he marveled, and said to those who followed him,

Jesus: Truly, I say to you, not even in Israel have I found such faith. I tell you, many will come from east and west and sit at table with Abraham, Isaac, and Jacob in the kingdom of heaven, while the sons of the kingdom will be thrown into the outer darkness; there men will weep and gnash their teeth.

St. Matthew: And to the centurion Jesus said,

Jesus: Go; be it done for you as you have believed.

St. Matthew: And the servant was healed at that very moment.

Jesus Heals Many at Peter's House (Mt 8:14–17); F3–517; S5–1505;

St. Matthew: And when Jesus entered Peter's house, he saw his mother-in-law lying sick with a fever; he touched her hand, and the fever left her, and she rose and served him. That evening they brought to him many who were possessed with demons; and he cast out the spirits with a word, and healed all who were sick. This was to fulfil what was spoken by the prophet Isaiah,

Isaiah: He took our infirmities and bore our diseases.

Would-be Followers of Jesus (Mt 8:18–22); C7–2444

St. Matthew: Now when Jesus saw great crowds around him, he gave orders to go over to the other side. And a scribe came up and said to him,

Scribe: Teacher, I will follow you wherever you go.

St. Matthew: And Jesus said to him,

Jesus: Foxes have holes, and birds of the air have nests; but the Son of man has nowhere to lay his head. Another of the disciples said to him,

Another disciple: Lord, let me first go and bury my father.

St. Matthew: But Jesus said to him,

Jesus: Follow me, and leave the dead to bury their own dead.

Jesus Calms the Storm at Sea (Mt 8:23–27); P-2610

St. Matthew: And when he got into the boat, his disciples followed him. And behold, there arose a great storm on the sea, so that the boat was being swamped by the waves; but he was asleep. And they went and woke him, saying,

Disciples: Save us, Lord; we are perishing.

St. Matthew: And he said to them,

Jesus: Why are you afraid, O men of little faith?

St. Matthew: Then he rose and rebuked the winds and the sea; and there was a great calm. And the men marveled, saying,

Disciples: What sort of man is this, that even winds and sea obey him?

~ Jesus Heals the Gadarene Demoniacs (Mt 8:28–34)

St. Matthew: And when he came to the other side, to the country of the Gadarenes, two demoniacs met him, coming out of the tombs, so fierce that no one could pass that way. And behold, they cried out,

Demoniacs: What have you to do with us, O Son of God? Have you come here to torment us before the time?

St. Matthew: Now a herd of many swine was feeding at some distance from them. And the demons begged him,

Demons: If you cast us out, send us away into the herd of swine.

St. Matthew: And he said to them,

Jesus: Go.

St. Matthew: So they came out and went into the swine; and behold, the whole herd rushed down the steep bank into the sea, and perished in the waters. The herdsmen fled, and going into the city they told everything, and what had happened to the demoniacs. And behold, all the city came out to meet Jesus; and when they saw him, they begged him to leave their neighborhood.

Matthew Chapter 9

~ Jesus Heals a Paralytic (Mt 9:1–8)

St. Matthew: And getting into a boat he crossed over and came to his own city. And behold, they brought to him a paralytic, lying on his bed; and when Jesus saw their faith he said to the paralytic,

Jesus: Take heart, my son; your sins are forgiven.

St. Matthew: And behold, some of the scribes said to themselves,

Scribes: This man is blaspheming.

St. Matthew: But Jesus, knowing their thoughts, said,

Jesus: Why do you think evil in your hearts? For which is easier, to say, "Your sins are forgiven," or to say, "Rise and walk?" But that you may know that the Son of man has authority on earth to forgive sins—

St. Matthew: he then said to the paralytic—

Jesus: Rise, take up your bed and go home.

* The Call of Matthew (Mt 9:9–13); F4–589; C1–2100

St. Matthew: And he rose and went home. When the crowds saw it, they were afraid, and they glorified God, who had given such authority to men. As Jesus passed on from there, he saw a man called Matthew sitting at the tax office; and he said to him,

Jesus: Follow me.

St. Matthew: And he rose and followed him. And as he sat at table in the house, behold, many tax collectors and sinners came and sat down with Jesus and his disciples. And when the Pharisees saw this, they said to his disciples,

Pharisees: Why does your teacher eat with tax collectors and sinners?

St. Matthew: But when he heard it, he said,

Jesus: Those who are well have no need of a physician, but those who are sick. Go and learn what this means, "I desire mercy, and not sacrifice." For I came not to call the righteous, but sinners.

~ The Question about Fasting (Mt 9:14–17)

St. Matthew: Then the disciples of John came to him, saying,

Disciples of John: Why do we and the Pharisees fast, but your disciples do not fast?

St. Matthew: And Jesus said to them,

Jesus: Can the wedding guests mourn as long as the bridegroom is with them? The days will come, when the bridegroom is taken away from them, and then they will fast. And no one puts a piece of unshrunk cloth on an old garment, for the patch tears away from the garment, and a worse tear is made. Neither is new wine put into old wineskins; if it is, the skins burst, and the wine is spilled, and the skins are destroyed; but new wine is put into fresh wineskins, and so both are preserved.

~ A Girl Restored to Life and a Woman Healed (Mt 9:18–26)

St. Matthew: While he was thus speaking to them, behold, a ruler came in and knelt before him, saying,

Ruler: My daughter has just died; but come and lay your hand on her, and she will live.

St. Matthew: And Jesus rose and followed him, with his disciples. And behold, a woman who had suffered from a hemorrhage for twelve years came up behind him and touched the fringe of his garment; for she said to herself,

Woman: If I only touch his garment, I shall be made well.

St. Matthew: Jesus turned, and seeing her he said,

Jesus: Take heart, daughter; your faith has made you well.

St. Matthew: And instantly the woman was made well. And when Jesus came to the ruler's house, and saw the flute players, and the crowd making a tumult, he said,

Jesus: Depart; for the girl is not dead but sleeping.

St. Matthew: And they laughed at him. But when the crowd had been put outside, he went in and took her by the hand, and the girl arose. And the report of this went through all that district.

Jesus Heals Two Blind Men (Mt 9:27–31); F2–439; P–2616;

St. Matthew: And as Jesus passed on from there, two blind men followed him, crying aloud,

Two Blind Men: Have mercy on us, Son of David.

St. Matthew: When he entered the house, the blind men came to him; and Jesus said to them,

Jesus: Do you believe that I am able to do this?

St. Matthew: They said to him,

Two Blind Men: Yes, Lord.

St. Matthew: Then he touched their eyes, saying,

Jesus: According to your faith be it done to you.

St. Matthew: And their eyes were opened. And Jesus sternly charged them,

Jesus: See that no one knows it.

St. Matthew: But they went away and spread his fame through all that district.

~ Jesus Heals a Man Who Was Mute (Mt 9:32–34)

St. Matthew: As they were going away, behold, a mute demoniac was brought to him. And when the demon had been cast out, the mute man spoke; and the crowds marveled, saying,

Crowds: Never was anything like this seen in Israel.

St. Matthew: But the Pharisees said,

Pharisees: He casts out demons by the prince of demons.

The Harvest is Plentiful, the Laborers Are Few (Mt 9:35–38); P–2611

St. Matthew: And Jesus went about all the cities and villages, teaching in their synagogues and preaching the gospel of the kingdom, and healing every disease and every infirmity. When he saw the crowds, he had compassion for them, because they were harassed and helpless, like sheep without a shepherd. Then he said to his disciples,

Jesus: The harvest is plentiful, but the laborers are few; pray therefore the Lord of the harvest to send out laborers into his harvest.

Matthew Chapter 10

~ The Twelve Disciples (Mt 10:1–4)

St. Matthew: And he called to him his twelve disciples and gave them authority over unclean spirits, to cast them out, and to heal every disease and every infirmity. The names of the twelve apostles are these: first, Simon, who is called Peter, and Andrew his brother; James the son of Zebedee, and John his brother; Philip and Bartholomew; Thomas and Matthew the tax collector; James the son of Alphaeus, and Thaddaeus; Simon the Cananaean, and Judas Iscariot, who betrayed him.

* The Mission of the Twelve (Mt 10:5–15); S5–1509; C1–2121

St. Matthew: These twelve Jesus sent out, charging them,

Jesus: Go nowhere among the Gentiles, and enter no town of the Samaritans, but go rather to the lost sheep of the house of Israel.

And preach as you go, saying, "The kingdom of heaven is at hand." Heal the sick, raise the dead, cleanse lepers, cast out demons. You received without paying, give without pay.

Take no gold, nor silver, nor copper in your belts, no bag for your journey, nor two tunics, nor sandals, nor a staff; for the laborer deserves his food.

Jesus 2: And whatever town or village you enter, find out who is worthy in it, and stay with him until you depart. As you enter the house, salute it. And if the house is worthy, let your peace come upon it; but if it is not worthy, let your peace return to you.

And if any one will not receive you or listen to your words, shake off the dust from your feet as you leave that house or town. Truly, I say to you, it shall be more tolerable on the day of judgment for the land of Sodom and Gomorrah than for that town.

*Coming Persecutions (Mt 10:16–25); PF3–161; LC–1821

Jesus 3: Behold, I send you out as sheep in the midst of wolves; so be wise as serpents and innocent as doves. Beware of men; for they will deliver you up to councils, and flog you in their synagogues, and you will be dragged before governors and kings for my sake, to bear testimony before them and the Gentiles.

Jesus 4: When they deliver you up, do not be anxious how you are to speak or what you are to say; for what you are to say will be given to you in that hour; for it is not you who speak, but the Spirit of your Father speaking through you.

Brother will deliver up brother to death, and the father his child, and children will rise against parents and have them put to death; and you will be hated by all for my name's sake. But he who endures to the end will be saved.

When they persecute you in one town, flee to the next; for truly, I say to you, you will not have gone through all the towns of Israel, before the Son of man comes.

Jesus 5: A disciple is not above his teacher, nor a servant above his master; it is enough for the disciple to be like his teacher, and the servant like his master. If they have called the master of the house Beelzebul, how much more will they malign those of his household.

* Whom to Fear (Mt 10:26–33); PLG–14; C2–2145

Jesus 6: What I tell you in the dark, utter in the light; and what you hear whispered, proclaim upon the housetops.

And do not fear those who kill the body but cannot kill the soul; rather fear him who can destroy both soul and body in hell.

Are not two sparrows sold for a penny? And not one of them will fall to the ground without your Father's will. But even the hairs of your head are all numbered. Fear not, therefore; you are of more value than many sparrows.

Jesus 7: So everyone who acknowledges me before men, I also will acknowledge before my Father who is in heaven; but whoever denies me before men, I also will deny before my Father who is in heaven.

Taking Up One's Cross (Mt 10:34–39); C4–2232; S5–1506

Jesus 8: He who loves father or mother more than me is not worthy of me; and he who loves son or daughter more than me is not worthy of me; and he who does not take his cross and follow me is not worthy of me.

He who finds his life will lose it, and he who loses his life for my sake will find it.

Rewards (Mt 10:40–42); F9–858

Jesus 8: He who receives you receives me, and he who receives me receives him who sent me.

He who receives a prophet because he is a prophet shall receive a prophet's reward, and he who receives a righteous man because he is a righteous man shall receive a righteous man's reward.

And whoever gives to one of these little ones even a cup of cold water because he is a disciple, truly, I say to you, he shall not lose his reward.

Matthew Chapter 11

St. Matthew: And when Jesus had finished instructing his twelve disciples, he went on from there to teach and preach in their cities.

* Messengers from John the Baptist (Mt 11:2–6); F3–549; C7–2443

St. Matthew: Now when John heard in prison about the deeds of the Christ, he sent word by his disciples and said to him,

Disciples of John: Are you he who is to come, or shall we look for another?

St. Matthew: And Jesus answered them,

Jesus: Go and tell John what you hear and see: the blind receive their sight and the lame walk, lepers are cleansed and the deaf hear, and the dead are raised up, and the poor have good news preached to them. And blessed is he who takes no offense at me.

Jesus Praises John the Baptist (Mt 11:7–19); F8–719; F3–523

St. Matthew: As they went away, Jesus began to speak to the crowds concerning John:

Jesus: What did you go out into the wilderness to behold? A reed shaken by the wind? Why then did you go out? To see a man dressed in soft robes?

Behold, those who wear soft robes are in kings' houses. Why then did you go out? To see a prophet? Yes, I tell you, and more than a prophet. This is he of whom it is written, "Behold, I send my messenger before your face, who shall prepare your way before you." Truly, I say to you, among those born of women there has risen no one greater than John the Baptist; yet he who is least in the kingdom of heaven is greater than he.

From the days of John the Baptist until now the kingdom of heaven has suffered violence, and men of violence take it by force. For all the prophets and the law prophesied until John; and if you are willing to accept it, he is Elijah who is to come. He who has ears to hear, let him hear.

But to what shall I compare this generation? It is like children sitting in the marketplaces and calling to their playmates,

Children in the marketplaces: We piped to you, and you did not dance; we wailed, and you did not mourn.

Jesus: For John came neither eating nor drinking, and they say, "He has a demon;" the Son of man came eating and drinking, and they say, "Behold, a glutton and a drunkard, a friend of tax collectors and sinners!" Yet wisdom is justified by her deeds.

Jesus Upbraids the Unrepentant Cities (Mt 11:20–24); F7–678

St. Matthew: Then he began to upbraid the cities where most of his mighty works had been done, because they did not repent.

Jesus: Woe to you, Chorazin! Woe to you, Bethsaida! For if the mighty works done in you had been done in Tyre and Sidon, they would have repented long ago in sackcloth and ashes. But I tell you, it shall be more tolerable on the day of judgment for Tyre and Sidon than for you.

And you, Capernaum, will you be exalted to heaven? You shall be brought down to Hades. For if the mighty works done in you had been done in Sodom, it would have remained until this day. But I tell you that it shall be more tolerable on the day of judgment for the land of Sodom than for you.

* Jesus Thanks His Father (Mt 11:25–30); P–2603; LP1–2779

St. Matthew: At that time Jesus declared,

Jesus: I thank you, Father, Lord of heaven and earth, that you have hidden these things from the wise and understanding and revealed them to babes; yea, Father, for such was your gracious will. All things have been delivered to me by my Father; and no one knows the Son except the Father, and no one knows the Father except the Son and any one to whom the Son chooses to reveal him.

Come to me, all who labor and are heavy laden, and I will give you rest. Take my yoke upon you, and learn from me; for I am gentle and lowly in heart, and you will find rest for your souls. For my yoke is easy, and my burden is light.

Matthew Chapter 12

* Plucking Grain on the Sabbath (Mt 12:1–8); F4–581; C3–2173

St. Matthew: At that time Jesus went through the grainfields on the sabbath; his disciples were hungry, and they began to pluck heads of grain and to eat. But when the Pharisees saw it, they said to him,

Pharisees: Look, your disciples are doing what is not lawful to do on the sabbath.

St. Matthew: He said to them,

Jesus: Have you not read what David did, when he was hungry, and those who were with him: how he entered the house of God and ate the showbread, which it was not lawful for him to eat nor for those who were with him, but only for the priests?

Or have you not read in the law how on the sabbath the priests in the temple profane the sabbath, and are guiltless?

I tell you, something greater than the temple is here. And if you had known what this means, "I desire mercy, and not sacrifice," you would not have condemned the guiltless. For the Son of man is Lord of the sabbath.

The Man with a Withered Hand (Mt 12:9–14); F1–342

St. Matthew: And he went on from there, and entered their synagogue. And behold, there was a man with a withered hand. And they asked him,

Pharisees: Is it lawful to heal on the sabbath?

St. Matthew: So that they might accuse him. He said to them,

Jesus: What man of you, if he has one sheep and it falls into a pit on the sabbath, will not lay hold of it and lift it out? Of how much more value is a man than a sheep! So it is lawful to do good on the sabbath.

St. Matthew: Then he said to the man,

Jesus: Stretch out your hand.

St. Matthew: And the man stretched it out, and it was restored, whole like the other. But the Pharisees went out and took counsel against him, how to destroy him.

God's Chosen Servant (Mt 12:15–21); F8–713

St. Matthew: Jesus, aware of this, withdrew from there. And many followed him, and he healed them all, and ordered them not to make him known. This was to fulfill what was spoken by the prophet Isaiah:

Isaiah: Behold, my servant whom I have chosen, my beloved with whom my soul is well pleased. I will put my Spirit upon him, and he shall proclaim justice to the Gentiles. He will not wrangle or cry aloud, nor will any one hear his voice in the streets; he will not break a bruised reed or quench a smoldering wick, till he brings justice to victory; and in his name will the Gentiles hope.

* Jesus and Beelzebul (Mt 12:22–32); F7–679; LC–1864

St. Matthew: Then a blind and mute demoniac was brought to him, and he healed him, so that the mute man spoke and saw. And all the people were amazed, and said,

People: Can this be the Son of David?

St. Matthew: But when the Pharisees heard it they said,

Pharisees: It is only by Beelzebul, the prince of demons, that this man casts out demons.

St. Matthew: Knowing their thoughts, he said to them,

Jesus: Every kingdom divided against itself is laid waste, and no city or house divided against itself will stand; and if Satan casts out Satan, he is divided against himself; how then will his kingdom stand?

And if I cast out demons by Beelzebul, by whom do your sons cast them out? Therefore they shall be your judges.

But if it is by the Spirit of God that I cast out demons, then the kingdom of God has come upon you.

Jesus 2: Or how can one enter a strong man's house and plunder his goods, unless he first binds the strong man? Then indeed he may plunder his house. He who is not with me is against me, and he who does not gather with me scatters.

Therefore I tell you, every sin and blasphemy will be forgiven men, but the blasphemy against the Spirit will not be forgiven.

Jesus 3: And whoever says a word against the Son of man will be forgiven; but whoever speaks against the Holy Spirit will not be forgiven, either in this age or in the age to come.

A Tree and Its Fruit (Mt 12:33–37); F4–590;

Jesus 3: Either make the tree good, and its fruit good; or make the tree bad, and its fruit bad; for the tree is known by its fruit.

Jesus 3: You brood of vipers! How can you speak good, when you are evil? For out of the abundance of the heart the mouth speaks.

The good man out of his good treasure brings forth good, and the evil man out of his evil treasure brings forth evil.

I tell you, on the day of judgment men will render account for every careless word they utter; for by your words you will be justified, and by your words you will be condemned.

* The Sign of Jonah (Mt 12:38–42); F4–590; F7–678

St. Matthew: Then some of the scribes and Pharisees said to him,

Scribes and Pharisees: Teacher, we wish to see a sign from you. But he answered them,

Jesus: An evil and adulterous generation seeks for a sign; but no sign shall be given to it except the sign of the prophet Jonah. For as Jonah was three days and three nights in the belly of the whale, so will the Son of man be three days and three nights in the heart of the earth.

Jesus 2: The men of Nineveh will arise at the judgment with this generation and condemn it; for they repented at the preaching of Jonah, and behold, something greater than Jonah is here.

Jesus 3: The queen of the South will arise at the judgment with this generation and condemn it; for she came from the ends of the earth to hear the wisdom of Solomon, and behold, something greater than Solomon is here.

~ The Return of the Unclean Spirit (Mt 12:43–45)

Jesus 4: When the unclean spirit has gone out of a man, he passes through waterless places seeking rest, but he finds none. Then he says,

Unclean spirit: I will return to my house from which I came.

Jesus 4: And when he comes he finds it empty, swept, and put in order. Then he goes and brings with him seven other spirits more evil than himself, and they enter and dwell there; and the last state of that man becomes worse than the first. So shall it be also with this evil generation.

The True Kindred of Jesus (Mt 12:46–50); F9–764; C4–2233

St. Matthew: While he was still speaking to the people, behold, his mother and his brethren stood outside, asking to speak to him. But he replied to the man who told him,

Jesus 5: Who is my mother, and who are my brethren?

St. Matthew: And stretching out his hand toward his disciples, he said,

Jesus 5: Here are my mother and my brethren! For whoever does the will of my Father in heaven is my brother, and sister, and mother.

Matthew Chapter 13

The Parable of the Sower (Mt 13:1–9); F3–546

St. Matthew: That same day Jesus went out of the house and sat beside the sea. And great crowds gathered about him, so that he got into a boat and sat there; and the whole crowd stood on the beach. And he told them many things in parables, saying:

Jesus: A sower went out to sow. And as he sowed, some seeds fell along the path, and the birds came and devoured them. Other seeds fell on rocky ground, where they had not much soil, and immediately they sprang up, since they had no depth of soil, but when the sun rose they were scorched; and since they had no root they withered away.

Other seeds fell upon thorns, and the thorns grew up and choked them. Other seeds fell on good soil and brought forth grain, some a hundredfold, some sixty, some thirty. He who has ears, let him hear.

* The Purpose of the Parables (Mt 13:10–17); F9–787; F3–546

St. Matthew: Then the disciples came and said to him,

Disciples: Why do you speak to them in parables?

St. Matthew: And he answered them,

Jesus: To you it has been given to know the secrets of the kingdom of heaven, but to them it has not been given. For to him who has will more be given, and he will have abundance; but from him who has not, even what he has will be taken away. This is why I speak to them in parables, because seeing they do not see, and hearing they do not hear, nor do they understand. With them indeed is fulfilled the prophecy of Isaiah which says:

Isaiah: You shall indeed hear but never understand, and you shall indeed see but never perceive. For this people's heart has grown dull, and their ears are heavy of hearing, and their eyes they have closed, lest they should perceive with their eyes, and hear with their ears, and understand with their heart, and turn for me to heal them.

Jesus: But blessed are your eyes, for they see, and your ears, for they hear. Truly, I say to you, many prophets and righteous men longed to see what you see, and did not see it, and to hear what you hear, and did not hear it.

The Parable of the Sower Explained (Mt 13:18–23); PF1–29

Jesus 1: Hear then the parable of the sower. When any one hears the word of the kingdom and does not understand it, the evil one comes and snatches away what is sown in his heart; this is what was sown along the path.

As for what was sown on rocky ground, this is he who hears the word and immediately receives it with joy; yet he has no root in himself, but endures for a while, and when tribulation or persecution arises on account of the word, immediately he falls away.

As for what was sown among thorns, this is he who hears the word, but the cares of the world and the delight in riches choke the word, and it proves unfruitful. As for what was sown on good soil, this is he who hears the word and understands it; he indeed bears fruit, and yields, in one case a hundredfold, in another sixty, and in another thirty.

The Parable of the Weeds Among the Wheat (Mt 13:24–30); F9–827

St. Matthew: Another parable he put before them, saying,

Jesus: The kingdom of heaven may be compared to a man who sowed good seed in his field; but while men were sleeping, his enemy came and sowed weeds among the wheat, and went away. So when the plants came up and bore grain, then the weeds appeared also. And the servants of the householder came and said to him,

Servants: Sir, did you not sow good seed in your field? How then has it weeds?

Jesus: He said to them,

Householder: An enemy has done this.

Jesus: The servants said to him,

Servants: Then do you want us to go and gather them?

Jesus: But he said,

Householder: No; lest in gathering the weeds you root up the wheat along with them. Let both grow together until the harvest; and at harvest time I will tell the reapers, "Gather the weeds first and bind them in bundles to be burned, but gather the wheat into my barn."

~ The Parables of the Mustard Seed (Mt 13:31–32)

St. Matthew: Another parable he put before them, saying,

Jesus 2: The kingdom of heaven is like a grain of mustard seed which a man took and sowed in his field; it is the smallest of all seeds, but when it has grown it is the greatest of shrubs and becomes a tree, so that the birds of the air come and make nests in its branches.

~ The Parable of the Leaven (Mt 13:33)

St. Matthew: He told them another parable.

Jesus 3: The kingdom of heaven is like leaven which a woman took and hid in three measures of flour, till it was all leavened.

~ Why Jesus Speaks in Parables (Mt 13:34–35)

St. Matthew: All this Jesus said to the crowds in parables; indeed he said nothing to them without a parable. This was to fulfil what was spoken by the prophet:

Prophet: I will open my mouth in parables, I will utter what has been hidden since the foundation of the world.

~ Jesus Explains the Parable of the Weeds (Mt 13:36–43)

St. Matthew: Then he left the crowds and went into the house. And his disciples came to him, saying,

Disciples: Explain to us the parable of the weeds of the field.

St. Matthew: He answered,

Jesus 4: He who sows the good seed is the Son of man; the field is the world, and the good seed means the sons of the kingdom; the weeds are the sons of the evil one, and the enemy who sowed them is the devil; the harvest is the close of the age, and the reapers are angels.

Just as the weeds are gathered and burned with fire, so will it be at the close of the age. The Son of man will send his angels, and they will gather out of his kingdom all causes of sin and all evildoers, and throw them into the furnace of fire; there men will weep and gnash their teeth.

Then the righteous will shine like the sun in the kingdom of their Father. He who has ears, let him hear.

Three Parables About the Kingdom (Mt 13:44–50); F3–546; F12–1034

Jesus: The kingdom of heaven is like treasure hidden in a field, which a man found and covered up; then in his joy he goes and sells all that he has and buys that field. Again, the kingdom of heaven is like a merchant in search of fine pearls, who, on finding one pearl of great value, went and sold all that he had and bought it.

Again, the kingdom of heaven is like a net which was thrown into the sea and gathered fish of every kind; when it was full, men drew it ashore and sat down and sorted the good into vessels but threw away the bad. So it will be at the close of the age.

The angels will come out and separate the evil from the righteous, and throw them into the furnace of fire; there men will weep and gnash their teeth.

Treasures New and Old (Mt 13:51–52); LT–1117

Jesus: Have you understood all this?

St. Matthew: They said to him,

Disciples: Yes.

St. Matthew: And he said to them,

Jesus: Therefore every scribe who has been trained for the kingdom of heaven is like a householder who brings out of his treasure what is new and what is old.

The Rejection of Jesus at Nazareth (Mt 13:53–58); F3–495; F3–500

St. Matthew: And when Jesus had finished these parables, he went away from there, and coming to his own country he taught them in their synagogue, so that they were astonished, and said,

People of Nazareth: Where did this man get this wisdom and these mighty works? Is not this the carpenter's son? Is not his mother called Mary? And are not his brethren James and Joseph and Simon and Judas? And are not all his sisters with us? Where then did this man get all this?

St. Matthew: And they took offense at him. But Jesus said to them,

Jesus: A prophet is not without honor except in his own country and in his own house.

St. Matthew: And he did not do many mighty works there, because of their unbelief.

Matthew Chapter 14

~ The Death of John the Baptist (Mt 14:1–12)

St. Matthew: At that time Herod the tetrarch heard about the fame of Jesus; and he said to his servants,

Herod: This is John the Baptist; he has been raised from the dead; that is why these powers are at work in him.

St. Matthew: For Herod had seized John and bound him and put him in prison, for the sake of Herodias, his brother Philip's wife; because John said to him,

John the Baptist: It is not lawful for you to have her.

St. Matthew: And though he wanted to put him to death, he feared the people, because they held him to be a prophet. But when Herod's birthday came, the daughter of Herodias danced before the company, and pleased Herod, so that he promised with an oath to give her whatever she might ask. Prompted by her mother, she said,

Daughter of Herodias: Give me the head of John the Baptist here on a platter.

St. Matthew: And the king was sorry; but because of his oaths and his guests he commanded it to be given; he sent and had John beheaded in the prison, and his head was brought on a platter and given to the girl, and she brought it to her mother. And his disciples came and took the body and buried it; and they went and told Jesus.

Feeding the Five Thousand (Mt 14:13–21); S3–1335; S3–1329

St. Matthew: Now when Jesus heard this, he withdrew from there in a boat to a lonely place apart. But when the crowds heard it, they followed him on foot from the towns. As he went ashore he saw a great throng; and he had compassion on them, and healed their sick. When it was evening, the disciples came to him and said,

Disciples: This is a lonely place, and the day is now over; send the crowds away to go into the villages and buy food for themselves.

St. Matthew: Jesus said,

Jesus: They need not go away; you give them something to eat.

St. Matthew: They said to him,

Disciples: We have only five loaves here and two fish.

St. Matthew: And he said,

Jesus: Bring them here to me.

St. Matthew: Then he ordered the crowds to sit down on the grass; and taking the five loaves and the two fish he looked up to heaven, and blessed, and broke and gave the loaves to the disciples, and the disciples gave them to the crowds. And they all ate and were satisfied. And they took up twelve baskets full of the broken pieces left over. And those who ate were about five thousand men, besides women and children.

Jesus Walks on the Sea (Mt 14:22–33); F2–448

St. Matthew: Then he made the disciples get into the boat and go before him to the other side, while he dismissed the crowds. And after he had dismissed the crowds, he went up on the mountain by himself to pray. When evening came, he was there alone, but the boat by this time was many furlongs distant from the land, beaten by the waves; for the wind was against them. And in the fourth watch of the night he came to them, walking on the sea. But when the disciples saw him walking on the sea, they were terrified, saying,

Disciples: It is a ghost!

St. Matthew: And they cried out for fear. But immediately he spoke to them, saying,

Jesus: Take heart, it is I; have no fear.

St. Matthew: And Peter answered him,

Peter: Lord, if it is you, bid me come to you on the water.

St. Matthew: He said,

Jesus: Come.

St. Matthew: So Peter got out of the boat and walked on the water and came to Jesus; but when he saw the wind, he was afraid, and beginning to sink he cried out,

Peter: Lord, save me.

St. Matthew: Jesus immediately reached out his hand and caught him, saying to him,

Jesus: You of little faith, why did you doubt?

St. Matthew: And when they got into the boat, the wind ceased. And those in the boat worshipped him, saying,

Disciples: Truly you are the Son of God.

~ Jesus Heals the Sick in Gennesaret (Mt 14:34–36)

St. Matthew: And when they had crossed over, they came to land at Gennesaret. And when the men of that place recognized him, they sent round to all that region and brought to him all that were sick, and besought him that they might only touch the fringe of his garment; and as many as touched it were made well.

Matthew Chapter 15

The Tradition of the Elders (Mt 15:1–9); F4–579

St. Matthew: Then Pharisees and scribes came to Jesus from Jerusalem and said,

Pharisees and scribes: Why do your disciples transgress the tradition of the elders? For they do not wash their hands when they eat.

St. Matthew: He answered them,

Jesus: And why do you transgress the commandment of God for the sake of your tradition? For God commanded, "Honor your father and your mother," and, "He who speaks evil of father or mother, let him surely die." But you say, "If any one tells his father or his mother, 'What you would have gained from me is given to God,' he need not honor his father." So, for the sake of your tradition, you have made void the word of God. You hypocrites! Well did Isaiah prophesy of you when he said:

Isaiah: This people honors me with their lips, but their heart is far from me; in vain do they worship me, teaching as doctrines the precepts of men.

* Things that Defile a Man (Mt 15:10–20); LC–1968; C9–2517

St. Matthew: And he called the people to him and said to them,

Jesus: Hear and understand: not what goes into the mouth defiles a man, but what comes out of the mouth, this defiles a man.

St. Matthew: Then the disciples came and said to him,

Disciples: Do you know that the Pharisees were offended when they heard this saying?

St. Matthew: He answered,

Jesus: Every plant which my heavenly Father has not planted will be rooted up. Let them alone; they are blind guides. And if a blind man leads a blind man, both will fall into a pit.

St. Matthew: But Peter said to him,

Peter: Explain the parable to us.

St. Matthew: And he said,

Jesus: Are you also still without understanding? Do you not see that whatever goes into the mouth passes into the stomach, and so passes on? But what comes out of the mouth proceeds from the heart, and this defiles a man. For out of the heart come evil thoughts, murder, adultery, fornication, theft, false witness, slander. These are what defile a man; but to eat with unwashed hands does not defile a man.

* The Canaanite Woman's Faith (Mt 15:21–28); F2–439; F2-448

St. Matthew: And Jesus went away from there and withdrew to the district of Tyre and Sidon. And behold, a Canaanite woman from that region came out and cried,

Canaanite woman: Have mercy on me, O Lord, Son of David; my daughter is severely possessed by a demon.

St. Matthew: But he did not answer her a word. And his disciples came and begged him, saying,

Disciples: Send her away, for she is crying after us.

St. Matthew: He answered,

Jesus: I was sent only to the lost sheep of the house of Israel.

St. Matthew: But she came and knelt before him, saying,

Canaanite woman: Lord, help me.

St. Matthew: And he answered,

Jesus: It is not fair to take the children's bread and throw it to the dogs.

St. Matthew: She said,

Canaanite woman: Yes, Lord, yet even the dogs eat the crumbs that fall from their masters' table.

St. Matthew: Then Jesus answered her,

Jesus: O woman, great is your faith! Be it done for you as you desire.

St. Matthew: And her daughter was healed instantly.

~ Jesus Heals Many People (Mt 15:29–31)

St. Matthew: And Jesus went on from there and passed along the Sea of Galilee. And he went up on the mountain, and sat down there. And great crowds came to him, bringing with them the lame, the maimed, the blind, the mute, and many others, and they put them at his feet, and he healed them, so that the throng wondered, when they saw the mute speaking, the maimed whole, the lame walking, and the blind seeing; and they glorified the God of Israel.

Feeding the Four Thousand (Mt 15:32–39); S3–1335; S3–1329

St. Matthew: Then Jesus called his disciples to him and said,

Jesus: I have compassion on the crowd, because they have been with me now three days, and have nothing to eat; and I am unwilling to send them away hungry, lest they faint on the way.

St. Matthew: And the disciples said to him,

Disciples: Where are we to get bread enough in the desert to feed so great a crowd?

St. Matthew: And Jesus said to them,

Jesus: How many loaves have you?

St. Matthew: They said,

Disciples: Seven, and a few small fish.

St. Matthew: And commanding the crowd to sit down on the ground, he took the seven loaves and the fish, and having given thanks he broke them and gave them to the disciples, and the disciples gave them to the crowds. And they all ate and were satisfied; and they took up seven baskets full of the broken pieces left over. Those who ate were four thousand men, besides women and children. And sending away the crowds, he got into the boat and went to the region of Magadan.

Matthew Chapter 16

~ The Demand for a Sign (Mt 16:1–4)

St. Matthew: And the Pharisees and Sadducees came, and to test him they asked him to show them a sign from heaven. He answered them,

Jesus: When it is evening, you say, "It will be fair weather; for the sky is red." And in the morning, "It will be stormy today, for the sky is red and threatening." You know how to interpret the appearance of the sky, but you cannot interpret the signs of the times. An evil and adulterous generation seeks for a sign, but no sign shall be given to it except the sign of Jonah.

St. Matthew: So he left them and departed.

~ The Leaven of the Pharisees and Sadducees (Mt 16:5–12)

St. Matthew: When the disciples reached the other side, they had forgotten to bring any bread. Jesus said to them,

Jesus: Take heed and beware of the leaven of the Pharisees and Sadducees.

St. Matthew: And they discussed it among themselves, saying,

Disciples: We brought no bread.

St. Matthew: But Jesus, aware of this, said,

Jesus: O men of little faith, why do you discuss among yourselves the fact that you have no bread? Do you not yet perceive? Do you not remember the five loaves of the five thousand, and how many baskets you gathered? Or the seven loaves of the four thousand, and how many baskets you gathered? How is it that you fail to perceive that I did not speak about bread? Beware of the leaven of the Pharisees and Sadducees.

St. Matthew: Then they understood that he did not tell them to beware of the leaven of bread, but of the teaching of the Pharisees and Sadducees.

* Peter's Declaration That Jesus Is the Christ (Mt 16:13–20); PF3–153; F9–881

St. Matthew: Now when Jesus came into the district of Caesarea Philippi, he asked his disciples,

Jesus: Who do men say that the Son of man is?

St. Matthew: And they said,

Disciples: Some say John the Baptist, others say Elijah, and others Jeremiah or one of the prophets.

St. Matthew: He said to them,

Jesus: But who do you say that I am?

St. Matthew: Simon Peter replied,

Peter: You are the Christ, the Son of the living God.

St. Matthew: And Jesus answered him,

Jesus: Blessed are you, Simon Bar-Jona! For flesh and blood has not revealed this to you, but my Father who is in heaven. And I tell you, you are Peter, and on this rock I will build my church, and the gates of Hades shall not prevail against it. I will give you the keys of the kingdom of heaven, and whatever you bind on earth shall be bound in heaven, and whatever you loose on earth shall be loosed in heaven.

St. Matthew: Then he strictly charged the disciples to tell no one that he was the Christ.

* Jesus Foretells His Death and Resurrection (Mt 16:21–23); F3–540; F4–607

St. Matthew: From that time Jesus began to show his disciples that he must go to Jerusalem and suffer many things from the elders and chief priests and scribes, and be killed, and on the third day be raised. And Peter took him and began to rebuke him, saying,

Peter: God forbid, Lord! This shall never happen to you.

St. Matthew: But he turned and said to Peter,

Jesus: Get behind me, Satan! You are a hindrance to me; for you are not on the side of God, but of men.

* The Cross and Self-Denial (Mt 16:24–28); F1–226; F4–618

St. Matthew: Then Jesus told his disciples,

Jesus: If any man would come after me, let him deny himself and take up his cross and follow me. For whoever would save his life will lose it, and whoever loses his life for my sake will find it. For what will it profit a man, if he gains the whole world and forfeits his life? Or what shall a man give in return for his life? For the Son of man is to come with his angels in the glory of his Father, and then he will repay every man for what he has done. Truly, I say to you, there are some standing here who will not taste death before they see the Son of man coming in his kingdom.

Matthew Chapter 17

* The Transfiguration of Jesus (Mt 17:1–13); F2–444; F8–718

St. Matthew: And after six days Jesus took with him Peter and James and John his brother, and led them up a high mountain apart. And he was transfigured before them, and his face shone like the sun, and his garments became white as light. And behold, there appeared to them Moses and Elijah, talking with him. And Peter said to Jesus,

Peter: Lord, it is well that we are here; if you wish, I will make three booths here, one for you and one for Moses and one for Elijah.

St. Matthew: He was still speaking, when behold, a bright cloud overshadowed them, and a voice from the cloud said,

God the Father: This is my beloved Son, with whom I am well pleased; listen to him.

St. Matthew: When the disciples heard this, they fell on their faces, and were filled with awe. But Jesus came and touched them, saying,

Jesus: Rise, and have no fear.

St. Matthew: And when they lifted up their eyes, they saw no one but Jesus only. And as they were coming down the mountain, Jesus commanded them,

Jesus: Tell no one the vision, until the Son of man is raised from the dead.

St. Matthew: And the disciples asked him,

Disciples: Then why do the scribes say that first Elijah must come?

Jesus: Elijah does come, and he is to restore all things; but I tell you that Elijah has already come, and they did not know him, but did to him whatever they pleased. So also the Son of man will suffer at their hands.

St. Matthew: Then the disciples understood that he was speaking to them of John the Baptist.

~ Jesus Cures an Epileptic Boy (Mt 17:14–21)

St. Matthew: And when they came to the crowd, a man came up to him and kneeling before him said,

Man: Lord, have mercy on my son, for he is an epileptic and he suffers terribly; for often he falls into the fire, and often into the water. And I brought him to your disciples, and they could not heal him.

St. Matthew: And Jesus answered,

Jesus: O faithless and perverse generation, how long am I to be with you? How long am I to bear with you? Bring him here to me.

St. Matthew: And Jesus rebuked him, and the demon came out of him, and the boy was cured instantly. Then the disciples came to Jesus privately and said,

Disciples: Why could we not cast it out?

St. Matthew: He said to them,

Jesus: Because of your little faith. For truly, I say to you, if you have faith as a grain of mustard seed, you will say to this mountain, "Move from here to there," and it will move; and nothing will be impossible to you.

Jesus Again Foretells His Death and Resurrection (Mt 17:22–23); F3–554

St. Matthew: As they were gathering in Galilee, Jesus said to them,

Jesus: The Son of man is to be delivered into the hands of men, and they will kill him, and he will be raised on the third day.

St. Matthew: And they were greatly distressed.

Jesus and the Temple Tax (Mt 17:24–27); F4–586

St. Matthew: When they came to Capernaum, the collectors of the half-shekel tax went up to Peter and said,

Tax collectors: Does not your teacher pay the tax?

St. Matthew: He said,

Peter: Yes.

St. Matthew: And when he came home, Jesus spoke to him first, saying,

Jesus: What do you think, Simon? From whom do kings of the earth take toll or tribute? From their sons or from others?

St. Matthew: And when he said,

Peter: From others,

St. Matthew: Jesus said to him,

Jesus: Then the sons are free. However, not to give offense to them, go to the sea and cast a hook, and take the first fish that comes up, and when you open its mouth you will find a shekel; take that and give it to them for me and for yourself.

Matthew Chapter 18

True Greatness (Mt 18:1–4); F3–526; LP1–2785

St. Matthew: At that time the disciples came to Jesus, saying,

Disciples: Who is the greatest in the kingdom of heaven?

St. Matthew: And calling to him a child, he put him in the midst of them, and said,

Jesus: Truly, I say to you, unless you turn and become like children, you will never enter the kingdom of heaven.

Whoever humbles himself like this child, he is the greatest in the kingdom of heaven.

Temptations to Sin (Mt 18:5–9); C5–2285

Jesus: Whoever receives one such child in my name receives me; but whoever causes one of these little ones who believe in me to sin, it would be better for him to have a great millstone fastened round his neck and to be drowned in the depth of the sea.

Jesus 2: Woe to the world for temptations to sin! For it is necessary that temptations come, but woe to the man by whom the temptation comes!

And if your hand or your foot causes you to sin, cut it off and throw it away; it is better for you to enter life maimed or lame than with two hands or two feet to be thrown into the eternal fire.

And if your eye causes you to sin, pluck it out and throw it away; it is better for you to enter life with one eye than with two eyes to be thrown into the hell of fire.

* The Parable of the Lost Sheep (Mt 18:10–14); F4–605; LP3–2822

Jesus 3: See that you do not despise one of these little ones; for I tell you that in heaven their angels always behold the face of my Father who is in heaven.

Jesus 4: What do you think? If a man has a hundred sheep, and one of them has gone astray, does he not leave the ninety-nine on the mountains and go in search of the one that went astray?

And if he finds it, truly, I say to you, he rejoices over it more than over the ninety-nine that never went astray.

So it is not the will of my Father who is in heaven that one of these little ones should perish.

* Binding and Loosing of Sins (Mt 18:15–20); F3–553; S4–1444

Jesus 5: If your brother sins against you, go and tell him his fault, between you and him alone. If he listens to you, you have gained your brother.

But if he does not listen, take one or two others along with you, that every word may be confirmed by the evidence of two or three witnesses.

If he refuses to listen to them, tell it to the church; and if he refuses to listen even to the church, let him be to you as a Gentile and a tax collector.

Jesus 6: Truly, I say to you, whatever you bind on earth shall be bound in heaven, and whatever you loose on earth shall be loosed in heaven.

Again I say to you, if two of you agree on earth about anything they ask, it will be done for them by my Father in heaven.

For where two or three are gathered in my name, there am I in the midst of them.

* Repeated Forgiveness (Mt 18:21–22); F10–982; LP5–2845

St. Matthew: Then Peter came up and said to him,

Peter: Lord, how often shall my brother sin against me, and I forgive him? As many as seven times?

St. Matthew: Jesus said to him,

Jesus: I do not say to you seven times, but seventy times seven.

The Parable of the Unmerciful Servant (Mt 18:23–35); LP5–2843

Jesus: Therefore the kingdom of heaven may be compared to a king who wished to settle accounts with his servants. When he began the reckoning, one was brought to him who owed him ten thousand talents; and as he could not pay, his lord ordered him to be sold, with his wife and children and all that he had, and payment to be made. So the servant fell on his knees, imploring him,

First servant: Lord, have patience with me, and I will pay you everything.

Jesus: And out of pity for him the lord of that servant released him and forgave him the debt. But that same servant, as he went out, came upon one of his fellow servants who owed him a hundred denarii; and seizing him by the throat he said,

First servant: Pay what you owe.

Jesus: So his fellow servant fell down and besought him,

Second servant: Have patience with me, and I will pay you.

Jesus: He refused and went and put him in prison till he should pay the debt. When his fellow servants saw what had taken place, they were greatly distressed, and they went and reported to their lord all that had taken place. Then his lord summoned him and said to him,

Lord: You wicked servant! I forgave you all that debt because you besought me; and should not you have had mercy on your fellow servant, as I had mercy on you?

Jesus: And in anger his lord delivered him to the jailers, till he should pay all his debt. So also my heavenly Father will do to every one of you, if you do not forgive your brother from your heart.

Matthew Chapter 19

* Teachings About Divorce (Mt 19:1–12); C6–2364; S7–1620

St. Matthew: Now when Jesus had finished these sayings, he went away from Galilee and entered the region of Judea beyond the Jordan; and large crowds followed him, and he healed them there. And Pharisees came up to him and tested him by asking,

Pharisees: Is it lawful to divorce one's wife for any cause?

St. Matthew: He answered,

Jesus: Have you not read that he who made them from the beginning made them male and female, and said,

God the Father: For this reason a man shall leave his father and mother and be joined to his wife, and the two shall become one.

Jesus: So they are no longer two but one. What therefore God has joined together, let not man put asunder.

St. Matthew: They said to him,

Pharisees: Why then did Moses command one to give a certificate of divorce, and to put her away?

St. Matthew: He said to them,

Jesus: For your hardness of heart Moses allowed you to divorce your wives, but from the beginning it was not so. And I say to you: whoever divorces his wife, except for unchastity, and marries another, commits adultery; and he who marries a divorced woman, commits adultery.

St. Matthew: The disciples said to him,

Disciples: If such is the case of a man with his wife, it is not expedient to marry.

St. Matthew: But he said to them,

Jesus: Not all men can receive this saying, but only those to whom it is given. For there are eunuchs who have been so from birth, and there are eunuchs who have been made eunuchs by men, and there are eunuchs who have made themselves eunuchs for the sake of the kingdom of heaven. He who is able to receive this, let him receive it.

~ Jesus Blesses the Children (Mt 19:13–15)

St. Matthew: Then children were brought to him that he might lay his hands on them and pray. The disciples rebuked the people; but Jesus said,

Jesus: Let the children come to me, and do not hinder them; for to such belongs the kingdom of heaven.

St. Matthew: And he laid his hands on them and went away.

~ The Rich Young Man (Mt 19:16–30)

St. Matthew: And behold, one came up to him, saying,

Young man: Teacher, what good deed must I do, to have eternal life?

St. Matthew: And he said to him,

Jesus: Why do you ask me about what is good? One there is who is good. If you would enter life, keep the commandments.

St. Matthew: He said to him,

Young man: Which?

St. Matthew: And Jesus said,

Jesus: You shall not kill, You shall not commit adultery, You shall not steal, You shall not bear false witness, Honor your father and mother, and, You shall love your neighbor as yourself.

St. Matthew: The young man said to him,

Young man: All these I have observed; what do I still lack?

St. Matthew: Jesus said to him,

Jesus: If you would be perfect, go, sell what you possess and give to the poor, and you will have treasure in heaven; and come, follow me.

St. Matthew: When the young man heard this he went away sorrowful; for he had great possessions. And Jesus said to his disciples,

Jesus: Truly, I say to you, it will be hard for a rich man to enter the kingdom of heaven. Again I tell you, it is easier for a camel to go through the eye of a needle than for a rich man to enter the kingdom of God.

St. Matthew: When the disciples heard this they were greatly astonished, saying,

Disciples: Who then can be saved?

St. Matthew: But Jesus looked at them and said to them,

Jesus: With men this is impossible, but with God all things are possible.

St. Matthew: Then Peter said in reply,

Peter: Behold, we have left everything and followed you. What then shall we have?

St. Matthew: Jesus said to them,

Jesus: Truly, I say to you, in the new world, when the Son of man shall sit on his glorious throne, you who have followed me will also sit on twelve thrones, judging the twelve tribes of Israel. And everyone who has left houses or brothers or sisters or father or mother or children or lands, for my name's sake, will receive a hundredfold, and inherit eternal life. But many that are first will be last, and the last first.

Matthew Chapter 20

~ The Laborers in the Vineyard (Mt 20:1–16)

Jesus: For the kingdom of heaven is like a householder who went out early in the morning to hire laborers for his vineyard. After agreeing with the laborers for a denarius a day, he sent them into his vineyard. And going out about the third hour he saw others standing idle in the marketplace; and to them he said,

Householder: You go into the vineyard too, and whatever is right I will give you.

Jesus: So they went. Going out again about the sixth hour and the ninth hour, he did the same. And about the eleventh hour he went out and found others standing; and he said to them,

Householder: Why do you stand here idle all day?

Jesus: They said to him,

Men: Because no one has hired us.

Jesus: He said to them,

Householder: You go into the vineyard too.

Jesus: And when evening came, the owner of the vineyard said to his steward,

Householder: Call the laborers and pay them their wages, beginning with the last, up to the first.

Jesus: And when those hired about the eleventh hour came, each of them received a denarius. Now when the first came, they thought they would receive more; but each of them also received a denarius. And on receiving it they grumbled at the householder, saying,

First hired men: These last worked only one hour, and you have made them equal to us who have borne the burden of the day and the scorching heat.

Jesus: But he replied to one of them,

Householder: Friend, I am doing you no wrong; did you not agree with me for a denarius? Take what belongs to you, and go; I choose to give to this last as I give to you. Am I not allowed to do what I choose with what belongs to me? Or do you begrudge my generosity?'

Jesus: So the last will be first, and the first last.

A Third Time Jesus Foretells His Death and Resurrection (Mt 20:17–19); F4–572

St. Matthew: And as Jesus was going up to Jerusalem, he took the twelve disciples aside, and on the way he said to them,

Jesus: Behold, we are going up to Jerusalem; and the Son of man will be delivered to the chief priests and scribes, and they will condemn him to death, and deliver him to the Gentiles to be mocked and scourged and crucified, and he will be raised on the third day.

* The Request of the Mother of James and John (Mt 20:20–28); F2–440; F4–601

St. Matthew: Then the mother of the sons of Zebedee came up to him, with her sons, and kneeling before him she asked him for something. And he said to her,

Jesus: What do you want?

St. Matthew: She said to him,

Mother of James and John: Command that these two sons of mine may sit, one at your right hand and one at your left, in your kingdom.

St. Matthew: But Jesus answered,

Jesus: You do not know what you are asking. Are you able to drink the chalise that I am to drink?

St. Matthew: They aid to him,

James and John: We are able.

St. Matthew: He said to them,

Jesus: You will drink my chalise, but to sit at my right hand and at my left is not mine to grant, but it is for those for whom it has been prepared by my Father.

St. Matthew: And when the ten heard it, they were indignant at the two brothers. But Jesus called them to him and said,

Jesus: You know that the rulers of the Gentiles lord it over them, and their great men exercise authority over them. It shall not be so among you; but whoever would be great among you must be your servant, and whoever would be first among you must be your slave; even as the Son of man came not to be served but to serve, and to give his life as a ransom for many.

Jesus Heals Two Blind Men (Mt 20:29–34); F2–439

St. Matthew: And as they went out of Jericho, a great crowd followed him. And behold, two blind men sitting by the roadside, when they heard that Jesus was passing by, cried out,

Blind men: Have mercy on us, Son of David!

St. Matthew: The crowd rebuked them, telling them to be silent; but they cried out the more,

Blind men: Lord, have mercy on us, Son of David!

St. Matthew: And Jesus stopped and called them, saying,

Jesus: What do you want me to do for you?

St. Matthew: They said to him,

Blind men: Lord, let our eyes be opened.

St. Matthew: And Jesus in pity touched their eyes, and immediately they received their sight and followed him.

Matthew Chapter 21

Jesus' Entry Into Jerusalem (Mt 21:1–11); F3–559; F2–439

St. Matthew: And when they drew near to Jerusalem and came to Bethphage, to the Mount of Olives, then Jesus sent two disciples, saying to them,

Jesus: Go into the village opposite you, and immediately you will find a donkey tied, and a colt with her; untie them and bring them to me. If any one says anything to you, you shall say, "The Lord has need of them," and he will send them immediately.

St. Matthew: This took place to fulfil what was spoken by the prophet, saying,

Prophet Zechariah: Tell the daughter of Zion, Behold, your king is coming to you, humble, and mounted on a donkey, and on a colt, the foal of a donkey.

St. Matthew: The disciples went and did as Jesus had directed them; they brought the donkey and the colt, and put their garments on them, and he sat thereon. Most of the crowd spread their garments on the road, and others cut branches from the trees and spread them on the road. And the crowds that went before him and that followed him shouted,

Crowds: Hosanna to the Son of David! Blessed is he who comes in the name of the Lord! Hosanna in the highest!

St. Matthew: And when he entered Jerusalem, all the city was stirred, saying,

People of Jerusalem: Who is this?

St. Matthew: And the crowds said,

Crowds: This is the prophet Jesus from Nazareth of Galilee.

* Jesus Cleanses the Temple (Mt 21:12–17); F4–584; F2–439

St. Matthew: And Jesus entered the temple of God and drove out all who sold and bought in the temple, and he overturned the tables of the moneychangers and the seats of those who sold pigeons. He said to them,

Jesus: It is written, "My house shall be called a house of prayer"; but you make it a den of robbers.

St. Matthew: And the blind and the lame came to him in the temple, and he healed them. But when the chief priests and the scribes saw the wonderful things that he did, and the children crying out in the temple,

Children in the temple: Hosanna to the Son of David!

St. Matthew: They were indignant; and they said to him,

Chief priests and scribes: Do you hear what these are saying?

St. Matthew: And Jesus said to them,

Jesus: Yes; have you never read, "Out of the mouth of babies and infants you have brought perfect praise?"

St. Matthew: And leaving them, he went out of the city to Bethany and lodged there.

Jesus Curses the Fig Tree (Mt 21:18–22); F3–544; P–2610

St. Matthew: In the morning, as he was returning to the city, he was hungry. And seeing a fig tree by the wayside he went to it, and found nothing on it but leaves only. And he said to it,

Jesus: May no fruit ever come from you again!

St. Matthew: And the fig tree withered at once. When the disciples saw it they marveled, saying,

Disciples: How did the fig tree wither at once?

St. Matthew: And Jesus answered them,

Jesus: Truly, I say to you, if you have faith and never doubt, you will not only do what has been done to the fig tree, but even if you say to this mountain, "Be taken up and cast into the sea," it will be done. And whatever you ask in prayer, you will receive, if you have faith.

~ The Authority of Jesus Questioned (Mt 21:23–27)

St. Matthew: And when he entered the temple, the chief priests and the elders of the people came up to him as he was teaching, and said,

Chief priests and elders: By what authority are you doing these things, and who gave you this authority?

St. Matthew: Jesus answered them,

Jesus: I also will ask you a question; and if you tell me the answer, then I also will tell you by what authority I do these things. The baptism of John, where was it from? From heaven or from men?

St. Matthew: And they argued with one another,

Chief priests and elders: If we say, "From heaven," he will say to us, "Why then did you not believe him?" But if we say, "From men," we are afraid of the multitude; for all hold that John was a prophet.

St. Matthew: So they answered Jesus,

Chief priests and elders: We do not know.

St. Matthew: And he said to them,

Jesus: Neither will I tell you by what authority I do these things.

The Parable of the Two Sons (Mt 21:28–32); F3–546; F3–535

Jesus: What do you think? A man had two sons; and he went to the first and said,

Man: Son, go and work in the vineyard today.

Jesus: And he answered,

First son: I will not;

Jesus: But afterward he repented and went. And he went to the second and said the same; and he answered,

Second son: I go, sir,

Jesus: But did not go. Which of the two did the will of his father?

St. Matthew: They said,

Chief priests and elders: The first.

St. Matthew: Jesus said to them,

Jesus: Truly, I say to you, the tax collectors and the harlots go into the kingdom of God before you. For John came to you in the way of righteousness, and you did not believe him, but the tax collectors and the harlots believed him; and even when you saw it, you did not afterward repent and believe him.

The Parable of the Wicked Tenants (Mt 21:33–41); F9–755; F2–443

Jesus: Hear another parable. There was a householder who planted a vineyard, and set a hedge around it, and dug a wine press in it, and built a tower, and let it out to tenants, and went into another country. When the season of fruit drew near, he sent his servants to the tenants, to get his fruit; and the tenants took his servants and beat one, killed another, and stoned another. Again he sent other servants, more than the first; and they did the same to them. Afterward he sent his son to them, saying,

Householder: They will respect my son. But when the tenants saw the son, they said to themselves,

Tenants: This is the heir; come, let us kill him and have his inheritance.

Jesus: And they took him and cast him out of the vineyard, and killed him. When therefore the owner of the vineyard comes, what will he do to those tenants?

St. Matthew: They said to him,

Chief priests and elders: He will put those wretches to a miserable death, and let out the vineyard to other tenants who will give him the fruits in their seasons.

The Stone Which the Builders Rejected (Mt 21:42–46); F9-756

St. Matthew: Jesus said to them,

Jesus: Have you never read in the Scriptures: "The very stone which the builders rejected has become the head of the corner; this was the Lord's doing, and it is marvelous in our eyes?" Therefore I tell you, the kingdom of God will be taken away from you and given to a nation producing the fruits of it. And he who falls on this stone will be broken to pieces; but when it falls on any one, it will crush him.

St. Matthew: When the chief priests and the Pharisees heard his parables, they perceived that he was speaking about them. But when they tried to arrest him, they feared the multitudes, because they held him to be a prophet.

Matthew Chapter 22

The Parable of the Marriage Feast (Mt 22:1–14); F3–546; F9–796

St. Matthew: And again Jesus spoke to them in parables, saying,

Jesus: The kingdom of heaven may be compared to a king who gave a marriage feast for his son, and sent his servants to call those who were invited to the marriage feast; but they would not come. Again he sent other servants, saying,

King: Tell those who are invited, Behold, I have made ready my dinner, my oxen and my fat calves are killed, and everything is ready; come to the marriage feast.

Jesus: But they made light of it and went off, one to his farm, another to his business, while the rest seized his servants, treated them shamefully, and killed them. The king was angry, and he sent his troops and destroyed those murderers and burned their city. Then he said to his servants,

King: The wedding is ready, but those invited were not worthy. Go therefore to the streets, and invite to the marriage feast as many as you find.

Jesus: And those servants went out into the streets and gathered all whom they found, both bad and good; so the wedding hall was filled with guests. But when the king came in to look at the guests, he saw there a man who had no wedding garment; and he said to him,

King: Friend, how did you get in here without a wedding garment?

Jesus: And he was speechless. Then the king said to the attendants,

King: Bind him hand and foot, and cast him into the outer darkness; where there will be weeping and gnashing of teeth. For many are called, but few are chosen.

The Question About Paying Taxes (Mt 22:15–22); C4–2242

St. Matthew: Then the Pharisees went and took counsel how to entangle him in his talk. And they sent their disciples to him, along with the Herodians, saying,

Disciples of the Pharisees: Teacher, we know that you are true, and teach the way of God truthfully, and care for no man; for you do not regard the position of men. Tell us, then, what you think. Is it lawful to pay taxes to Caesar, or not?

St. Matthew: But Jesus, aware of their malice, said,

Jesus: Why put me to the test, you hypocrites? Show me the money for the tax.

St. Matthew: And they brought him a coin. And Jesus said to them,

Jesus: Whose likeness and inscription is this?

St. Matthew: They said,

Disciples of the Pharisees: Caesar's.

St. Matthew: Then he said to them,

Jesus: Render therefore to Caesar the things that are Caesar's, and to God the things that are God's.

St. Matthew: When they heard it, they marveled; and they left him and went away.

* The Question About Man's Resurrection (Mt 22:23–33); F4–575; F4–581

St. Matthew: The same day Sadducees came to him, who say that there is no resurrection; and they asked him a question, saying,

Sadducees: Teacher, Moses said,

Moses: If a man dies, having no children, his brother must marry the widow, and raise up children for his brother.

Sadducees: Now there were seven brothers among us; the first married, and died, and having no children left his wife to his brother. So too the second and third, down to the seventh. After them all, the woman died. In the resurrection, therefore, to which of the seven will she be wife? For they all had her.

St. Matthew: But Jesus answered them,

Jesus: You are wrong, because you know neither the Scriptures nor the power of God. For in the resurrection they neither marry nor are given in marriage, but are like angels in heaven. And as for the resurrection of the dead, have you not read what was said to you by God,

God the Father: "I am the God of Abraham, and the God of Isaac, and the God of Jacob."

Jesus: He is not God of the dead, but of the living.

St. Matthew: And when the crowd heard it, they were astonished at his teaching.

* The Greatest Commandment (Mt 22:34–40); LC–2055; LC–1824

St. Matthew: But when the Pharisees heard that he had silenced the Sadducees, they came together. And one of them, a lawyer, asked him a question, to test him.

Lawyer: Teacher, which is the great commandment in the law?

St. Matthew: And he said to him,

Jesus: "You shall love the Lord your God with all your heart, and with all your soul, and with all your mind." This is the great and first commandment. And a second is like it, "You shall love your neighbor as yourself." On these two commandments depend all the law and the prophets.

* A Question About the Christ (Mt 22:41–46); F2–439; F2–447

St. Matthew: Now while the Pharisees were gathered together, Jesus asked them a question, saying,

Jesus: What do you think of the Christ? Whose son is he?

St. Matthew: They said to him,

Pharisees: The son of David.

St. Matthew: He said to them,

Jesus: How is it then that David, inspired by the Spirit, calls him Lord, saying,

David: The Lord said to my Lord, Sit at my right hand, till I put your enemies under your feet.

Jesus: If David thus calls him Lord, how is he his son?

St. Matthew: And no one was able to answer him a word, nor from that day did any one dare to ask him any more questions.

Matthew Chapter 23

* Jesus Denounces the Hypocrisy of the Scribes and Pharisees (Mt 23:1–36); C6–2367; C1–2111

St. Matthew: Then said Jesus to the crowds and to his disciples,

Jesus: The scribes and the Pharisees sit on Moses' seat; so practice and observe whatever they tell you, but not what they do; for they preach, but do not practice.

They bind heavy burdens, hard to bear, and lay them on men's shoulders; but they themselves will not move them with their finger.

They do all their deeds to be seen by men; for they make their phylacteries broad and their fringes long, and they love the place of honor at feasts and the best seats in the synagogues, and salutations in the market places, and being called rabbi by men.

Jesus 2: But you are not to be called rabbi, for you have one teacher, and you are all brethren.

And call no man your father on earth, for you have one Father, who is in heaven.

Neither be called masters, for you have one master, the Christ.

He who is greatest among you shall be your servant; whoever exalts himself will be humbled, and whoever humbles himself will be exalted.

Jesus 3: But woe to you, scribes and Pharisees, hypocrites! because you shut the kingdom of heaven against men; for you neither enter yourselves, nor allow those who would enter to go in.

Woe to you, scribes and Pharisees, hypocrites! for you traverse sea and land to make a single proselyte, and when he becomes a proselyte, you make him twice as much a child of hell as yourselves.

Woe to you, blind guides, who say,

Scribes and Pharisees: If any one swears by the temple, it is nothing; but if any one swears by the gold of the temple, he is bound by his oath.

Jesus 4: You blind fools! For which is greater, the gold or the temple that has made the gold sacred? And you say,

Scribes and Pharisees: If any one swears by the altar, it is nothing; but if any one swears by the gift that is on the altar, he is bound by his oath.

Jesus 5: You blind men! For which is greater, the gift or the altar that makes the gift sacred? So he who swears by the altar, swears by it and by everything on it; and he who swears by the temple, swears by it and by him who dwells in it; and he who swears by heaven, swears by the throne of God and by him who sits upon it.

Jesus 6: Woe to you, scribes and Pharisees, hypocrites! for you tithe mint and dill and cummin, and have neglected the weightier matters of the law, justice and mercy and faith; these you ought to have done, without neglecting the others. You blind guides, straining out a gnat and swallowing a camel!

Jesus 7: Woe to you, scribes and Pharisees, hypocrites! for you cleanse the outside of the cup and of the plate, but inside they are full of extortion and rapacity.

You blind Pharisee! first cleanse the inside of the cup and of the plate, that the outside also may be clean.

Jesus 8: Woe to you, scribes and Pharisees, hypocrites! for you are like whitewashed tombs, which outwardly appear beautiful, but within they are full of dead men's bones and all uncleanness.

So you also outwardly appear righteous to men, but within you are full of hypocrisy and iniquity.

Woe to you, scribes and Pharisees, hypocrites! for you build the tombs of the prophets and adorn the monuments of the righteous, saying,

Scribes and Pharisees: If we had lived in the days of our fathers, we would not have taken part with them in shedding the blood of the prophets.

Jesus 9: Thus you witness against yourselves, that you are sons of those who murdered the prophets.

Fill up, then, the measure of your fathers.

You serpents, you brood of vipers, how are you to escape being sentenced to hell?

Therefore I send you prophets and wise men and scribes, some of whom you will kill and crucify, and some you will scourge in your synagogues and persecute from town to town, that upon you may come all the righteous blood shed on earth, from the blood of innocent Abel to the blood of Zechariah the son of Barachiah, whom you murdered between the sanctuary and the altar.

Truly, I say to you, all this will come upon this generation.

The Lament Over Jerusalem (Mt 23:37–39); F3–558; F7–674

Jesus: O Jerusalem, Jerusalem, killing the prophets and stoning those who are sent to you! How often would I have gathered your children together as a hen gathers her brood under her wings, and you would not! Behold, your house is forsaken and desolate. For I tell you, you will not see me again, until you say, "Blessed is he who comes in the name of the Lord."

Matthew Chapter 24

The Destruction of the Temple Foretold (Mt 24:1–2); F4–585

St. Matthew: Jesus left the temple and was going away, when his disciples came to point out to him the buildings of the temple. But he answered them,

Jesus: You see all these, do you not? Truly, I say to you, there will not be left here one stone upon another, that will not be thrown down.

Signs of Jesus' Coming and the Close of the Age (Mt 24:3–8); F4–585

St. Matthew: As he sat on the Mount of Olives, the disciples came to him privately, saying,

Disciples: Tell us, when will this be, and what will be the sign of your coming and of the close of the age? And Jesus answered them,

Jesus: Take heed that no one leads you astray. For many will come in my name, saying,

First false prophet: I am the Christ,

Jesus: And they will lead many astray.

And you will hear of wars and rumors of wars; see that you are not alarmed; for this must take place, but the end is not yet.

For nation will rise against nation, and kingdom against kingdom, and there will be famines and earthquakes in various places: all this is but the beginning of the birth-pangs.

Persecutions Foretold (Mt 24:9–14); F7–675; PF3–161

Jesus 2: Then they will deliver you up to tribulation, and put you to death; and you will be hated by all nations for my name's sake.

And then many will fall away, and betray one another, and hate one another.

And many false prophets will arise and lead many astray.

And because wickedness is multiplied, most men's love will grow cold.

But he who endures to the end will be saved.

And this gospel of the kingdom will be preached throughout the whole world, as a testimony to all nations; and then the end will come.

~ The Desolating Sacrilege (Mt 24:15–28)

Jesus: So when you see the desolating sacrilege spoken of by the prophet Daniel, standing in the holy place (let the reader understand), then let those who are in Judea flee to the mountains;

let him who is on the housetop not go down to take what is in his house;

and let him who is in the field not turn back to take his mantle.

And alas for those who are with child and for those who are nursing in those days!

Pray that your flight may not be in winter or on a sabbath.

For then there will be great tribulation, such as has not been from the beginning of the world until now, no, and never will be.

And if those days had not been shortened, no human being would be saved; but for the sake of the elect those days will be shortened.

Then if any one says to you,

Second false prophet: Behold, here is the Christ!

Jesus: Or

Third false prophet: There he is!

Jesus: Do not believe it. For false Christs and false prophets will arise and show great signs and wonders, so as to lead astray, if possible, even the elect. Behold, I have told you beforehand. So, if they say to you,

Fourth false prophet: Behold, he is in the wilderness,

Jesus: Do not go out; if they say,

Fifth false prophet: Behold, he is in the inner rooms,

Jesus: Do not believe it.

For as the lightning comes from the east and shines as far as the west, so will be the coming of the Son of man.

Wherever the body is, there the eagles will be gathered together.

~ The Coming of the Son of Man (Mt 24:29–31)

Jesus: Immediately after the tribulation of those days the sun will be darkened, and the moon will not give its light, and the stars will fall from heaven, and the powers of the heavens will be shaken;

then will appear the sign of the Son of man in heaven, and then all the tribes of the earth will mourn, and they will see the Son of man coming on the clouds of heaven with power and great glory;

and he will send out his angels with a loud trumpet call, and they will gather his elect from the four winds, from one end of heaven to the other.

~ The Lesson of the Fig Tree (Mt 24:32–35)

Jesus 2: From the fig tree learn its lesson: as soon as its branch becomes tender and puts forth its leaves, you know that summer is near.

So also, when you see all these things, you know that he is near, at the very gates.

Truly, I say to you, this generation will not pass away till all these things take place.

Heaven and earth will pass away, but my words will not pass away.

The Necessity for Watchfulness (Mt 24:36–44); F2–443; F7–673

Jesus 3: But of that day and hour no one knows, not even the angels of heaven, nor the Son, but the Father only.

As were the days of Noah, so will be the coming of the Son of man.

For as in those days before the flood they were eating and drinking, marrying and giving in marriage, until the day when Noah entered the ark, and they did not know until the flood came and swept them all away, so will be the coming of the Son of man.

Then two men will be in the field; one is taken and one is left.

Two women will be grinding at the mill; one is taken and one is left.

Watch therefore, for you do not know on what day your Lord is coming.

Jesus 4: But know this, that if the householder had known in what part of the night the thief was coming, he would have watched and would not have let his house be broken into.

Therefore you also must be ready; for the Son of man is coming at an hour you do not expect.

~ The Faithful and the Unfaithful Servant (Mt 24:45–51)

Jesus 4: Who then is the faithful and wise servant, whom his master has set over his household, to give them their food at the proper time? Blessed is that servant whom his master when he comes will find so doing. Truly, I say to you, he will set him over all his possessions. But if that wicked servant says to himself,

Wicked servant: My master is delayed,

Jesus 4: And begins to beat his fellow servants, and eats and drinks with the drunken, the master of that servant will come on a day when he does not expect him and at an hour he does not know, and will punish him, and put him with the hypocrites; there men will weep and gnash their teeth.

Matthew Chapter 25

The Parable of the Wise and the Foolish Maidens (Mt 25:1–13); F7–672; F9–796

Jesus: Then the kingdom of heaven shall be compared to ten maidens who took their lamps and went to meet the bridegroom. Five of them were foolish, and five were wise. For when the foolish took their lamps, they took no oil with them; but the wise took flasks of oil with their lamps. As the bridegroom was delayed, they all slumbered and slept. But at midnight there was a cry,

Crier: Behold, the bridegroom! Come out to meet him.

Jesus: Then all those maidens rose and trimmed their lamps. And the foolish said to the wise,

Foolish maidens: Give us some of your oil, for our lamps are going out.

Jesus: But the wise replied,

Wise maidens: Perhaps there will not be enough for us and for you; go rather to the dealers and buy for yourselves.

Jesus: And while they went to buy, the bridegroom came, and those who were ready went in with him to the marriage feast; and the door was shut. Afterward the other maidens came also, saying,

Foolish maidens: Lord, lord, open to us.

Jesus: But he replied,

Bridegroom: Truly, I say to you, I do not know you.

Jesus: Watch therefore, for you know neither the day nor the hour.

* The Parable of the Talents (Mt 25:14–30); F3–546; LC–1936

Jesus: For it will be as when a man going on a journey called his servants and entrusted to them his property; to one he gave five talents, to another two, to another one, to each according to his ability.

Then he went away. He who had received the five talents went at once and traded with them; and he made five talents more. So also, he who had the two talents made two talents more. But he who had received the one talent went and dug in the ground and hid his master's money.

Now after a long time the master of those servants came and settled accounts with them. And he who had received the five talents came forward, bringing five talents more, saying,

Servant: Master, you delivered to me five talents; here I have made five talents more.

Jesus: His master said to him,

Master: Well done, good and faithful servant; you have been faithful over a little, I will set you over much; enter into the joy of your master.

Jesus: And he also who had the two talents came forward, saying,

Servant 2: Master, you delivered to me two talents; here I have made two talents more.

Jesus: His master said to him,

Master: Well done, good and faithful servant; you have been faithful over a little, I will set you over much; enter into the joy of your master.

Jesus: He also who had received the one talent came forward, saying,

Servant 3: Master, I knew you to be a hard man, reaping where you did not sow, and gathering where you did not winnow; so I was afraid, and I went and hid your talent in the ground. Here you have what is yours.

Jesus: But his master answered him,

Master: You wicked and slothful servant! You knew that I reap where I have not sowed, and gather where I have not winnowed? Then you ought to have invested my money with the bankers, and at my coming I should have received what was my own with interest. So take the talent from him, and give it to him who has the ten talents. For to everyone who has will more be given, and he will have abundance; but from him who has not, even what he has will be taken away. And cast the worthless servant into the outer darkness; where there will be weeping and gnashing of teeth.

* The Judgment of the Nations (Mt 25:31–46); F12–1033; LP4–2831

Jesus: When the Son of man comes in his glory, and all the angels with him, then he will sit on his glorious throne. Before him will be gathered all the nations, and he will separate them one from another as a shepherd separates the sheep from the goats, and he will place the sheep at his right hand, but the goats at the left. Then the King will say to those at his right hand,

Jesus, King of Glory: Come, O blessed of my Father, inherit the kingdom prepared for you from the foundation of the world; for I was hungry and you gave me food, I was thirsty and you gave me drink, I was a stranger and you welcomed me, I was naked and you clothed me, I was sick and you visited me, I was in prison and you came to me.

Jesus: Then the righteous will answer him,

Righteous: Lord, when did we see you hungry and feed you, or thirsty and give you drink? And when did we see you a stranger and welcome you, or naked and clothe you? And when did we see you sick or in prison and visit you?

Jesus: And the King will answer them,

Jesus, King of Glory: Truly, I say to you, as you did it to one of the least of these my brethren, you did it to me.

Jesus: Then he will say to those at his left hand,

Jesus, King of Glory: Depart from me, you cursed, into the eternal fire prepared for the devil and his angels; for I was hungry and you gave me no food, I was thirsty and you gave me no drink, I was a stranger and you did not welcome me, naked and you did not clothe me, sick and in prison and you did not visit me.

Jesus: Then they also will answer,

Unrighteous: Lord, when did we see you hungry or thirsty or a stranger or naked or sick or in prison, and did not minister to you?

Jesus: Then he will answer them,

Jesus, King of Glory: Truly, I say to you, as you did it not to one of the least of these, you did it not to me.

Jesus: And they will go away into eternal punishment, but the righteous into eternal life.

Matthew Chapter 26

~ The Conspiracy to Kill Jesus (Mt 26:1–5)

St. Matthew: When Jesus had finished all these sayings, he said to his disciples,

Jesus: You know that after two days the Passover is coming, and the Son of man will be delivered up to be crucified.

St. Matthew: Then the chief priests and the elders of the people gathered in the palace of the high priest, who was called Caiaphas, and took counsel together in order to arrest Jesus by stealth and kill him. But they said,

Chief priests and elders: Not during the feast, lest there be a tumult among the people.

~ The Anointing at Bethany (Mt 26:6–13)

St. Matthew: Now when Jesus was at Bethany in the house of Simon the leper, a woman came up to him with an alabaster flask of very expensive ointment, and she poured it on his head, as he sat at table. But when the disciples saw it, they were indignant, saying,

Disciples: Why this waste? For this ointment might have been sold for a large sum, and given to the poor.

St. Matthew: But Jesus, aware of this, said to them,

Jesus: Why do you trouble the woman? For she has done a beautiful thing to me. For you always have the poor with you, but you will not always have me. In pouring this ointment on my body she has done it to prepare me for burial. Truly, I say to you, wherever this gospel is preached in the whole world, what she has done will be told in memory of her.

~ Judas Agrees to Betray Jesus (Mt 26:14–16)

St. Matthew: Then one of the twelve, who was called Judas Iscariot, went to the chief priests and said,

Judas: What will you give me if I deliver him to you?

St. Matthew: And they paid him thirty pieces of silver. And from that moment he sought an opportunity to betray him.

The Passover with the Disciples (Mt 26:17–25); F4–610; S3–1339

St. Matthew: Now on the first day of Unleavened Bread the disciples came to Jesus, saying,

Disciples: Where will you have us prepare for you to eat the Passover?

St. Matthew: He said,

Jesus: Go into the city to a certain one, and say to him, "The Teacher says, My time is at hand; I will keep the Passover at your house with my disciples."

St. Matthew: And the disciples did as Jesus had directed them, and they prepared the Passover. When it was evening, he sat at table with the twelve disciples; and as they were eating, he said,

Jesus: Truly, I say to you, one of you will betray me.

St. Matthew: And they were very sorrowful, and began to say to him one after another,

Each disciple: Is it I, Lord?

St. Matthew: He answered,

Jesus: He who has dipped his hand in the dish with me, will betray me. The Son of man goes as it is written of him, but woe to that man by whom the Son of man is betrayed! It would have been better for that man if he had not been born.

St. Matthew: Judas, who betrayed him, said,

Judas: Is it I, Master?

St. Matthew: He said to him,

Jesus: You have said so.

* The Institution of the Eucharist (Mt 26:26–29); S3–1365; LP5–2839

St. Matthew: Now as they were eating, Jesus took bread, and blessed, and broke it, and gave it to the disciples and said,

Jesus: Take, eat; this is my body.

St. Matthew: And he took a chalice, and when he had given thanks he gave it to them, saying,

Jesus: Drink of it, all of you; for this is my blood of the covenant, which is poured out for many for the forgiveness of sins. I tell you I shall not drink again of this fruit of the vine until that day when I drink it new with you in my Father's kingdom.

Peter's Denial Foretold (Mt 26:30–35); F9–764

St. Matthew: And when they had sung a hymn, they went out to the Mount of Olives. Then Jesus said to them,

Jesus: You will all fall away because of me this night; for it is written, "I will strike the shepherd, and the sheep of the flock will be scattered." But after I am raised up, I will go before you to Galilee.

St. Matthew: Peter declared to him,

Peter: Though they all fall away because of you, I will never fall away.

St. Matthew: Jesus said to him,

Jesus: Truly, I say to you, this very night, before the cock crows, you will deny me three times.

St. Matthew: Peter said to him,

Peter: Even if I must die with you, I will not deny you.

St. Matthew: And so said all the disciples.

* Jesus Prays in Gethsemane (Mt 26:36–46); LP6–2849; F1–363

St. Matthew: Then Jesus went with them to a place called Gethsemane, and he said to his disciples,

Jesus: Sit here, while I go yonder and pray.

St. Matthew: And taking with him Peter and the two sons of Zebedee, he began to be sorrowful and troubled. Then he said to them,

Jesus: My soul is very sorrowful, even to death; remain here, and watch with me.

St. Matthew: And going a little farther he fell on his face and prayed,

Jesus: My Father, if it be possible, let this chalice pass from me; nevertheless, not as I will, but as you will.

St. Matthew: And he came to the disciples and found them sleeping; and he said to Peter,

Jesus: So, could you not watch with me one hour? Watch and pray that you may not enter into temptation; the spirit indeed is willing, but the flesh is weak.

St. Matthew: Again, for the second time, he went away and prayed,

Jesus: My Father, if this cannot pass unless I drink it, your will be done.

St. Matthew: And again he came and found them sleeping, for their eyes were heavy. So, leaving them again, he went away and prayed for the third time, saying the same words. Then he came to the disciples and said to them,

Jesus: Are you still sleeping and taking your rest? Behold, the hour is at hand, and the Son of man is betrayed into the hands of sinners. Rise, let us be going; see, my betrayer is at hand.

* The Betrayal and Arrest of Jesus (Mt 26:47–56); F1–333; F4–609

St. Matthew: While he was still speaking, Judas came, one of the twelve, and with him a great crowd with swords and clubs, from the chief priests and the elders of the people. Now the betrayer had given them a sign, saying,

Judas: The one I shall kiss is the man; seize him.

St. Matthew: And he came up to Jesus at once and said,

Judas: Hail, Master!

St. Matthew: And he kissed him. Jesus said to him,

Jesus: Friend, why are you here?

St. Matthew: Then they came up and laid hands on Jesus and seized him. And behold, one of those who were with Jesus stretched out his hand and drew his sword, and struck the slave of the high priest, and cut off his ear. Then Jesus said to him,

Jesus: Put your sword back into its place; for all who take the sword will perish by the sword. Do you think that I cannot appeal to my Father, and he will at once send me more than twelve legions of angels? But how then should the Scriptures be fulfilled, that it must be so?

St. Matthew: At that hour Jesus said to the crowds,

Jesus: Have you come out as against a robber, with swords and clubs to capture me? Day after day I sat in the temple teaching, and you did not seize me. But all this has taken place, that the Scriptures of the prophets might be fulfilled.

St. Matthew: Then all the disciples forsook him and fled.

* Jesus Before the High Priest (Mt 26:57–68); F2–443; F4–591

St. Matthew: Then those who had seized Jesus led him to Caiaphas the high priest, where the scribes and the elders had gathered. But Peter followed him at a distance, as far as the courtyard of the high priest, and going inside he sat with the guards to see the end. Now the chief priests and the whole council sought false testimony against Jesus that they might put him to death, but they found none, though many false witnesses came forward. At last two came forward and said,

Two false witnesses: This fellow said, "I am able to destroy the temple of God, and to build it in three days."

St. Matthew: And the high priest stood up and said,

High priest: Have you no answer to make? What is it that these men testify against you?

St. Matthew: But Jesus was silent. And the high priest said to him,

High priest: I adjure you by the living God, tell us if you are the Christ, the Son of God.

St. Matthew: Jesus said to him,

Jesus: You have said so. But I tell you, hereafter you will see the Son of man seated at the right hand of Power, and coming on the clouds of heaven.

St. Matthew: Then the high priest tore his robes, and said,

High priest: He has uttered blasphemy. Why do we still need witnesses? You have now heard his blasphemy. What is your judgment?

St. Matthew: They answered,

Scribes and elders: He deserves death.

St. Matthew: Then they spat in his face, and struck him; and some slapped him, saying,

Scribes and elders: Prophesy to us, you Christ! Who is it that struck you?

~ Peter Denies Jesus (Mt 26:69–75)

St. Matthew: Now Peter was sitting outside in the courtyard. And a maid came up to him, and said,

First maid: You also were with Jesus the Galilean.

St. Matthew: But he denied it before them all, saying,

Peter: I do not know what you mean.

St. Matthew: And when he went out to the porch, another maid saw him, and she said to the bystanders,

Second maid: This man was with Jesus of Nazareth.

St. Matthew: And again he denied it with an oath,

Peter: I do not know the man.

St. Matthew: After a little while the bystanders came up and said to Peter,

Bystanders: Certainly you are also one of them, for your accent betrays you.

St. Matthew: Then he began to invoke a curse on himself and to swear,

Peter: I do not know the man.

St. Matthew: And immediately the cock crowed. And Peter remembered the saying of Jesus, "Before the cock crows, you will deny me three times." And he went out and wept bitterly.

Matthew Chapter 27

~ Jesus Brought Before Pilate (Mt 27:1–2)

St. Matthew: When morning came, all the chief priests and the elders of the people took counsel against Jesus to put him to death; and they bound him and led him away and delivered him to Pilate the governor.

~ Judas Hangs Himself (Mt 27:3–10)

St. Matthew: When Judas, his betrayer, saw that he was condemned, he repented and brought back the thirty pieces of silver to the chief priests and the elders, saying,

Judas: I have sinned in betraying innocent blood.

St. Matthew: They said,

Chief priests and elders: What is that to us? See to it yourself.

St. Matthew: And throwing down the pieces of silver in the temple, he departed; and he went and hanged himself. But the chief priests, taking the pieces of silver, said,

Chief priests: It is not lawful to put them into the treasury, since they are blood money.

St. Matthew: So they took counsel, and bought with them the potter's field, to bury strangers in. Therefore that field has been called the Field of Blood to this day. Then was fulfilled what had been spoken by the prophet Jeremiah, saying,

Prophet Jeremiah: And they took the thirty pieces of silver, the price of him on whom a price had been set by some of the sons of Israel, and they gave them for the potter's field, as the Lord directed me.

~ Pilate Questions Jesus (Mt 27:11–14)

St. Matthew: Now Jesus stood before the governor; and the governor asked him,

Pilate: Are you the King of the Jews?

St. Matthew: Jesus said,

Jesus: You have said so.

St. Matthew: But when he was accused by the chief priests and elders, he made no answer. Then Pilate said to him,

Pilate: Do you not hear how many things they testify against you?

St. Matthew: But he gave him no answer, not even to a single charge; so that the governor wondered greatly.

~ Barabbas or Jesus? (Mt 27:15–23)

St. Matthew: Now at the feast the governor was accustomed to release for the crowd any one prisoner whom they wanted. And they had then a notorious prisoner, called Barabbas. So when they had gathered, Pilate said to them,

Pilate: Whom do you want me to release for you, Barabbas or Jesus who is called Christ?

St. Matthew: For he knew that it was out of envy that they had delivered him up. Besides, while he was sitting on the judgment seat, his wife sent word to him,

Pilate's wife: Have nothing to do with that righteous man, for I have suffered much over him today in a dream.

St. Matthew: Now the chief priests and the elders persuaded the people to ask for Barabbas and destroy Jesus. The governor again said to them,

Pilate: Which of the two do you want me to release for you?

St. Matthew: And they said,

People: Barabbas.

St. Matthew: Pilate said to them,

Pilate: Then what shall I do with Jesus who is called Christ?

St. Matthew: They all said,

People: Let him be crucified.

St. Matthew: And he said,

Pilate: Why, what evil has he done?

St. Matthew: But they shouted all the more,

People: Let him be crucified.

Pilate Delivers Jesus to Be Crucified (Mt 27:24–26)

St. Matthew: So when Pilate saw that he was gaining nothing, but rather that a riot was beginning, he took water and washed his hands before the crowd, saying,

Pilate: I am innocent of this righteous man's blood; see to it yourselves.

St. Matthew: And all the people answered,

People: His blood be on us and on our children!

St. Matthew: Then he released for them Barabbas, and having scourged Jesus, delivered him to be crucified.

~ The Soldiers Mock Jesus (Mt 27:27–31)

St. Matthew: Then the soldiers of the governor took Jesus into the praetorium, and they gathered the whole battalion before him. And they stripped him and put a scarlet robe upon him, and plaiting a crown of thorns they put it on his head, and put a reed in his right hand. And kneeling before him they mocked him, saying,

Soldiers: Hail, King of the Jews!

~ The Crucifixion of Jesus (Mt 27:32–44); F4–585

St. Matthew: And they spat upon him, and took the reed and struck him on the head. And when they had mocked him, they stripped him of the robe, and put his own clothes on him, and led him away to crucify him.

As they were marching out, they came upon a man of Cyrene, Simon by name; this man they compelled to carry his cross. And when they came to a place called Golgotha (which means the place of a skull), they offered him wine to drink, mingled with gall; but when he tasted it, he would not drink it.

And when they had crucified him, they divided his garments among them by casting lots; then they sat down and kept watch over him there.

And over his head they put the charge against him, which read, “This is Jesus the King of the Jews.” Then two robbers were crucified with him, one on the right and one on the left.

And those who passed by derided him, wagging their heads and saying,

Passersby: You who would destroy the temple and build it in three days, save yourself! If you are the Son of God, come down from the cross.

St. Matthew: So also the chief priests, with the scribes and elders, mocked him, saying,

Chief priests, scribes, and elders: He saved others; he cannot save himself. He is the King of Israel; let him come down now from the cross, and we will believe in him. He trusts in God; let God deliver him now, if he desires him; for he said, “I am the Son of God.”

St. Matthew: And the robbers who were crucified with him also reviled him in the same way.

* The Death of Jesus (Mt 27:45–56); F4–586; F5–633

St. Matthew: Now from the sixth hour there was darkness over all the land until the ninth hour. And about the ninth hour Jesus cried with a loud voice,

Jesus: Eli, Eli, lama sabach–thani?

St. Matthew: That is,

Jesus: My God, my God, why have you forsaken me?

St. Matthew: And some of the bystanders hearing it said,

Bystanders: This man is calling Elijah.

St. Matthew: And one of them at once ran and took a sponge, filled it with vinegar, and put it on a reed, and gave it to him to drink. But the others said,

Bystanders: Wait, let us see whether Elijah will come to save him.

St. Matthew: And Jesus cried again with a loud voice and yielded up his spirit.

And behold, the curtain of the temple was torn in two, from top to bottom; and the earth shook, and the rocks were split; the tombs also were opened, and many bodies of the saints who had fallen asleep were raised, and coming out of the tombs after his resurrection they went into the holy city and appeared to many.

When the centurion and those who were with him, keeping watch over Jesus, saw the earthquake and what took place, they were filled with awe, and said,

Centurion: Truly this was the Son of God!

St. Matthew: There were also many women there, looking on from afar, who had followed Jesus from Galilee, ministering to him; among whom were Mary Magdalene, and Mary the mother of James and Joseph, and the mother of the sons of Zebedee.

~ The Burial of Jesus (Mt 27:57–61)

St. Matthew: When it was evening, there came a rich man from Arimathea, named Joseph, who also was a disciple of Jesus. He went to Pilate and asked for the body of Jesus. Then Pilate ordered it to be given to him. And Joseph took the body, and wrapped it in a clean linen shroud, and laid it in his own new tomb, which he had hewn in the rock; and he rolled a great stone to the door of the tomb, and departed. Mary Magdalene and the other Mary were there, sitting opposite the sepulchre.

~ The Guard at the Tomb (Mt 27:62–66)

St. Matthew: Next day, that is, after the day of Preparation, the chief priests and the Pharisees gathered before Pilate and said,

Chief priests and Pharisees: Sir, we remember how that impostor said, while he was still alive, "After three days I will rise again." Therefore order the sepulchre to be made secure until the third day, lest his disciples go and steal him away, and tell the people, "He has risen from the dead," and the last fraud will be worse than the first.

St. Matthew: Pilate said to them,

Pilate: You have a guard of soldiers; go, make it as secure as you can.

St. Matthew: So they went and made the sepulchre secure by sealing the stone and setting a guard.

Matthew Chapter 28

* The Resurrection of Jesus (Mt 28:1–10); F3–500; C3–2174

St. Matthew: Now after the sabbath, toward the dawn of the first day of the week, Mary Magdalene and the other Mary went to see the sepulchre. And behold, there was a great earthquake; for an angel of the Lord descended from heaven and came and rolled back the stone, and sat upon it. His appearance was like lightning, and his raiment white as snow. And for fear of him the guards trembled and became like dead men. But the angel said to the women,

Angel: Do not be afraid; for I know that you seek Jesus who was crucified. He is not here; for he has risen, as he said. Come, see the place where he lay. Then go quickly and tell his disciples that he has risen from the dead, and behold, he is going before you to Galilee; there you will see him. Lo, I have told you.

St. Matthew: So they departed quickly from the tomb with fear and great joy, and ran to tell his disciples. And behold, Jesus met them and said,

Jesus: Hail!

St. Matthew: And they came up and took hold of his feet and worshipped him. Then Jesus said to them,

Jesus: Do not be afraid; go and tell my brethren to go to Galilee, and there they will see me.

The Report of the Guard (Mt 28:11–15); F5–640

St. Matthew: While they were going, behold, some of the guard went into the city and told the chief priests all that had taken place. And when they had assembled with the elders and taken counsel, they gave a sum of money to the soldiers and said,

Chief priests and elders: Tell people, "His disciples came by night and stole him away while we were asleep." And if this comes to the governor's ears, we will satisfy him and keep you out of trouble.

St. Matthew: So they took the money and did as they were directed; and this story has been spread among the Jews to this day.

* Jesus Commissions the Disciples (Mt 28:16–20); F9–849; S1–1223

St. Matthew: Now the eleven disciples went to Galilee, to the mountain to which Jesus had directed them. And when they saw him they worshipped him; but some doubted. And Jesus came and said to them,

Jesus: All authority in heaven and on earth has been given to me. Go therefore and make disciples of all nations, baptizing them in the name of the Father and of the Son and of the Holy Spirit, teaching them to observe all that I have commanded you; and lo, I am with you always, to the close of the age.

THE GOSPEL OF ST. MARK

Mark Chapter 1

The Preaching of John the Baptist (Mk 1:1–8); F2–422; F3–515

St. Mark: The beginning of the gospel of Jesus Christ, the Son of God. As it is written in Isaiah the prophet,

Isaiah: Behold, I send my messenger before your face, who shall prepare your way; the voice of one crying in the wilderness: Prepare the way of the Lord, make his paths straight.

St. Mark: John the Baptist appeared in the wilderness, preaching a baptism of repentance for the forgiveness of sins. And there went out to him all the country of Judea, and all the people of Jerusalem; and they were baptized by him in the river Jordan, confessing their sins. Now John was clothed with camel's hair, and had a leather belt around his waist, and ate locusts and wild honey. And he preached, saying,

John the Baptist: After me comes he who is mightier than I, the thong of whose sandals I am not worthy to stoop down and untie. I have baptized you with water; but he will baptize you with the Holy Spirit.

The Baptism of Jesus (Mk 1:9–11); PF3–151; F2–422

St. Mark: In those days Jesus came from Nazareth of Galilee and was baptized by John in the Jordan. And when he came up out of the water, immediately he saw the heavens opened and the Spirit descending upon him like a dove; and a voice came from heaven,

God the Father: You are my beloved Son; with you I am well pleased.

The Temptation of Jesus (Mk 1:12–13); F1–333; F3–538

St. Mark: The Spirit immediately drove him out into the wilderness. And he was in the wilderness forty days, tempted by Satan; and he was with the wild beasts; and the angels ministered to him.

* Jesus Preaches the Gospel in Galilee (Mk 1:14–15); S4–1423; S4–1427

St. Mark: Now after John was arrested, Jesus came into Galilee, preaching the gospel of God, and saying,

Jesus: The time is fulfilled, and the kingdom of God is at hand; repent, and believe in the gospel.

Jesus Calls the First Disciples (Mk 1:16–20); F9–787

St. Mark: And passing along by the Sea of Galilee, he saw Simon and Andrew the brother of Simon casting a net in the sea; for they were fishermen. And Jesus said to them,

Jesus: Follow me and I will make you become fishers of men.

St. Mark: And immediately they left their nets and followed him. And going on a little farther, he saw James the son of Zebedee and John his brother, who were in their boat mending the nets. And immediately he called them; and they left their father Zebedee in the boat with the hired servants, and followed him.

* The Man with an Unclean Spirit (Mk 1:21–28); C3–2173; STL–1673

St. Mark: And they went into Capernaum; and immediately on the sabbath he entered the synagogue and taught. And they were astonished at his teaching, for he taught them as one who had authority, and not as the scribes. And immediately there was in their synagogue a man with an unclean spirit; and he cried out,

Unclean spirit: What have you to do with us, Jesus of Nazareth? Have you come to destroy us? I know who you are, the Holy One of God.

St. Mark: But Jesus rebuked him, saying,

Jesus: Be silent, and come out of him!

St. Mark: And the unclean spirit, convulsing him and crying with a loud voice, came out of him. And they were all amazed, so that they questioned among themselves, saying,

All: What is this? A new teaching! With authority he commands even the unclean spirits, and they obey him.

St. Mark: And at once his fame spread everywhere throughout all the surrounding region of Galilee.

~ Healings at Simon's House (Mk 1:29–34)

St. Mark: And immediately he left the synagogue, and entered the house of Simon and Andrew, with James and John. Now Simon's mother-in-law lay sick with a fever, and immediately they told him of her. And he came and took her by the hand and lifted her up, and the fever left her; and she served them. That evening, at sundown, they brought to him all who were sick or possessed with demons. And the whole city was gathered together about the door. And he healed many who were sick with various diseases, and cast out many demons; and he would not permit the demons to speak, because they knew him.

Jesus Preaches and Heals Throughout Galilee (Mk 1:35–39); P-2602

St. Mark: And in the morning, a great while before day, he rose and went out to a lonely place, and there he prayed. And Simon and those who were with him pursued him, and they found him and said to him,

Simon: Everyone is searching for you.

St. Mark: And he said to them,

Jesus: Let us go on to the next towns, that I may preach there also; for that is why I came out.

St. Mark: And he went throughout all Galilee, preaching in their synagogues and casting out demons.

Jesus Cleanses a Leper (Mk 1:40–45); S5–1504; P-2616

St. Mark: And a leper came to him beseeching him, and kneeling said to him,

Leper: If you will, you can make me clean.

St. Mark: Moved with pity, he stretched out his hand and touched him, and said to him,

Jesus: I will; be clean.

St. Mark: And immediately the leprosy left him, and he was made clean. And he sternly charged him, and sent him away at once, and said to him,

Jesus: See that you say nothing to any one; but go, show yourself to the priest, and offer for your cleansing what Moses commanded, for a proof to the people.

St. Mark: But he went out and began to talk freely about it, and to spread the news, so that Jesus could no longer openly enter a town, but was out in the country; and people came to him from every quarter.

Mark Chapter 2

* Jesus Heals a Paralytic (Mk 2:1–12); S5–1502; S5–1503

St. Mark: And when he returned to Capernaum after some days, it was reported that he was at home. And many were gathered together, so that there was no longer room for them, not even about the door; and he was preaching the word to them. And they came, bringing to him a paralytic carried by four men. And when they could not get near him because of the crowd, they removed the roof above him; and when they had made an opening, they let down the pallet on which the paralytic lay. And when Jesus saw their faith, he said to the paralytic,

Jesus: My son, your sins are forgiven.

St. Mark: Now some of the scribes were sitting there, questioning in their hearts,

Scribes: Why does this man speak thus? It is blasphemy! Who can forgive sins but God alone?

St. Mark: And immediately Jesus, perceiving in his spirit that they thus questioned within themselves, said to them,

Jesus: Why do you question thus in your hearts? Which is easier, to say to the paralytic, "Your sins are forgiven," or to say, "Rise, take up your pallet and walk?" But that you may know that the Son of man has authority on earth to forgive sins—

St. Mark: He said to the paralytic—

Jesus: I say to you, rise, take up your pallet and go home.

St. Mark: And he rose, and immediately took up the pallet and went out before them all; so that they were all amazed and glorified God, saying,

All: We never saw anything like this!

* Jesus Calls Levi (Mk 2:13–17); S4–1484; S5–1503

St. Mark: He went out again beside the sea; and all the crowd gathered about him, and he taught them. And as he passed on, he saw Levi the son of Alphaeus sitting at the tax office, and he said to him,

Jesus: Follow me.

St. Mark: And he rose and followed him. And as he sat at table in his house, many tax collectors and sinners were sitting with Jesus and his disciples; for there were many who followed him. And the scribes of the Pharisees, when they saw that he was eating with sinners and tax collectors, said to his disciples,

Scribes: Why does he eat with tax collectors and sinners?

St. Mark: And when Jesus heard it, he said to them,

Jesus: Those who are well have no need of a physician, but those who are sick; I came not to call the righteous, but sinners.

The Question About Fasting (Mk 2:18–22); F9–796

St. Mark: Now John's disciples and the Pharisees were fasting; and people came and said to him,

People: Why do John's disciples and the disciples of the Pharisees fast, but your disciples do not fast?

St. Mark: And Jesus said to them,

Jesus: Can the wedding guests fast while the bridegroom is with them? As long as they have the bridegroom with them, they cannot fast. The days will come, when the bridegroom is taken away from them, and then they will fast in that day.

No one sews a piece of unshrunk cloth on an old garment; if he does, the patch tears away from it, the new from the old, and a worse tear is made.

And no one puts new wine into old wineskins; if he does, the wine will burst the skins, and the wine is lost, and so are the skins; but new wine is for fresh skins.

* A Teaching About the Sabbath (Mk 2:23–28); F4–581; F3–544

St. Mark: One sabbath he was going through the grainfields; and as they made their way his disciples began to pluck heads of grain. And the Pharisees said to him,

Pharisees: Look, why are they doing what is not lawful on the sabbath?

St. Mark: And he said to them,

Jesus: Have you never read what David did, when he was in need and was hungry, he and those who were with him: how he entered the house of God, when Abiathar was high priest, and ate the showbread, which it is not lawful for any but the priests to eat, and also gave it to those who were with him?

St. Mark: And he said to them,

Jesus: The sabbath was made for man, not man for the sabbath; so the Son of man is Lord even of the sabbath.

Mark Chapter 3

* The Man With a Withered Hand (Mk 3:1–6); C3–2173; F4–591

St. Mark: Again he entered the synagogue, and a man was there who had a withered hand. And they watched him, to see whether he would heal him on the sabbath, so that they might accuse him. And he said to the man who had the withered hand,

Jesus: Come here.

St. Mark: And he said to them,

Jesus: Is it lawful on the sabbath to do good or to do harm, to save life or to kill?

St. Mark: But they were silent. And he looked around at them with anger, grieved at their hardness of heart, and said to the man,

Jesus: Stretch out your hand.

St. Mark: He stretched it out, and his hand was restored. The Pharisees went out, and immediately held counsel with the Herodians against him, how to destroy him.

A Multitude by the Sea (Mk 3:7–12); S5–1504

St. Mark: Jesus withdrew with his disciples to the sea, and a great multitude from Galilee followed; also from Judea and Jerusalem and Idumea and from beyond the Jordan and from about Tyre and Sidon a great multitude, hearing all that he did, came to him.

And he told his disciples to have a boat ready for him because of the crowd, lest they should crush him; for he had healed many, so that all who had diseases pressed upon him to touch him. And whenever the unclean spirits beheld him, they fell down before him and cried out,

Unclean spirits: You are the Son of God.

St. Mark: And he strictly ordered them not to make him known.

* Jesus Appoints the Twelve (Mk 3:13–19); F9–787; STL–1673

St. Mark: And he went up on the mountain, and called to him those whom he desired; and they came to him. And he appointed twelve, to be with him, and to be sent out to preach and have authority to cast out demons: Simon whom he surnamed Peter; James the son of Zebedee and John the brother of James, whom he surnamed Boanerges, that is, sons of thunder; Andrew, and Philip, and Bartholomew, and Matthew, and Thomas, and James the son of Alphaeus, and Thaddaeus, and Simon the Cananaean, and Judas Iscariot, who betrayed him.

* Jesus and Beelzebul (Mk 3:20–30); F3–548; F4–574

St. Mark: Then he went home; and the crowd came together again, so that they could not even eat. And when his family heard it, they went out to seize him, for people were saying,

People: He is beside himself.

St. Mark: And the scribes who came down from Jerusalem said,

Scribes: He is possessed by Beelzebul, and by the prince of demons he casts out the demons.

St. Mark: And he called them to him, and said to them in parables,

Jesus: How can Satan cast out Satan? If a kingdom is divided against itself, that kingdom cannot stand. And if a house is divided against itself, that house will not be able to stand. And if Satan has risen up against himself and is divided, he cannot stand, but is coming to an end. But no one can enter a strong man's house and plunder his goods, unless he first binds the strong man; then indeed he may plunder his house.

Truly, I say to you, all sins will be forgiven the sons of men, and whatever blasphemies they utter; but whoever blasphemes against the Holy Spirit never has forgiveness, but is guilty of an eternal sin.

St. Mark: For they had said,

Scribes: He has an unclean spirit.

The True Kindred of Jesus (Mk 3:31–35); F3–500

St. Mark: And his mother and his brethren came; and standing outside they sent to him and called him. And a crowd was sitting about him; and they said to him,

Crowd: Your mother and your brethren are outside, asking for you.

St. Mark: And he replied,

Jesus: Who are my mother and my brethren?

St. Mark: And looking around on those who sat about him, he said,

Jesus: Here are my mother and my brethren! Whoever does the will of God is my brother, and sister, and mother.

Mark Chapter 4

The Parable of the Sower (Mk 4:1–9); P–2707

St. Mark: Again he began to teach beside the sea. And a very large crowd gathered about him, so that he got into a boat and sat in it on the sea; and the whole crowd was beside the sea on the land. And he taught them many things in parables, and in his teaching he said to them:

Jesus: Listen! A sower went out to sow. And as he sowed, some seed fell along the path, and the birds came and devoured it. Other seed fell on rocky ground, where it had not much soil, and immediately it sprang up, since it had no depth of soil; and when the sun rose it was scorched, and since it had no root it withered away. Other seed fell among thorns and the thorns grew up and choked it, and it yielded no grain. And other seeds fell into good soil and brought forth grain, growing up and increasing and yielding thirtyfold and sixtyfold and a hundredfold.

St. Mark: And he said,

Jesus: He who has ears to hear, let him hear.

Explanation of the Parable (Mk 4:10–20); F3–546; P–2707

St. Mark: And when he was alone, those who were about him with the twelve asked him concerning the parables. And he said to them,

Jesus: To you has been given the secret of the kingdom of God, but for those outside everything is in parables; so that they may indeed see but not perceive, and may indeed hear but not understand; lest they should turn again, and be forgiven.

St. Mark: And he said to them,

Jesus: Do you not understand this parable? How then will you understand all the parables? The sower sows the word. And these are the ones along the path, where the word is sown; when they hear, Satan immediately comes and takes away the word which is sown in them.

And these in like manner are the ones sown upon rocky ground, who, when they hear the word, immediately receive it with joy; and they have no root in themselves, but endure for a while; then, when tribulation or persecution arises on account of the word, immediately they fall away.

And others are the ones sown among thorns; they are those who hear the word, but the cares of the world, and the delight in riches, and the desire for other things, enter in and choke the word, and it proves unfruitful. But those that were sown upon the good soil are the ones who hear the word and accept it and bear fruit, thirtyfold and sixtyfold and a hundredfold.

~ A Lamp Is Not Hidden (Mk 4:21–25)

St. Mark: And he said to them,

Jesus: Is a lamp brought in to be put under a bushel, or under a bed, and not on a stand? For there is nothing hid, except to be made manifest; nor is anything secret, except to come to light. If any man has ears to hear, let him hear.

St. Mark: And he said to them,

Jesus: Take heed what you hear; the measure you give will be the measure you get, and still more will be given you. For to him who has will more be given; and from him who has not, even what he has will be taken away.

~ A Parable About Seeds (Mk 4:26–32)

St. Mark: And he said,

Jesus: The kingdom of God is as if a man should scatter seed upon the ground, and should sleep and rise night and day, and the seed should sprout and grow, he knows not how. The earth produces of itself, first the blade, then the ear, then the full grain in the ear. But when the grain is ripe, at once he puts in the sickle, because the harvest has come.

St. Mark: And he said,

Jesus: With what can we compare the kingdom of God, or what parable shall we use for it? It is like a grain of mustard seed, which, when sown upon the ground, is the smallest of all the seeds on earth; yet when it is sown it grows up and becomes the greatest of all shrubs, and puts forth large branches, so that the birds of the air can make nests in its shade.

The Use of Parables (Mk 4:33–34); F3–546

St. Mark: With many such parables he spoke the word to them, as they were able to hear it; he did not speak to them without a parable, but privately to his own disciples he explained everything.

~ Jesus Calms a Storm on the Sea (Mk 4:35–41)

St. Mark: On that day, when evening had come, he said to them,

Jesus: Let us go across to the other side.

St. Mark: And leaving the crowd, they took him with them in the boat, just as he was. And other boats were with him. And a great storm of wind arose, and the waves beat into the boat, so that the boat was already filling. But he was in the stern, asleep on the cushion; and they woke him and said to him,

Disciples: Teacher, do you not care if we perish?

St. Mark: And he awoke and rebuked the wind, and said to the sea,

Jesus: Peace! Be still!

St. Mark: And the wind ceased, and there was a great calm. He said to them,

Jesus: Why are you afraid? Have you no faith?

St. Mark: And they were filled with awe, and said to one another,

Disciples: Who then is this, that even wind and sea obey him?

Mark Chapter 5

~ Jesus Heals the Gerasene Demoniac (Mk 5:1–20)

St. Mark: They came to the other side of the sea, to the country of the Gerasenes. And when he had come out of the boat, there met him out of the tombs a man with an unclean spirit, who lived among the tombs; and no one could bind him anymore, even with a chain; for he had often been bound with fetters and chains, but the chains he wrenched apart, and the fetters he broke in pieces; and no one had the strength to subdue him. Night and day among the tombs and on the mountains he was always crying out, and bruising himself with stones. And when he saw Jesus from afar, he ran and worshiped him; and crying out with a loud voice, he said,

Man with unclean spirit: What have you to do with me, Jesus, Son of the Most High God? I adjure you by God, do not torment me.

St. Mark: For he had said to him,

Jesus: Come out of the man, you unclean spirit!

St. Mark: And Jesus asked him,

Jesus: What is your name?

St. Mark: He replied,

Unclean spirits: My name is Legion; for we are many.

St. Mark: And he begged him eagerly not to send them out of the country. Now a great herd of swine was feeding there on the hillside; and they begged him,

Unclean spirits: Send us to the swine, let us enter them.

St. Mark: So he gave them leave. And the unclean spirits came out, and entered the swine; and the herd, numbering about two thousand, rushed down the steep bank into the sea, and were drowned in the sea.

The herdsmen fled, and told it in the city and in the country. And people came to see what it was that had happened. And they came to Jesus, and saw the demoniac sitting there, clothed and in his right mind, the man who had had the legion; and they were afraid. And those who had seen it told what had happened to the demoniac and to the swine. And they began to beg Jesus to depart from their neighborhood.

And as he was getting into the boat, the man who had been possessed with demons begged him that he might be with him. But he refused, and said to him,

Jesus: Go home to your friends, and tell them how much the Lord has done for you, and how he has had mercy on you.

St. Mark: And he went away and began to proclaim in the Decapolis how much Jesus had done for him; and all men marveled.

* A Girl Restored to Life and a Woman Healed (Mk 5:21–43); F11–994; F3–548

St. Mark: And when Jesus had crossed again in the boat to the other side, a great crowd gathered about him; and he was beside the sea. Then came one of the rulers of the synagogue, Jairus by name; and seeing him, he fell at his feet, and besought him, saying,

Jairus: My little daughter is at the point of death. Come and lay your hands on her, so that she may be made well, and live.

St. Mark: And he went with him. And a great crowd followed him and thronged about him. And there was a woman who had had a flow of blood for twelve years, and who had suffered much under many physicians, and had spent all that she had, and was no better but rather grew worse. She had heard the reports about Jesus, and came up behind him in the crowd and touched his garment. For she said,

Woman with flow of blood: If I touch even his garments, I shall be made well.

St. Mark: And immediately the hemorrhage ceased; and she felt in her body that she was healed of her disease. And Jesus, perceiving in himself that power had gone forth from him, immediately turned about in the crowd, and said,

Jesus: Who touched my garments?

St. Mark: And his disciples said to him,

Disciples: You see the crowd pressing around you, and yet you say, "Who touched me?"

St. Mark: And he looked around to see who had done it. But the woman, knowing what had been done to her, came in fear and trembling and fell down before him, and told him the whole truth. And he said to her,

Jesus: Daughter, your faith has made you well; go in peace, and be healed of your disease.

St. Mark: While he was still speaking, there came from the ruler's house some who said,

Some from Jairus' house: Your daughter is dead. Why trouble the Teacher any further?

St. Mark: But ignoring what they said, Jesus said to the ruler of the synagogue,

Jesus: Do not fear, only believe.

St. Mark: And he allowed no one to follow him except Peter and James and John the brother of James. When they came to the house of the ruler of the synagogue, he saw a tumult, and people weeping and wailing loudly. And when he had entered, he said to them,

Jesus: Why do you make a tumult and weep? The child is not dead but sleeping.

St. Mark: And they laughed at him. But he put them all outside, and took the child's father and mother and those who were with him, and went in where the child was. Taking her by the hand he said to her,

Jesus: Talitha cumi;

St. Mark: Which means,

Jesus: Little girl, I say to you, arise.

St. Mark: And immediately the girl got up and walked (she was twelve years of age), and they were immediately overcome with amazement. And he strictly charged them that no one should know this, and told them to give her something to eat.

Mark Chapter 6

* The Rejection of Jesus at Nazareth (Mk 6:1–6); F8–699; F3–500

St. Mark: He went away from there and came to his own country; and his disciples followed him. And on the sabbath he began to teach in the synagogue; and many who heard him were astonished, saying,

Many: Where did this man get all this? What is the wisdom given to him? What mighty works are wrought by his hands! Is not this the carpenter, the son of Mary and brother of James and Joseph and Judas and Simon, and are not his sisters here with us?

St. Mark: And they took offense at him. And Jesus said to them,

Jesus: A prophet is not without honor, except in his own country, and among his own kin, and in his own house.

St. Mark: And he could do no mighty work there, except that he laid his hands upon a few sick people and healed them. And he marveled because of their unbelief.

St. Mark: And he went about among the villages teaching.

* The Mission of the Twelve (Mk 6:7–13); S5–1506; STL–1673

St. Mark: And he called to him the twelve, and began to send them out two by two, and gave them authority over the unclean spirits. He charged them to take nothing for their journey except a staff; no bread, no bag, no money in their belts; but to wear sandals and not put on two tunics. And he said to them,

Jesus: Where you enter a house, stay there until you leave the place. And if any place will not receive you and they refuse to hear you, when you leave, shake off the dust that is on your feet for a testimony against them.

St. Mark: So they went out and preached that men should repent. And they cast out many demons, and anointed with oil many that were sick and healed them.

The Death of John the Baptist (Mk 6:14–29); F3–523

St. Mark: King Herod heard of it; for Jesus' name had become known. Some said,

Some: John the baptizer has been raised from the dead; that is why these powers are at work in him.

St. Mark: But others said,

Others: It is Elijah.

St. Mark: And others said,

Second group of others: It is a prophet, like one of the prophets of old.

St. Mark: But when Herod heard of it he said,

Herod: John, whom I beheaded, has been raised.

St. Mark: For Herod had sent and seized John, and bound him in prison for the sake of Herodias, his brother Philip's wife; because he had married her. For John said to Herod,

John the Baptist: It is not lawful for you to have your brother's wife.

St. Mark: And Herodias had a grudge against him, and wanted to kill him. But she could not, for Herod feared John, knowing that he was a righteous and holy man, and kept him safe. When he heard him, he was much perplexed; and yet he heard him gladly.

But an opportunity came when Herod on his birthday gave a banquet for his courtiers and officers and the leading men of Galilee. For when Herodias' daughter came in and danced, she pleased Herod and his guests; and the king said to the girl,

Herod: Ask me for whatever you wish, and I will grant it.

St. Mark: And he vowed to her,

Herod: Whatever you ask me, I will give you, even half of my kingdom.

St. Mark: And she went out, and said to her mother,

Herodias' daughter: What shall I ask?

St. Mark: And she said,

Herodias: The head of John the baptizer.

St. Mark: And she came in immediately with haste to the king, and asked, saying,

Herodias' daughter: I want you to give me at once the head of John the Baptist on a platter.

St. Mark: And the king was exceedingly sorry; but because of his oaths and his guests he did not want to break his word to her. And immediately the king sent a soldier of the guard and gave orders to bring his head. He went and beheaded him in the prison, and brought his head on a platter, and gave it to the girl; and the girl gave it to her mother.

When his disciples heard of it, they came and took his body, and laid it in a tomb.

Feeding the Five Thousand (Mk 6:30–44); F3–472

St. Mark: The apostles returned to Jesus, and told him all that they had done and taught. And he said to them,

Jesus: Come away by yourselves to a lonely place, and rest a while.

St. Mark: For many were coming and going, and they had no leisure even to eat. And they went away in the boat to a lonely place by themselves. Now many saw them going, and knew them, and they ran there on foot from all the towns, and got there ahead of them.

As he went ashore he saw a great throng, and he had compassion on them, because they were like sheep without a shepherd; and he began to teach them many things. And when it grew late, his disciples came to him and said,

Disciples: This is a lonely place, and the hour is now late; send them away, to go into the country and villages round about and buy themselves something to eat.

St. Mark: But he answered them,

Jesus: You give them something to eat.

St. Mark: And they said to him,

Disciples: Shall we go and buy two hundred denarii worth of bread, and give it to them to eat?

St. Mark: And he said to them,

Jesus: How many loaves have you? Go and see.

St. Mark: And when they had found out, they said,

Disciples: Five, and two fish.

St. Mark: Then he commanded them all to sit down by companies upon the green grass. So they sat down in groups, by hundreds and by fifties. And taking the five loaves and the two fish he looked up to heaven, and blessed, and broke the loaves, and gave them to the disciples to set before the people; and he divided the two fish among them all. And they all ate and were satisfied. And they took up twelve baskets full of broken pieces and of the fish. And those who ate the loaves were five thousand men.

Jesus Walks on the Sea (Mk 6:45–52); P–2602

St. Mark: Immediately he made his disciples get into the boat and go before him to the other side, to Bethsaida, while he dismissed the crowd. And after he had taken leave of them, he went up on the mountain to pray. And when evening came, the boat was out on the sea, and he was alone on the land. And he saw that they were making headway painfully, for the wind was against them.

And about the fourth watch of the night he came to them, walking on the sea. He meant to pass by them, but when they saw him walking on the sea they thought it was a ghost, and cried out; for they all saw him, and were terrified. But immediately he spoke to them and said,

Jesus: Take heart, it is I; have no fear.

St. Mark: And he got into the boat with them and the wind ceased. And they were utterly astounded, for they did not understand about the loaves, but their hearts were hardened.

Jesus Heals the Sick in Gennesaret (Mk 6:53–56); S5–1504

St. Mark: And when they had crossed over, they came to land at Gennesaret, and moored to the shore. And when they got out of the boat, immediately the people recognized him, and ran about the whole neighborhood and began to bring sick people on their pallets to any place where they heard he was.

And wherever he came, in villages, cities, or country, they laid the sick in the marketplaces, and besought him that they might touch even the fringe of his garment; and as many as touched it were made well.

Mark Chapter 7

* The Tradition of the Elders (Mk 7:1–23); F4–581; C4–2218

St. Mark: Now when the Pharisees gathered together to him, with some of the scribes, who had come from Jerusalem, they saw that some of his disciples ate with hands defiled, that is, unwashed. (For the Pharisees, and all the Jews, do not eat unless they wash their hands, observing the tradition of the elders; and when they come from the market place, they do not eat unless they purify themselves; and there are many other traditions which they observe, the washing of cups and pots and vessels of bronze.) And the Pharisees and the scribes asked him,

Pharisees and scribes: Why do your disciples not live according to the tradition of the elders, but eat with hands defiled?

St. Mark: And he said to them,

Jesus: Well did Isaiah prophesy of you hypocrites, as it is written,

Isaiah: This people honors me with their lips, but their heart is far from me; in vain do they worship me, teaching as doctrines the precepts of men.

Jesus: You leave the commandment of God, and hold fast the tradition of men.

St. Mark: And he said to them,

Jesus: You have a fine way of rejecting the commandment of God, in order to keep your tradition! For Moses said,

Moses: Honor your father and your mother;

Jesus: And,

Moses: He who speaks evil of father or mother, let him surely die;

Jesus: But you say, "If a man tells his father or his mother, What you would have gained from me is Corban (that is, given to God);" then you no longer permit him to do anything for his father or mother, thus making void the word of God through your tradition which you hand on. And many such things you do.

St. Mark: And he called the people to him again, and said to them,

Jesus: Hear me, all of you, and understand: there is nothing outside a man which by going into him can defile him; but the things which come out of a man are what defile him.

St. Mark: And when he had entered the house, and left the people, his disciples asked him about the parable. And he said to them,

Jesus: Then are you also without understanding? Do you not see that whatever goes into a man from outside cannot defile him, since it enters, not his heart but his stomach, and so passes on?

St. Mark: (Thus he declared all foods clean.) And he said,

Jesus: What comes out of a man is what defiles a man. For from within, out of the heart of man, come evil thoughts, fornication, theft, murder, adultery, coveting, wickedness, deceit, licentiousness, envy, slander, pride, foolishness. All these evil things come from within, and they defile a man.

The Syrophoenician Woman's Faith (Mk 7:24–30); P–2616

St. Mark: And from there he arose and went away to the region of Tyre and Sidon. And he entered a house, and would not have any one know it; yet he could not be hid. But immediately a woman, whose little daughter was possessed by an unclean spirit, heard of him, and came and fell down at his feet. Now the woman was a Greek, a Syrophoenician by birth. And she begged him to cast the demon out of her daughter. And he said to her,

Jesus: Let the children first be fed, for it is not right to take the children's bread and throw it to the dogs.

St. Mark: But she answered him,

Syrophoenician woman: Yes, Lord; yet even the dogs under the table eat the children's crumbs.

St. Mark: And he said to her,

Jesus: For this saying you may go your way; the demon has left your daughter.

St. Mark: And she went home, and found the child lying in bed, and the demon gone.

* Jesus Cures a Deaf Man (Mk 7:31–37); S5–1504; LT–1151;

St. Mark: Then he returned from the region of Tyre, and went through Sidon to the Sea of Galilee, through the region of the Decapolis. And they brought to him a man who was deaf and had an impediment in his speech; and they besought him to lay his hand upon him. And taking him aside from the multitude privately, he put his fingers into his ears, and he spat and touched his tongue; and looking up to heaven, he sighed, and said to him,

Jesus: Ephphatha,

St. Mark: That is,

Jesus: Be opened.

St. Mark: And his ears were opened, his tongue was released, and he spoke plainly. And he charged them to tell no one; but the more he charged them, the more zealously they proclaimed it. And they were astonished beyond measure, saying,

People: He has done all things well; he even makes the deaf hear and the mute speak.

Mark Chapter 8

Feeding the Four Thousand (Mk 8:1–10); S3–1329

St. Mark: In those days, when again a great crowd had gathered, and they had nothing to eat, he called his disciples to him, and said to them,

Jesus: I have compassion on the crowd, because they have been with me now three days, and have nothing to eat; and if I send them away hungry to their homes, they will faint on the way; and some of them have come a long way.

St. Mark: And his disciples answered him,

Disciples: How can one feed these men with bread here in the desert?

St. Mark: And he asked them,

Jesus: How many loaves have you?

St. Mark: They said,

Disciples: Seven.

St. Mark: And he commanded the crowd to sit down on the ground; and he took the seven loaves, and having given thanks he broke them and gave them to his disciples to set before the people; and they set them before the crowd. And they had a few small fish; and having blessed them, he commanded that these also should be set before them. And they ate, and were satisfied; and they took up the broken pieces left over, seven baskets full. And there were about four thousand people.

St. Mark: And he sent them away; and immediately he got into the boat with his disciples, and went to the district of Dalmanutha.

~ The Demand for a Sign (Mk 8:11–13)

St. Mark: The Pharisees came and began to argue with him, seeking from him a sign from heaven, to test him. And he sighed deeply in his spirit, and said,

Jesus: Why does this generation seek a sign? Truly, I say to you, no sign shall be given to this generation.

St. Mark: And he left them, and getting into the boat again he departed to the other side.

The Leaven of the Pharisees and of Herod (Mk 8:14–21); S3–1329

St. Mark: Now they had forgotten to bring bread; and they had only one loaf with them in the boat. And he cautioned them, saying,

Jesus: Take heed, beware of the leaven of the Pharisees and the leaven of Herod.

St. Mark: And they discussed it with one another, saying,

Disciples: We have no bread.

St. Mark: And being aware of it, Jesus said to them,

Jesus: Why do you discuss the fact that you have no bread? Do you not yet perceive or understand? Are your hearts hardened? Having eyes do you not see, and having ears do you not hear? And do you not remember? When I broke the five loaves for the five thousand, how many baskets full of broken pieces did you take up?

St. Mark: They said to him,

Disciples: Twelve.

Jesus: And the seven for the four thousand, how many baskets full of broken pieces did you take up?

St. Mark: And they said to him,

Disciples: Seven.

St. Mark: And he said to them,

Jesus: Do you not yet understand?

* Jesus Cures a Blind Man at Bethsaida (Mk 8:22–26); LT–1151; S5–1504

St. Mark: And they came to Bethsaida. And some people brought to him a blind man, and begged him to touch him. And he took the blind man by the hand, and led him out of the village; and when he had spit on his eyes and laid his hands upon him, he asked him,

Jesus: Do you see anything?

St. Mark: And he looked up and said,

Blind man: I see men; but they look like trees, walking.

St. Mark: Then again he laid his hands upon his eyes; and he looked intently and was restored, and saw everything clearly. And he sent him away to his home, saying,

Jesus: Do not even enter the village.

Peter's Declaration That Jesus Is the Christ (Mk 8:27–30); F3–472

St. Mark: And Jesus went on with his disciples, to the villages of Caesarea Philippi; and on the way he asked his disciples,

Jesus: Who do men say that I am?

St. Mark: And they told him,

Disciples: John the Baptist; and others say, Elijah; and others one of the prophets.

St. Mark: And he asked them,

Jesus: But who do you say that I am?

St. Mark: Peter answered him,

Peter: You are the Christ.

St. Mark: And he charged them to tell no one about him.

* Jesus Foretells His Death and Resurrection (Mk 8:31–38); F3–557; C10–2544

St. Mark: And he began to teach them that the Son of man must suffer many things, and be rejected by the elders and the chief priests and the scribes, and be killed, and after three days rise again. And he said this plainly. And Peter took him, and began to rebuke him. But turning and seeing his disciples, he rebuked Peter, and said,

Jesus: Get behind me, Satan! For you are not on the side of God, but of men.

St. Mark: And he called to him the multitude with his disciples, and said to them,

Jesus: If any man would come after me, let him deny himself and take up his cross and follow me. For whoever would save his life will lose it; and whoever loses his life for my sake and the gospel's will save it. For what does it profit a man, to gain the whole world and forfeit his life? For what can a man give in return for his life? For whoever is ashamed of me and of my words in this adulterous and sinful generation, of him will the Son of man also be ashamed, when he comes in the glory of his Father with the holy angels.

Mark Chapter 9

St. Mark: And he said to them,

Jesus: Truly, I say to you, there are some standing here who will not taste death before they see that the kingdom of God has come with power.

* The Transfiguration (Mk 9:2–8); PF3–151; F3–459

St. Mark: And after six days Jesus took with him Peter and James and John, and led them up a high mountain apart by themselves; and he was transfigured before them, and his garments became glistening, intensely white, as no fuller on earth could bleach them. And there appeared to them Elijah with Moses; and they were talking to Jesus. And Peter said to Jesus,

Peter: Master, it is well that we are here; let us make three booths, one for you and one for Moses and one for Elijah.

St. Mark: For he did not know what to say, for they were exceedingly afraid. And a cloud overshadowed them, and a voice came out of the cloud,

God the Father: This is my beloved Son; listen to him.

St. Mark: And suddenly looking around they no longer saw any one with them but Jesus only.

The Coming of Elijah (Mk 9:9–13); F5–649

St. Mark: And as they were coming down the mountain, he charged them to tell no one what they had seen, until the Son of man should have risen from the dead. So they kept the matter to themselves, questioning what the rising from the dead meant. And they asked him,

Peter, James, and John: Why do the scribes say that first Elijah must come?

St. Mark: And he said to them,

Jesus: Elijah does come first to restore all things; and how is it written of the Son of man, that he should suffer many things and be treated with contempt? But I tell you that Elijah has come, and they did to him whatever they pleased, as it is written of him.

* The Healing of a Boy with a Mute Spirit (Mk 9:14–29); S5–1504; P–2610

St. Mark: And when they came to the disciples, they saw a great crowd about them, and scribes arguing with them. And immediately all the crowd, when they saw him, were greatly amazed, and ran up to him and greeted him. And he asked them,

Jesus: What are you discussing with them?

St. Mark: And one of the crowd answered him,

Father of boy: Teacher, I brought my son to you, for he has a mute spirit; and wherever it seizes him, it dashes him down; and he foams and grinds his teeth and becomes rigid; and I asked your disciples to cast it out, and they were not able.

St. Mark: And he answered them,

Jesus: O faithless generation, how long am I to be with you? How long am I to bear with you? Bring him to me.

St. Mark: And they brought the boy to him; and when the spirit saw him, immediately it convulsed the boy, and he fell on the ground and rolled about, foaming at the mouth. And Jesus asked his father,

Jesus: How long has he had this?

St. Mark: And he said,

Father of boy: From childhood. And it has often cast him into the fire and into the water, to destroy him; but if you can do anything, have pity on us and help us.

St. Mark: And Jesus said to him,

Jesus: If you can! All things are possible to him who believes.

St. Mark: Immediately the father of the child cried out and said,

Father of boy: I believe; help my unbelief!

St. Mark: And when Jesus saw that a crowd came running together, he rebuked the unclean spirit, saying to it,

Jesus: You mute and deaf spirit, I command you, come out of him, and never enter him again.

St. Mark: And after crying out and convulsing him terribly, it came out, and the boy was like a corpse; so that most of them said,

People: He is dead.

St. Mark: But Jesus took him by the hand and lifted him up, and he arose. And when he had entered the house, his disciples asked him privately,

Disciples: Why could we not cast it out?

St. Mark: And he said to them,

Jesus: This kind cannot be driven out by anything but prayer and fasting.

Jesus Again Foretells His Death and Resurrection (Mk 9:30–32); F3–557; F3–474

St. Mark: They went on from there and passed through Galilee. And he would not have any one know it; for he was teaching his disciples, saying to them,

Jesus: The Son of man will be delivered into the hands of men, and they will kill him; and when he is killed, after three days he will rise.

St. Mark: But they did not understand the saying, and they were afraid to ask him.

True Greatness (Mk 9:33–37); LC–1825

St. Mark: And they came to Capernaum; and when he was in the house he asked them,

Jesus: What were you discussing on the way?

St. Mark: But they were silent; for on the way they had discussed with one another who was the greatest. And he sat down and called the twelve; and he said to them,

Jesus: If any one would be first, he must be last of all and servant of all.

St. Mark: And he took a child, and put him in the midst of them; and taking him in his arms, he said to them,

Jesus: Whoever receives one such child in my name receives me; and whoever receives me, receives not me but him who sent me.

~ Another Exorcist (Mk 9:38–41)

St. Mark: John said to him,

John: Teacher, we saw a man casting out demons in your name, and we forbade him, because he was not following us.

St. Mark: But Jesus said,

Jesus: Do not forbid him; for no one who does a mighty work in my name will be able soon after to speak evil of me. For he that is not against us is for us. For truly, I say to you, whoever gives you a cup of water to drink because you bear the name of Christ, will by no means lose his reward.

Temptations to Sin (Mk 9:42–50); F12–1034

Jesus: Whoever causes one of these little ones who believe in me to sin, it would be better for him if a great millstone were hung round his neck and he were thrown into the sea.

And if your hand causes you to sin, cut it off; it is better for you to enter life maimed than with two hands to go to hell, to the unquenchable fire. And if your foot causes you to sin, cut it off; it is better for you to enter life lame than with two feet to be thrown into hell. And if your eye causes you to sin, pluck it out; it is better for you to enter the kingdom of God with one eye than with two eyes to be thrown into hell, where their worm does not die, and the fire is not quenched.

For everyone will be salted with fire. Salt is good; but if the salt has lost its saltiness, how will you season it? Have salt in yourselves, and be at peace with one another.

Mark Chapter 10

* Teachings About Divorce (Mk 10:1–12); S7–1639; C6–2364

St. Mark: And he left there and went to the region of Judea and beyond the Jordan, and crowds gathered to him again; and again, as his custom was, he taught them. And Pharisees came up and in order to test him asked,

Pharisees: Is it lawful for a man to divorce his wife?

St. Mark: He answered them,

Jesus: What did Moses command you?

St. Mark: They said,

Pharisees: Moses allowed a man to write a certificate of divorce, and to put her away.

St. Mark: But Jesus said to them,

Jesus: For your hardness of heart he wrote you this commandment. But from the beginning of creation, God made them male and female. For this reason a man shall leave his father and mother and be joined to his wife, and the two shall become one. So they are no longer two but one. What therefore God has joined together, let not man put asunder.

St. Mark: And in the house the disciples asked him again about this matter. And he said to them,

Jesus: Whoever divorces his wife and marries another, commits adultery against her; and if she divorces her husband and marries another, she commits adultery.

* Jesus Blesses the Children (Mk 10:13–16); S1–1244; S1–1261

St. Mark: And they were bringing children to him, that he might touch them; and the disciples rebuked them. But when Jesus saw it he was indignant, and said to them,

Jesus: Let the children come to me, do not hinder them; for to such belongs the kingdom of God. Truly, I say to you, whoever does not receive the kingdom of God like a child shall not enter it.

St. Mark: And he took them in his arms and blessed them, laying his hands upon them.

* The Rich Man (Mk 10:17–31); S7–1618; P–2728

St. Mark: And as he was setting out on his journey, a man ran up and knelt before him, and asked him,

Rich young man: Good Teacher, what must I do to inherit eternal life?

St. Mark: And Jesus said to him,

Jesus: Why do you call me good? No one is good but God alone. You know the commandments: "Do not kill, Do not commit adultery, Do not steal, Do not bear false witness, Do not defraud, Honor your father and mother."

St. Mark: And he said to him,

Rich young man: Teacher, all these I have observed from my youth.

St. Mark: And Jesus looking upon him loved him, and said to him,

Jesus: You lack one thing; go, sell what you have, and give to the poor, and you will have treasure in heaven; and come, follow me.

St. Mark: At that saying his countenance fell, and he went away sorrowful; for he had great possessions. And Jesus looked around and said to his disciples,

Jesus: How hard it will be for those who trust in riches to enter the kingdom of God!

St. Mark: And the disciples were amazed at his words. But Jesus said to them again,

Jesus: Children, how hard it is for those who trust in riches to enter the kingdom of God! It is easier for a camel to go through the eye of a needle than for a rich man to enter the kingdom of God.

St. Mark: And they were exceedingly astonished, and said to him,

Disciples: Then who can be saved?

St. Mark: Jesus looked at them and said,

Jesus: With men it is impossible, but not with God; for all things are possible with God.

St. Mark: Peter began to say to him,

Peter: Lo, we have left everything and followed you.

St. Mark: Jesus said,

Jesus: Truly, I say to you, there is no one who has left house or brothers or sisters or mother or father or children or lands, for my sake and for the gospel, who will not receive a hundredfold now in this time, houses and brothers and sisters and mothers and children and lands, with persecutions, and in the age to come eternal life. But many that are first will be last, and the last first.

* A Third Time Jesus Foretells His Death and Resurrection (Mk 10:32–34); F3–557; F3–474

St. Mark: And they were on the road, going up to Jerusalem, and Jesus was walking ahead of them; and they were amazed, and those who followed were afraid. And taking the twelve again, he began to tell them what was to happen to him, saying,

Jesus: Behold, we are going up to Jerusalem; and the Son of man will be delivered to the chief priests and the scribes, and they will condemn him to death, and deliver him to the Gentiles; and they will mock him, and spit upon him, and scourge him, and kill him; and after three days he will rise.

* The Request of James and John (Mk 10:35–45); S6–1551; S1–1225

St. Mark: And James and John, the sons of Zebedee, came forward to him, and said to him,

James and John: Teacher, we want you to do for us whatever we ask of you.

St. Mark: And he said to them,

Jesus: What do you want me to do for you?

St. Mark: And they said to him,

James and John: Grant us to sit, one at your right hand and one at your left, in your glory.

St. Mark: But Jesus said to them,

Jesus: You do not know what you are asking. Are you able to drink the chalice that I drink, or to be baptized with the baptism with which I am baptized?

St. Mark: And they said to him,

James and John: We are able.

St. Mark: And Jesus said to them,

Jesus: The chalice that I drink you will drink; and with the baptism with which I am baptized, you will be baptized; but to sit at my right hand or at my left is not mine to grant, but it is for those for whom it has been prepared.

St. Mark: And when the ten heard it, they began to be indignant at James and John. And Jesus called them to him and said to them,

Jesus: You know that those who are supposed to rule over the Gentiles lord it over them, and their great men exercise authority over them. But it shall not be so among you; but whoever would be great among you must be your servant, and whoever would be first among you must be slave of all. For the Son of man also came not to be served but to serve, and to give his life as a ransom for many.

* Bartimaeus Receives His Sight (Mk 10:46–52); P–2667; P–2616

St. Mark: And they came to Jericho; and as he was leaving Jericho with his disciples and a great multitude, Bartimaeus, a blind beggar, the son of Timaeus, was sitting by the roadside. And when he heard that it was Jesus of Nazareth, he began to cry out and say,

Bartimaeus: Jesus, Son of David, have mercy on me!

St. Mark: And many rebuked him, telling him to be silent; but he cried out all the more,

Bartimaeus: Son of David, have mercy on me!

St. Mark: And Jesus stopped and said,

Jesus: Call him.

St. Mark: And they called the blind man, saying to him,

People: Take heart; rise, he is calling you.

St. Mark: And throwing off his mantle he sprang up and came to Jesus. And Jesus said to him,

Jesus: What do you want me to do for you?

St. Mark: And the blind man said to him,

Bartimaeus: Master, let me receive my sight.

St. Mark: And Jesus said to him,

Jesus: Go your way; your faith has made you well.

St. Mark: And immediately he received his sight and followed him on the way.

Mark Chapter 11

~ Jesus' Entry into Jerusalem (Mk 11:1–11)

St. Mark: And when they drew near to Jerusalem, to Bethphage and Bethany, at the Mount of Olives, he sent two of his disciples, and said to them,

Jesus: Go into the village opposite you, and immediately as you enter it you will find a colt tied, on which no one has ever sat; untie it and bring it. If any one says to you, "Why are you doing this?" say, "The Lord has need of it and will send it back here immediately."

St. Mark: And they went away, and found a colt tied at the door out in the open street; and they untied it. And those who stood there said to them,

Bystanders: What are you doing, untying the colt?

St. Mark: And they told them what Jesus had said; and they let them go. And they brought the colt to Jesus, and threw their garments on it; and he sat upon it. And many spread their garments on the road, and others spread leafy branches which they had cut from the fields. And those who went before and those who followed cried out,

Crowds: Hosanna! Blessed is he who comes in the name of the Lord! Blessed is the kingdom of our father David that is coming! Hosanna in the highest!

St. Mark: And he entered Jerusalem, and went into the temple; and when he had looked round at everything, as it was already late, he went out to Bethany with the twelve.

~ Jesus Curses the Fig Tree (Mk 11:12–14)

St. Mark: On the following day, when they came from Bethany, he was hungry. And seeing in the distance a fig tree in leaf, he went to see if he could find anything on it. When he came to it, he found nothing but leaves, for it was not the season for figs. And he said to it,

Jesus: May no one ever eat fruit from you again.

St. Mark: And his disciples heard it.

~ Jesus Cleanses the Temple (Mk 11:15–19)

St. Mark: And they came to Jerusalem. And he entered the temple and began to drive out those who sold and those who bought in the temple, and he overturned the tables of the money-changers and the seats of those who sold pigeons; and he would not allow any one to carry anything through the temple. And he taught, and said to them,

Jesus: Is it not written, "My house shall be called a house of prayer for all the nations?" But you have made it a den of robbers.

St. Mark: And the chief priests and the scribes heard it and sought a way to destroy him; for they feared him, because all the multitude was astonished at his teaching. And when evening came they went out of the city.

* The Lesson from the Withered Fig Tree (Mk 11:20–26); LP5–2841; P–2610

St. Mark: As they passed by in the morning, they saw the fig tree withered away to its roots. And Peter remembered and said to him,

Peter: Master, look! The fig tree which you cursed has withered.

St. Mark: And Jesus answered them,

Jesus: Have faith in God. Truly, I say to you, whoever says to this mountain, "Be taken up and cast into the sea," and does not doubt in his heart, but believes that what he says will come to pass, it will be done for him. Therefore I tell you, whatever you ask in prayer, believe that you have received it, and it will be yours. And whenever you stand praying, forgive, if you have anything against any one; so that your Father also who is in heaven may forgive you your trespasses.

~ Jesus' Authority is Questioned (Mk 11:27–33)

St. Mark: And they came again to Jerusalem. And as he was walking in the temple, the chief priests and the scribes and the elders came to him, and they said to him,

Chief priests, scribes, and elders: By what authority are you doing these things, or who gave you this authority to do them?

St. Mark: Jesus said to them,

Jesus: I will ask you a question; answer me, and I will tell you by what authority I do these things. Was the baptism of John from heaven or from men? Answer me.

St. Mark: And they argued with one another,

Chief priests, scribes, and elders: If we say, "From heaven," he will say, "Why then did you not believe him?" But shall we say, "From men?"

St. Mark: They were afraid of the people, for all held that John was a real prophet. So they answered Jesus,

Chief priests, scribes, and elders: We do not know.

St. Mark: And Jesus said to them,

Jesus: Neither will I tell you by what authority I do these things.

Mark Chapter 12

~ The Parable of the Wicked Tenants (Mk 12:1–12)

St. Mark: And he began to speak to them in parables.

Jesus: A man planted a vineyard, and set a hedge around it, and dug a pit for the wine press, and built a tower, and let it out to tenants, and went into another country. When the time came, he sent a servant to the tenants, to get from them some of the fruit of the vineyard. And they took him and beat him, and sent him away empty-handed. Again he sent to them another servant, and they wounded him in the head, and treated him shamefully. And he sent another, and him they killed; and so with many others, some they beat and some they killed. He had still one other, a beloved son; finally he sent him to them, saying,

Owner of the vineyard: They will respect my son.

Jesus: But those tenants said to one another,

Tenants: This is the heir; come, let us kill him, and the inheritance will be ours.

Jesus: And they took him and killed him, and cast him out of the vineyard. What will the owner of the vineyard do? He will come and destroy the tenants, and give the vineyard to others. Have you not read this Scripture: "The very stone which the builders rejected has become the cornerstone; this was the Lord's doing, and it is marvelous in our eyes?"

St. Mark: And they tried to arrest him, but feared the multitude, for they perceived that he had told the parable against them; so they left him and went away.

The Question About Paying Taxes (Mk 12:13–17); F2–450

St. Mark: And they sent to him some of the Pharisees and some of the Herodians, to entrap him in his talk. And they came and said to him,

Pharisees and Herodians: Teacher, we know that you are true, and care for no man; for you do not regard the position of men, but truly teach the way of God. Is it lawful to pay taxes to Caesar, or not? Should we pay them, or should we not?

St. Mark: But knowing their hypocrisy, he said to them,

Jesus: Why put me to the test? Bring me a coin, and let me look at it.

St. Mark: And they brought one. And he said to them,

Jesus: Whose likeness and inscription is this?

St. Mark: They said to him,

Pharisees and Herodians: Caesar's.

St. Mark: Jesus said to them,

Jesus: Render to Caesar the things that are Caesar's, and to God the things that are God's.

St. Mark: And they were amazed at him.

The Question About Man's Resurrection (Mk 12:18–27); F11–993; S7–1619

St. Mark: And Sadducees came to him, who say that there is no resurrection; and they asked him a question, saying,

Sadducees: Teacher, Moses wrote for us that if a man's brother dies and leaves a wife, but leaves no child, the man must take the wife, and raise up children for his brother. There were seven brothers; the first took a wife, and when he died left no children; and the second took her, and died, leaving no children; and the third likewise; and the seven left no children. Last of all the woman also died. In the resurrection whose wife will she be? For the seven had her as wife.

St. Mark: Jesus said to them,

Jesus: Is not this why you are wrong, that you know neither the Scriptures nor the power of God? For when they rise from the dead, they neither marry nor are given in marriage, but are like angels in heaven. And as for the dead being raised, have you not read in the book of Moses, in the passage about the bush, how God said to him,

God the Father: I am the God of Abraham, and the God of Isaac, and the God of Jacob.

Jesus: He is not God of the dead, but of the living; you are quite wrong.

* The First Commandment (Mk 12:28–34); PF3–129; F4–575

St. Mark: And one of the scribes came up and heard them disputing with one another, and seeing that he answered them well, asked him,

Scribe: Which commandment is the first of all?

St. Mark: Jesus answered,

Jesus: The first is, "Hear, O Israel: The Lord our God, the Lord is one; and you shall love the Lord your God with all your heart, and with all your soul, and with all your mind, and with all your strength." The second is this, "You shall love your neighbor as yourself." There is no other commandment greater than these.

St. Mark: And the scribe said to him,

Scribe: You are right, Teacher; you have truly said that he is one, and there is no other but he; and to love him with all the heart, and with all the understanding, and with all the strength, and to love one's neighbor as oneself, is much more than all whole burnt offerings and sacrifices.

St. Mark: And when Jesus saw that he answered wisely, he said to him,

Jesus: You are not far from the kingdom of God.

St. Mark: And after that no one dared to ask him any question.

A Question About the Christ (Mk 12:35–37); F1–202

St. Mark: And as Jesus taught in the temple, he said,

Jesus: How can the scribes say that the Christ is the son of David? David himself, inspired by the Holy Spirit, declared,

David: The Lord said to my Lord, Sit at my right hand, till I put your enemies under your feet.

Jesus: David himself calls him Lord; so how is he his son?

St. Mark: And the great throng heard him gladly.

Jesus Denounces the Hypocrisy of the Scribes (Mk 12:38–40); F7–678

St. Mark: And in his teaching he said,

Jesus: Beware of the scribes, who like to go about in long robes, and to have salutations in the marketplaces and the best seats in the synagogues and the places of honor at feasts, who devour widows' houses and for a pretense make long prayers. They will receive the greater condemnation.

The Widow's Offering (Mk 12:41–44); C7–2444

St. Mark: And he sat down opposite the treasury, and watched the multitude putting money into the treasury. Many rich people put in large sums. And a poor widow came, and put in two copper coins, which make a penny. And he called his disciples to him, and said to them,

Jesus: Truly, I say to you, this poor widow has put in more than all those who are contributing to the treasury. For they all contributed out of their abundance; but she out of her poverty has put in everything she had, her whole living.

Mark Chapter 13

The Destruction of the Temple Foretold (Mk 13:1–8); P–2612

St. Mark: And as he came out of the temple, one of his disciples said to him,

Disciples: Look, Teacher, what wonderful stones and what wonderful buildings!

St. Mark: And Jesus said to him,

Jesus: Do you see these great buildings? There will not be left here one stone upon another, that will not be thrown down.

St. Mark: And as he sat on the Mount of Olives opposite the temple, Peter and James and John and Andrew asked him privately,

Peter, James, John, and Andrew: Tell us, when will this be, and what will be the sign when these things are all to be accomplished?

St. Mark: And Jesus began to say to them,

Jesus: Take heed that no one leads you astray. Many will come in my name, saying,

Many: I am he!

Jesus: And they will lead many astray. And when you hear of wars and rumors of wars, do not be alarmed; this must take place, but the end is not yet. For nation will rise against nation, and kingdom against kingdom; there will be earthquakes in various places, there will be famines; this is but the beginning of the birth-pangs.

Persecutions Foretold (Mk 13:9–13); LP6–2849

Jesus 2: But take heed to yourselves; for they will deliver you up to councils; and you will be beaten in synagogues; and you will stand before governors and kings for my sake, to bear testimony before them. And the gospel must first be preached to all nations.

And when they bring you to trial and deliver you up, do not be anxious beforehand what you are to say; but say whatever is given you in that hour, for it is not you who speak, but the Holy Spirit.

And brother will deliver up brother to death, and the father his child, and children will rise against parents and have them put to death; and you will be hated by all for my name's sake. But he who endures to the end will be saved.

The Desolating Sacrilege (Mk 13:14–23); LP6–2849

Jesus 3: But when you see the desolating sacrilege set up where it ought not to be (let the reader understand), then let those who are in Judea flee to the mountains; let him who is on the housetop not go down, nor enter his house, to take anything away; and let him who is in the field not turn back to take his mantle.

And alas for those who are with child and for those who give suck in those days! Pray that it may not happen in winter.

For in those days there will be such tribulation as has not been from the beginning of the creation which God created until now, and never will be. And if the Lord had not shortened the days, no human being would be saved; but for the sake of the elect, whom he chose, he shortened the days.

Jesus 4: And then if any one says to you,

First false prophet: Look, here is the Christ!

Jesus 4: Or

Second false prophet: Look, there he is!

Jesus 4: Do not believe it. False Christs and false prophets will arise and show signs and wonders, to lead astray, if possible, the elect. But take heed; I have told you all things beforehand.

~ The Coming of the Son of Man (Mk 13:24–27)

Jesus 4: But in those days, after that tribulation, the sun will be darkened, and the moon will not give its light, and the stars will be falling from heaven, and the powers in the heavens will be shaken. And then they will see the Son of man coming in clouds with great power and glory. And then he will send out the angels, and gather his elect from the four winds, from the ends of the earth to the ends of heaven.

~ The Lesson of the Fig Tree (Mk 13:28–31)

Jesus 5: From the fig tree learn its lesson: as soon as its branch becomes tender and puts forth its leaves, you know that summer is near. So also, when you see these things taking place, you know that he is near, at the very gates.

Jesus 6: Truly, I say to you, this generation will not pass away before all these things take place. Heaven and earth will pass away, but my words will not pass away.

* The Necessity for Watchfulness (Mk 13:32–37); F7–672; LP6–2849

Jesus 6: But of that day or that hour no one knows, not even the angels in heaven, nor the Son, but only the Father. Take heed, watch and pray; for you do not know when the time will come.

It is like a man going on a journey, when he leaves home and puts his servants in charge, each with his work, and commands the doorkeeper to be on the watch. Watch therefore—for you do not know when the master of the house will come, in the evening, or at midnight, or at cockcrow, or in the morning—lest he come suddenly and find you asleep.

And what I say to you I say to all: Watch.

Mark Chapter 14

~ The Conspiracy to Kill Jesus (Mk 14:1–2)

St. Mark: It was now two days before the Passover and the feast of Unleavened Bread. And the chief priests and the scribes were seeking how to arrest him by stealth, and kill him; for they said,

Chief priests and scribes: Not during the feast, lest there be a tumult of the people.

The Anointing at Bethany (Mk 14:3–9)

St. Mark: And while he was at Bethany in the house of Simon the leper, as he sat at table, a woman came with an alabaster flask of ointment of pure nard, very costly, and she broke the flask and poured it over his head. But there were some who said to themselves indignantly,

Some disciples: Why was the ointment thus wasted? For this ointment might have been sold for more than three hundred denarii, and given to the poor.

St. Mark: And they reproached her. But Jesus said,

Jesus: Let her alone; why do you trouble her? She has done a beautiful thing to me. For you always have the poor with you, and whenever you will, you can do good to them; but you will not always have me. She has done what she could; she has anointed my body beforehand for burying. And truly, I say to you, wherever the gospel is preached in the whole world, what she has done will be told in memory of her.

~ Judas Agrees to Betray Jesus (Mk 14:10–11)

St. Mark: Then Judas Iscariot, who was one of the twelve, went to the chief priests in order to betray him to them. And when they heard it they were glad, and promised to give him money. And he sought an opportunity to betray him.

The Passover with the Disciples (Mk 14:12–21); S3–1339; F3–474

St. Mark: And on the first day of Unleavened Bread, when they sacrificed the Passover lamb, his disciples said to him,

Disciples: Where will you have us go and prepare for you to eat the Passover?

St. Mark: And he sent two of his disciples, and said to them,

Jesus: Go into the city, and a man carrying a jar of water will meet you; follow him, and wherever he enters, say to the householder, "The Teacher says, 'Where is my guest room, where I am to eat the Passover with my disciples?'" And he will show you a large upper room furnished and ready; there prepare for us.

St. Mark: And the disciples set out and went to the city, and found it as he had told them; and they prepared the Passover. And when it was evening he came with the twelve. And as they were at table eating, Jesus said,

Jesus: Truly, I say to you, one of you will betray me, one who is eating with me.

St. Mark: They began to be sorrowful, and to say to him one after another,

Disciples: Is it I?

St. Mark: He said to them,

Jesus: It is one of the twelve, one who is dipping bread into the dish with me. For the Son of man goes as it is written of him, but woe to that man by whom the Son of man is betrayed! It would have been better for that man if he had not been born.

* The Institution of the Last Supper (Mk 14:22–25); S3–1335; S3–1403

St. Mark: And as they were eating, he took bread, and blessed, and broke it, and gave it to them, and said,

Jesus: Take; this is my body.

St. Mark: And he took a chalice, and when he had given thanks he gave it to them, and they all drank of it. And he said to them,

Jesus: This is my blood of the covenant, which is poured out for many. Truly, I say to you, I shall not drink again of the fruit of the vine until that day when I drink it new in the kingdom of God.

Peter's Denial Foretold (Mk 14:26–31); F3–474

St. Mark: And when they had sung a hymn, they went out to the Mount of Olives. And Jesus said to them,

Jesus: You will all fall away; for it is written, "I will strike the shepherd, and the sheep will be scattered." But after I am raised up, I will go before you to Galilee.

St. Mark: Peter said to him,

Peter: Even though they all fall away, I will not.

St. Mark: And Jesus said to him,

Jesus: Truly, I say to you, this very night, before the cock crows twice, you will deny me three times.

St. Mark: But he said vehemently,

Peter: If I must die with you, I will not deny you.

St. Mark: And they all said the same.

* Jesus Prays in Gethsemane (Mk 14:32–42); F3–473; P–2701

St. Mark: And they went to a place which was called Gethsemane; and he said to his disciples,

Jesus: Sit here, while I pray.

St. Mark: And he took with him Peter and James and John, and began to be greatly distressed and troubled. And he said to them,

Jesus: My soul is very sorrowful, even to death; remain here, and watch.

St. Mark: And going a little farther, he fell on the ground and prayed that, if it were possible, the hour might pass from him. And he said,

Jesus: Abba, Father, all things are possible to you; remove this chalice from me; yet not what I will, but what you will.

St. Mark: And he came and found them sleeping, and he said to Peter,

Jesus: Simon, are you asleep? Could you not watch one hour? Watch and pray that you may not enter into temptation; the spirit indeed is willing, but the flesh is weak.

St. Mark: And again he went away and prayed, saying the same words. And again he came and found them sleeping, for their eyes were very heavy; and they did not know what to answer him. And he came the third time, and said to them,

Jesus: Are you still sleeping and taking your rest? It is enough; the hour has come; the Son of man is betrayed into the hands of sinners. Rise, let us be going; see, my betrayer is at hand.

~ The Betrayal and Arrest of Jesus (Mk 14:43–52)

St. Mark: And immediately, while he was still speaking, Judas came, one of the twelve, and with him a crowd with swords and clubs, from the chief priests and the scribes and the elders. Now the betrayer had given them a sign, saying,

Judas: The one I shall kiss is the man; seize him and lead him away under guard.

St. Mark: And when he came, he went up to him at once, and said,

Judas: Master!

St. Mark: And he kissed him. And they laid hands on him and seized him. But one of those who stood by drew his sword, and struck the slave of the high priest and cut off his ear. And Jesus said to them,

Jesus: Have you come out as against a robber, with swords and clubs to capture me? Day after day I was with you in the temple teaching, and you did not seize me. But let the Scriptures be fulfilled.

St. Mark: And they all deserted him, and fled. And a young man followed him, with nothing but a linen cloth about his body; and they seized him, but he left the linen cloth and ran away naked.

Jesus Before the Council (Mk 14:53–65); F4–585; F2–443

St. Mark: And they led Jesus to the high priest; and all the chief priests and the elders and the scribes were assembled.

And Peter had followed him at a distance, right into the courtyard of the high priest; and he was sitting with the guards, and warming himself at the fire.

Now the chief priests and the whole council sought testimony against Jesus to put him to death; but they found none. For many bore false witness against him, and their witness did not agree. And some stood up and bore false witness against him, saying,

False witnesses: We heard him say, "I will destroy this temple that is made with hands, and in three days I will build another, not made with hands."

St. Mark: Yet not even so did their testimony agree. And the high priest stood up in the midst, and asked Jesus,

High priest: Have you no answer to make? What is it that these men testify against you?

St. Mark: But he was silent and made no answer. Again the high priest asked him,

High priest: Are you the Christ, the Son of the Blessed?

St. Mark: And Jesus said,

Jesus: I am; and you will see the Son of man seated at the right hand of Power, and coming with the clouds of heaven.

St. Mark: And the high priest tore his garments, and said,

High priest: Why do we still need witnesses? You have heard his blasphemy. What is your decision?

St. Mark: And they all condemned him as deserving death. And some began to spit on him, and to cover his face, and to strike him, saying to him,

Chief priests, elders, and scribes: Prophesy!

St. Mark: And the guards received him with blows.

~ Peter Denies Jesus (Mk 14:66–72)

St. Mark: And as Peter was below in the courtyard, one of the maids of the high priest came; and seeing Peter warming himself, she looked at him, and said,

Maid: You also were with the Nazarene, Jesus.

St. Mark: But he denied it, saying,

Peter: I neither know nor understand what you mean.

St. Mark: And he went out into the gateway. And the maid saw him, and began again to say to the bystanders,

Maid: This man is one of them.

St. Mark: But again he denied it. And after a little while again the bystanders said to Peter,

Bystanders: Certainly you are one of them; for you are a Galilean.

St. Mark: But he began to invoke a curse on himself and to swear,

Peter: I do not know this man of whom you speak.

St. Mark: And immediately the cock crowed a second time. And Peter remembered how Jesus had said to him, "Before the cock crows twice, you will deny me three times." And he broke down and wept.

Mark Chapter 15

~ Jesus Before Pilate (Mk 15:1–5)

St. Mark: And as soon as it was morning the chief priests, with the elders and scribes, and the whole council held a consultation; and they bound Jesus and led him away and delivered him to Pilate. And Pilate asked him,

Pilate: Are you the King of the Jews?

St. Mark: And he answered him,

Jesus: You have said so.

St. Mark: And the chief priests accused him of many things. And Pilate again asked him,

Pilate: Have you no answer to make? See how many charges they bring against you.

St. Mark: But Jesus made no further answer, so that Pilate wondered.

Pilate Delivers Jesus to be Crucified (Mk 15:6–15); F4–597

St. Mark: Now at the feast he used to release for them one prisoner for whom they asked. And among the rebels in prison, who had committed murder in the insurrection, there was a man called Barabbas. And the crowd came up and began to ask Pilate to do as he was wont to do for them. And he answered them,

Pilate: Do you want me to release for you the King of the Jews?

St. Mark: For he perceived that it was out of envy that the chief priests had delivered him up. But the chief priests stirred up the crowd to have him release for them Barabbas instead. And Pilate again said to them,

Pilate: Then what shall I do with the man whom you call the King of the Jews?

St. Mark: And they cried out again,

Crowd: Crucify him.

St. Mark: And Pilate said to them,

Pilate: Why, what evil has he done?

St. Mark: But they shouted all the more,

Crowd: Crucify him.

St. Mark: So Pilate, wishing to satisfy the crowd, released for them Barabbas; and having scourged Jesus, he delivered him to be crucified.

~ The Soldiers Mock Jesus (Mk 15:16–20)

St. Mark: And the soldiers led him away inside the palace (that is, the praetorium); and they called together the whole battalion. And they clothed him in a purple cloak, and plaiting a crown of thorns they put it on him. And they began to salute him,

Soldiers: Hail, King of the Jews!

St. Mark: And they struck his head with a reed, and spat upon him, and they knelt down in homage to him. And when they had mocked him, they stripped him of the purple cloak, and put his own clothes on him. And they led him out to crucify him.

~ The Crucifixion of Jesus (Mk 15:21–32)

St. Mark: And they compelled a passer-by, Simon of Cyrene, who was coming in from the country, the father of Alexander and Rufus, to carry his cross.

And they brought him to the place called Golgotha (which means the place of a skull). And they offered him wine mingled with myrrh; but he did not take it. And they crucified him, and divided his garments among them, casting lots for them, to decide what each should take. And it was the third hour, when they crucified him. And the inscription of the charge against him read, "The King of the Jews." And with him they crucified two robbers, one on his right and one on his left. And those who passed by derided him, wagging their heads, and saying,

Passersby: Aha! You who would destroy the temple and build it in three days, save yourself, and come down from the cross!

St. Mark: So also the chief priests mocked him to one another with the scribes, saying,

Chief priests: He saved others; he cannot save himself. Let the Christ, the King of Israel, come down now from the cross, that we may see and believe.

St. Mark: Those who were crucified with him also reviled him.

* The Death of Jesus (Mk 15:33–41); F4–603; P–2605

St. Mark: And when the sixth hour had come, there was darkness over the whole land until the ninth hour. And at the ninth hour Jesus cried with a loud voice,

Jesus: Elo-i, Elo-i, lama sabach-thani?

St. Mark: Which means,

Jesus: My God, my God, why have you forsaken me?

St. Mark: And some of the bystanders hearing it said,

Bystanders: Behold, he is calling Elijah.

St. Mark: And one ran and, filling a sponge full of vinegar, put it on a reed and gave it to him to drink, saying,

One bystander: Wait, let us see whether Elijah will come to take him down.

St. Mark: And Jesus uttered a loud cry, and breathed his last. And the curtain of the temple was torn in two, from top to bottom. And when the centurion, who stood facing him, saw that he thus breathed his last, he said,

Centurion: Truly this man was the Son of God!

St. Mark: There were also women looking on from afar, among whom were Mary Magdalene, and Mary the mother of James the younger and of Joseph, and Salome, who, when he was in Galilee, followed him, and ministered to him; and also many other women who came up with him to Jerusalem.

~ The Burial of Jesus (Mk 15:42–47)

St. Mark: And when evening had come, since it was the day of Preparation, that is, the day before the sabbath, Joseph of Arimathea, a respected member of the council, who was also himself looking for the kingdom of God, took courage and went to Pilate, and asked for the body of Jesus. And Pilate wondered if he were already dead; and summoning the centurion, he asked him whether he was already dead. And when he learned from the centurion that he was dead, he granted the body to Joseph.

And he bought a linen shroud, and taking him down, wrapped him in the linen shroud, and laid him in a tomb which had been hewn out of the rock; and he rolled a stone against the door of the tomb. Mary Magdalene and Mary the mother of Joseph saw where he was laid.

Mark Chapter 16

* The Resurrection of Jesus (Mk 16:1–8); F5–641; C3–2174

St. Mark: And when the sabbath was past, Mary Magdalene, and Mary the mother of James, and Salome, bought spices, so that they might go and anoint him. And very early on the first day of the week they went to the tomb when the sun had risen. And they were saying to one another,

Mary Magdalene, Mary the mother of James, Salome: Who will roll away the stone for us from the door of the tomb?

St. Mark: And looking up, they saw that the stone was rolled back; —it was very large. And entering the tomb, they saw a young man sitting on the right side, dressed in a white robe; and they were amazed. And he said to them,

Angel: Do not be amazed; you seek Jesus of Nazareth, who was crucified. He has risen, he is not here; see the place where they laid him. But go, tell his disciples and Peter that he is going before you to Galilee; there you will see him, as he told you.

St. Mark: And they went out and fled from the tomb; for trembling and astonishment had come upon them; and they said nothing to any one, for they were afraid.

Jesus Appears to Mary Magdalene (Mk 16:9–11); F5–643

St. Mark: Now when he rose early on the first day of the week, he appeared first to Mary Magdalene, from whom he had cast out seven demons. She went and told those who had been with him, as they mourned and wept. But when they heard that he was alive and had been seen by her, they would not believe it.

* Jesus Appears to Two Disciples (Mk 16:12–13); F5–645; F6–659

St. Mark: After this he appeared in another form to two of them, as they were walking into the country. And they went back and told the rest, but they did not believe them.

* Jesus Commissions the Disciples (Mk 16:14–18); F10–977; S1–1223

St. Mark: Afterward he appeared to the eleven themselves as they sat at table; and he upbraided them for their unbelief and hardness of heart, because they had not believed those who saw him after he had risen. And he said to them,

Jesus: Go into all the world and preach the gospel to the whole creation. He who believes and is baptized will be saved; but he who does not believe will be condemned. And these signs will accompany those who believe: in my name they will cast out demons; they will speak in new tongues; they will pick up serpents, and if they drink any deadly thing, it will not hurt them; they will lay their hands on the sick, and they will recover.

* The Ascension of Jesus (Mk 16:19–20); PLG–2; F7–670

St. Mark: So then the Lord Jesus, after he had spoken to them, was taken up into heaven, and sat down at the right hand of God. And they went forth and preached everywhere, while the Lord worked with them and confirmed the message by the signs that attended it. Amen.

The Gospel of St. Luke

Luke Chapter 1

~ Dedication to Theophilus (Lk 1:1–4)

St. Luke: Inasmuch as many have undertaken to compile a narrative of the things which have been accomplished among us, just as they were delivered to us by those who from the beginning were eyewitnesses and ministers of the word, it seemed good to me also, having followed all things closely for some time past, to write an orderly account for you, most excellent Theophilus, that you may know the truth concerning the things of which you have been informed.

* The Birth of John the Baptist Foretold (Lk 1:5–25); F3–523; F8–696

St. Luke: In the days of Herod, king of Judea, there was a priest named Zechariah, of the division of Abijah; and he had a wife of the daughters of Aaron, and her name was Elizabeth. And they were both righteous before God, walking in all the commandments and ordinances of the Lord blameless. But they had no child, because Elizabeth was barren, and both were advanced in years.

Now while he was serving as priest before God when his division was on duty, according to the custom of the priesthood, it fell to him by lot to enter the temple of the Lord and burn incense. And the whole multitude of the people were praying outside at the hour of incense.

And there appeared to him an angel of the Lord standing on the right side of the altar of incense. And Zechariah was troubled when he saw him, and fear fell upon him. But the angel said to him,

Archangel Gabriel: Do not be afraid, Zechariah, for your prayer is heard, and your wife Elizabeth will bear you a son, and you shall call his name John. And you will have joy and gladness, and many will rejoice at his birth; for he will be great before the Lord, and he shall drink no wine nor strong drink, and he will be filled with the Holy Spirit, even from his mother's womb. And he will turn many of the sons of Israel to the Lord their God, and he will go before him in the spirit and power of Elijah, to turn the hearts of the fathers to the children, and the disobedient to the wisdom of the just, to make ready for the Lord a people prepared.

St. Luke: And Zechariah said to the angel,

Zechariah: How shall I know this? For I am an old man, and my wife is advanced in years.

St. Luke: And the angel answered him,

Archangel Gabriel: I am Gabriel, who stand in the presence of God; and I was sent to speak to you, and to bring you this good news. And behold, you will be silent and unable to speak until the day that these things come to pass, because you did not believe my words, which will be fulfilled in their time.

St. Luke: And the people were waiting for Zechariah, and they wondered at his delay in the temple. And when he came out, he could not speak to them, and they perceived that he had seen a vision in the temple; and he made signs to them and remained mute. And when his time of service was ended, he went to his home. After these days his wife Elizabeth conceived, and for five months she hid herself, saying,

Elizabeth: Thus the Lord has done to me in the days when he looked on me, to take away my reproach among men.

* The Birth of Jesus Foretold (Lk 1:26–38); PF3–64; DOX–2856

St. Luke: In the sixth month the angel Gabriel was sent from God to a city of Galilee named Nazareth, to a virgin betrothed to a man whose name was Joseph, of the house of David; and the virgin's name was Mary. And he came to her and said,

Archangel Gabriel: Hail, full of grace, the Lord is with you!

St. Luke: But she was greatly troubled at the saying, and considered in her mind what sort of greeting this might be. And the angel said to her,

Archangel Gabriel: Do not be afraid, Mary, for you have found favor with God. And behold, you will conceive in your womb and bear a son, and you shall call his name Jesus. He will be great, and will be called the Son of the Most High; and the Lord God will give to him the throne of his father David, and he will reign over the house of Jacob forever; and of his kingdom there will be no end.

St. Luke: And Mary said to the angel,

Blessed Virgin Mary: How shall this happen since I do not know man?*

St. Luke: And the angel said to her,

Archangel Gabriel: The Holy Spirit will come upon you, and the power of the Most High will overshadow you; therefore the child to be born will be called holy, the Son of God. And behold, your kinswoman Elizabeth in her old age has also conceived a son; and this is the sixth month with her who was called barren. For with God nothing will be impossible.

St. Luke: And Mary said,

Blessed Virgin Mary: Behold, I am the handmaid of the Lord; let it be to me according to your word.

St. Luke: And the angel departed from her.

* Mary Visits Elizabeth; and Mary's Song of Praise (Lk 1:39–56); F7–722; P–2619

St. Luke: In those days Mary arose and went with haste into the hill country, to a city of Judah, and she entered the house of Zechariah and greeted Elizabeth. And when Elizabeth heard the greeting of Mary, the babe leaped in her womb; and Elizabeth was filled with the Holy Spirit and she exclaimed with a loud cry,

Elizabeth: Blessed are you among women, and blessed is the fruit of your womb! And why is this granted me, that the mother of my Lord should come to me? For behold, when the voice of your greeting came to my ears, the babe in my womb leaped for joy. And blessed is she who believed that there would be a fulfilment of what was spoken to her from the Lord.

St. Luke: And Mary said,

Blessed Virgin Mary: My soul magnifies the Lord, and my spirit rejoices in God my Savior, for he has regarded the low estate of his handmaiden. For behold, henceforth all generations will call me blessed; for he who is mighty has done great things for me, and holy is his name. And his mercy is on those who fear him from generation to generation. He has shown strength with his arm, he has scattered the proud in the imagination of their hearts, he has put down the mighty from their thrones, and exalted those of low degree; he has filled the hungry with good things, and the rich he has sent empty away. He has helped his servant Israel, in remembrance of his mercy, as he spoke to our fathers, to Abraham and to his posterity forever.

St. Luke: And Mary remained with her about three months, and returned to her home.

~ The Birth of John the Baptist (Lk 1:57–66)

St. Luke: Now the time came for Elizabeth to be delivered, and she gave birth to a son. And her neighbors and kinsfolk heard that the Lord had shown great mercy to her, and they rejoiced with her. And on the eighth day they came to circumcise the child; and they would have named him Zechariah after his father, but his mother said,

Elizabeth: Not so; he shall be called John.

St. Luke: And they said to her,

Neighbors and Relatives: None of your kindred is called by this name.

St. Luke: And they kept inquiring by signs of his father what he would have him called. And he asked for a writing tablet, and wrote, "His name is John." And they all marveled. And immediately his mouth was opened and his tongue loosed, and he spoke, blessing God. And fear came on all their neighbors. And all these things were talked about through all the hill country of Judea; and all who heard them laid them up in their hearts, saying,

Neighbors and Relatives: What then will this child be?

St. Luke: For the hand of the Lord was with him.

* Zechariah's Prophecy (Lk 1:67–80); F2–422; F8–717

St. Luke: And his father Zechariah was filled with the Holy Spirit, and prophesied, saying,

Zechariah: Blessed be the Lord God of Israel, for he has visited and redeemed his people, and has raised up a horn of salvation for us in the house of his servant David, as he spoke by the mouth of his holy prophets from of old, that we should be saved from our enemies, and from the hand of all who hate us; to perform the mercy promised to our fathers, and to remember his holy covenant, the oath which he swore to our father Abraham, to grant us that we, being delivered from the hand of our enemies, might serve him without fear, in holiness and righteousness before him all the days of our life.

And you, child, will be called the prophet of the Most High; for you will go before the Lord to prepare his ways, to give knowledge of salvation to his people in the forgiveness of their sins, through the tender mercy of our God, when the day shall dawn upon us from on high to give light to those who sit in darkness and in the shadow of death, to guide our feet into the way of peace.

St. Luke: And the child grew and became strong in spirit, and he was in the wilderness till the day of his manifestation to Israel.

Luke Chapter 2

The Birth of Jesus (Lk 2:1–7); F3–525; F3–515

St. Luke: In those days a decree went out from Caesar Augustus that all the world should be enrolled. This was the first enrollment, when Quirinius was governor of Syria. And all went to be enrolled, each to his own city.

And Joseph also went up from Galilee, from the city of Nazareth, to Judea, to the city of David, which is called Bethlehem, because he was of the house and lineage of David, to be enrolled with Mary, his betrothed, who was with child.

And while they were there, the time came for her to be delivered. And she gave birth to her first-born son and wrapped him in swaddling cloths, and laid him in a manger, because there was no place for them in the inn.

* The Shepherds and the Angels (Lk 2:8–20); F3–486; F3–525

St. Luke: And in that region there were shepherds out in the field, keeping watch over their flock by night. And an angel of the Lord appeared to them, and the glory of the Lord shone around them, and they were filled with fear. And the angel said to them,

Angel: Be not afraid; for behold, I bring you good news of a great joy which will come to all the people; for to you is born this day in the city of David a Savior, who is Christ the Lord. And this will be a sign for you: you will find a babe wrapped in swaddling cloths and lying in a manger.

St. Luke: And suddenly there was with the angel a multitude of the heavenly host praising God and saying,

Multitude of Angels: Glory to God in the highest, and on earth peace among men with whom he is pleased!

St. Luke: When the angels went away from them into heaven, the shepherds said to one another,

Shepherds: Let us go over to Bethlehem and see this thing that has happened, which the Lord has made known to us.

St. Luke: And they went with haste, and found Mary and Joseph, and the babe lying in a manger. And when they saw it they made known the saying which had been told them concerning this child; and all who heard it wondered at what the shepherds told them. But Mary kept all these things, pondering them in her heart. And the shepherds returned, glorifying and praising God for all they had heard and seen, as it had been told them.

Jesus is Circumcised and Named (Lk 2:21); F3–527

St. Luke: And at the end of eight days, when he was circumcised, he was called Jesus, the name given by the angel before he was conceived in the womb.

* Jesus is Presented in the Temple (Lk 2:22–38); F3–529; F4–583

St. Luke: And when the time came for their purification according to the law of Moses, they brought him up to Jerusalem to present him to the Lord (as it is written in the law of the Lord, "Every male that opens the womb shall be called holy to the Lord") and to offer a sacrifice according to what is said in the law of the Lord, "a pair of turtledoves, or two young pigeons."

Now there was a man in Jerusalem, whose name was Simeon, and this man was righteous and devout, looking for the consolation of Israel, and the Holy Spirit was upon him. And it had been revealed to him by the Holy Spirit that he should not see death before he had seen the Lord's Christ.

And inspired by the Spirit he came into the temple; and when the parents brought in the child Jesus, to do for him according to the custom of the law, he took him up in his arms and blessed God and said,

Simeon: Lord, now let your servant depart in peace, according to your word; for mine eyes have seen your salvation which you have prepared in the presence of all peoples, a light for revelation to the Gentiles, and for glory to your people Israel.

St. Luke: And his father and his mother marveled at what was said about him; and Simeon blessed them and said to Mary his mother,

Simeon: Behold, this child is set for the fall and rising of many in Israel, and for a sign that is spoken against (and a sword will pierce through your own soul also), that thoughts out of many hearts may be revealed.

St. Luke: And there was a prophetess, Anna, the daughter of Phanuel, of the tribe of Asher; she was of a great age, having lived with her husband seven years from her virginity, and as a widow till she was eighty-four. She did not depart from the temple, worshiping with fasting and prayer night and day.

And coming up at that very hour she gave thanks to God, and spoke of him to all who were looking for the redemption of Jerusalem.

~ The Return to Nazareth (Lk 2:39–40)

St. Luke: And when they had performed everything according to the law of the Lord, they returned into Galilee, to their own city, Nazareth. And the child grew and became strong, filled with wisdom; and the favor of God was upon him.

* The Boy Jesus in the Temple (Lk 2:41–52); F3–534; F4–583

St. Luke: Now his parents went to Jerusalem every year at the feast of the Passover. And when he was twelve years old, they went up according to custom; and when the feast was ended, as they were returning, the boy Jesus stayed behind in Jerusalem. His parents did not know it, but supposing him to be in the company they went a day's journey, and they sought him among their kinsfolk and acquaintances; and when they did not find him, they returned to Jerusalem, seeking him.

After three days they found him in the temple, sitting among the teachers, listening to them and asking them questions; and all who heard him were amazed at his understanding and his answers. And when they saw him they were astonished; and his mother said to him,

Mary: Son, why have you treated us so? Behold, your father and I have been looking for you anxiously.

St. Luke: And he said to them,

Jesus: How is it that you sought me? Did you not know that I must be in my Father's house?

St. Luke: And they did not understand the saying which he spoke to them. And he went down with them and came to Nazareth, and was obedient to them; and his mother kept all these things in her heart. And Jesus increased in wisdom and in stature, and in favor with God and man.

Luke Chapter 3

* The Preaching of John the Baptist (Lk 3:1–20); S4–1460; C7–2447

St. Luke: In the fifteenth year of the reign of Tiberius Caesar, Pontius Pilate being governor of Judea, and Herod being tetrarch of Galilee, and his brother Philip tetrarch of the region of Ituraea and Trachonitis, and Lysanias tetrarch of Abilene, in the high priesthood of Annas and Caiaphas, the word of God came to John the son of Zechariah in the wilderness; and he went into all the region about the Jordan, preaching a baptism of repentance for the forgiveness of sins. As it is written in the book of the words of Isaiah the prophet,

Isaiah: The voice of one crying in the wilderness: Prepare the way of the Lord, make his paths straight. Every valley shall be filled, and every mountain and hill shall be brought low, and the crooked shall be made straight, and the rough ways shall be made smooth; and all flesh shall see the salvation of God.

St. Luke: He said therefore to the multitudes that came out to be baptized by him,

John the Baptist: You brood of vipers! Who warned you to flee from the wrath to come? Bear fruits that befit repentance, and do not begin to say to yourselves, "We have Abraham as our father"; for I tell you, God is able from these stones to raise up children to Abraham. Even now the axe is laid to the root of the trees; every tree therefore that does not bear good fruit is cut down and thrown into the fire.

St. Luke: And the multitudes asked him,

Multitudes: What then shall we do?

St. Luke: And he answered them,

John the Baptist: He who has two coats, let him share with him who has none; and he who has food, let him do likewise.

St. Luke: Tax collectors also came to be baptized, and said to him,

Tax collectors: Teacher, what shall we do?

St. Luke: And he said to them,

John the Baptist: Collect no more than is appointed you.

St. Luke: Soldiers also asked him,

Soldiers: And we, what shall we do?

St. Luke: And he said to them,

John the Baptist: Rob no one by violence or by false accusation, and be content with your wages.

St. Luke: As the people were in expectation, and all men questioned in their hearts concerning John, whether perhaps he were the Christ, John answered them all,

John the Baptist: I baptize you with water; but he who is mightier than I is coming, the thong of whose sandals I am not worthy to untie; he will baptize you with the Holy Spirit and with fire. His winnowing fork is in his hand, to clear his threshing floor, and to gather the wheat into his granary, but the chaff he will burn with unquenchable fire.

St. Luke: So, with many other exhortations, he preached good news to the people. But Herod the tetrarch, who had been reproved by him for Herodias, his brother's wife, and for all the evil things that Herod had done, added this to them all, that he shut up John in prison.

* The Baptism of Jesus (Lk 3:21–22); F4–608; P–2600

St. Luke: Now when all the people were baptized, and when Jesus also had been baptized and was praying, the heaven was opened, and the Holy Spirit descended upon him in bodily form, as a dove, and a voice came from heaven,

God the Father: You are my beloved Son; with you I am well pleased.

The Ancestry of Jesus (Lk 3:23–38); F3–535

St. Luke: Jesus, when he began his ministry, was about thirty years of age, being the son (as was supposed) of Joseph, the son of Heli, the son of Matthat, the son of Levi, the son of Melchi, the son of Janna-i, the son of Joseph, the son of Mattathias, the son of Amos, the son of Nahum, the son of Esli, the son of Naggai, the son of Maath, the son of Mattathias, the son of Seme-in, the son of Josech, the son of Joda, the son of Joanan, the son of Rhesa, the son of Zerubbabel, the son of Shealti-el, the son of Neri, the son of Melchi, the son of Addi, the son of Cosam, the son of Elmadam, the son of Er, the son of Joshua, the son of Eliezer, the son of Jorim, the son of Matthat, the son of Levi, the son of Simeon, the son of Judah, the son of Joseph, the son of Jonam, the son of Eliakim, the son of Mele-a, the son of Menna, the son of Mattatha, the son of Nathan, the son of David, the son of Jesse, the son of Obed, the son of Boaz, the son of Sala, the son of Nahshon, the son of Amminadab, the son of Admin, the son of Arni, the son of Hezron, the son of Perez, the son of Judah, the son of Jacob, the son of Isaac, the son of Abraham, the son of Terah, the son of Nahor, the son of Serug, the son of Reu, the son of Peleg, the son of Eber, the son of Shelah, the son of Ca-inan, the son of Arphaxad, the son of Shem, the son of Noah, the son of Lamech, the son of Methuselah, the son of Enoch, the son of Jared, the son of Mahalale-el, the son of Ca-inan, the son of Enos, the son of Seth, the son of Adam, the son of God.

Luke Chapter 4

* The Temptation of Jesus (Lk 4:1–13); DOX–2855

St. Luke: And Jesus, full of the Holy Spirit, returned from the Jordan, and was led by the Spirit for forty days in the wilderness, tempted by the devil. And he ate nothing in those days; and when they were ended, he was hungry. The devil said to him,

Devil: If you are the Son of God, command this stone to become bread.

St. Luke: And Jesus answered him,

Jesus: It is written, "Man shall not live by bread alone."

St. Luke: And the devil took him up, and showed him all the kingdoms of the world in a moment of time, and said to him,

Devil: To you I will give all this authority and their glory; for it has been delivered to me, and I give it to whom I will. If you, then, will worship me, it shall all be yours.

St. Luke: And Jesus answered him,

Jesus: It is written, "You shall worship the Lord your God, and him only shall you serve."

St. Luke: And he took him to Jerusalem, and set him on the pinnacle of the temple, and said to him,

Devil: If you are the Son of God, throw yourself down from here; for it is written, "He will give his angels charge of you, to guard you," and "On their hands they will bear you up, lest you strike your foot against a stone."

St. Luke: And Jesus answered him,

Jesus: It is said, "You shall not tempt the Lord your God."

St. Luke: And when the devil had ended every temptation, he departed from him until an opportune time.

~ Jesus Begins Preaching and Teaching in Galilee (Lk 4:14–15)

St. Luke: And Jesus returned in the power of the Spirit into Galilee, and a report concerning him went out through all the surrounding country. And he taught in their synagogues, being glorified by all.

* The Rejection of Jesus at Nazareth (Lk 4:16–30); S2–1286; F2–436

St. Luke: And he came to Nazareth, where he had been brought up; and he went to the synagogue, as his custom was, on the sabbath day. And he stood up to read; and there was given to him the book of the prophet Isaiah. He opened the book and found the place where it was written,

Jesus: The Spirit of the Lord is upon me, because he has anointed me to preach good news to the poor. He has sent me to proclaim release to the captives and recovering of sight to the blind, to set at liberty those who are oppressed, to proclaim the acceptable year of the Lord.

St. Luke: And he closed the book, and gave it back to the attendant, and sat down; and the eyes of all in the synagogue were fixed on him. And he began to say to them,

Jesus: Today this Scripture has been fulfilled in your hearing.

St. Luke: And all spoke well of him, and wondered at the gracious words which proceeded out of his mouth; and they said,

All: Is not this Joseph's son?

St. Luke: And he said to them,

Jesus: Doubtless you will quote to me this proverb, "Physician, heal yourself"; what we have heard you did at Capernaum, do here also in your own country.

St. Luke: And he said,

Jesus: Truly, I say to you, no prophet is acceptable in his own country. But in truth, I tell you, there were many widows in Israel in the days of Elijah, when the heaven was shut up three years and six months, when there came a great famine over all the land; and Elijah was sent to none of them but only to Zarephath, in the land of Sidon, to a woman who was a widow. And there were many lepers in Israel in the time of the prophet Elisha; and none of them was cleansed, but only Naaman the Syrian.

St. Luke: When they heard this, all in the synagogue were filled with wrath. And they rose up and put him out of the city, and led him to the brow of the hill on which their city was built, that they might throw him down headlong. But passing through the midst of them he went away.

~ The Man with an Unclean Spirit (Lk 4:31–37)

St. Luke: And he went down to Capernaum, a city of Galilee. And he was teaching them on the sabbath; and they were astonished at his teaching, for his word was with authority. And in the synagogue there was a man who had the spirit of an unclean demon; and he cried out with a loud voice,

Demon: Ah! What have you to do with us, Jesus of Nazareth? Have you come to destroy us? I know who you are, the Holy One of God.

St. Luke: But Jesus rebuked him, saying,

Jesus: Be silent, and come out of him!

St. Luke: And when the demon had thrown him down in the midst, he came out of him, having done him no harm. And they were all amazed and said to one another,

All: What is this word? For with authority and power he commands the unclean spirits, and they come out.

St. Luke: And reports of him went out into every place in the surrounding region.

~ Healings at Simon's House (Lk 4:38–41)

St. Luke: And he arose and left the synagogue, and entered Simon's house. Now Simon's mother-in-law was ill with a high fever, and they besought him for her. And he stood over her and rebuked the fever, and it left her; and immediately she rose and served them. Now when the sun was setting, all those who had any that were sick with various diseases brought them to him; and he laid his hands on every one of them and healed them. And demons also came out of many, crying,

Demons: You are the Son of God!

St. Luke: But he rebuked them, and would not allow them to speak, because they knew that he was the Christ.

~ Jesus Preaches in the Synagogues of Judea (Lk 4:42–44)

St. Luke: And when it was day he departed and went into a lonely place. And the people sought him and came to him, and would have kept him from leaving them; but he said to them,

Jesus: I must preach the good news of the kingdom of God to the other cities also; for I was sent for this purpose.

St. Luke: And he was preaching in the synagogues of Judea.

Luke Chapter 5

Jesus Calls the First Disciples (Lk 5:1–11); F1–208

St. Luke: While the people pressed upon him to hear the word of God, he was standing by the lake of Gennesaret. And he saw two boats by the lake; but the fishermen had gone out of them and were washing their nets. Getting into one of the boats, which was Simon's, he asked him to put out a little from the land. And he sat down and taught the people from the boat. And when he had ceased speaking, he said to Simon,

Jesus: Put out into the deep and let down your nets for a catch.

St. Luke: And Simon answered,

Simon Peter: Master, we toiled all night and took nothing! But at your word I will let down the nets.

St. Luke: And when they had done this, they enclosed a great shoal of fish; and as their nets were breaking, they beckoned to their partners in the other boat to come and help them. And they came and filled both the boats, so that they began to sink. But when Simon Peter saw it, he fell down at Jesus' knees, saying,

Simon Peter: Depart from me, for I am a sinful man, O Lord.

St. Luke: For he was astonished, and all that were with him, at the catch of fish which they had taken; and so also were James and John, sons of Zebedee, who were partners with Simon. And Jesus said to Simon,

Jesus: Do not be afraid; henceforth you will be catching men.

St. Luke: And when they had brought their boats to land, they left everything and followed him.

* Jesus Cleanses a Leper (Lk 5:12–16); P–2602

St. Luke: While he was in one of the cities, there came a man full of leprosy; and when he saw Jesus, he fell on his face and besought him,

Leper: Lord, if you will, you can make me clean.

St. Luke: And he stretched out his hand, and touched him, saying,

Jesus: I will; be clean.

St. Luke: And immediately the leprosy left him. And he charged him to

Jesus: Tell no one; but go and show yourself to the priest, and make an offering for your cleansing, as Moses commanded, for a proof to the people.

St. Luke: But so much the more the report went abroad concerning him; and great multitudes gathered to hear and to be healed of their infirmities. But he withdrew to the wilderness and prayed.

Jesus Heals a Paralytic (Lk 5:17–26); LT–1116

St. Luke: On one of those days, as he was teaching, there were Pharisees and teachers of the law sitting by, who had come from every village of Galilee and Judea and from Jerusalem; and the power of the Lord was with him to heal. And behold, men were bringing on a bed a man who was paralyzed, and they sought to bring him in and lay him before Jesus; but finding no way to bring him in, because of the crowd, they went up on the roof and let him down with his bed through the tiles into the midst before Jesus. And when he saw their faith he said,

Jesus: Man, your sins are forgiven you.

St. Luke: And the scribes and the Pharisees began to question, saying,

Scribes and Pharisees: Who is this that speaks blasphemies? Who can forgive sins but God only?

St. Luke: When Jesus perceived their questionings, he answered them,

Jesus: Why do you question in your hearts? Which is easier, to say, "Your sins are forgiven you," or to say, "Rise and walk?" But that you may know that the Son of man has authority on earth to forgive sins—

St. Luke: He said to the man who was paralyzed—

Jesus: I say to you, rise, take up your bed and go home.

St. Luke: And immediately he rose before them, and took up that on which he lay, and went home, glorifying God. And amazement seized them all, and they glorified God and were filled with awe, saying,

All: We have seen strange things today.

Jesus Calls Levi (Lk 5:27–32); F4–588

St. Luke: After this he went out, and saw a tax collector, named Levi, sitting at the tax office; and he said to him,

Jesus: Follow me.

St. Luke: And he left everything, and rose and followed him. And Levi made him a great feast in his house; and there was a large company of tax collectors and others sitting at table with them. And the Pharisees and their scribes murmured against his disciples, saying,

Scribes and Pharisees: Why do you eat and drink with tax collectors and sinners?

St. Luke: And Jesus answered them,

Jesus: Those who are well have no need of a physician, but those who are sick; I have not come to call the righteous, but sinners to repentance.

~ The Question About Fasting (Lk 5:33–39)

St. Luke: And they said to him,

Scribes and Pharisees: The disciples of John fast often and offer prayers, and so do the disciples of the Pharisees, but yours eat and drink.

St. Luke: And Jesus said to them,

Jesus: Can you make wedding guests fast while the bridegroom is with them? The days will come, when the bridegroom is taken away from them, and then they will fast in those days.

St. Luke: He told them a parable also:

Jesus: No one tears a piece from a new garment and puts it upon an old garment; if he does, he will tear the new, and the piece from the new will not match the old. And no one puts new wine into old wineskins; if he does, the new wine will burst the skins and it will be spilled, and the skins will be destroyed. But new wine must be put into fresh wineskins. And no one after drinking old wine desires new; for he says, "The old is good."

Luke Chapter 6

~ A Teaching About the Sabbath (Lk 6:1–5)

St. Luke: On a sabbath, while he was going through the grainfields, his disciples plucked and ate some heads of grain, rubbing them in their hands. But some of the Pharisees said,

Pharisees: Why are you doing what is not lawful to do on the sabbath?

St. Luke: And Jesus answered,

Jesus: Have you not read what David did when he was hungry, he and those who were with him: how he entered the house of God, and took and ate the showbread, which it is not lawful for any but the priests to eat, and also gave it to those with him?

St. Luke: And he said to them,

Jesus: The Son of man is Lord of the sabbath.

The Man with a Withered Hand (Lk 6:6–11); F4–581

St. Luke: On another sabbath, when he entered the synagogue and taught, a man was there whose right hand was withered. And the scribes and the Pharisees watched him, to see whether he would heal on the sabbath, so that they might find an accusation against him. But he knew their thoughts, and he said to the man who had the withered hand,

Jesus: Come and stand here.

St. Luke: And he rose and stood there. And Jesus said to them,

Jesus: I ask you, is it lawful on the sabbath to do good or to do harm, to save life or to destroy it?

St. Luke: And he looked around on them all, and said to him,

Jesus: Stretch out your hand.

St. Luke: And he did so, and his hand was restored. But they were filled with fury and discussed with one another what they might do to Jesus.

Jesus Chooses the Twelve Disciples (Lk 6:12–16); S6–1577; P–2600

St. Luke: In these days he went out to the mountain to pray; and all night he continued in prayer to God. And when it was day, he called his disciples, and chose from them twelve, whom he named apostles: Simon, whom he named Peter, and Andrew his brother, and James and John, and Philip, and Bartholomew, and Matthew, and Thomas, and James the son of Alphaeus, and Simon who was called the Zealot, and Judas the son of James, and Judas Iscariot, who became a traitor.

* Jesus Teaches and Heals (Lk 6:17–19); LT–1116; S5–1514

St. Luke: And he came down with them and stood on a level place, with a great crowd of his disciples and a great multitude of people from all Judea and Jerusalem and the seacoast of Tyre and Sidon, who came to hear him and to be healed of their diseases; and those who were troubled with unclean spirits were cured. And all the crowd sought to touch him, for power came forth from him and healed them all.

* Blessings and Woes (Lk 6:20–26); C7–2444; C10–2546

St. Luke: And he lifted up his eyes on his disciples, and said:

Jesus: Blessed are you poor, for yours is the kingdom of God. Blessed are you that hunger now, for you shall be satisfied. Blessed are you that weep now, for you shall laugh. Blessed are you when men hate you, and when they exclude you and revile you, and cast out your name as evil, on account of the Son of man!

Rejoice in that day, and leap for joy, for behold, your reward is great in heaven; for so their fathers did to the prophets. But woe to you that are rich, for you have received your consolation. Woe to you that are full now, for you shall hunger. Woe to you that laugh now, for you shall mourn and weep. Woe to you, when all men speak well of you, for so their fathers did to the false prophets.

* Love for Enemies (Lk 6:27–36); STL–1669; LP5–2842

Jesus 2: But I say to you that hear, Love your enemies, do good to those who hate you, bless those who curse you, pray for those who abuse you. To him who strikes you on the cheek, offer the other also; and from him who takes away your coat do not withhold even your shirt. Give to everyone who begs from you; and of him who takes away your goods do not ask them again. And as you wish that men would do to you, do so to them.

If you love those who love you, what credit is that to you? For even sinners love those who love them. And if you do good to those who do good to you, what credit is that to you? For even sinners do the same. And if you lend to those from whom you hope to receive, what credit is that to you? Even sinners lend to sinners, to receive as much again.

But love your enemies, and do good, and lend, expecting nothing in return; and your reward will be great, and you will be sons of the Most High; for he is kind to the ungrateful and the selfish. Be merciful, even as your Father is merciful.

~ Judging Others (Lk 6:37–42)

Jesus 3: Judge not, and you will not be judged; condemn not, and you will not be condemned; forgive, and you will be forgiven; give, and it will be given to you; good measure, pressed down, shaken together, running over, will be put into your lap. For the measure you give will be the measure you get back.

St. Luke: He also told them a parable:

Jesus: Can a blind man lead a blind man? Will they not both fall into a pit? A disciple is not above his teacher, but everyone when he is fully taught will be like his teacher.

Why do you see the speck that is in your brother's eye, but do not notice the log that is in your own eye? Or how can you say to your brother, "Brother, let me take out the speck that is in your eye," when you yourself do not see the log that is in your own eye? You hypocrite, first take the log out of your own eye, and then you will see clearly to take out the speck that is in your brother's eye.

~ A Tree and Its Fruit (Lk 6:43–45)

Jesus 2: For no good tree bears bad fruit, nor again does a bad tree bear good fruit; for each tree is known by its own fruit. For figs are not gathered from thorns, nor are grapes picked from a bramble bush.

The good man out of the good treasure of his heart produces good, and the evil man out of his evil treasure produces evil; for out of the abundance of the heart his mouth speaks.

~ Hearers and Doers (Lk 6:46–49)

Jesus 3: Why do you call me "Lord, Lord," and not do what I tell you? Everyone who comes to me and hears my words and does them, I will show you what he is like: he is like a man building a house, who dug deep, and laid the foundation upon rock; and when a flood arose, the stream broke against that house, and could not shake it, because it had been well built.

But he who hears and does not do them is like a man who built a house on the ground without a foundation; against which the stream broke, and immediately it fell, and the ruin of that house was great.

Luke Chapter 7

~ Jesus Heals a Centurion's Slave (Lk 7:1–10)

St. Luke: After he had ended all his sayings in the hearing of the people he entered Capernaum. Now a centurion had a slave who was dear to him, who was sick and at the point of death. When he heard of Jesus, he sent to him elders of the Jews, asking him to come and heal his slave. And when they came to Jesus, they besought him earnestly, saying,

Elders of the Jews: He is worthy to have you do this for him, for he loves our nation, and he built us our synagogue.

St. Luke: And Jesus went with them. When he was not far from the house, the centurion sent friends to him, saying to him,

Centurion: Lord, do not trouble yourself, for I am not worthy to have you come under my roof; therefore I did not presume to come to you. But say the word, and let my servant be healed. For I am a man set under authority, with soldiers under me: and I say to one, "Go," and he goes; and to another, "Come," and he comes; and to my slave, "Do this," and he does it.

St. Luke: When Jesus heard this he marveled at him, and turned and said to the multitude that followed him,

Jesus: I tell you, not even in Israel have I found such faith.

St. Luke: And when those who had been sent returned to the house, they found the slave well.

Jesus Raises a Widow's Son at Nain (Lk 7:11–17); F11–994; S5–1503

St. Luke: Soon afterward he went to a city called Nain, and his disciples and a great crowd went with him. As he drew near to the gate of the city, behold, a man who had died was being carried out, the only son of his mother, and she was a widow; and a large crowd from the city was with her. And when the Lord saw her, he had compassion on her and said to her,

Jesus: Do not weep.

St. Luke: And he came and touched the bier, and the bearers stood still. And he said,

Jesus: Young man, I say to you, arise.

St. Luke: And the dead man sat up, and began to speak. And he gave him to his mother. Fear seized them all; and they glorified God, saying,

All: A great prophet has arisen among us!

St. Luke: And

All: God has visited his people!

St. Luke: And this report concerning him spread through the whole of Judea and all the surrounding country.

* Messengers From John the Baptist (Lk 7:18–35); F3–547; F2–453

St. Luke: The disciples of John told him of all these things. And John, calling to him two of his disciples, sent them to the Lord, saying,

John the Baptist: Are you he who is to come, or shall we look for another?

St. Luke: And when the men had come to him, they said,

Disciples of John: John the Baptist has sent us to you, saying, "Are you he who is to come, or shall we look for another?"

St. Luke: In that hour he cured many of diseases and plagues and evil spirits, and on many that were blind he bestowed sight. And he answered them,

Jesus: Go and tell John what you have seen and heard: the blind receive their sight, the lame walk, lepers are cleansed, and the deaf hear, the dead are raised up, the poor have good news preached to them. And blessed is he who takes no offense at me.

St. Luke: When the messengers of John had gone, he began to speak to the crowds concerning John:

Jesus: What did you go out into the wilderness to behold? A reed shaken by the wind? What then did you go out to see? A man clothed in soft clothing? Behold, those who are gorgeously appareled and live in luxury are in kings' courts. What then did you go out to see? A prophet? Yes, I tell you, and more than a prophet.

This is he of whom it is written,

Malachi: Behold, I send my messenger before your face, who shall prepare your way before you.

Jesus: I tell you, among those born of women none is greater than John; yet he who is least in the kingdom of God is greater than he.

St. Luke: When they heard this all the people and the tax collectors justified God, having been baptized with the baptism of John; but the Pharisees and the lawyers rejected the purpose of God for themselves, not having been baptized by him.

Jesus: To what then shall I compare the men of this generation, and what are they like? They are like children sitting in the marketplace and calling to one another, "We piped to you, and you did not dance; we wailed, and you did not weep." For John the Baptist has come eating no bread and drinking no wine; and you say, "He has a demon." The Son of man has come eating and drinking; and you say, "Behold, a glutton and a drunkard, a friend of tax collectors and sinners!" Yet wisdom is justified by all her children.

* A Sinful Woman is Forgiven (Lk 7:36–50); P–2712; F4–588

St. Luke: One of the Pharisees asked him to eat with him, and he went into the Pharisee's house, and took his place at table.

And behold, a woman of the city, who was a sinner, when she learned that he was at table in the Pharisee's house, brought an alabaster flask of ointment, and standing behind him at his feet, weeping, she began to wet his feet with her tears, and wiped them with the hair of her head, and kissed his feet, and anointed them with the ointment. Now when the Pharisee who had invited him saw it, he said to himself,

Simon: If this man were a prophet, he would have known who and what sort of woman this is who is touching him, for she is a sinner.

St. Luke: And Jesus answering said to him,

Jesus: Simon, I have something to say to you.

St. Luke: And he answered,

Simon: What is it, Teacher?

Jesus: A certain creditor had two debtors; one owed five hundred denarii, and the other fifty. When they could not pay, he forgave them both. Now which of them will love him more?

St. Luke: Simon answered,

Simon: The one, I suppose, to whom he forgave more.

St. Luke: And he said to him,

Jesus: You have judged rightly.

St. Luke: Then turning toward the woman he said to Simon,

Jesus: Do you see this woman? I entered your house, you gave me no water for my feet, but she has wet my feet with her tears and wiped them with her hair. You gave me no kiss, but from the time I came in she has not ceased to kiss my feet. You did not anoint my head with oil, but she has anointed my feet with ointment. Therefore I tell you, her sins, which are many, are forgiven, for she loved much; but he who is forgiven little, loves little.

St. Luke: And he said to her,

Jesus: Your sins are forgiven.

St. Luke: Then those who were at table with him began to say among themselves,

Pharisees: Who is this, who even forgives sins?

St. Luke: And he said to the woman,

Jesus: Your faith has saved you; go in peace.

Luke Chapter 8

~ Some Women Accompany Jesus (Lk 8:1–3)

St. Luke: Soon afterward he went on through cities and villages, preaching and bringing the good news of the kingdom of God. And the twelve were with him, and also some women who had been healed of evil spirits and infirmities: Mary, called Magdalene, from whom seven demons had gone out, and Joanna, the wife of Chuza, Herod's steward, and Susanna, and many others, who provided for them out of their means.

The Parable of the Sower (Lk 8:4–8); P–2731

St. Luke: And when a great crowd came together and people from town after town came to him, he said in a parable:

Jesus: A sower went out to sow his seed; and as he sowed, some fell along the path, and was trodden under foot, and the birds of the air devoured it. And some fell on the rock; and as it grew up, it withered away, because it had no moisture. And some fell among thorns; and the thorns grew with it and choked it. And some fell into good soil and grew, and yielded a hundredfold.

St. Luke: As he said this, he called out,

Jesus: He who has ears to hear, let him hear.

* The Explanation of the Parable (Lk 8:9–15); LP6–2847; F1–368

St. Luke: And when his disciples asked him what this parable meant, he said,

Jesus: To you it has been given to know the secrets of the kingdom of God; but for others they are in parables, so that seeing they may not see, and hearing they may not understand.

Jesus 2: Now the parable is this: The seed is the word of God. The ones along the path are those who have heard; then the devil comes and takes away the word from their hearts, that they may not believe and be saved.

And the ones on the rock are those who, when they hear the word, receive it with joy; but these have no root, they believe for a while and in time of temptation fall away.

And as for what fell among the thorns, they are those who hear, but as they go on their way they are choked by the cares and riches and pleasures of life, and their fruit does not mature.

And as for that in the good soil, they are those who, hearing the word, hold it fast in an honest and good heart, and bring forth fruit with patience.

~ A Lamp Is Not Hidden (Lk 8:16–18)

Jesus 3: No one after lighting a lamp covers it with a vessel, or puts it under a bed, but puts it on a stand, that those who enter may see the light. For nothing is hid that shall not be made manifest, nor anything secret that shall not be known and come to light.

Take heed then how you hear; for to him who has will more be given, and from him who has not, even what he thinks that he has will be taken away.

~ The True Kindred of Jesus (Lk 8:19–21)

St. Luke: Then his mother and his brethren came to him, but they could not reach him for the crowd. And he was told,

One of the crowd: Your mother and your brethren are standing outside, desiring to see you.

St. Luke: But he said to them,

Jesus: My mother and my brethren are those who hear the word of God and do it.

Jesus Calms a Storm on the Sea (Lk 8:22–25); P–2743

St. Luke: One day he got into a boat with his disciples, and he said to them,

Jesus: Let us go across to the other side of the lake.

St. Luke: So they set out, and as they sailed he fell asleep. And a storm of wind came down on the lake, and they were filling with water, and were in danger. And they went and woke him, saying,

Disciples: Master, Master, we are perishing!

St. Luke: And he awoke and rebuked the wind and the raging waves; and they ceased, and there was a calm. He said to them,

Jesus: Where is your faith?

St. Luke: And they were afraid, and they marveled, saying to one another,

Disciples: Who then is this, that he commands even wind and water, and they obey him?

Jesus Heals the Gerasene Demoniac (Lk 8:26–39); F3–550

St. Luke: Then they arrived at the country of the Gerasenes, which is opposite Galilee. And as he stepped out on land, there met him a man from the city who had demons; for a long time he had worn no clothes, and he lived not in a house but among the tombs. When he saw Jesus, he cried out and fell down before him, and said with a loud voice,

Possessed man: What have you to do with me, Jesus, Son of the Most High God? I beseech you, do not torment me.

St. Luke: For he had commanded the unclean spirit to come out of the man. (For many a time it had seized him; he was kept under guard, and bound with chains and fetters, but he broke the bonds and was driven by the demon into the desert.) Jesus then asked him,

Jesus: What is your name?

St. Luke: And he said,

Possessed man: Legion;

St. Luke: For many demons had entered him. And they begged him not to command them to depart into the abyss.

Now a large herd of swine was feeding there on the hillside; and they begged him to let them enter these. So he gave them leave.

Then the demons came out of the man and entered the swine, and the herd rushed down the steep bank into the lake and were drowned.

When the herdsmen saw what had happened, they fled, and told it in the city and in the country.

Then people went out to see what had happened, and they came to Jesus, and found the man from whom the demons had gone, sitting at the feet of Jesus, clothed and in his right mind; and they were afraid.

And those who had seen it told them how he who had been possessed with demons was healed.

Then all the people of the surrounding country of the Gerasenes asked him to depart from them; for they were seized with great fear; so he got into the boat and returned. The man from whom the demons had gone begged that he might be with him; but he sent him away, saying,

Jesus: Return to your home, and declare how much God has done for you.

St. Luke: And he went away, proclaiming throughout the whole city how much Jesus had done for him.

A Girl Restored to Life and a Woman Healed (Lk 8:40–56); F8–695; LT–1116

St. Luke: Now when Jesus returned, the crowd welcomed him, for they were all waiting for him. And there came a man named Jairus, who was a ruler of the synagogue; and falling at Jesus' feet he besought him to come to his house, for he had an only daughter, about twelve years of age, and she was dying.

As he went, the people pressed round him. And a woman who had had a flow of blood for twelve years and had spent all her living upon physicians, and could not be healed by any one came up behind him, and touched the fringe of his garment; and immediately her flow of blood ceased. And Jesus said,

Jesus: Who was it that touched me?

St. Luke: When all denied it, Peter said,

Peter: Master, the multitudes surround you and press upon you!

St. Luke: But Jesus said,

Jesus: Someone touched me; for I perceive that power has gone forth from me.

St. Luke: And when the woman saw that she was not hidden, she came trembling, and falling down before him declared in the presence of all the people why she had touched him, and how she had been immediately healed. And he said to her,

Jesus: Daughter, your faith has made you well; go in peace.

St. Luke: While he was still speaking, a man from the ruler's house came and said,

Man: Your daughter is dead; do not trouble the Teacher anymore.

St. Luke: But Jesus on hearing this answered him,

Jesus: Do not fear; only believe, and she shall be well.

St. Luke: And when he came to the house, he permitted no one to enter with him, except Peter and John and James, and the father and mother of the child. And all were weeping and bewailing her; but he said,

Jesus: Do not weep; for she is not dead but sleeping.

St. Luke: And they laughed at him, knowing that she was dead. But taking her by the hand he called, saying,

Jesus: Child, arise.

St. Luke: And her spirit returned, and she got up at once; and he directed that something should be given her to eat. And her parents were amazed; but he charged them to tell no one what had happened.

Luke Chapter 9

The Mission of the Twelve (Lk 9:1–6); F3–551

St. Luke: And he called the twelve together and gave them power and authority over all demons and to cure diseases, and he sent them out to preach the kingdom of God and to heal. And he said to them,

Jesus: Take nothing for your journey, no staff, nor bag, nor bread, nor money; and do not have two tunics. And whatever house you enter, stay there, and from there depart. And wherever they do not receive you, when you leave that town shake off the dust from your feet as a testimony against them.

St. Luke: And they departed and went through the villages, preaching the gospel and healing everywhere.

~ Herod's Perplexity (Lk 9:7–9)

St. Luke: Now Herod the tetrarch heard of all that was done, and he was perplexed, because it was said by some that John had been raised from the dead, by some that Elijah had appeared, and by others that one of the old prophets had risen. Herod said,

Herod: John I beheaded; but who is this about whom I hear such things?

St. Luke: And he sought to see him.

~ Feeding the Five Thousand (Lk 9:10–17)

St. Luke: On their return the apostles told him what they had done. And he took them and withdrew apart to a city called Bethsaida. When the crowds learned it, they followed him;

and he welcomed them and spoke to them of the kingdom of God, and cured those who had need of healing. Now the day began to wear away; and the twelve came and said to him,

Apostles: Send the crowd away, to go into the villages and country round about, to lodge and get provisions; for we are here in a lonely place.

St. Luke: But he said to them,

Jesus: You give them something to eat.

St. Luke: They said,

Apostles: We have no more than five loaves and two fish—unless we are to go and buy food for all these people.

St. Luke: For there were about five thousand men. And he said to his disciples,

Jesus: Make them sit down in companies, about fifty each.

St. Luke: And they did so, and made them all sit down. And taking the five loaves and the two fish he looked up to heaven, and blessed and broke them, and gave them to the disciples to set before the crowd. And all ate and were satisfied. And they took up what was left over, twelve baskets of broken pieces.

Peter's Declaration that Jesus is the Christ (Lk 9:18–22); P–2600

St. Luke: Now it happened that as he was praying alone the disciples were with him; and he asked them,

Jesus: Who do the people say that I am?

St. Luke: And they answered,

Disciples: John the Baptist; but others say, Elijah; and others, that one of the old prophets has risen.

St. Luke: And he said to them,

Jesus: But who do you say that I am?

St. Luke: And Peter answered,

Peter: The Christ of God.

St. Luke: But he charged and commanded them to tell this to no one, saying,

Jesus: The Son of man must suffer many things, and be rejected by the elders and chief priests and scribes, and be killed, and on the third day be raised.

Taking Up One's Cross (Lk 9:23–27); S4–1435

St. Luke: And he said to all,

Jesus: If any man would come after me, let him deny himself and take up his cross daily and follow me. For whoever would save his life will lose it; and whoever loses his life for my sake, he will save it. For what does it profit a man if he gains the whole world and loses or forfeits himself? For whoever is ashamed of me and of my words, of him will the Son of man be ashamed when he comes in his glory and the glory of the Father and of the holy angels. But I tell you truly, there are some standing here who will not taste death before they see the kingdom of God.

* The Transfiguration (Lk 9:28–36); F3–554; LT–1151

St. Luke: Now about eight days after these sayings he took with him Peter and John and James, and went up on the mountain to pray. And as he was praying, the appearance of his countenance was altered, and his raiment became dazzling white. And behold, two men talked with him, Moses and Elijah, who appeared in glory and spoke of his departure, which he was to accomplish at Jerusalem. Now Peter and those who were with him were heavy with sleep, and when they wakened they saw his glory and the two men who stood with him. And as the men were parting from him, Peter said to Jesus,

Peter: Master, it is well that we are here; let us make three booths, one for you and one for Moses and one for Elijah—

St. Luke: —not knowing what he said. As he said this, a cloud came and overshadowed them; and they were afraid as they entered the cloud. And a voice came out of the cloud, saying,

God the Father: This is my Son, my Chosen; listen to him!

St. Luke: And when the voice had spoken, Jesus was found alone. And they kept silence and told no one in those days anything of what they had seen.

~ Jesus Heals a Boy with a Demon (Lk 9:37–43)

St. Luke: On the next day, when they had come down from the mountain, a great crowd met him. And behold, a man from the crowd cried,

Man from the crowd: Teacher, I beg you to look upon my son, for he is my only child; and behold, a spirit seizes him, and he suddenly cries out; it convulses him till he foams, and shatters him, and will hardly leave him. And I begged your disciples to cast it out, but they could not.

St. Luke: Jesus answered,

Jesus: O faithless and perverse generation, how long am I to be with you and bear with you? Bring your son here.

St. Luke: While he was coming, the demon tore him and convulsed him. But Jesus rebuked the unclean spirit, and healed the boy, and gave him back to his father. And all were astonished at the majesty of God.

Jesus Again Foretells His Death (Lk 9:44–45); F3–554

St. Luke: But while they were all marveling at everything he did, he said to his disciples,

Jesus: Let these words sink into your ears; for the Son of man is to be delivered into the hands of men.

St. Luke: But they did not understand this saying, and it was concealed from them, that they should not perceive it; and they were afraid to ask him about this saying.

~ True Greatness (Lk 9:46–48)

St. Luke: And an argument arose among them as to which of them was the greatest. But when Jesus perceived the thought of their hearts, he took a child and put him by his side, and said to them,

Jesus: Whoever receives this child in my name receives me, and whoever receives me receives him who sent me; for he who is least among you all is the one who is great.

~ Another Exorcist (Lk 9:49–50)

St. Luke: John answered,

John: Master, we saw a man casting out demons in your name, and we forbade him, because he does not follow with us.

St. Luke: But Jesus said to him,

Jesus: Do not forbid him; for he that is not against you is for you.

A Samaritan Village Refuses to Receive Jesus (Lk 9:51–56); F3–557

St. Luke: When the days drew near for him to be received up, he set his face to go to Jerusalem. And he sent messengers ahead of him, who went and entered a village of the Samaritans, to make ready for him; but the people would not receive him, because his face was set toward Jerusalem. And when his disciples James and John saw it, they said,

James and John: Lord, do you want us to bid fire come down from heaven and consume them?

St. Luke: But he turned and rebuked them. And they went on to another village.

Would-Be Followers of Jesus (Lk 9:57–62); F3–544

St. Luke: As they were going along the road, a man said to him,

First man: I will follow you wherever you go.

St. Luke: And Jesus said to him,

Jesus: Foxes have holes, and birds of the air have nests; but the Son of man has nowhere to lay his head.

St. Luke: To another he said,

Jesus: Follow me.

St. Luke: But he said,

Second man: Lord, let me first go and bury my father.

St. Luke: But he said to him,

Jesus: Leave the dead to bury their own dead; but as for you, go and proclaim the kingdom of God.

St. Luke: Another said,

Third man: I will follow you, Lord; but let me first say farewell to those at my home.

St. Luke: Jesus said to him,

Jesus: No one who puts his hand to the plow and looks back is fit for the kingdom of God.

Luke Chapter 10

* The Mission of the Seventy (Lk 10:1–12); F9–765; C1–2122

St. Luke: After this the Lord appointed seventy others, and sent them on ahead of him, two by two, into every town and place where he himself was about to come. And he said to them,

Jesus: The harvest is plentiful, but the laborers are few; pray therefore the Lord of the harvest to send out laborers into his harvest. Go your way; behold, I send you out as lambs in the midst of wolves. Carry no purse, no bag, no sandals; and salute no one on the road.

Whatever house you enter, first say, "Peace be to this house!" And if a son of peace is there, your peace shall rest upon him; but if not, it shall return to you. And remain in the same house, eating and drinking what they provide, for the laborer deserves his wages; do not go from house to house.

Whenever you enter a town and they receive you, eat what is set before you; heal the sick in it and say to them, "The kingdom of God has come near to you." But whenever you enter a town and they do not receive you, go into its streets and say, "Even the dust of your town that clings to our feet, we wipe off against you; nevertheless know this, that the kingdom of God has come near." I tell you, it shall be more tolerable on that day for Sodom than for that town.

Woes to Unrepentant Cities (Lk 10:13–16); PF2–87; F9–858

Jesus 1: Woe to you, Chorazin! Woe to you, Bethsaida! For if the mighty works done in you had been done in Tyre and Sidon, they would have repented long ago, sitting in sackcloth and ashes. But it shall be more tolerable in the judgment for Tyre and Sidon than for you.

And you, Capernaum, will you be exalted to heaven? You shall be brought down to Hades.

He who hears you hears me, and he who rejects you rejects me, and he who rejects me rejects him who sent me.

The Return of the Seventy (Lk 10:17–20); F9–787

St. Luke: The seventy returned with joy, saying

Seventy: Lord, even the demons are subject to us in your name!

St. Luke: And he said to them,

Jesus: I saw Satan fall like lightning from heaven. Behold, I have given you authority to tread upon serpents and scorpions, and over all the power of the enemy; and nothing shall hurt you. Nevertheless do not rejoice in this, that the spirits are subject to you; but rejoice that your names are written in heaven.

Jesus Rejoices and Thanks the Father (Lk 10:21–23); P–2603; LT–1083

St. Luke: In that same hour he rejoiced in the Holy Spirit and said,

Jesus: I thank you, Father, Lord of heaven and earth, that you have hidden these things from the wise and understanding and revealed them to infants; yes, Father, for such was your gracious will. All things have been delivered to me by my Father; and no one knows who the Son is except the Father, or who the Father is except the Son and any one to whom the Son chooses to reveal him.

St. Luke: Then turning to the disciples he said privately,

Jesus: Blessed are the eyes which see what you see! For I tell you that many prophets and kings desired to see what you see, and did not see it, and to hear what you hear, and did not hear it.

* The Parable of the Good Samaritan (Lk 10:25–37); LP3–2822; LC–2083

St. Luke: And behold, a lawyer stood up to put him to the test, saying,

Lawyer: Teacher, what shall I do to inherit eternal life?

St. Luke: He said to him,

Jesus: What is written in the law? How do you read?

St. Luke: And he answered,

Lawyer: You shall love the Lord your God with all your heart, and with all your soul, and with all your strength, and with all your mind; and your neighbor as yourself.

St. Luke: And he said to him,

Jesus: You have answered right; do this, and you will live.

St. Luke: But he, desiring to justify himself, said to Jesus,

Lawyer: And who is my neighbor?

St. Luke: Jesus replied,

Jesus: A man was going down from Jerusalem to Jericho, and he fell among robbers, who stripped him and beat him, and departed, leaving him half dead.

Now by chance a priest was going down that road; and when he saw him he passed by on the other side.

So likewise a Levite, when he came to the place and saw him, passed by on the other side.

But a Samaritan, as he journeyed, came to where he was; and when he saw him, he had compassion, and went to him and bound up his wounds, pouring on oil and wine; then he set him on his own beast and brought him to an inn, and took care of him. And the next day he took out two denarii and gave them to the innkeeper, saying,

Samaritan: Take care of him; and whatever more you spend, I will repay you when I come back.

Jesus: Which of these three, do you think, proved neighbor to the man who fell among the robbers?

St. Luke: He said,

Lawyer: The one who showed mercy on him.

St. Luke: And Jesus said to him,

Jesus: Go and do likewise.

~ Jesus Visits Martha and Mary (Lk 10:38–42)

St. Luke: Now as they went on their way, he entered a village; and a woman named Martha received him into her house. And she had a sister called Mary, who sat at the Lord's feet and listened to his teaching. But Martha was distracted with much serving; and she went to him and said,

Martha: Lord, do you not care that my sister has left me to serve alone? Tell her then to help me.

St. Luke: But the Lord answered her,

Jesus: Martha, Martha, you are anxious and troubled about many things; one thing is needful. Mary has chosen the good portion, which shall not be taken away from her.

Luke Chapter 11

* The Lord's Prayer (Lk 11:1–4); LP5–2845; P–2759

St. Luke: He was praying in a certain place, and when he ceased, one of his disciples said to him,

Disciple: Lord, teach us to pray, as John taught his disciples.

St. Luke: And he said to them,

Jesus: When you pray, say: "Father, hallowed be your name. Your kingdom come. Give us each day our daily bread; and forgive us our sins, for we ourselves forgive everyone who is indebted to us; and lead us not into temptation."

* Perseverance in Prayer (Lk 11:5–13); P–2613; F2–443

St. Luke: And he said to them,

Jesus: Which of you who has a friend will go to him at midnight and say to him,

First man: Friend, lend me three loaves; for a friend of mine has arrived on a journey, and I have nothing to set before him;

Jesus: And he will answer from within,

Second man: Do not bother me; the door is now shut, and my children are with me in bed; I cannot get up and give you anything.

Jesus: I tell you, though he will not get up and give him anything because he is his friend, yet because of his importunity he will rise and give him whatever he needs. And I tell you, Ask, and it will be given you; seek, and you will find; knock, and it will be opened to you. For everyone who asks receives, and he who seeks finds, and to him who knocks it will be opened.

What father among you, if his son asks for a fish, will instead of a fish give him a serpent; or if he asks for an egg, will give him a scorpion? If you then, who are evil, know how to give good gifts to your children, how much more will the heavenly Father give the Holy Spirit to those who ask him!

Jesus and Beelzebul (Lk 11:14–23); F8–700; F1–385

St. Luke: Now he was casting out a demon that was mute; when the demon had gone out, the mute man spoke, and the people marveled. But some of them said,

Some people: He casts out demons by Beelzebul, the prince of demons;

St. Luke: While others, to test him, sought from him a sign from heaven. But he, knowing their thoughts, said to them,

Jesus: Every kingdom divided against itself is laid waste, and a divided household falls. And if Satan also is divided against himself, how will his kingdom stand? For you say that I cast out demons by Beelzebul. And if I cast out demons by Beelzebul, by whom do your sons cast them out? Therefore they shall be your judges. But if it is by the finger of God that I cast out demons, then the kingdom of God has come upon you.

When a strong man, fully armed, guards his own palace, his goods are in peace; but when one stronger than he assails him and overcomes him, he takes away his armor in which he trusted, and divides his spoil.

He who is not with me is against me, and he who does not gather with me scatters.

~ The Return of the Unclean Spirit (Lk 11:24–26)

Jesus: When the unclean spirit has gone out of a man, he passes through waterless places seeking rest; and finding none he says,

Unclean spirit: I will return to my house from which I came.

Jesus: And when he comes he finds it swept and put in order. Then he goes and brings seven other spirits more evil than himself, and they enter and dwell there; and the last state of that man becomes worse than the first.

~ True Blessedness (Lk 11:27–28)

St. Luke: As he said this, a woman in the crowd raised her voice and said to him,

Woman in the crowd: Blessed is the womb that bore you, and the breasts that you sucked!

St. Luke: But he said,

Jesus: Blessed rather are those who hear the word of God and keep it!

~ The Sign of Jonah (Lk 11:29–32)

St. Luke: When the crowds were increasing, he began to say,

Jesus: This generation is an evil generation; it seeks a sign, but no sign shall be given to it except the sign of Jonah. For as Jonah became a sign to the men of Nineveh, so will the Son of man be to this generation.

The queen of the South will arise at the judgment with the men of this generation and condemn them; for she came from the ends of the earth to hear the wisdom of Solomon, and behold, something greater than Solomon is here.

The men of Nineveh will arise at the judgment with this generation and condemn it; for they repented at the preaching of Jonah, and behold, something greater than Jonah is here.

~ The Light of the Body (Lk 11:33–36)

Jesus 2: No one after lighting a lamp puts it in a cellar or under a bushel, but on a stand, that those who enter may see the light. Your eye is the lamp of your body; when your eye is sound, your whole body is full of light; but when it is not sound, your body is full of darkness.

Therefore be careful lest the light in you be darkness. If then your whole body is full of light, having no part dark, it will be wholly bright, as when a lamp with its rays gives you light.

* Jesus Denounces the Hypocrisy of the Pharisees and Lawyers (Lk 11:37–54); F4–579; C7–2447

St. Luke: While he was speaking, a Pharisee asked him to dine with him; so he went in and sat at table. The Pharisee was astonished to see that he did not first wash before dinner. And the Lord said to him,

Jesus: Now you Pharisees cleanse the outside of the cup and of the dish, but inside you are full of extortion and wickedness. You fools! Did not he who made the outside make the inside also? But give for alms those things which are within; and behold, everything is clean for you.

But woe to you Pharisees! for you tithe mint and rue and every herb, and neglect justice and the love of God; these you ought to have done, without neglecting the others. Woe to you Pharisees! for you love the best seat in the synagogues and salutations in the marketplaces.

Woe to you! for you are like graves which are not seen, and men walk over them without knowing it.

St. Luke: One of the lawyers answered him,

Lawyer: Teacher, in saying this you reproach us also.

St. Luke: And he said,

Jesus: Woe to you lawyers also! for you load men with burdens hard to bear, and you yourselves do not touch the burdens with one of your fingers. Woe to you! for you build the tombs of the prophets whom your fathers killed. So you are witnesses and consent to the deeds of your fathers; for they killed them, and you build their tombs.

Therefore also the Wisdom of God said,

God the Father: "I will send them prophets and apostles, some of whom they will kill and persecute, that the blood of all the prophets, shed from the foundation of the world, may be required of this generation, from the blood of Abel to the blood of Zechariah, who perished between the altar and the sanctuary."

Yes, I tell you, it shall be required of this generation. Woe to you lawyers! for you have taken away the key of knowledge; you did not enter yourselves, and you hindered those who were entering.

St. Luke: As he went away from there, the scribes and the Pharisees began to press him hard, and to provoke him to speak of many things, lying in wait for him, to catch at something he might say.

Luke Chapter 12

A Warning Against Hypocrisy (Lk 12:1–3); F7–678

St. Luke: In the meantime, when so many thousands of the multitude had gathered together that they trod upon one another, he began to say to his disciples first,

Jesus: Beware of the leaven of the Pharisees, which is hypocrisy. Nothing is covered up that will not be revealed, or hidden that will not be known. Therefore whatever you have said in the dark shall be heard in the light, and what you have whispered in private rooms shall be proclaimed upon the housetops.

* Whom to Fear (Lk 12:4–12); LC–1864; S2–1287

Jesus 2: I tell you, my friends, do not fear those who kill the body, and after that have no more that they can do. But I will warn you whom to fear: fear him who, after he has killed, has power to cast into hell; yes, I tell you, fear him!

Jesus 3: Are not five sparrows sold for two pennies? And not one of them is forgotten before God. Why, even the hairs of your head are all numbered. Fear not; you are of more value than many sparrows.

Jesus 4: And I tell you, everyone who acknowledges me before men, the Son of man also will acknowledge before the angels of God; but he who denies me before men will be denied before the angels of God.

And everyone who speaks a word against the Son of man will be forgiven; but he who blasphemes against the Holy Spirit will not be forgiven.

Jesus 5: And when they bring you before the synagogues and the rulers and the authorities, do not be anxious how or what you are to answer or what you are to say; for the Holy Spirit will teach you in that very hour what you ought to say.

The Parable of the Rich Fool (Lk 12:13–21); F3–549

St. Luke: One of the multitude said to him,

Man in the crowd: Teacher, bid my brother divide the inheritance with me.

St. Luke: But he said to him,

Jesus: Man, who made me a judge or divider over you?

St. Luke: And he said to them,

Jesus: Take heed, and beware of all covetousness; for a man's life does not consist in the abundance of his possessions.

St. Luke: And he told them a parable, saying,

Jesus: The land of a rich man brought forth plentifully; and he thought to himself,

Rich man: What shall I do, for I have nowhere to store my crops?

Jesus: And he said,

Rich man: I will do this: I will pull down my barns, and build larger ones; and there I will store all my grain and my goods. And I will say to my soul, "Soul, you have ample goods laid up for many years; take your ease, eat, drink, be merry."

Jesus: But God said to him,

God the Father: Fool! This night your soul is required of you; and the things you have prepared, whose will they be? So is he who lays up treasure for himself, and is not rich toward God.

Do Not be Anxious (Lk 12:22–34); F9–764

St. Luke: And he said to his disciples,

Jesus: Therefore I tell you, do not be anxious about your life, what you shall eat, nor about your body, what you shall put on. For life is more than food, and the body more than clothing.

Consider the ravens: they neither sow nor reap, they have neither storehouse nor barn, and yet God feeds them. Of how much more value are you than the birds! And which of you by being anxious can add a cubit to his span of life? If then you are not able to do as small a thing as that, why are you anxious about the rest?

Jesus 2: Consider the lilies, how they grow; they neither toil nor spin; yet I tell you, even Solomon in all his glory was not arrayed like one of these. But if God so clothes the grass which is alive in the field today and tomorrow is thrown into the oven, how much more will he clothe you, O men of little faith!

Jesus 3: And do not seek what you are to eat and what you are to drink, nor be of anxious mind. For all the nations of the world seek these things; and your Father knows that you need them. Instead, seek his kingdom, and these things shall be yours as well.

Fear not, little flock, for it is your Father's good pleasure to give you the kingdom. Sell your possessions, and give alms; provide yourselves with purses that do not grow old, with a treasure in the heavens that does not fail, where no thief approaches and no moth destroys. For where your treasure is, there will your heart be also.

The Necessity of Watchfulness (Lk 12:35–40); LP6–2849

Jesus: Let your loins be girded and your lamps burning, and be like men who are waiting for their master to come home from the marriage feast, so that they may open to him at once when he comes and knocks. Blessed are those servants whom the master finds awake when he comes; truly, I say to you, he will gird himself and have them sit at table, and he will come and serve them.

If he comes in the second watch, or in the third, and finds them so, blessed are those servants! But know this, that if the householder had known at what hour the thief was coming, he would have been awake and would not have left his house to be broken into. You also must be ready; for the Son of man is coming at an unexpected hour.

~ The Faithful and the Unfaithful Servant (Lk 12:41–48)

St. Luke: Peter said,

Peter: Lord, are you telling this parable for us or for all?

St. Luke: And the Lord said,

Jesus: Who then is the faithful and wise steward, whom his master will set over his household, to give them their portion of food at the proper time? Blessed is that servant whom his master when he comes will find so doing. Truly, I say to you, he will set him over all his possessions. But if that servant says to himself,

Servant: My master is delayed in coming,

Jesus: And begins to beat the menservants and the maidservants, and to eat and drink and get drunk, the master of that servant will come on a day when he does not expect him and at an hour he does not know, and will punish him, and put him with the unfaithful. And that servant who knew his master's will, but did not make ready or act according to his will, shall receive a severe beating. But he who did not know, and did what deserved a beating, shall receive a light beating.

Everyone to whom much is given, of him will much be required; and of him to whom men commit much they will demand the more.

* Jesus the Cause of Division (Lk 12:49–53); S1–1225; LP1–2804

Jesus 2: I came to cast fire upon the earth; and would that it were already kindled! I have a baptism to be baptized with; and how I am constrained until it is accomplished! Do you think that I have come to give peace on earth?

No, I tell you, but rather division; for henceforth in one house there will be five divided, three against two and two against three; they will be divided, father against son and son against father, mother against daughter and daughter against her mother, mother-in-law against her daughter-in-law and daughter-in-law against her mother-in-law.

~ Interpreting the Present Time (Lk 12:54–56)

St. Luke: He also said to the multitudes,

Jesus: When you see a cloud rising in the west, you say at once,

Person: A shower is coming;

Jesus: And so it happens. And when you see the south wind blowing, you say,

Person: There will be scorching heat;

Jesus: And it happens. You hypocrites! You know how to interpret the appearance of earth and sky; but why do you not know how to interpret the present time?

~ Settling with Your Accuser (Lk 12:57–59)

Jesus: And why do you not judge for yourselves what is right? As you go with your accuser before the magistrate, make an effort to settle with him on the way, lest he drag you to the judge, and the judge hand you over to the officer, and the officer put you in prison. I tell you, you will never get out till you have paid the very last copper.

Luke Chapter 13

~ Repent or Perish (Lk 13:1–5)

St. Luke: There were some present at that very time who told him of the Galileans whose blood Pilate had mingled with their sacrifices. And he answered them,

Jesus: Do you think that these Galileans were worse sinners than all the other Galileans, because they suffered thus? I tell you, No; but unless you repent you will all likewise perish.

Or those eighteen upon whom the tower in Siloam fell and killed them, do you think that they were worse offenders than all the others who dwelt in Jerusalem? I tell you, No; but unless you repent you will all likewise perish.

~ The Parable of the Barren Fig Tree (Lk 13:6–9)

St. Luke: And he told this parable:

Jesus: A man had a fig tree planted in his vineyard; and he came seeking fruit on it and found none. And he said to the vinedresser,

Man: Lo, these three years I have come seeking fruit on this fig tree, and I find none. Cut it down; why should it use up the ground?

St. Luke: And he answered him,

Vinedresser: Let it alone, sir, this year also, till I dig about it and put on manure. And if it bears fruit next year, well and good; but if not, you can cut it down.

Jesus Heals a Crippled Woman (Lk 13:10–17); F4–582

St. Luke: Now he was teaching in one of the synagogues on the sabbath. And there was a woman who had had a spirit of infirmity for eighteen years; she was bent over and could not fully straighten herself. And when Jesus saw her, he called her and said to her,

Jesus: Woman, you are freed from your infirmity.

St. Luke: And he laid his hands upon her, and immediately she was made straight, and she praised God. But the ruler of the synagogue, indignant because Jesus had healed on the sabbath, said to the people,

Ruler of the synagogue: There are six days on which work ought to be done; come on those days and be healed, and not on the sabbath day.

St. Luke: Then the Lord answered him,

Jesus: You hypocrites! Does not each of you on the sabbath untie his ox or his donkey from the manger, and lead it away to water it? And ought not this woman, a daughter of Abraham whom Satan bound for eighteen years, be loosed from this bond on the sabbath day?

St. Luke: As he said this, all his adversaries were put to shame; and all the people rejoiced at all the glorious things that were done by him.

~ The Parable of the Mustard Seed (Lk 13:18–19)

St. Luke: He said therefore,

Jesus: What is the kingdom of God like? And to what shall I compare it? It is like a grain of mustard seed which a man took and sowed in his garden; and it grew and became a tree, and the birds of the air made nests in its branches.

* The Parable of the Leaven (Lk 13:20–21); P–2660

St. Luke: And again he said,

Jesus: To what shall I compare the kingdom of God? It is like leaven which a woman took and hid in three measures of flour, till it was all leavened.

~ The Narrow Door (Lk 13:22–30)

St. Luke: He went on his way through towns and villages, teaching, and journeying toward Jerusalem. And someone said to him,

Someone: Lord, will those who are saved be few?

St. Luke: And he said to them,

Jesus: Strive to enter by the narrow door; for many, I tell you, will seek to enter and will not be able. When once the householder has risen up and shut the door, you will begin to stand outside and to knock at the door, saying,

People: Lord, open to us.

Jesus: He will answer you,

Householder: I do not know where you come from.

Jesus: Then you will begin to say,

People: We ate and drank in your presence, and you taught in our streets.

Jesus: But he will say,

Householder: I tell you, I do not know where you come from; depart from me, all you workers of iniquity!

Jesus: There you will weep and gnash your teeth, when you see Abraham and Isaac and Jacob and all the prophets in the kingdom of God and you yourselves thrust out. And men will come from east and west, and from north and south, and sit at table in the kingdom of God. And behold, some are last who will be first, and some are first who will be last.

* The Lament over Jerusalem (Lk 13:31–35); F4–575; F3–557

St. Luke: At that very hour some Pharisees came, and said to him,

Pharisees: Get away from here, for Herod wants to kill you.

St. Luke: And he said to them,

Jesus: Go and tell that fox, "Behold, I cast out demons and perform cures today and tomorrow, and the third day I finish my course. Nevertheless I must go on my way today and tomorrow and the day following; for it cannot be that a prophet should perish away from Jerusalem." O Jerusalem, Jerusalem, killing the prophets and stoning those who are sent to you! How often would I have gathered your children together as a hen gathers her brood under her wings, and you would not! Behold, your house is forsaken. And I tell you, you will not see me until you say, "Blessed is he who comes in the name of the Lord!"

Luke Chapter 14

* Jesus Heals the Man with Dropsy on the Sabbath (Lk 14:1–6); F4–575; F4–588

St. Luke: One sabbath when he went to dine at the house of a ruler who belonged to the Pharisees, they were watching him. And behold, there was a man before him who had dropsy. And Jesus spoke to the lawyers and Pharisees, saying,

Jesus: Is it lawful to heal on the sabbath, or not?

St. Luke: But they were silent. Then he took him and healed him, and let him go. And he said to them,

Jesus: Which of you, having an ass or an ox that has fallen into a well, will not immediately pull him out on a sabbath day?

St. Luke: And they could not reply to this.

~ Humility and Hospitality (Lk 14:7–14)

St. Luke: Now he told a parable to those who were invited, when he marked how they chose the places of honor, saying to them,

Jesus: When you are invited by any one to a marriage feast, do not sit down in a place of honor, lest a more eminent man than you be invited by him; and he who invited you both will come and say to you,

Host: Give place to this man,

Jesus: And then you will begin with shame to take the lowest place. But when you are invited, go and sit in the lowest place, so that when your host comes he may say to you,

Host: Friend, go up higher;

Jesus: Then you will be honored in the presence of all who sit at table with you. For everyone who exalts himself will be humbled, and he who humbles himself will be exalted.

St. Luke: He said also to the man who had invited him,

Jesus: When you give a dinner or a banquet, do not invite your friends or your brothers or your kinsmen or rich neighbors, lest they also invite you in return, and you be repaid. But when you give a feast, invite the poor, the maimed, the lame, the blind, and you will be blessed, because they cannot repay you. You will be repaid at the resurrection of the just.

~ The Parable of the Great Banquet (Lk 14:15–24)

St. Luke: When one of those who sat at table with him heard this, he said to him,

Man at Table: Blessed is he who shall eat bread in the kingdom of God!

St. Luke: But he said to him,

Jesus: A man once gave a great banquet, and invited many; and at the time for the banquet he sent his servant to say to those who had been invited,

Householder: Come; for all is now ready.

Jesus: But they all alike began to make excuses. The first said to him,

First man: I have bought a field, and I must go out and see it; I pray you, have me excused.

Jesus: And another said,

Second man: I have bought five yoke of oxen, and I go to examine them; I pray you, have me excused.

Jesus: And another said,

Third man: I have married a wife, and therefore I cannot come.

Jesus: So the servant came and reported this to his master. Then the householder in anger said to his servant,

Householder: Go out quickly to the streets and lanes of the city, and bring in the poor and maimed and blind and lame.

Jesus: And the servant said,

Servant: Sir, what you commanded has been done, and still there is room.

Jesus: And the master said to the servant,

Householder: Go out to the highways and hedges, and compel people to come in, that my house may be filled. For I tell you, none of those men who were invited shall taste my banquet

The Cost of Discipleship (Lk 14:25–33); S7–1618; C10–2544

St. Luke: Now great multitudes accompanied him; and he turned and said to them,

Jesus: If any one comes to me and does not hate his own father and mother and wife and children and brothers and sisters, yes, and even his own life, he cannot be my disciple. Whoever does not bear his own cross and come after me, cannot be my disciple.

Jesus1: For which of you, desiring to build a tower, does not first sit down and count the cost, whether he has enough to complete it? Otherwise, when he has laid a foundation, and is not able to finish, all who see it begin to mock him, saying,

All: This man began to build, and was not able to finish.

Jesus 2: Or what king, going to encounter another king in war, will not sit down first and take counsel whether he is able with ten thousand to meet him who comes against him with twenty thousand? And if not, while the other is yet a great way off, he sends an embassy and asks terms of peace. So therefore, whoever of you does not renounce all that he has cannot be my disciple.

~ About Salt (Lk 14:34–35)

Jesus 3: Salt is good; but if salt has lost its taste, how shall its saltiness be restored? It is fit neither for the land nor for the dunghill; men throw it away. He who has ears to hear, let him hear.

Luke Chapter 15

The Parable of the Lost Sheep (Lk 15:1–7); S4–1443; LC–1846

St. Luke: Now the tax collectors and sinners were all drawing near to hear him. And the Pharisees and the scribes murmured, saying,

Pharisees and scribes: This man receives sinners and eats with them.

St. Luke: So he told them this parable:

Jesus: What man of you, having a hundred sheep, if he has lost one of them, does not leave the ninety-nine in the wilderness, and go after the one which is lost, until he finds it? And when he has found it, he lays it on his shoulders, rejoicing. And when he comes home, he calls together his friends and his neighbors, saying to them,

Shepherd: Rejoice with me, for I have found my sheep which was lost.

Jesus: Just so, I tell you, there will be more joy in heaven over one sinner who repents than over ninety-nine righteous persons who need no repentance.

~ The Parable of the Lost Coin (Lk 15:8–10)

Jesus: Or what woman, having ten silver coins, if she loses one coin, does not light a lamp and sweep the house and seek diligently until she finds it? And when she has found it, she calls together her friends and neighbors, saying,

Woman: Rejoice with me, for I have found the coin which I had lost.

Jesus: Just so, I tell you, there is joy before the angels of God over one sinner who repents.

* The Parable of the Prodigal and His Brother (Lk 15:11–32); F3–545; LP5–2839

St. Luke: And he said,

Jesus: There was a man who had two sons; and the younger of them said to his father,

Younger son: Father, give me the share of property that falls to me.

Jesus: And he divided his living between them. Not many days later, the younger son gathered all he had and took his journey into a far country, and there he squandered his property in loose living. And when he had spent everything, a great famine arose in that country, and he began to be in want. So he went and joined himself to one of the citizens of that country, who sent him into his fields to feed swine. And he would gladly have fed on the pods that the swine ate; and no one gave him anything. But when he came to himself he said,

Younger son: How many of my father's hired servants have bread enough and to spare, but I perish here with hunger! I will arise and go to my father, and I will say to him, "Father, I have sinned against heaven and before you; I am no longer worthy to be called your son; treat me as one of your hired servants."

Jesus: And he arose and came to his father. But while he was yet at a distance, his father saw him and had compassion, and ran and embraced him and kissed him. And the son said to him,

Younger son: Father, I have sinned against heaven and before you; I am no longer worthy to be called your son.

Jesus: But the father said to his servants,

Father: Bring quickly the best robe, and put it on him; and put a ring on his hand, and shoes on his feet; and bring the fatted calf and kill it, and let us eat and make merry; for this my son was dead, and is alive again; he was lost, and is found.

Jesus: And they began to make merry. Now his elder son was in the field; and as he came and drew near to the house, he heard music and dancing. And he called one of the servants and asked what this meant. And he said to him,

Servant: Your brother has come, and your father has killed the fatted calf, because he has received him safe and sound.

Jesus: But he was angry and refused to go in. His father came out and entreated him, but he answered his father,

Older son: Lo, these many years I have served you, and I never disobeyed your command; yet you never gave me a kid, that I might make merry with my friends. But when this son of yours came, who has devoured your living with harlots, you killed for him the fatted calf!

Jesus: And he said to him,

Father: Son, you are always with me, and all that is mine is yours. It was fitting to make merry and be glad, for this your brother was dead, and is alive; he was lost, and is found.

Luke Chapter 16

The Parable of the Dishonest Steward (Lk 16:1–13); C7–2424; F9–952

St. Luke: He also said to the disciples,

Jesus: There was a rich man who had a steward, and charges were brought to him that this man was wasting his goods. And he called him and said to him,

Rich man: What is this that I hear about you? Turn in the account of your stewardship, for you can no longer be steward.

Jesus: And the steward said to himself,

Steward: What shall I do, since my master is taking the stewardship away from me? I am not strong enough to dig, and I am ashamed to beg. I have decided what to do, so that people may receive me into their houses when I am put out of the stewardship.

Jesus: So, summoning his master's debtors one by one, he said to the first,

Steward: How much do you owe my master?

Jesus: He said,

First debtor: A hundred measures of oil.

Jesus: And he said to him,

Steward: Take your bill, and sit down quickly and write fifty.

Jesus: Then he said to another,

Steward: And how much do you owe?

Jesus: He said,

Second debtor: A hundred measures of wheat.

Jesus: He said to him,

Steward: Take your bill, and write eighty.

Jesus: The master commended the dishonest steward for his shrewdness; for the sons of this world are more shrewd in dealing with their own generation than the sons of light. And I tell you, make friends for yourselves by means of unrighteous mammon, so that when it fails they may receive you into the eternal habitations.

He who is faithful in a very little is faithful also in much; and he who is dishonest in a very little is dishonest also in much. If then you have not been faithful in the unrighteous mammon, who will entrust to you the true riches? And if you have not been faithful in that which is another's, who will give you that which is your own?

No servant can serve two masters; for either he will hate the one and love the other, or he will be devoted to the one and despise the other. You cannot serve God and mammon.

The Law and the Kingdom of God (Lk 16:14–18); C6–2382; F3–523

St. Luke: The Pharisees, who were lovers of money, heard all this, and they scoffed at him. But he said to them,

Jesus: You are those who justify yourselves before men, but God knows your hearts; for what is exalted among men is an abomination in the sight of God.

The law and the prophets were until John; since then the good news of the kingdom of God is preached, and everyone enters it violently.

But it is easier for heaven and earth to pass away, than for one dot of the law to become void.

Everyone who divorces his wife and marries another commits adultery, and he who marries a woman divorced from her husband commits adultery.

* The Rich Man and Lazarus (Lk 16:19–31); LC–1859; LP4–2839–31

Jesus 2: There was a rich man, who was clothed in purple and fine linen and who feasted sumptuously every day. And at his gate lay a poor man named Lazarus, full of sores, who desired to be fed with what fell from the rich man's table; moreover the dogs came and licked his sores. The poor man died and was carried by the angels to Abraham's bosom. The rich man also died and was buried; and in Hades, being in torment, he lifted up his eyes, and saw Abraham far off and Lazarus in his bosom. And he called out,

Rich man: Father Abraham, have mercy upon me, and send Lazarus to dip the end of his finger in water and cool my tongue; for I am in anguish in this flame.

Jesus 2: But Abraham said,

Abraham: Son, remember that you in your lifetime received your good things, and Lazarus in like manner evil things; but now he is comforted here, and you are in anguish. And besides all this, between us and you a great chasm has been fixed, in order that those who would pass from here to you may not be able, and none may cross from there to us.

Jesus 2: And he said,

Rich man: Then I beg you, father, to send him to my father's house, for I have five brothers, so that he may warn them, lest they also come into this place of torment.

Jesus 2: But Abraham said,

Abraham: They have Moses and the prophets; let them hear them.

Jesus 2: And he said,

Rich man: No, father Abraham; but if someone goes to them from the dead, they will repent.

Jesus 2: He said to him,

Abraham: If they do not hear Moses and the prophets, neither will they be convinced if someone should rise from the dead.

Luke Chapter 17

* Some Sayings of Jesus (Lk 17:1–10); LP5–2845; PF3–162

St. Luke: And he said to his disciples,

Jesus: Temptations to sin are sure to come; but woe to him by whom they come! It would be better for him if a millstone were hung round his neck and he were cast into the sea, than that he should cause one of these little ones to sin.

Take heed to yourselves; if your brother sins, rebuke him, and if he repents, forgive him; and if he sins against you seven times in the day, and turns to you seven times, and says, "I repent," you must forgive him.

St. Luke: The apostles said to the Lord,

Apostles: Increase our faith!

St. Luke: And the Lord said,

Jesus: If you had faith as a grain of mustard seed, you could say to this sycamore tree,

Person: Be rooted up, and be planted in the sea,

Jesus: And it would obey you. Will any one of you, who has a servant plowing or keeping sheep, say to him when he has come in from the field,

Master: Come at once and sit down at table?

Jesus: Will he not rather say to him,

Master: Prepare supper for me, and put on your apron and serve me, till I eat and drink; and afterward you shall eat and drink?

Jesus: Does he thank the servant because he did what was commanded? So you also, when you have done all that is commanded you, say, "We are unworthy servants; we have only done what was our duty."

Jesus Cleanses Ten Lepers (Lk 17:11–19); F4–586; Lk 17:14

St. Luke: On the way to Jerusalem he was passing along between Samaria and Galilee. And as he entered a village, he was met by ten lepers, who stood at a distance and lifted up their voices and said,

Ten lepers: Jesus, Master, have mercy on us.

St. Luke: When he saw them he said to them,

Jesus: Go and show yourselves to the priests.

St. Luke: And as they went they were cleansed. Then one of them, when he saw that he was healed, turned back, praising God with a loud voice; and he fell on his face at Jesus' feet, giving him thanks. Now he was a Samaritan. Then said Jesus,

Jesus: Were not ten cleansed? Where are the nine? Was no one found to return and give praise to God except this foreigner?

St. Luke: And he said to him,

Jesus: Rise and go your way; your faith has made you well.

The Coming of the Kingdom (Lk 17:20–37); C7–2463; LC–1889

St. Luke: Being asked by the Pharisees when the kingdom of God was coming, he answered them,

Jesus: The kingdom of God is not coming with signs to be observed; nor will they say,

Person: Behold, here it is!

Jesus: or

Other person: There!

Jesus: For behold, the kingdom of God is in the midst of you.

St. Luke: And he said to the disciples,

Jesus: The days are coming when you will desire to see one of the days of the Son of man, and you will not see it. And they will say to you,

Person: Behold, there!

Jesus: or

Other person: Behold, here!

Jesus: Do not go, do not follow them. For as the lightning flashes and lights up the sky from one side to the other, so will the Son of man be in his day. But first he must suffer many things and be rejected by this generation.

As it was in the days of Noah, so will it be in the days of the Son of man. They ate, they drank, they married, they were given in marriage, until the day when Noah entered the ark, and the flood came and destroyed them all.

Jesus 2: Likewise as it was in the days of Lot—they ate, they drank, they bought, they sold, they planted, they built, but on the day when Lot went out from Sodom fire and sulphur rained from heaven and destroyed them all—so will it be on the day when the Son of man is revealed.

On that day, let him who is on the housetop, with his goods in the house, not come down to take them away; and likewise let him who is in the field not turn back.

Remember Lot's wife.

Whoever seeks to gain his life will lose it, but whoever loses his life will preserve it. I tell you, in that night there will be two in one bed; one will be taken and the other left. There will be two women grinding together; one will be taken and the other left.

St. Luke: And they said to him,

Disciples: Where, Lord?

St. Luke: He said to them,

Jesus: Where the body is, there the eagles will be gathered together.

Luke Chapter 18

* The Parable of the Widow and the Unrighteous Judge (Lk 18:1–8); P–2573; P–2613

St. Luke: And he told them a parable, to the effect that they ought always to pray and not lose heart. He said,

Jesus: In a certain city there was a judge who neither feared God nor regarded man; and there was a widow in that city who kept coming to him and saying,

Widow: Vindicate me against my adversary.

Jesus: For a while he refused; but afterward he said to himself,

Judge: Though I neither fear God nor regard man, yet because this widow bothers me, I will vindicate her, or she will wear me out by her continual coming.

St. Luke: And the Lord said,

Jesus: Hear what the unrighteous judge says. And will not God vindicate his elect, who cry to him day and night? Will he delay long over them? I tell you, he will vindicate them speedily. Nevertheless, when the Son of man comes, will he find faith on earth?

* The Parable of the Pharisee and the Tax Collector (Lk 18:9–14); LP5–2839; P–2613

St. Luke: He also told this parable to some who trusted in themselves that they were righteous and despised others:

Jesus: Two men went up into the temple to pray, one a Pharisee and the other a tax collector. The Pharisee stood and prayed thus with himself,

Pharisee: God, I thank you that I am not like other men, extortioners, unjust, adulterers, or even like this tax collector. I fast twice a week, I give tithes of all that I get.

Jesus: But the tax collector, standing far off, would not even lift up his eyes to heaven, but beat his breast, saying,

Tax collector: God, be merciful to me a sinner!

Jesus: I tell you, this man went down to his house justified rather than the other; for everyone who exalts himself will be humbled, but he who humbles himself will be exalted.

~ Jesus Blesses the Children (Lk 18:15–17)

St. Luke: Now they were bringing even infants to him that he might touch them; and when the disciples saw it, they rebuked them. But Jesus called them to him, saying,

Jesus: Let the children come to me, and do not hinder them; for to such belongs the kingdom of God. Truly, I say to you, whoever does not receive the kingdom of God like a child shall not enter it.

~ The Rich Ruler (Lk 18:18–30)

St. Luke: And a ruler asked him,

Ruler: Good Teacher, what shall I do to inherit eternal life?

St. Luke: And Jesus said to him,

Jesus: Why do you call me good? No one is good but God alone. You know the commandments: "Do not commit adultery, Do not kill, Do not steal, Do not bear false witness, Honor your father and mother."

St. Luke: And he said,

Ruler: All these I have observed from my youth.

St. Luke: And when Jesus heard it, he said to him,

Jesus: One thing you still lack. Sell all that you have and distribute to the poor, and you will have treasure in heaven; and come, follow me.

St. Luke: But when he heard this he became sad, for he was very rich. Jesus looking at him said,

Jesus: How hard it is for those who have riches to enter the kingdom of God! For it is easier for a camel to go through the eye of a needle than for a rich man to enter the kingdom of God.

St. Luke: Those who heard it said,

Disciples: Then who can be saved?

St. Luke: But he said,

Jesus: What is impossible with men is possible with God.

St. Luke: And Peter said,

Peter: Lo, we have left our homes and followed you.

St. Luke: And he said to them,

Jesus: Truly, I say to you, there is no man who has left house or wife or brothers or parents or children, for the sake of the kingdom of God, who will not receive manifold more in this time, and in the age to come eternal life.

~ A Third Time Jesus Foretells His Death and Resurrection (Lk 18:31–34)

St. Luke: And taking the twelve, he said to them,

Jesus: Behold, we are going up to Jerusalem, and everything that is written of the Son of man by the prophets will be accomplished. For he will be delivered to the Gentiles, and will be mocked and shamefully treated and spit upon; they will scourge him and kill him, and on the third day he will rise.

St. Luke: But they understood none of these things; this saying was hid from them, and they did not grasp what was said.

~ Jesus Heals a Blind Beggar near Jericho (Lk 18:35–43)

St. Luke: As he drew near to Jericho, a blind man was sitting by the roadside begging and hearing a multitude going by, he inquired what this meant. They told him,

Crowd: Jesus of Nazareth is passing by.

St. Luke: And he cried,

Blind man: Jesus, Son of David, have mercy on me!

St. Luke: And those who were in front rebuked him, telling him to be silent; but he cried out all the more,

Blind man: Son of David, have mercy on me!

St. Luke: And Jesus stopped, and commanded him to be brought to him; and when he came near, he asked him,

Jesus: What do you want me to do for you?

St. Luke: He said,

Blind man: Lord, let me receive my sight.

St. Luke: And Jesus said to him,

Jesus: Receive your sight; your faith has made you well.

St. Luke: And immediately he received his sight and followed him, glorifying God; and all the people, when they saw it, gave praise to God.

Luke Chapter 19

* Jesus and Zacchaeus (Lk 19:1–10); S4–1443; C7–2412

St. Luke: He entered Jericho and was passing through. And there was a man named Zacchaeus; he was a chief tax collector, and rich. And he sought to see who Jesus was, but could not, on account of the crowd, because he was small of stature. So he ran on ahead and climbed up into a sycamore tree to see him, for he was to pass that way. And when Jesus came to the place, he looked up and said to him,

Jesus: Zacchaeus, make haste and come down; for I must stay at your house today.

St. Luke: So he made haste and came down, and received him joyfully. And when they saw it they all murmured,

All: He has gone in to be the guest of a man who is a sinner.

St. Luke: And Zacchaeus stood and said to the Lord,

Zacchaeus: Behold, Lord, the half of my goods I give to the poor; and if I have defrauded any one of anything, I restore it fourfold.

St. Luke: And Jesus said to him,

Jesus: Today salvation has come to this house, since he also is a son of Abraham. For the Son of man came to seek and to save the lost.

The Parable of the Ten Pounds (Lk 19:11–27); LC–1936; LC–1880

St. Luke: As they heard these things, he proceeded to tell a parable, because he was near to Jerusalem, and because they supposed that the kingdom of God was to appear immediately. He said therefore,

Jesus: A nobleman went into a far country to receive a kingly power and then return. Calling ten of his servants, he gave them ten pounds, and said to them,

Nobleman: Trade with these till I come.

Jesus: But his citizens hated him and sent an embassy after him, saying,

Citizens: We do not want this man to reign over us.

Jesus: When he returned, having received the kingly power, he commanded these servants, to whom he had given the money, to be called to him, that he might know what they had gained by trading. The first came before him, saying,

First servant: Lord, your pound has made ten pounds more.

Jesus: And he said to him,

Nobleman: Well done, good servant! Because you have been faithful in a very little, you shall have authority over ten cities.

Jesus: And the second came, saying,

Second servant: Lord, your pound has made five pounds.

Jesus: And he said to him,

Nobleman: And you are to be over five cities.

Jesus: Then another came, saying,

Third servant: Lord, here is your pound, which I kept laid away in a napkin; for I was afraid of you, because you are a severe man; you take up what you did not lay down, and reap what you did not sow.

Jesus: He said to him,

Nobleman: I will condemn you out of your own mouth, you wicked servant! You knew that I was a severe man, taking up what I did not lay down and reaping what I did not sow? Why then did you not put my money into the bank, and at my coming I should have collected it with interest?

Jesus: And he said to those who stood by,

Nobleman: Take the pound from him, and give it to him who has the ten pounds.

Jesus: And they said to him,

Other people: Lord, he has ten pounds!

Nobleman: I tell you, that to everyone who has will more be given; but from him who has not, even what he has will be taken away. But as for these enemies of mine, who did not want me to reign over them, bring them here and slay them before me.

Jesus' Entry Into Jerusalem (Lk 19:28–40); F3–559

St. Luke: And when he had said this, he went on ahead, going up to Jerusalem. When he drew near to Bethphage and Bethany, at the mount that is called Olivet, he sent two of the disciples, saying,

Jesus: Go into the village opposite, where on entering you will find a colt tied, on which no one has ever yet sat; untie it and bring it here. If any one asks you, "Why are you untying it?" you shall say this, "The Lord has need of it."

St. Luke: So those who were sent went away and found it as he had told them. And as they were untying the colt, its owners said to them,

Owners: Why are you untying the colt?

St. Luke: And they said,

Two disciples: The Lord has need of it.

St. Luke: And they brought it to Jesus, and throwing their garments on the colt they set Jesus upon it. And as he rode along, they spread their garments on the road. As he was now drawing near, at the descent of the Mount of Olives, the whole multitude of the disciples began to rejoice and praise God with a loud voice for all the mighty works that they had seen, saying,

Multitude of disciples: Blessed is the King who comes in the name of the Lord! Peace in heaven and glory in the highest!

St. Luke: And some of the Pharisees in the multitude said to him,

Pharisees: Teacher, rebuke your disciples.

St. Luke: He answered,

Jesus: I tell you, if these were silent, the very stones would cry out.

Jesus Weeps over Jerusalem (Lk 19:41–44); F3–558

St. Luke: And when he drew near and saw the city he wept over it, saying,

Jesus: Would that even today you knew the things that make for peace! But now they are hid from your eyes. For the days shall come upon you, when your enemies will cast up a bank about you and surround you, and hem you in on every side, and dash you to the ground, you and your children within you, and they will not leave one stone upon another in you; because you did not know the time of your visitation.

~ Jesus Cleanses the Temple (Lk 19:45–48)

St. Luke: And he entered the temple and began to drive out those who sold, saying to them,

Jesus: It is written, "My house shall be a house of prayer"; but you have made it a den of robbers.

St. Luke: And he was teaching daily in the temple. The chief priests and the scribes and the principal men of the people sought to destroy him; but they did not find anything they could do, for all the people hung upon his words.

Luke Chapter 20

~ The Authority of Jesus Questioned (Lk 20:1–8)

St. Luke: One day, as he was teaching the people in the temple and preaching the gospel, the chief priests and the scribes with the elders came up and said to him,

Chief priests, scribes, and elders: Tell us by what authority you do these things, or who it is that gave you this authority.

St. Luke: He answered them,

Jesus: I also will ask you a question; now tell me, Was the baptism of John from heaven or from men?

St. Luke: And they discussed it with one another, saying,

Chief priests, scribes, and elders: If we say, "From heaven," he will say, "Why did you not believe him?" But if we say, "From men," all the people will stone us; for they are convinced that John was a prophet.

St. Luke: So they answered that they did not know whence it was. And Jesus said to them,

Jesus: Neither will I tell you by what authority I do these things.

The Parable of the Wicked Tenants (Lk 20:9–18); F4–587

St. Luke: And he began to tell the people this parable:

Jesus: A man planted a vineyard, and let it out to tenants, and went into another country for a long while. When the time came, he sent a servant to the tenants, that they should give him some of the fruit of the vineyard; but the tenants beat him, and sent him away empty-handed. And he sent another servant; him also they beat and treated shamefully, and sent him away empty-handed. And he sent yet a third; this one they wounded and cast out. Then the owner of the vineyard said,

Owner: What shall I do? I will send my beloved son; it may be they will respect him.

Jesus: But when the tenants saw him, they said to themselves,

Tenants: This is the heir; let us kill him, that the inheritance may be ours.

Jesus: And they cast him out of the vineyard and killed him. What then will the owner of the vineyard do to them? He will come and destroy those tenants, and give the vineyard to others.

St. Luke: When they heard this, they said,

Chief priests, scribes, and elders: God forbid!

St. Luke: But he looked at them and said,

Jesus: What then is this that is written: "The very stone which the builders rejected has become the head of the corner? Everyone who falls on that stone will be broken to pieces; but when it falls on any one it will crush him."

~ The Question about Paying Taxes (Lk 20:19–26)

St. Luke: The scribes and the chief priests tried to lay hands on him at that very hour, but they feared the people; for they perceived that he had told this parable against them. So they watched him, and sent spies, who pretended to be sincere, that they might take hold of what he said, so as to deliver him up to the authority and jurisdiction of the governor. They asked him,

Spies: Teacher, we know that you speak and teach rightly, and show no partiality, but truly teach the way of God. Is it lawful for us to give tribute to Caesar, or not?

St. Luke: But he perceived their craftiness, and said to them,

Jesus: Show me a coin. Whose likeness and inscription has it?

St. Luke: They said,

Spies: Caesar's.

St. Luke: He said to them,

Jesus: Then render to Caesar the things that are Caesar's, and to God the things that are God's.

St. Luke: And they were not able in the presence of the people to catch him by what he said; but marveling at his answer they were silent.

The Question about Man's Resurrection (Lk 20:27–40); F1–330; F4–575

St. Luke: There came to him some Sadducees, those who say that there is no resurrection, and they asked him a question, saying,

Sadducees: Teacher, Moses wrote for us that if a man's brother dies, having a wife but no children, the man must take the wife and raise up children for his brother. Now there were seven brothers; the first took a wife, and died without children; and the second and the third took her, and likewise all seven left no children and died.

Afterward the woman also died. In the resurrection, therefore, whose wife will the woman be? For the seven had her as wife.

St. Luke: And Jesus said to them,

Jesus: The sons of this age marry and are given in marriage; but those who are accounted worthy to attain to that age and to the resurrection from the dead neither marry nor are given in marriage, for they cannot die anymore, because they are equal to angels and are sons of God, being sons of the resurrection. But that the dead are raised, even Moses showed, in the passage about the bush, where he calls the Lord the God of Abraham and the God of Isaac and the God of Jacob. Now he is not God of the dead, but of the living; for all live to him.

St. Luke: And some of the scribes answered,

Scribes: Teacher, you have spoken well.

St. Luke: For they no longer dared to ask him any question.

~ A Question about the Messiah (Lk 20:41–44)

St. Luke: But he said to them,

Jesus: How can they say that the Christ is David's son? For David himself says in the Book of Psalms,

David: The Lord said to my Lord, Sit at my right hand, till I make your enemies a stool for your feet.

Jesus: David thus calls him Lord; so how is he his son?

~ Jesus Denounces the Hypocrisy of the Scribes (Lk 20:45–47)

St. Luke: And in the hearing of all the people he said to his disciples,

Jesus: Beware of the scribes, who like to go about in long robes, and love salutations in the marketplaces and the best seats in the synagogues and the places of honor at feasts, who devour widows' houses and for a pretense make long prayers. They will receive the greater condemnation.

Luke Chapter 21

The Widow's Offering (Lk 21:1–4); C10–2544

St. Luke: He looked up and saw the rich putting their gifts into the treasury; and he saw a poor widow put in two copper coins. And he said,

Jesus: Truly I tell you, this poor widow has put in more than all of them; for they all contributed out of their abundance, but she out of her poverty put in all the living that she had.

~ The Destruction of the Temple Foretold (Lk 21:5–9)

St. Luke: And as some spoke of the temple, how it was adorned with noble stones and offerings, he said,

Jesus: As for these things which you see, the days will come when there shall not be left here one stone upon another that will not be thrown down.

St. Luke: And they asked him,

Disciples: Teacher, when will this be, and what will be the sign when this is about to take place?

St. Luke: And he said,

Jesus: Take heed that you are not led astray; for many will come in my name, saying,

False prophet: I am he!

Jesus: and,

Second false prophet: The time is at hand!

Jesus: Do not go after them. And when you hear of wars and tumults, do not be terrified; for this must first take place, but the end will not be at once.

Signs and Persecutions (Lk 21:10–19); F7–675

St. Luke: Then he said to them,

Jesus: Nation will rise against nation, and kingdom against kingdom; there will be great earthquakes, and in various places famines and pestilences; and there will be terrors and great signs from heaven.

Jesus: But before all this they will lay their hands on you and persecute you, delivering you up to the synagogues and prisons, and you will be brought before kings and governors for my name's sake. This will be a time for you to bear testimony.

Settle it therefore in your minds, not to meditate beforehand how to answer; for I will give you a mouth and wisdom, which none of your adversaries will be able to withstand or contradict.

You will be delivered up even by parents and brothers and kinsmen and friends, and some of you they will put to death; you will be hated by all for my name's sake. But not a hair of your head will perish. By your endurance you will gain your lives.

The Destruction of Jerusalem Foretold (Lk 21:20–24); PF2–58; F7–674

Jesus: But when you see Jerusalem surrounded by armies, then know that its desolation has come near. Then let those who are in Judea flee to the mountains, and let those who are inside the city depart, and let not those who are out in the country enter it; for these are days of vengeance, to fulfil all that is written.

Alas for those who are with child and for those who give suck in those days! For great distress shall be upon the earth and wrath upon this people; they will fall by the edge of the sword, and be led captive among all nations; and Jerusalem will be trodden down by the Gentiles, until the times of the Gentiles are fulfilled.

The Coming of the Son of Man (Lk 21:25–28); F7–671; F8–697

Jesus: And there will be signs in sun and moon and stars, and upon the earth distress of nations in perplexity at the roaring of the sea and the waves, men fainting with fear and with foreboding of what is coming on the world; for the powers of the heavens will be shaken.

And then they will see the Son of man coming in a cloud with power and great glory. Now when these things begin to take place, look up and raise your heads, because your redemption is drawing near.

~ The Lesson of the Fig Tree (Lk 21:29–33)

St. Luke: And he told them a parable:

Jesus: Look at the fig tree, and all the trees; as soon as they come out in leaf, you see for yourselves and know that the summer is already near. So also, when you see these things taking place, you know that the kingdom of God is near.

Truly, I say to you, this generation will not pass away till all has taken place. Heaven and earth will pass away, but my words will not pass away.

Exhortation to Watchfulness (Lk 21:34–38); P–2612

Jesus: But take heed to yourselves lest your hearts be weighed down with dissipation and drunkenness and cares of this life, and that day come upon you suddenly like a snare; for it will come upon all who dwell upon the face of the whole earth. But watch at all times, praying that you may have strength to escape all these things that will take place, and to stand before the Son of man.

St. Luke: And every day he was teaching in the temple, but at night he went out and lodged on the mount called Olivet. And early in the morning all the people came to him in the temple to hear him.

Luke Chapter 22

~ The Conspiracy to Kill Jesus (Lk 22:1–6)

St. Luke: Now the feast of Unleavened Bread drew near, which is called the Passover. And the chief priests and the scribes were seeking how to put him to death; for they feared the people.

Then Satan entered into Judas called Iscariot, who was of the number of the twelve; he went away and conferred with the chief priests and officers how he might betray him to them. And they were glad, and engaged to give him money. So he agreed, and sought an opportunity to betray him to them in the absence of the multitude.

The Preparation of the Passover (Lk 22:7–13); LT–1151; S3–1339

St. Luke: Then came the day of Unleavened Bread, on which the Passover lamb had to be sacrificed.

St. Luke: So Jesus sent Peter and John, saying,

Jesus: Go and prepare the Passover for us, that we may eat it.

St. Luke: They said to him,

Peter and John: Where will you have us prepare it?

St. Luke: He said to them,

Jesus: Behold, when you have entered the city, a man carrying a jar of water will meet you; follow him into the house which he enters, and tell the householder, "The Teacher says to you, 'Where is the guest room, where I am to eat the Passover with my disciples?'" And he will show you a large upper room furnished; there make ready.

St. Luke: And they went, and found it as he had told them; and they prepared the Passover.

* Jesus Institutes the Eucharist (Lk 22:14–23); F4–610; S3–1328

St. Luke: And when the hour came, he sat at table, and the apostles with him. And he said to them,

Jesus: I have earnestly desired to eat this Passover with you before I suffer; for I tell you I shall not eat it until it is fulfilled in the kingdom of God.

St. Luke: And he took a chalice, and when he had given thanks he said,

Jesus: Take this, and divide it among yourselves; for I tell you that from now on I shall not drink of the fruit of the vine until the kingdom of God comes.

St. Luke: And he took bread, and when he had given thanks he broke it and gave it to them, saying,

Jesus: This is my body which is given for you. Do this in remembrance of me.

St. Luke: And likewise the chalice after supper, saying,

Jesus: This chalice which is poured out for you is the new covenant in my blood. But behold the hand of him who betrays me is with me on the table. For the Son of man goes as it has been determined; but woe to that man by whom he is betrayed!

St. Luke: And they began to question one another, which of them it was that would do this.

* The Dispute about Greatness (Lk 22:24–30); S6–1570; F9–787

St. Luke: A dispute also arose among them, which of them was to be regarded as the greatest. And he said to them,

Jesus: The kings of the Gentiles exercise lordship over them; and those in authority over them are called benefactors. But not so with you; rather let the greatest among you become as the youngest, and the leader as one who serves. For which is the greater, one who sits at table, or one who serves? Is it not the one who sits at table? But I am among you as one who serves. You are those who have continued with me in my trials; and I assign to you, as my Father assigned to me, a kingdom, that you may eat and drink at my table in my kingdom, and sit on thrones judging the twelve tribes of Israel.

* Peter's Denial Foretold (Lk 22:31–34); PF3–162; F3–552

Jesus: Simon, Simon, behold, Satan demanded to have you, that he might sift you like wheat, but I have prayed for you that your faith may not fail; and when you have turned again, strengthen your brethren.

St. Luke: And he said to him,

Peter: Lord, I am ready to go with you to prison and to death.

St. Luke: He said,

Jesus: I tell you, Peter, the cock will not crow this day, until you three times deny that you know me.

~ Purse, Bag, and Sword (Lk 22:35–38)

St. Luke: And he said to them,

Jesus: When I sent you out with no purse or bag or sandals, did you lack anything?

St. Luke: They said,

Apostles: Nothing.

St. Luke: He said to them,

Jesus: But now, let him who has a purse take it, and likewise a bag. And let him who has no sword sell his mantle and buy one. For I tell you that this Scripture must be fulfilled in me, "And he was reckoned with transgressors"; for what is written about me has its fulfilment.

St. Luke: And they said,

Apostles: Look, Lord, here are two swords.

St. Luke: And he said to them,

Jesus: It is enough.

* Jesus Prays on the Mount of Olives (Lk 22:39–46); F3–532; LP3–2824

St. Luke: And he came out, and went, as was his custom, to the Mount of Olives; and the disciples followed him. And when he came to the place he said to them,

Jesus: Pray that you may not enter into temptation.

St. Luke: And he withdrew from them about a stone's throw, and knelt down and prayed,

Jesus: Father, if you are willing, remove this chalise from me; nevertheless not my will, but yours, be done.

St. Luke: And there appeared to him an angel from heaven, strengthening him. And being in an agony he prayed more earnestly; and his sweat became like great drops of blood falling upon the ground. And when he rose from prayer, he came to the disciples and found them sleeping for sorrow, and he said to them,

Jesus: Why do you sleep? Rise and pray that you may not enter into temptation.

~ The Betrayal and Arrest of Jesus (Lk 22:47–53)

St. Luke: While he was still speaking, there came a crowd, and the man called Judas, one of the twelve, was leading them. He drew near to Jesus to kiss him; but Jesus said to him,

Jesus: Judas, would you betray the Son of man with a kiss?

St. Luke: And when those who were about him saw what would follow, they said,

Peter: Lord, shall we strike with the sword?

St. Luke: And one of them struck the slave of the high priest and cut off his right ear. But Jesus said,

Jesus: No more of this!

St. Luke: And he touched his ear and healed him. Then Jesus said to the chief priests and officers of the temple and elders, who had come out against him,

Jesus: Have you come out as against a robber, with swords and clubs? When I was with you day after day in the temple, you did not lay hands on me. But this is your hour, and the power of darkness.

Peter Denies Jesus (Lk 22:54–62); S4–1429

St. Luke: Then they seized him and led him away, bringing him into the high priest's house. Peter followed at a distance; and when they had kindled a fire in the middle of the courtyard and sat down together, Peter sat among them. Then a maid, seeing him as he sat in the light and gazing at him, said,

Maid: This man also was with him.

St. Luke: But he denied it, saying,

Peter: Woman, I do not know him.

St. Luke: And a little later someone else saw him and said,

Someone else: You also are one of them.

St. Luke: But Peter said,

Peter: Man, I am not.

St. Luke: And after an interval of about an hour still another insisted, saying,

Another person: Certainly this man also was with him; for he is a Galilean.

St. Luke: But Peter said,

Peter: Man, I do not know what you are saying.

St. Luke: And immediately, while he was still speaking, the cock crowed. And the Lord turned and looked at Peter. And Peter remembered the word of the Lord, how he had said to him, "Before the cock crows today, you will deny me three times." And he went out and wept bitterly.

~ The Mocking and Beating of Jesus (Lk 22:63–65)

St. Luke: Now the men who were holding Jesus mocked him and beat him; they also blindfolded him and asked him,

Men: Prophesy! Who is it that struck you?

St. Luke: And they spoke many other words against him, reviling him.

Jesus Before the Council (Lk 22:66–71); F2–443

St. Luke: When day came, the assembly of the elders of the people gathered together, both chief priests and scribes; and they led him away to their council, and they said,

Chief priests, scribes, and elders: If you are the Christ, tell us.

St. Luke: But he said to them,

Jesus: If I tell you, you will not believe; and if I ask you, you will not answer. But from now on the Son of man shall be seated at the right hand of the power of God.

St. Luke: And they all said,

Chief priests, scribes, and elders: Are you the Son of God, then?

St. Luke: And he said to them,

Jesus: You say that I am.

St. Luke: And they said,

Chief priests, scribes, and elders: What further testimony do we need? We have heard it ourselves from his own lips.

Luke Chapter 23

Jesus Before Pilate (Lk 23:1–5); F4–596

St. Luke: Then the whole company of them arose, and brought him before Pilate. And they began to accuse him, saying,

Chief priests, scribes, and elders: We found this man perverting our nation, and forbidding us to give tribute to Caesar, and saying that he himself is Christ a king.

St. Luke: And Pilate asked him,

Pilate: Are you the King of the Jews?

St. Luke: And he answered him,

Jesus: You have said so.

St. Luke: And Pilate said to the chief priests and the multitudes,

Pilate: I find no crime in this man.

St. Luke: But they were urgent, saying,

Chief priests and multitudes: He stirs up the people, teaching throughout all Judea, from Galilee even to this place.

~ Jesus Before Herod (Lk 23:6–12)

St. Luke: When Pilate heard this, he asked whether the man was a Galilean. And when he learned that he belonged to Herod's jurisdiction, he sent him over to Herod, who was himself in Jerusalem at that time.

When Herod saw Jesus, he was very glad, for he had long desired to see him, because he had heard about him, and he was hoping to see some sign done by him. So he questioned him at some length; but he made no answer. The chief priests and the scribes stood by, vehemently accusing him.

And Herod with his soldiers treated him with contempt and mocked him; then, arraying him in gorgeous apparel, he sent him back to Pilate.

And Herod and Pilate became friends with each other that very day, for before this they had been at enmity with each other.

Jesus Sentenced to Death (Lk 23:13–25); F4–596

St. Luke: Pilate then called together the chief priests and the rulers and the people, and said to them,

Pilate: You brought me this man as one who was perverting the people; and after examining him before you, behold, I did not find this man guilty of any of your charges against him; neither did Herod, for he sent him back to us. Behold, nothing deserving death has been done by him; I will therefore chastise him and release him.

St. Luke: But they all cried out together,

Chief priests, rulers, and people: Away with this man, and release to us Barabbas

St. Luke: —a man who had been thrown into prison for an insurrection started in the city, and for murder. Pilate addressed them once more, desiring to release Jesus; but they shouted out,

Chief priests, rulers, and people: Crucify, crucify him!

St. Luke: A third time he said to them,

Pilate: Why, what evil has he done? I have found in him no crime deserving death; I will therefore chastise him and release him.

St. Luke: But they were urgent, demanding with loud cries that he should be crucified. And their voices prevailed. So Pilate gave sentence that their demand should be granted. He released the man who had been thrown into prison for insurrection and murder, whom they asked for; but Jesus he delivered up to their will.

* The Crucifixion of Jesus (Lk 23:26–43); F4–591; P–2605

St. Luke: And as they led him away, they seized one Simon of Cyrene, who was coming in from the country, and laid on him the cross, to carry it behind Jesus. And there followed him a great multitude of the people, and of women who bewailed and lamented him. But Jesus turning to them said,

Jesus: Daughters of Jerusalem, do not weep for me, but weep for yourselves and for your children. For behold, the days are coming when they will say, "Blessed are the barren, and the wombs that never bore, and the breasts that never gave suck!" Then they will begin to say to the mountains, "Fall on us;" and to the hills, "Cover us." For if they do this when the wood is green, what will happen when it is dry?

St. Luke: Two others also, who were criminals, were led away to be put to death with him. And when they came to the place which is called The Skull, there they crucified him, and the criminals, one on the right and one on the left. And Jesus said,

Jesus: Father, forgive them; for they know not what they do.

St. Luke: And they cast lots to divide his garments. And the people stood by, watching; but the rulers scoffed at him, saying,

Rulers: He saved others; let him save himself, if he is the Christ of God, his Chosen One!

St. Luke: The soldiers also mocked him, coming up and offering him vinegar, and saying,

Soldiers: If you are the King of the Jews, save yourself!

St. Luke: There was also an inscription over him, "This is the King of the Jews." One of the criminals who were hanged railed at him, saying,

First criminal: Are you not the Christ? Save yourself and us!

St. Luke: But the other rebuked him, saying,

Second criminal: Do you not fear God, since you are under the same sentence of condemnation? And we indeed justly; for we are receiving the due reward of our deeds; but this man has done nothing wrong.

St. Luke: And he said,

Second criminal: Jesus, remember me when you come into your kingdom.

St. Luke: And he said to him,

Jesus: Truly, I say to you, today you will be with me in Paradise.

* The Death of Jesus (Lk 23:44–49); F8–730; F11–1011

St. Luke: It was now about the sixth hour, and there was darkness over the whole land until the ninth hour, while the sun's light failed; and the curtain of the temple was torn in two. Then Jesus, crying with a loud voice, said,

Jesus: Father, into your hands I commit my spirit!

St. Luke: And having said this he breathed his last. Now when the centurion saw what had taken place, he praised God, and said,

Centurion: Certainly this man was innocent!

St. Luke: And all the multitudes who assembled to see the sight, when they saw what had taken place, returned home beating their breasts. And all his acquaintances and the women who had followed him from Galilee stood at a distance and saw these things.

~ The Burial of Jesus (Lk 23:50–56)

St. Luke: Now there was a man named Joseph from the Jewish town of Arimathea. He was a member of the council, a good and righteous man, who had not consented to their purpose and deed, and he was looking for the kingdom of God. This man went to Pilate and asked for the body of Jesus.

Then he took it down and wrapped it in a linen shroud, and laid him in a rock-hewn tomb, where no one had ever yet been laid. It was the day of Preparation, and the sabbath was beginning.

The women who had come with him from Galilee followed, and saw the tomb, and how his body was laid; then they returned, and prepared spices and ointments. On the sabbath they rested according to the commandment.

Luke Chapter 24

* The Resurrection of Jesus (Lk 24:1–12); F5–641; C3–2174

St. Luke: But on the first day of the week, at early dawn, they went to the tomb, taking the spices which they had prepared. And they found the stone rolled away from the tomb, but when they went in they did not find the body. While they were perplexed about this, behold, two men stood by them in dazzling apparel; and as they were frightened and bowed their faces to the ground, the men said to them,

Angels: Why do you seek the living among the dead? He is not here, but has risen. Remember how he told you, while he was still in Galilee, that the Son of man must be delivered into the hands of sinful men, and be crucified, and on the third day rise.

St. Luke: And they remembered his words, and returning from the tomb they told all this to the eleven and to all the rest. Now it was Mary Magdalene and Joanna and Mary the mother of James and the other women with them who told this to the apostles; but these words seemed to them an idle tale, and they did not believe them.

But Peter rose and ran to the tomb; stooping and looking in, he saw the linen clothes by themselves; and he went home wondering at what had happened.

* The Walk to Emmaus (Lk 24:13–35); S3–1329; S3–1347

St. Luke: That very day two of them were going to a village named Emmaus, about seven miles from Jerusalem, and talking with each other about all these things that had happened. While they were talking and discussing together, Jesus himself drew near and went with them. But their eyes were kept from recognizing him. And he said to them,

Jesus: What is this conversation which you are holding with each other as you walk?

St. Luke: And they stood still, looking sad. Then one of them, named Cleopas, answered him,

Cleopas: Are you the only visitor to Jerusalem who does not know the things that have happened there in these days?

St. Luke: And he said to them,

Jesus: What things?

St. Luke: And they said to him,

Cleopas and the other man: Concerning Jesus of Nazareth, who was a prophet mighty in deed and word before God and all the people, and how our chief priests and rulers delivered him up to be condemned to death, and crucified him. But we had hoped that he was the one to redeem Israel. Yes, and besides all this, it is now the third day since this happened. Moreover, some women of our company amazed us. They were at the tomb early in the morning and did not find his body; and they came back saying that they had even seen a vision of angels, who said that he was alive. Some of those who were with us went to the tomb, and found it just as the women had said; but him they did not see.

St. Luke: And he said to them,

Jesus: O foolish men, and slow of heart to believe all that the prophets have spoken! Was it not necessary that the Christ should suffer these things and enter into his glory?

St. Luke: And beginning with Moses and all the prophets, he interpreted to them in all the Scriptures the things concerning himself. So they drew near to the village to which they were going. He appeared to be going further, but they constrained him, saying,

Cleopas and the other man: Stay with us, for it is toward evening and the day is now far spent.

St. Luke: So he went in to stay with them. When he was at table with them, he took the bread and blessed, and broke it, and gave it to them. And their eyes were opened and they recognized him; and he vanished out of their sight. They said to each other,

Cleopas and the other man: Did not our hearts burn within us while he talked to us on the road, while he opened to us the Scriptures?

St. Luke: And they rose that same hour and returned to Jerusalem; and they found the eleven gathered together and those who were with them, who said,

Apostles: The Lord has risen indeed, and has appeared to Simon!

St. Luke: Then they told what had happened on the road, and how he was known to them in the breaking of the bread.

* Jesus Appears to His Disciples (Lk 24:36–49); F10–981; LT–1120

St. Luke: As they were saying this, Jesus himself stood among them, and said to them,

Jesus: Peace to you.

St. Luke: But they were startled and frightened, and supposed that they saw a spirit. And he said to them,

Jesus: Why are you troubled, and why do questionings rise in your hearts? See my hands and my feet, that it is I myself; handle me, and see; for a spirit has not flesh and bones as you see that I have.

St. Luke: And when he had said this, he showed them his hands and his feet. And while they still disbelieved for joy, and wondered, he said to them,

Jesus: Have you anything here to eat?

St. Luke: They gave him a piece of broiled fish, and he took it and ate before them. Then he said to them,

Jesus: These are my words which I spoke to you, while I was still with you, that everything written about me in the law of Moses and the prophets and the psalms must be fulfilled.

St. Luke: Then he opened their minds to understand the Scriptures, and said to them,

Jesus: Thus it is written, that the Christ should suffer and on the third day rise from the dead, and that repentance and forgiveness of sins should be preached in his name to all nations, beginning from Jerusalem. You are witnesses of these things. And behold, I send the promise of my Father upon you; but stay in the city, until you are clothed with power from on high.

The Ascension of Jesus (Lk 24:50–53); F6–659

St. Luke: Then he led them out as far as Bethany, and lifting up his hands he blessed them. While he blessed them, he parted from them, and was carried up into heaven. And they worshipped him, and returned to Jerusalem with great joy, and were continually in the temple blessing God.

THE GOSPEL OF ST. JOHN

John Chapter 1

* The Word Became Flesh (Jn 1:1–18); F1–241; LP1–2780

St. John: In the beginning was the Word, and the Word was with God, and the Word was God. He was in the beginning with God; all things were made through him, and without him was not anything made that was made.

In him was life, and the life was the light of men. The light shines in the darkness, and the darkness has not overcome it.

There was a man sent from God, whose name was John. He came for testimony, to bear witness to the light, that all might believe through him. He was not the light, but came to bear witness to the light.

The true light that enlightens every man was coming into the world. He was in the world, and the world was made through him, yet the world knew him not. He came to his own home, and his own people received him not.

But to all who received him, who believed in his name, he gave power to become children of God; who were born, not of blood nor of the will of the flesh nor of the will of man, but of God.

And the Word became flesh and dwelt among us, full of grace and truth; we have beheld his glory, glory as of the only Son from the Father. John bore witness to him and cried,

John the Baptist: This was he of whom I said, "He who comes after me ranks before me, for he was before me."

St. John: And from his fullness have we all received, grace upon grace. For the law was given through Moses; grace and truth came through Jesus Christ. No one has ever seen God; the only Son, who is in the bosom of the Father, he has made him known.

* The Testimony of John The Baptist (Jn 1:19–28); F4–575; F4–613

St. John: And this is the testimony of John, when the Jews sent priests and Levites from Jerusalem to ask him,

Priests and Levites: Who are you?

St. John: He confessed, he did not deny, but confessed,

John the Baptist: I am not the Christ.

St. John: And they asked him,

Priests and Levites: What then? Are you Elijah?

St. John: He said,

John the Baptist: I am not.

Priests and Levites: Are you the prophet?

St. John: And he answered,

John the Baptist: No.

St. John: They said to him then,

Priests and Levites: Who are you? Let us have an answer for those who sent us. What do you say about yourself?

St. John: He said,

John the Baptist: I am the voice of one crying in the wilderness, "Make straight the way of the Lord," as the prophet Isaiah said.

St. John: Now they had been sent from the Pharisees. They asked him,

Priests and Levites: Then why are you baptizing, if you are neither the Christ, nor Elijah, nor the prophet?

St. John: John answered them,

John the Baptist: I baptize with water; but among you stands one whom you do not know, even he who comes after me, the thong of whose sandal I am not worthy to untie.

St. John: This took place in Bethany beyond the Jordan, where John was baptizing.

* The Lamb of God (Jn 1:29–34); F3–523; S5–1505

St. John: The next day he saw Jesus coming toward him, and said,

John the Baptist: Behold, the Lamb of God, who takes away the sin of the world! This is he of whom I said, "After me comes a man who ranks before me, for he was before me." I myself did not know him; but for this I came baptizing with water, that he might be revealed to Israel.

St. John: And John bore witness,

John the Baptist: I saw the Spirit descend as a dove from heaven, and it remained on him. I myself did not know him; but he who sent me to baptize with water said to me, "He on whom you see the Spirit descend and remain, this is he who baptizes with the Holy Spirit." And I have seen and have borne witness that this is the Son of God.

The First Disciples of Jesus (Jn 1:35–42); F4–608; F9–878

St. John: The next day again John was standing with two of his disciples; and he looked at Jesus as he walked, and said,

John the Baptist: Behold, the Lamb of God!

St. John: The two disciples heard him say this, and they followed Jesus. Jesus turned, and saw them following, and said to them,

Jesus: What do you seek?

St. John: And they said to him,

Two disciples: Rabbi,

St. John: (which means Teacher),

Two disciples: Where are you staying?

St. John: He said to them,

Jesus: Come and see.

St. John: They came and saw where he was staying; and they stayed with him that day, for it was about the tenth hour. One of the two who heard John speak, and followed him, was Andrew, Simon Peter's brother. He first found his brother Simon, and said to him,

Andrew: We have found the Messiah.

St. John: (which means Christ). He brought him to Jesus. Jesus looked at him, and said,

Jesus: So you are Simon the son of John? You shall be called Cephas (which means Peter).

Jesus Calls Philip and Nathanael (Jn 1:43–51); F9–878

St. John: The next day Jesus decided to go to Galilee. And he found Philip and said to him,

Jesus: Follow me.

St. John: Now Philip was from Bethsaida, the city of Andrew and Peter. Philip found Nathanael, and said to him,

Philip: We have found him of whom Moses in the law and also the prophets wrote, Jesus of Nazareth, the son of Joseph.

St. John: Nathanael said to him,

Nathanael: Can anything good come out of Nazareth?

St. John: Philip said to him,

Philip: Come and see.

St. John: Jesus saw Nathanael coming to him, and said of him,

Jesus: Behold, an Israelite indeed, in whom is no guile!

St. John: Nathanael said to him,

Nathanael: How do you know me?

St. John: Jesus answered him,

Jesus: Before Philip called you, when you were under the fig tree, I saw you.

St. John: Nathanael answered him,

Nathanael: Rabbi, you are the Son of God! You are the King of Israel!

St. John: Jesus answered him,

Jesus: Because I said to you, I saw you under the fig tree, do you believe? You shall see greater things than these.

St. John: And he said to him,

Jesus: Truly, truly, I say to you, you will see heaven opened, and the angels of God ascending and descending upon the Son of man.

John Chapter 2

* The Marriage at Cana (Jn 2:1–12); F3–486; S3–1335

St. John: On the third day there was a marriage at Cana in Galilee, and the mother of Jesus was there; Jesus also was invited to the marriage, with his disciples. When the wine failed, the mother of Jesus said to him,

Mother of Jesus: They have no wine.

St. John: And Jesus said to her,

Jesus: O woman, what have you to do with me? My hour has not yet come.

St. John: His mother said to the servants,

Mother of Jesus: Do whatever he tells you.

St. John: Now six stone jars were standing there, for the Jewish rites of purification, each holding twenty or thirty gallons. Jesus said to them,

Jesus: Fill the jars with water.

St. John: And they filled them up to the brim. He said to them,

Jesus: Now draw some out, and take it to the steward of the feast.

St. John: So they took it. When the steward of the feast tasted the water now become wine, and did not know where it came from (though the servants who had drawn the water knew), the steward of the feast called the bridegroom and said to him,

Steward: Every man serves the good wine first; and when men have drunk freely, then the poor wine; but you have kept the good wine until now.

St. John: This, the first of his signs, Jesus did at Cana in Galilee, and manifested his glory; and his disciples believed in him. After this he went down to Capernaum, with his mother and his brethren and his disciples; and there they stayed for a few days.

* The Cleansing of the Temple (Jn 2:13–25); F4–586; F11–994

St. John: The Passover of the Jews was at hand, and Jesus went up to Jerusalem. In the temple he found those who were selling oxen and sheep and pigeons, and the moneychangers at their business. And making a whip of cords, he drove them all, with the sheep and oxen, out of the temple; and he poured out the coins of the moneychangers and overturned their tables. And he told those who sold the pigeons,

Jesus: Take these things away; you shall not make my Father's house a house of trade.

St. John: His disciples remembered that it was written, "Zeal for your house will consume me." The Jews then said to him,

Jews: What sign have you to show us for doing this?

St. John: Jesus answered them,

Jesus: Destroy this temple, and in three days I will raise it up.

St. John: The Jews then said,

Jews: It has taken forty-six years to build this temple, and will you raise it up in three days?

St. John: But he spoke of the temple of his body. When therefore he was raised from the dead, his disciples remembered that he had said this; and they believed the Scripture and the word which Jesus had spoken. Now when he was in Jerusalem at the Passover feast, many believed in his name when they saw the signs which he did; but Jesus did not trust himself to them, because he knew all men and needed no one to bear witness of man; for he himself knew what was in man.

John Chapter 3

* Nicodemus Visits Jesus (Jn 3:1–21); F8–728; S2–1287

St. John: Now there was a man of the Pharisees, named Nicodemus, a ruler of the Jews. This man came to Jesus by night and said to him,

Nicodemus: Rabbi, we know that you are a teacher come from God; for no one can do these signs that you do, unless God is with him.

St. John: Jesus answered him,

Jesus: Truly, truly, I say to you, unless one is born anew, he cannot see the kingdom of God.

St. John: Nicodemus said to him,

Nicodemus: How can a man be born when he is old? Can he enter a second time into his mother's womb and be born?

St. John: Jesus answered,

Jesus: Truly, truly, I say to you, unless one is born of water and the Spirit, he cannot enter the kingdom of God. That which is born of the flesh is flesh, and that which is born of the Spirit is spirit. Do not marvel that I said to you, "You must be born anew." The wind blows where it wills, and you hear the sound of it, but you do not know whence it comes or whither it goes; so it is with everyone who is born of the Spirit.

St. John: Nicodemus said to him,

Nicodemus: How can this be?

St. John: Jesus answered him,

Jesus: Are you a teacher of Israel, and yet you do not understand this? Truly, truly, I say to you, we speak of what we know, and bear witness to what we have seen; but you do not receive our testimony. If I have told you earthly things and you do not believe, how can you believe if I tell you heavenly things?

No one has ascended into heaven but he who descended from heaven, the Son of man. And as Moses lifted up the serpent in the wilderness, so must the Son of man be lifted up, that whoever believes in him may have eternal life.

For God so loved the world that he gave his only Son, that whoever believes in him should not perish but have eternal life. For God sent the Son into the world, not to condemn the world, but that the world might be saved through him.

He who believes in him is not condemned; he who does not believe is condemned already, because he has not believed in the name of the only Son of God.

And this is the judgment, that the light has come into the world, and men loved darkness rather than light, because their deeds were evil. For everyone who does evil hates the light, and does not come to the light, lest his deeds should be exposed.

But he who does what is true comes to the light, that it may be clearly seen that his deeds have been wrought in God.

* Jesus and John the Baptist (Jn 3:22–30); F3–523; F9–796

St. John: After this Jesus and his disciples went into the land of Judea; there he remained with them and baptized. John also was baptizing at Aenon near Salim, because there was much water there; and people came and were baptized. For John had not yet been put in prison.

Now a discussion arose between John's disciples and a Jew over purifying. And they came to John, and said to him,

John's disciples: Rabbi, he who was with you beyond the Jordan, to whom you bore witness, here he is, baptizing, and all are going to him.

St. John: John answered,

John the Baptist: No one can receive anything except what is given him from heaven. You yourselves bear me witness, that I said, I am not the Christ, but I have been sent before him. He who has the bride is the bridegroom; the friend of the bridegroom, who stands and hears him, rejoices greatly at the bridegroom's voice; therefore this joy of mine is now full. He must increase, but I must decrease.

* He Who Comes from Heaven (Jn 3:31–36); F3–504; F8–690

St. John: He who comes from above is above all; he who is of the earth belongs to the earth, and of the earth he speaks; he who comes from heaven is above all. He bears witness to what he has seen and heard, yet no one receives his testimony; he who receives his testimony sets his seal to this, that God is true.

For he whom God has sent utters the words of God, for it is not by measure that he gives the Spirit; the Father loves the Son, and has given all things into his hand. He who believes in the Son has eternal life; he who does not obey the Son shall not see life, but the wrath of God rests upon him.

John Chapter 4

* Jesus and the Woman of Samaria (Jn 4:1–42); F2–439; LP3–2824

St. John: Now when the LORD knew that the Pharisees had heard that Jesus was making and baptizing more disciples than John (although Jesus himself did not baptize, but only his disciples), he left Judea and departed again to Galilee.

He had to pass through Samaria. So he came to a city of Samaria, called Sychar, near the field that Jacob gave to his son Joseph.

Jacob's well was there, and so Jesus, wearied as he was with his journey, sat down beside the well. It was about the sixth hour. There came a woman of Samaria to draw water. Jesus said to her,

Jesus: Give me a drink.

St. John: For his disciples had gone away into the city to buy food. The Samaritan woman said to him,

Samaritan woman: How is it that you, a Jew, ask a drink of me, a woman of Samaria?

St. John: For Jews have no dealings with Samaritans. Jesus answered her,

Jesus: If you knew the gift of God, and who it is that is saying to you, "Give me a drink," you would have asked him, and he would have given you living water.

St. John: The woman said to him,

Samaritan woman: Sir, you have nothing to draw with, and the well is deep; where do you get that living water? Are you greater than our father Jacob, who gave us the well, and drank from it himself, and his sons, and his cattle?

St. John: Jesus said to her,

Jesus: Everyone who drinks of this water will thirst again, but whoever drinks of the water that I shall give him will never thirst; the water that I shall give him will become in him a spring of water welling up to eternal life.

St. John: The woman said to him,

Samaritan woman: Sir, give me this water, that I may not thirst, nor come here to draw.

St. John: Jesus said to her,

Jesus: Go, call your husband, and come here.

St. John: The woman answered him,

Samaritan woman: I have no husband.

St. John: Jesus said to her,

Jesus: You are right in saying, "I have no husband," for you have had five husbands, and he whom you now have is not your husband; this you said truly.

St. John: The woman said to him,

Samaritan woman: Sir, I perceive that you are a prophet. Our fathers worshiped on this mountain; and you say that in Jerusalem is the place where men ought to worship.

St. John: Jesus said to her,

Jesus: Woman, believe me, the hour is coming when neither on this mountain nor in Jerusalem will you worship the Father. You worship what you do not know; we worship what we know, for salvation is from the Jews. But the hour is coming, and now is, when the true worshipers will worship the Father in spirit and truth, for such the Father seeks to worship him. God is Spirit, and those who worship him must worship in spirit and truth.

St. John: The woman said to him,

Samaritan woman: I know that Messiah is coming (he who is called Christ); when he comes, he will show us all things.

St. John: Jesus said to her,

Jesus: I who speak to you am he.

St. John: Just then his disciples came. They marveled that he was talking with a woman, but none said, "What do you wish?" or, "Why are you talking with her?" So the woman left her water jar, and went away into the city, and said to the people,

Samaritan woman: Come, see a man who told me all that I ever did. Can this be the Christ?

St. John: They went out of the city and were coming to him. Meanwhile the disciples besought him, saying,

Disciples: Rabbi, eat.

St. John: But he said to them,

Jesus: I have food to eat of which you do not know.

St. John: So the disciples said to one another,

Disciples: Has any one brought him food?

St. John: Jesus said to them,

Jesus: My food is to do the will of him who sent me, and to accomplish his work. Do you not say, "There are yet four months, then comes the harvest?" I tell you, lift up your eyes, and see how the fields are already white for harvest. He who reaps receives wages, and gathers fruit for eternal life, so that sower and reaper may rejoice together. For here the saying holds true, "One sows and another reaps." I sent you to reap that for which you did not labor; others have labored, and you have entered into their labor.

St. John: Many Samaritans from that city believed in him because of the woman's testimony, "He told me all that I ever did." So when the Samaritans came to him, they asked him to stay with them; and he stayed there two days. And many more believed because of his word. They said to the woman,

Samaritans: It is no longer because of your words that we believe, for we have heard for ourselves, and we know that this is indeed the Savior of the world.

~ Jesus Departs for Galilee (Jn 4:43–45)

St. John: After the two days he departed to Galilee. For Jesus himself testified that a prophet has no honor in his own country. So when he came to Galilee, the Galileans welcomed him, having seen all that he had done in Jerusalem at the feast, for they too had gone to the feast.

~ Jesus Heals an Official's Son (Jn 4:46–54)

St. John: So he came again to Cana in Galilee, where he had made the water wine. And at Capernaum there was an official whose son was ill. When he heard that Jesus had come from Judea to Galilee, he went and begged him to come down and heal his son, for he was at the point of death. Jesus therefore said to him,

Jesus: Unless you see signs and wonders you will not believe.

St. John: The official said to him,

Official: Sir, come down before my child dies.

St. John: Jesus said to him,

Jesus: Go; your son will live.

St. John: The man believed the word that Jesus spoke to him and went his way. As he was going down, his servants met him and told him that his son was living. So he asked them the hour when he began to mend, and they said to him,

Servants: Yesterday at the seventh hour the fever left him.

St. John: The father knew that was the hour when Jesus had said to him, "Your son will live;" And he himself believed, and all his household. This was now the second sign that Jesus did when he had come from Judea to Galilee.

John Chapter 5

* Jesus Heals on the Sabbath (Jn 5:1–18); F4–574; F4–589

St. John: After this there was a feast of the Jews, and Jesus went up to Jerusalem. Now there is in Jerusalem by the Sheep Gate a pool, in Hebrew called Bethzatha, which has five porticoes.

In these lay a multitude of invalids, blind, lame, paralyzed. One man was there, who had been ill for thirty-eight years. When Jesus saw him and knew that he had been lying there a long time, he said to him,

Jesus: Do you want to be healed?

St. John: The sick man answered him,

Sick man: Sir, I have no man to put me into the pool when the water is troubled, and while I am going another steps down before me.

St. John: Jesus said to him,

Jesus: Rise, take up your pallet, and walk.

St. John: And at once the man was healed, and he took up his pallet and walked. Now that day was the sabbath. So the Jews said to the man who was cured,

Jews: It is the sabbath, it is not lawful for you to carry your pallet.

St. John: But he answered them,

Healed man: The man who healed me said to me, "Take up your pallet, and walk."

St. John: They asked him,

Jews: Who is the man who said to you, "Take up your pallet, and walk?"

St. John: Now the man who had been healed did not know who it was, for Jesus had withdrawn, as there was a crowd in the place. Afterward, Jesus found him in the temple, and said to him,

Jesus: See, you are well! Sin no more, that nothing worse befall you.

St. John: The man went away and told the Jews that it was Jesus who had healed him.

St. John: And this was why the Jews persecuted Jesus, because he did this on the sabbath. But Jesus answered them,

Jesus: My Father is working still, and I am working.

St. John: This was why the Jews sought all the more to kill him, because he not only broke the sabbath but also called God his Father, making himself equal with God.

* The Authority of the Son (Jn 5:19–29); F12–1063; S4–1470

St. John: Jesus said to them,

Jesus: Truly, truly, I say to you, the Son can do nothing of his own accord, but only what he sees the Father doing; for whatever he does, that the Son does likewise. For the Father loves the Son, and shows him all that he himself is doing; and greater works than these will he show him, that you may marvel.

For as the Father raises the dead and gives them life, so also the Son gives life to whom he will. The Father judges no one, but has given all judgment to the Son, that all may honor the Son, even as they honor the Father. He who does not honor the Son does not honor the Father who sent him.

Jesus 2: Truly, truly, I say to you, he who hears my word and believes him who sent me, has eternal life; he does not come into judgment, but has passed from death to life.

Truly, truly, I say to you, the hour is coming, and now is, when the dead will hear the voice of the Son of God, and those who hear will live. For as the Father has life in himself, so he has granted the Son also to have life in himself, and has given him authority to execute judgment, because he is the Son of man.

Do not marvel at this; for the hour is coming when all who are in the tombs will hear his voice and come forth, those who have done good, to the resurrection of life, and those who have done evil, to the resurrection of judgment.

* The Testimony to Jesus (Jn 5:30–47); F9–859; LP3–2824

Jesus 3: I can do nothing on my own authority; as I hear, I judge; and my judgment is just, because I seek not my own will but the will of him who sent me.

If I bear witness to myself, my testimony is not true; there is another who bears witness to me, and I know that the testimony which he bears to me is true. You sent to John, and he has borne witness to the truth.

Not that the testimony which I receive is from man; but I say this that you may be saved.

He was a burning and shining lamp, and you were willing to rejoice for a while in his light. But the testimony which I have is greater than that of John; for the works which the Father has granted me to accomplish, these very works which I am doing, bear me witness that the Father has sent me.

And the Father who sent me has himself borne witness to me. His voice you have never heard, his form you have never seen; and you do not have his word abiding in you, for you do not believe him whom he has sent.

Jesus 4: You search the Scriptures, because you think that in them you have eternal life; and it is they that bear witness to me; yet you refuse to come to me that you may have life.

I do not receive glory from men. But I know that you have not the love of God within you. I have come in my Father's name, and you do not receive me; if another comes in his own name, him you will receive.

How can you believe, who receive glory from one another and do not seek the glory that comes from the only God? Do not think that I shall accuse you to the Father; it is Moses who accuses you, on whom you set your hope. If you believed Moses, you would believe me, for he wrote of me. But if you do not believe his writings, how will you believe my words?

John Chapter 6

* Feeding the Five Thousand (Jn 6:1–15); F2–439; F3–559

St. John: After this Jesus went to the other side of the Sea of Galilee, which is the Sea of Tiberias. And a multitude followed him, because they saw the signs which he did on those who were diseased. Jesus went up on the mountain, and there sat down with his disciples. Now the Passover, the feast of the Jews, was at hand. Lifting up his eyes, then, and seeing that a multitude was coming to him, Jesus said to Philip,

Jesus: How are we to buy bread, so that these people may eat?

St. John: This he said to test him, for he himself knew what he would do. Philip answered him,

Philip: Two hundred denarii would not buy enough bread for each of them to get a little.

St. John: One of his disciples, Andrew, Simon Peter's brother, said to him,

Andrew: There is a lad here who has five barley loaves and two fish; but what are they among so many?

St. John: Jesus said,

Jesus: Make the people sit down.

St. John: Now there was much grass in the place; so the men sat down, in number about five thousand. Jesus then took the loaves, and when he had given thanks, he distributed them to those who were seated; so also the fish, as much as they wanted. And when they had eaten their fill, he told his disciples,

Jesus: Gather up the fragments left over, that nothing may be lost.

St. John: So they gathered them up and filled twelve baskets with fragments from the five barley loaves, left by those who had eaten. When the people saw the sign which he had done, they said,

People: This is indeed the prophet who is to come into the world!

St. John: Perceiving then that they were about to come and take him by force to make him king, Jesus withdrew again to the mountain by himself.

~ Jesus Walks on the Sea (Jn 6:16–21)

St. John: When evening came, his disciples went down to the sea, got into a boat, and started across the sea to Capernaum. It was now dark, and Jesus had not yet come to them. The sea rose because a strong wind was blowing.

When they had rowed about three or four miles, they saw Jesus walking on the sea and drawing near to the boat. They were frightened, but he said to them,

Jesus: It is I; do not be afraid.

St. John: Then they were glad to take him into the boat, and immediately the boat was at the land to which they were going.

* The Bread from Heaven (Jn 6:22–59); LP4–2835; S3–1406

St. John: On the next day the people who remained on the other side of the sea saw that there had been only one boat there, and that Jesus had not entered the boat with his disciples, but that his disciples had gone away alone. However, boats from Tiberias came near the place where they ate the bread after the Lord had given thanks. So when the people saw that Jesus was not there, nor his disciples, they themselves got into the boats and went to Capernaum, seeking Jesus. When they found him on the other side of the sea, they said to him,

People: Rabbi, when did you come here?

St. John: Jesus answered them,

Jesus: Truly, truly, I say to you, you seek me, not because you saw signs, but because you ate your fill of the loaves. Do not labor for the food which perishes, but for the food which endures to eternal life, which the Son of man will give to you; for on him has God the Father set his seal.

St. John: Then they said to him,

People: What must we do, to be doing the works of God?

St. John: Jesus answered them,

Jesus: This is the work of God, that you believe in him whom he has sent.

St. John: So they said to him,

People: Then what sign do you do, that we may see, and believe you? What work do you perform? Our fathers ate the manna in the wilderness; as it is written, "He gave them bread from heaven to eat."

St. John: Jesus then said to them,

Jesus: Truly, truly, I say to you, it was not Moses who gave you the bread from heaven; my Father gives you the true bread from heaven. For the bread of God is that which comes down from heaven, and gives life to the world.

St. John: They said to him,

People: Lord, give us this bread always.

St. John: Jesus said to them,

Jesus: I am the bread of life; he who comes to me shall not hunger, and he who believes in me shall never thirst. But I said to you that you have seen me and yet do not believe. All that the Father gives me will come to me; and him who comes to me I will not cast out. For I have come down from heaven, not to do my own will, but the will of him who sent me; and this is the will of him who sent me, that I should lose nothing of all that he has given me, but raise it up at the last day. For this is the will of my Father, that everyone who sees the Son and believes in him should have eternal life; and I will raise him up at the last day.

St. John: The Jews then murmured at him, because he said,

Jesus: I am the bread which came down from heaven.

St. John: They said,

Jews: Is not this Jesus, the son of Joseph, whose father and mother we know? How does he now say, "I have come down from heaven?"

St. John: Jesus answered them,

Jesus: Do not murmur among yourselves. No one can come to me unless the Father who sent me draws him; and I will raise him up at the last day. It is written in the prophets, "And they shall all be taught by God." Everyone who has heard and learned from the Father comes to me. Not that any one has seen the Father except him who is from God; he has seen the Father. Truly, truly, I say to you, he who believes has eternal life. I am the bread of life. Your fathers ate the manna in the wilderness, and they died. This is the bread which comes down from heaven, that a man may eat of it and not die.

I am the living bread which came down from heaven; if any one eats of this bread, he will live forever; and the bread which I shall give for the life of the world is my flesh.

St. John: The Jews then disputed among themselves, saying,

Jews: How can this man give us his flesh to eat?

St. John: So Jesus said to them,

Jesus: Truly, truly, I say to you, unless you eat the flesh of the Son of man and drink his blood, you have no life in you; he who eats my flesh and drinks my blood has eternal life, and I will raise him up at the last day. For my flesh is food indeed, and my blood is drink indeed. He who eats my flesh and drinks my blood abides in me, and I in him. As the living Father sent me, and I live because of the Father, so he who eats me will live because of me. This is the bread which came down from heaven, not such as the fathers ate and died; he who eats this bread will live forever.

* The Words of Eternal Life (Jn 6:60–71); F2–440; F8–728

St. John: This he said in the synagogue, as he taught at Capernaum. Many of his disciples, when they heard it, said,

Many disciples: This is a hard saying; who can listen to it?

St. John: But Jesus, knowing in himself that his disciples murmured at it, said to them,

Jesus: Do you take offense at this? Then what if you were to see the Son of man ascending where he was before? It is the spirit that gives life, the flesh is of no avail; the words that I have spoken to you are spirit and life. But there are some of you that do not believe.

St. John: For Jesus knew from the first who those were that did not believe, and who it was that would betray him. And he said,

Jesus: This is why I told you that no one can come to me unless it is granted him by the Father.

St. John: After this many of his disciples drew back and no longer went about with him. Jesus said to the twelve,

Jesus: Do you also wish to go away?

St. John: Simon Peter answered him,

Peter: Lord, to whom shall we go? You have the words of eternal life; and we have believed, and have come to know, that you are the Holy One of God.

St. John: Jesus answered them,

Jesus: Did I not choose you, the twelve, and one of you is a devil?

St. John: He spoke of Judas the son of Simon Iscariot, for he, one of the twelve, was to betray him.

John Chapter 7

The Unbelief of Jesus' Brethren (Jn 7:1–9); F4–583

St. John: After this Jesus went about in Galilee; he would not go about in Judea, because the Jews sought to kill him. Now the Jews' feast of Tabernacles was at hand. So his brethren said to him,

Brethren: Leave here and go to Judea, that your disciples may see the works you are doing. For no man works in secret if he seeks to be known openly. If you do these things, show yourself to the world.

St. John: For even his brethren did not believe in him. Jesus said to them,

Jesus: My time has not yet come, but your time is always here. The world cannot hate you, but it hates me because I testify of it that its works are evil. Go to the feast yourselves; I am not going up to this feast, for my time has not yet fully come.

St. John: So saying, he remained in Galilee.

* Jesus at the Feast of Tabernacles (Jn 7:10–24); F4–581; F4–582

St. John: But after his brethren had gone up to the feast, then he also went up, not publicly but in private. The Jews were looking for him at the feast, and saying,

Jews: Where is he?

St. John: And there was much muttering about him among the people. While some said,

Some people: He is a good man,

St. John: Others said,

Other people: No, he is leading the people astray.

St. John: Yet for fear of the Jews no one spoke openly of him.

St. John: About the middle of the feast Jesus went up into the temple and taught. The Jews marveled at it, saying,

Jews: How is it that this man has learning, when he has never studied?

St. John: So Jesus answered them,

Jesus: My teaching is not mine, but his who sent me; if any man's will is to do his will, he shall know whether the teaching is from God or whether I am speaking on my own authority. He who speaks on his own authority seeks his own glory; but he who seeks the glory of him who sent him is true, and in him there is no falsehood. Did not Moses give you the law? Yet none of you keeps the law. Why do you seek to kill me?

St. John: The people answered,

People: You have a demon! Who is seeking to kill you?

St. John: Jesus answered them,

Jesus: I did one deed, and you all marvel at it. Moses gave you circumcision (not that it is from Moses, but from the fathers), and you circumcise a man upon the sabbath. If on the sabbath a man receives circumcision, so that the law of Moses may not be broken, are you angry with me because on the sabbath I made a man's whole body well? Do not judge by appearances, but judge with right judgment.

~ Is This the Christ? (Jn 7:25–31)

St. John: Some of the people of Jerusalem therefore said,

Some people: Is not this the man whom they seek to kill? And here he is, speaking openly, and they say nothing to him! Can it be that the authorities really know that this is the Christ? Yet we know where this man comes from; and when the Christ appears, no one will know where he comes from.

St. John: So Jesus proclaimed, as he taught in the temple,

Jesus: You know me, and you know where I come from? But I have not come of my own accord; he who sent me is true, and him you do not know. I know him, for I come from him, and he sent me.

St. John: So they sought to arrest him; but no one laid hands on him, because his hour had not yet come. Yet many of the people believed in him; they said,

Many people: When the Christ appears, will he do more signs than this man has done?

~ Officers Are Sent to Arrest Jesus (Jn 7:32–36)

St. John: The Pharisees heard the crowd thus muttering about him, and the chief priests and Pharisees sent officers to arrest him. Jesus then said,

Jesus: I shall be with you a little longer, and then I go to him who sent me; you will seek me and you will not find me; where I am you cannot come.

St. John: The Jews said to one another,

Jews: Where does this man intend to go that we shall not find him? Does he intend to go to the Dispersion among the Greeks and teach the Greeks? What does he mean by saying, "You will seek me and you will not find me," and, "Where I am you cannot come?"

* Rivers of Living Water (Jn 7:37–39); F8–728; S2–1287

St. John: On the last day of the feast, the great day, Jesus stood up and proclaimed,

Jesus: If any one thirst, let him come to me and drink. He who believes in me, as the Scripture has said, "Out of his heart shall flow rivers of living water."

St. John: Now this he said about the Spirit, which those who believed in him were to receive; for as yet the Spirit had not been given, because Jesus was not yet glorified.

~ Division among the People (Jn 7:40–44)

St. John: When they heard these words, some of the people said,

Some people: This is really the prophet.

St. John: Others said,

Other people: This is the Christ.

St. John: But some said,

group of people: Is the Christ to come from Galilee? Has not the Scripture said that the Christ is descended from David, and comes from Bethlehem, the village where David was?

St. John: So there was a division among the people over him. Some of them wanted to arrest him, but no one laid hands on him.

* The Authorities and the Woman Caught in Adultery (Jn 7:45–8:11); F4–575; F4–588

St. John: The officers then went back to the chief priests and Pharisees, who said to them,

Chief priests and Pharisees: Why did you not bring him?

St. John: The officers answered,

Officers: No man ever spoke like this man!

St. John: The Pharisees answered them,

Pharisees: Are you led astray, you also? Have any of the authorities or of the Pharisees believed in him? But this crowd, who do not know the law, are accursed.

St. John: Nicodemus, who had gone to him before, and who was one of them, said to them,

Nicodemus: Does our law judge a man without first giving him a hearing and learning what he does?

St. John: They replied,

Chief priests and Pharisees: Are you from Galilee too? Search and you will see that no prophet is to rise from Galilee.

St. John: They went each to his own house.

John Chapter 8

The Adulteress (Jn 8:1–11)

St. John: But Jesus went to the Mount of Olives. Early in the morning he came again to the temple; all the people came to him, and he sat down and taught them. The scribes and the Pharisees brought a woman who had been caught in adultery, and placing her in the midst they said to him,

Scribes and Pharisees: Teacher, this woman has been caught in the act of adultery. Now in the law Moses commanded us to stone such. What do you say about her?

St. John: This they said to test him, that they might have some charge to bring against him. Jesus bent down and wrote with his finger on the ground. And as they continued to ask him, he stood up and said to them,

Jesus: Let him who is without sin among you be the first to throw a stone at her.

St. John: And once more he bent down and wrote with his finger on the ground. But when they heard it, they went away, one by one, beginning with the eldest, and Jesus was left alone with the woman standing before him. Jesus looked up and said to her,

Jesus: Woman, where are they? Has no one condemned you?

St. John: She said,

Accused woman: No one, Lord.

St. John: And Jesus said,

Jesus: Neither do I condemn you; go, and do not sin again.

Jesus and the Light of the World (Jn 8:12–20); C8–2466

St. John: Again Jesus spoke to them, saying,

Jesus: I am the light of the world; he who follows me will not walk in darkness, but will have the light of life.

St. John: The Pharisees then said to him,

Pharisees: You are bearing witness to yourself; your testimony is not true.

St. John: Jesus answered,

Jesus: Even if I do bear witness to myself, my testimony is true, for I know where I have come from and where I am going, but you do not know whence I come or whither I am going. You judge according to the flesh, I judge no one. Yet even if I do judge, my judgment is true, for it is not I alone that judge, but I and he who sent me. In your law it is written that the testimony of two men is true; I bear witness to myself, and the Father who sent me bears witness to me.

St. John: They said to him therefore,

Pharisees: Where is your Father?

St. John: Jesus answered,

Jesus: You know neither me nor my Father; if you knew me, you would know my Father also.

St. John: These words he spoke in the treasury, as he taught in the temple; but no one arrested him, because his hour had not yet come.

* Jesus Alludes to His Death (Jn 8:21–30); F4–603; LP3–2824

St. John: Again he said to them,

Jesus: I go away, and you will seek me and die in your sin; where I am going, you cannot come.

St. John: Then said the Jews,

Jews: Will he kill himself, since he says, "Where I am going, you cannot come?"

St. John: He said to them,

Jesus: You are from below, I am from above; you are of this world, I am not of this world. I told you that you would die in your sins, for you will die in your sins unless you believe that I am he.

St. John: They said to him,

Pharisees: Who are you?

St. John: Jesus said to them,

Jesus: Even what I have told you from the beginning. I have much to say about you and much to judge; but he who sent me is true, and I declare to the world what I have heard from him.

St. John: They did not understand that he spoke to them of the Father. So Jesus said,

Jesus: When you have lifted up the Son of man, then you will know that I am he, and that I do nothing on my own authority but speak thus as the Father taught me. And he who sent me is with me; he has not left me alone, for I always do what is pleasing to him.

St. John: As he spoke thus, many believed in him.

* True Disciples of Jesus (Jn 8:31–38); PF2–89; C8–2466

St. John: Jesus then said to the Jews who had believed in him,

Jesus: If you continue in my word, you are truly my disciples, and you will know the truth, and the truth will make you free.

St. John: They answered him,

Jews: We are descendants of Abraham, and have never been in bondage to any one. How is it that you say, "You will be made free?"

St. John: Jesus answered them,

Jesus: Truly, truly, I say to you, everyone who commits sin is a slave to sin. The slave does not continue in the house for ever; the son continues for ever. So if the Son makes you free, you will be free indeed. I know that you are descendants of Abraham; yet you seek to kill me, because my word finds no place in you. I speak of what I have seen with my Father, and you do what you have heard from your father.

* Jesus and Abraham (Jn 8:39–59); F1–391; LP7–2852

St. John: They answered him,

Jews: Abraham is our father.

St. John: Jesus said to them,

Jesus: If you were Abraham's children, you would do what Abraham did, but now you seek to kill me, a man who has told you the truth which I heard from God; this is not what Abraham did. You do what your father did.

St. John: They said to him,

Jews: We were not born of fornication; we have one Father, even God.

St. John: Jesus said to them,

Jesus: If God were your Father, you would love me, for I proceeded and came forth from God; I came not of my own accord, but he sent me. Why do you not understand what I say? It is because you cannot bear to hear my word. You are of your father the devil, and your will is to do your father's desires. He was a murderer from the beginning, and has nothing to do with the truth, because there is no truth in him. When he lies, he speaks according to his own nature, for he is a liar and the father of lies. But, because I tell the truth, you do not believe me. Which of you convicts me of sin? If I tell the truth, why do you not believe me? He who is of God hears the words of God; the reason why you do not hear them is that you are not of God.

St. John: The Jews answered him,

Jews: Are we not right in saying that you are a Samaritan and have a demon?

St. John: Jesus answered,

Jesus: I have not a demon; but I honor my Father, and you dishonor me. Yet I do not seek my own glory; there is One who seeks it and he will be the judge. Truly, truly, I say to you, if any one keeps my word, he will never see death.

St. John: The Jews said to him,

Jews: Now we know that you have a demon. Abraham died, as did the prophets; and you say, "If any one keeps my word, he will never taste death." Are you greater than our father Abraham, who died? And the prophets died! Who do you claim to be?

St. John: Jesus answered,

Jesus: If I glorify myself, my glory is nothing; it is my Father who glorifies me, of whom you say that he is your God. But you have not known him; I know him. If I said, "I do not know him," I should be a liar like you; but I do know him and I keep his word. Your father Abraham rejoiced that he was to see my day; he saw it and was glad.

St. John: The Jews then said to him,

Jews: You are not yet fifty years old, and have you seen Abraham?

St. John: Jesus said to them,

Jesus: Truly, truly, I say to you, before Abraham was, I am.

St. John: So they took up stones to throw at him; but Jesus hid himself, and went out of the temple.

John Chapter 9

* Healing of the Blind Man (Jn 9:1–12); LT–1151; S5–1504

St. John: As he passed by, he saw a man blind from his birth. And his disciples asked him,

Disciples: Rabbi, who sinned, this man or his parents, that he was born blind?

St. John: Jesus answered,

Jesus: It was not that this man sinned, or his parents, but that the works of God might be made manifest in him. We must work the works of him who sent me, while it is day; night comes, when no one can work. As long as I am in the world, I am the light of the world.

St. John: As he said this, he spat on the ground and made clay of the spittle and anointed the man's eyes with the clay, saying to him,

Jesus: Go, wash in the pool of Siloam (which means Sent).

St. John: So he went and washed and came back seeing. The neighbors and those who had seen him before as a beggar, said,

Neighbors: Is not this the man who used to sit and beg?

St. John: Some said,

Some people: It is he;

St. John: Others said,

Other people: No, but he is like him.

St. John: He said,

Formerly blind man: I am the man.

St. John: They said to him,

People: Then how were your eyes opened?

St. John: He answered,

Formerly blind man: The man called Jesus made clay and anointed my eyes and said to me, "Go to Siloam and wash," so I went and washed and received my sight.

St. John: They said to him,

People: Where is he?

St. John: He said,

Formerly blind man: I do not know.

* The Pharisees Investigate the Healing (Jn 9:13–34); F4–596; C3–2173

St. John: They brought to the Pharisees the man who had formerly been blind. Now it was a sabbath day when Jesus made the clay and opened his eyes. The Pharisees again asked him how he had received his sight. And he said to them,

Formerly blind man: He put clay on my eyes, and I washed, and I see.

St. John: Some of the Pharisees said,

Some Pharisees: This man is not from God, for he does not keep the sabbath.

St. John: But others said,

Other Pharisees: How can a man who is a sinner do such signs?

St. John: There was a division among them. So they again said to the blind man,

Pharisees: What do you say about him, since he has opened your eyes?

St. John: He said,

Formerly blind man: He is a prophet.

St. John: The Jews did not believe that he had been blind and had received his sight, until they called the parents of the man who had received his sight, and asked them,

Jews: Is this your son, who you say was born blind? How then does he now see?

St. John: His parents answered,

Parents of formerly blind man: We know that this is our son, and that he was born blind; but how he now sees we do not know, nor do we know who opened his eyes. Ask him; he is of age, he will speak for himself.

St. John: His parents said this because they feared the Jews, for the Jews had already agreed that if any one should confess him to be Christ, he was to be put out of the synagogue. Therefore his parents said,

Parents of formerly blind man: He is of age, ask him.

St. John: So for the second time they called the man who had been blind, and said to him,

Jews: Give God the praise; we know that this man is a sinner.

St. John: He answered,

Formerly blind man: Whether he is a sinner, I do not know; one thing I know, that though I was blind, now I see.

St. John: They said to him,

Jews: What did he do to you? How did he open your eyes?

St. John: He answered them,

Formerly blind man: I have told you already, and you would not listen. Why do you want to hear it again? Do you too want to become his disciples?

St. John: And they reviled him, saying,

Jews: You are his disciple, but we are disciples of Moses. We know that God has spoken to Moses, but as for this man, we do not know where he comes from.

St. John: The man answered,

Formerly blind man: Why, this is a marvel! You do not know where he comes from, and yet he opened my eyes. We know that God does not listen to sinners, but if any one is a worshiper of God and does his will, God listens to him. Never since the world began has it been heard that any one opened the eyes of a man born blind. If this man were not from God, he could do nothing.

St. John: They answered him,

Jews: You were born in utter sin, and would you teach us?

St. John: And they cast him out.

Spiritual Blindness (Jn 9:35–41); F4–588

St. John: Jesus heard that they had cast him out, and having found him he said,

Jesus: Do you believe in the Son of man?

St. John: He answered,

Formerly blind man: And who is he, sir, that I may believe in him?

St. John: Jesus said to him,

Jesus: You have seen him, and it is he who speaks to you.

St. John: He said,

Formerly blind man: Lord, I believe;

St. John: And he worshipped him. Jesus said,

Jesus: For judgment I came into this world, that those who do not see may see, and that those who see may become blind.

St. John: Some of the Pharisees near him heard this, and they said to him,

Some Pharisees: Are we also blind?

St. John: Jesus said to them,

Jesus: If you were blind, you would have no guilt; but now that you say, "We see," your guilt remains.

John Chapter 10

* Jesus the Good Shepherd (Jn 10:1–21); F9–764; C2–2158

Jesus: Truly, truly, I say to you, he who does not enter the sheepfold by the door but climbs in by another way, that man is a thief and a robber; but he who enters by the door is the shepherd of the sheep. To him the gatekeeper opens; the sheep hear his voice, and he calls his own sheep by name and leads them out. When he has brought out all his own, he goes before them, and the sheep follow him, for they know his voice. A stranger they will not follow, but they will flee from him, for they do not know the voice of strangers.

St. John: This figure Jesus used with them, but they did not understand what he was saying to them. So Jesus again said to them,

Jesus: Truly, truly, I say to you, I am the door of the sheep. All who came before me are thieves and robbers; but the sheep did not heed them.

I am the door; if any one enters by me, he will be saved, and will go in and out and find pasture. The thief comes only to steal and kill and destroy; I came that they may have life, and have it abundantly.

I am the good shepherd. The good shepherd lays down his life for the sheep. He who is a hireling and not a shepherd, whose own the sheep are not, sees the wolf coming and leaves the sheep and flees; and the wolf snatches them and scatters them. He flees because he is a hireling and cares nothing for the sheep.

I am the good shepherd; I know my own and my own know me, as the Father knows me and I know the Father; and I lay down my life for the sheep. And I have other sheep, that are not of this fold; I must bring them also, and they will heed my voice.

So there shall be one flock, one shepherd. For this reason the Father loves me, because I lay down my life, that I may take it again. No one takes it from me, but I lay it down of my own accord. I have power to lay it down, and I have power to take it again; this charge I have received from my Father.

St. John: There was again a division among the Jews because of these words. Many of them said,

Many Jews: He has a demon, and he is mad; why listen to him?

St. John: Others said,

Other Jews: These are not the sayings of one who has a demon. Can a demon open the eyes of the blind?

* Jesus Is Rejected by the Jews (Jn 10:22–42); F2–437; S6–1562

St. John: It was the feast of the Dedication at Jerusalem; it was winter, and Jesus was walking in the temple, in the portico of Solomon. So the Jews gathered round him and said to him,

Jews: How long will you keep us in suspense? If you are the Christ, tell us plainly.

St. John: Jesus answered them,

Jesus: I told you, and you do not believe. The works that I do in my Father's name, they bear witness to me; but you do not believe, because you do not belong to my sheep. My sheep hear my voice, and I know them, and they follow me; and I give them eternal life, and they shall never perish, and no one shall snatch them out of my hand. My Father, who has given them to me, is greater than all, and no one is able to snatch them out of the Father's hand. I and the Father are one.

St. John: The Jews took up stones again to stone him. Jesus answered them,

Jesus: I have shown you many good works from the Father; for which of these do you stone me?

St. John: The Jews answered him,

Jews: It is not for a good work that we stone you but for blasphemy; because you, being a man, make yourself God.

St. John: Jesus answered them,

Jesus: Is it not written in your law, "I said, you are gods?" If he called them gods to whom the word of God came (and Scripture cannot be nullified), do you say of him whom the Father consecrated and sent into the world, "You are blaspheming," because I said, "I am the Son of God?" If I am not doing the works of my Father, then do not believe me; but if I do them, even though you do not believe me, believe the works, that you may know and understand that the Father is in me and I am in the Father.

St. John: Again they tried to arrest him, but he escaped from their hands. He went away again across the Jordan to the place where John at first baptized, and there he remained. And many came to him; and they said,

Many people: John did no sign, but everything that John said about this man was true.

St. John: And many believed in him there.

John Chapter 11

The Death of Lazarus (Jn 11:1–16); F11–994

St. John: Now a certain man was ill, Lazarus of Bethany, the village of Mary and her sister Martha. It was Mary who anointed the Lord with ointment and wiped his feet with her hair, whose brother Lazarus was ill. So the sisters sent to him, saying,

Sisters of Lazarus: Lord, he whom you love is ill.

St. John: But when Jesus heard it he said,

Jesus: This illness is not unto death; it is for the glory of God, so that the Son of God may be glorified by means of it.

St. John: Now Jesus loved Martha and her sister and Lazarus. So when he heard that he was ill, he stayed two days longer in the place where he was. Then after this he said to the disciples,

Jesus: Let us go into Judea again.

St. John: The disciples said to him,

Disciples: Rabbi, the Jews were but now seeking to stone you, and are you going there again?

St. John: Jesus answered,

Jesus: Are there not twelve hours in the day? If any one walks in the day, he does not stumble, because he sees the light of this world. But if any one walks in the night, he stumbles, because the light is not in him.

St. John: Thus he spoke, and then he said to them,

Jesus: Our friend Lazarus has fallen asleep, but I go to awake him out of sleep.

St. John: The disciples said to him,

Disciples: Lord, if he has fallen asleep, he will recover.

St. John: Now Jesus had spoken of his death, but they thought that he meant taking rest in sleep. Then Jesus told them plainly,

Jesus: Lazarus is dead; and for your sake I am glad that I was not there, so that you may believe. But let us go to him.

St. John: Thomas, called the Twin, said to his fellow disciples,

Thomas: Let us also go, that we may die with him.

* Jesus the Resurrection and the Life (Jn 11:17–27); F11–993; F11–1001

St. John: Now when Jesus came, he found that Lazarus had already been in the tomb four days. Bethany was near Jerusalem, about two miles off, and many of the Jews had come to Martha and Mary to console them concerning their brother. When Martha heard that Jesus was coming, she went and met him, while Mary sat in the house. Martha said to Jesus,

Martha: Lord, if you had been here, my brother would not have died. And even now I know that whatever you ask from God, God will give you.

St. John: Jesus said to her,

Jesus: Your brother will rise again.

St. John: Martha said to him,

Martha: I know that he will rise again in the resurrection at the last day.

St. John: Jesus said to her,

Jesus: I am the resurrection and the life; he who believes in me, though he die, yet shall he live, and whoever lives and believes in me shall never die. Do you believe this?

St. John: She said to him,

Martha: Yes, Lord; I believe that you are the Christ, the Son of God, he who is coming into the world.

Jesus Weeps (Jn 11:28–37); F4–581; F3–472

St. John: When she had said this, she went and called her sister Mary, saying quietly,

Martha: The Teacher is here and is calling for you.

St. John: And when she heard it, she rose quickly and went to him. Now Jesus had not yet come to the village, but was still in the place where Martha had met him. When the Jews who were with her in the house, consoling her, saw Mary rise quickly and go out, they followed her, supposing that she was going to the tomb to weep there. Then Mary, when she came where Jesus was and saw him, fell at his feet, saying to him,

Mary: Lord, if you had been here, my brother would not have died.

St. John: When Jesus saw her weeping, and the Jews who came with her also weeping, he was deeply moved in spirit and troubled; and he said,

Jesus: Where have you laid him?

St. John: They said to him,

Martha and Mary: Lord, come and see.

St. John: Jesus wept. So the Jews said,

Some Jews: See how he loved him!

St. John: But some of them said,

Other Jews: Could not he who opened the eyes of the blind man have kept this man from dying?

* Jesus Raises Lazarus to Life (Jn 11:38–44); P–2604; F5–640

St. John: Then Jesus, deeply moved again, came to the tomb; it was a cave, and a stone lay upon it. Jesus said,

Jesus: Take away the stone.

St. John: Martha, the sister of the dead man, said to him,

Martha: Lord, by this time there will be an odor, for he has been dead four days.

St. John: Jesus said to her,

Jesus: Did I not tell you that if you would believe you would see the glory of God?

St. John: So they took away the stone. And Jesus lifted up his eyes and said,

Jesus: Father, I thank you that you have heard me. I knew that you hear me always, but I have said this on account of the people standing by, that they may believe that you did send me.

St. John: When he had said this, he cried with a loud voice,

Jesus: Lazarus, come out.

St. John: The dead man came out, his hands and feet bound with bandages, and his face wrapped with a cloth. Jesus said to them,

Jesus: Unbind him, and let him go.

* The Plot to Put Jesus to Death (Jn 11:45–57); PF2–58; LP1–2793

St. John: Many of the Jews therefore, who had come with Mary and had seen what he did, believed in him; but some of them went to the Pharisees and told them what Jesus had done. So the chief priests and the Pharisees gathered the council, and said,

Chief priests and Pharisees: What are we to do? For this man performs many signs. If we let him go on thus, everyone will believe in him, and the Romans will come and destroy both our holy place and our nation.

St. John: But one of them, Caiaphas, who was high priest that year, said to them,

Caiaphas: You know nothing at all; you do not understand that it is expedient for you that one man should die for the people, and that the whole nation should not perish.

St. John: He did not say this of his own accord, but being high priest that year he prophesied that Jesus should die for the nation, and not for the nation only, but to gather into one the children of God who are scattered abroad.

So from that day on they took counsel how to put him to death. Jesus therefore no longer went about openly among the Jews, but went from there to the country near the wilderness, to a town called Ephraim; and there he stayed with the disciples.

Now the Passover of the Jews was at hand, and many went up from the country to Jerusalem before the Passover, to purify themselves. They were looking for Jesus and saying to one another as they stood in the temple,

People in the Temple: What do you think? That he will not come to the feast?

St. John: Now the chief priests and the Pharisees had given orders that if any one knew where he was, he should let them know, so that they might arrest him.

John Chapter 12

Mary of Bethany Anoints Jesus (Jn 12:1–8); C7–2449

St. John: Six days before the Passover, Jesus came to Bethany, where Lazarus was, whom Jesus had raised from the dead. There they made him a supper; Martha served, and Lazarus was one of those at table with him. Mary took a pound of costly ointment of pure nard and anointed the feet of Jesus and wiped his feet with her hair; and the house was filled with the fragrance of the ointment. But Judas Iscariot, one of his disciples (he who was to betray him), said,

Judas Iscariot: Why was this ointment not sold for three hundred denarii and given to the poor?

St. John: This he said, not that he cared for the poor but because he was a thief, and as he had the money box he used to take what was put into it. Jesus said,

Jesus: Let her alone; let her keep it for the day of my burial. The poor you always have with you, but you do not always have me.

~ The Plot to Put Lazarus to Death (Jn 12:9–11)

St. John: When the great crowd of the Jews learned that he was there, they came, not only on account of Jesus but also to see Lazarus, whom he had raised from the dead. So the chief priests planned to put Lazarus also to death, because on account of him many of the Jews were going away and believing in Jesus.

~ Jesus' Triumphal Entry into Jerusalem (Jn 12:12–19)

St. John: The next day a great crowd who had come to the feast heard that Jesus was coming to Jerusalem. So they took branches of palm trees and went out to meet him, crying,

Crowd of the Jews: Hosanna! Blessed is he who comes in the name of the Lord, even the King of Israel!

St. John: And Jesus found a young donkey and sat upon it; as it is written, "Fear not, daughter of Zion; behold, your king is coming, sitting on a donkey's colt!" His disciples did not understand this at first; but when Jesus was glorified, then they remembered that this had been written of him and had been done to him. The crowd that had been with him when he called Lazarus out of the tomb and raised him from the dead bore witness. The reason why the crowd went to meet him was that they heard he had done this sign. The Pharisees then said to one another,

Pharisees: You see that you can do nothing; look, the world has gone after him.

Some Greeks Wish to See Jesus (Jn 12:20–26); P–2731

St. John: Now among those who went up to worship at the feast were some Greeks. So these came to Philip, who was from Bethsaida in Galilee, and said to him,

Some Greeks: Sir, we wish to see Jesus.

St. John: Philip went and told Andrew; Andrew went with Philip and they told Jesus. And Jesus answered them,

Jesus: The hour has come for the Son of man to be glorified. Truly, truly, I say to you, unless a grain of wheat falls into the earth and dies, it remains alone; but if it dies, it bears much fruit. He who loves his life loses it, and he who hates his life in this world will keep it for eternal life. If any one serves me, he must follow me; and where I am, there shall my servant be also; if any one serves me, the Father will honor him.

* Jesus Speaks about His Death (Jn 12:27–36); S4–1428; LP1–2795

Jesus: Now is my soul troubled. And what shall I say? "Father, save me from this hour?" No, for this purpose I have come to this hour. Father, glorify your name.

St. John: Then a voice came from heaven,

God the Father: I have glorified it, and I will glorify it again.

St. John: The crowd standing by heard it and said that it had thundered. Others said,

Some of the crowd: An angel has spoken to him.

St. John: Jesus answered,

Jesus: This voice has come for your sake, not for mine. Now is the judgment of this world, now shall the ruler of this world be cast out; and I, when I am lifted up from the earth, will draw all men to myself.

St. John: He said this to show by what death he was to die. The crowd answered him,

Crowd: We have heard from the law that the Christ remains forever. How can you say that the Son of man must be lifted up? Who is this Son of man?

St. John: Jesus said to them,

Jesus: The light is with you for a little longer. Walk while you have the light, lest the darkness overtake you; he who walks in the darkness does not know where he goes. While you have the light, believe in the light, that you may become sons of light.

* The Unbelief of the People (Jn 12:37–43); F4–582; F8–712

St. John: When Jesus had said this, he departed and hid himself from them. Though he had done so many signs before them, yet they did not believe in him; it was that the word spoken by the prophet Isaiah might be fulfilled:

Isaiah: Lord, who has believed our report, and to whom has the arm of the Lord been revealed?

St. John: Therefore they could not believe. For Isaiah again said,

Isaiah: He has blinded their eyes and hardened their heart, lest they should see with their eyes and perceive with their heart, and turn for me to heal them.

St. John: Isaiah said this because he saw his glory and spoke of him. Nevertheless many even of the authorities believed in him, but for fear of the Pharisees they did not confess it, lest they should be put out of the synagogue: for they loved the praise of men more than the praise of God.

* Summary of Jesus' Teaching (Jn 12:44–50); F7–679; F12–1039

St. John: And Jesus cried out and said,

Jesus: He who believes in me, believes not in me but in him who sent me. And he who sees me sees him who sent me. I have come as light into the world, that whoever believes in me may not remain in darkness. If any one hears my sayings and does not keep them, I do not judge him; for I did not come to judge the world but to save the world.

He who rejects me and does not receive my sayings has a judge; the word that I have spoken will be his judge on the last day. For I have not spoken on my own authority; the Father who sent me has himself given me commandment what to say and what to speak. And I know that his commandment is eternal life. What I say, therefore, I say as the Father has bidden me.

John Chapter 13

* Jesus Washes the Disciples' Feet (Jn 13:1–20); S5–1524; LP5–2843

St. John: Now before the feast of the Passover, when Jesus knew that his hour had come to depart out of this world to the Father, having loved his own who were in the world, he loved them to the end. And during supper, when the devil had already put it into the heart of Judas Iscariot, Simon's son, to betray him, Jesus, knowing that the Father had given all things into his hands, and that he had come from God and was going to God, rose from supper, laid aside his garments, and tied a towel around himself. Then he poured water into a basin, and began to wash the disciples' feet, and to wipe them with the towel that was tied around him. He came to Simon Peter; and Peter said to him,

Peter: Lord, do you wash my feet?

St. John: Jesus answered him,

Jesus: What I am doing you do not know now, but afterward you will understand.

St. John: Peter said to him,

Peter: You shall never wash my feet.

St. John: Jesus answered him,

Jesus: If I do not wash you, you have no part in me.

St. John: Simon Peter said to him,

Peter: Lord, not my feet only but also my hands and my head!

St. John: Jesus said to him,

Jesus: He who has bathed does not need to wash, except for his feet, but he is clean all over; and you are clean, but not every one of you.

St. John: For he knew who was to betray him; that was why he said,

Jesus: You are not all clean.

St. John: When he had washed their feet, and taken his garments, and resumed his place, he said to them,

Jesus: Do you know what I have done to you? You call me Teacher and Lord; and you are right, for so I am. If I then, your Lord and Teacher, have washed your feet, you also ought to wash one another's feet. For I have given you an example, that you also should do as I have done to you. Truly, truly, I say to you, a servant is not greater than his master; nor is he who is sent greater than he who sent him. If you know these things, blessed are you if you do them.

I am not speaking of you all; I know whom I have chosen; it is that the Scripture may be fulfilled, "He who ate my bread has lifted his heel against me." I tell you this now, before it takes place, that when it does take place you may believe that I am he. Truly, truly, I say to you, he who receives any one whom I send receives me; and he who receives me receives him who sent me.

~ Jesus Foretells His Betrayal (Jn 13:21–30)

St. John: When Jesus had thus spoken, he was troubled in spirit, and testified,

Jesus: Truly, truly, I say to you, one of you will betray me.

St. John: The disciples looked at one another, uncertain of whom he spoke. One of his disciples, whom Jesus loved, was lying close to the breast of Jesus; so Simon Peter beckoned to him and said,

Peter: Tell us who it is of whom he speaks.

St. John: So lying thus, close to the breast of Jesus, he said to him,

Disciple whom Jesus loved: Lord, who is it?

St. John: Jesus answered,

Jesus: It is he to whom I shall give this morsel when I have dipped it.

St. John: So when he had dipped the morsel, he gave it to Judas, the son of Simon Iscariot. Then after the morsel, Satan entered into him. Jesus said to him,

Jesus: What you are going to do, do quickly.

St. John: Now no one at the table knew why he said this to him. Some thought that, because Judas had the money box, Jesus was telling him, "Buy what we need for the feast;" or, that he should give something to the poor. So, after receiving the morsel, he immediately went out; and it was night.

* The New Commandment (Jn 13:31–35); C3–2195; LP3–2822

St. John: When he had gone out, Jesus said,

Jesus: Now is the Son of man glorified, and in him God is glorified; if God is glorified in him, God will also glorify him in himself, and glorify him at once. Little children, yet a little while I am with you. You will seek me; and as I said to the Jews so now I say to you, "Where I am going you cannot come." A new commandment I give to you, that you love one another; even as I have loved you, that you also love one another. By this all men will know that you are my disciples, if you have love for one another.

~ Jesus Foretells Peter's Denial (Jn 13:36–38)

St. John: Simon Peter said to him,

Peter: Lord, where are you going?

St. John: Jesus answered,

Jesus: Where I am going you cannot follow me now; but you shall follow afterward.

St. John: Peter said to him,

Peter: Lord, why cannot I follow you now? I will lay down my life for you.

St. John: Jesus answered,

Jesus: Will you lay down your life for me? Truly, truly, I say to you, the cock will not crow, till you have denied me three times.

John Chapter 14

* Jesus the Way, the Truth, and the Life (Jn 14:1–14); PF2–74; C8–2466

Jesus: Let not your hearts be troubled; believe in God, believe also in me. In my Father's house are many rooms; if it were not so, would I have told you that I go to prepare a place for you? And when I go and prepare a place for you, I will come again and will take you to myself, that where I am you may be also. And you know the way where I am going.

St. John: Thomas said to him,

Thomas: Lord, we do not know where you are going; how can we know the way?

St. John: Jesus said to him,

Jesus: I am the way, and the truth, and the life; no one comes to the Father, but by me. If you had known me, you would have known my Father also; henceforth you know him and have seen him.

St. John: Philip said to him,

Philip: Lord, show us the Father, and we shall be satisfied.

St. John: Jesus said to him,

Jesus: Have I been with you so long, and yet you do not know me, Philip? He who has seen me has seen the Father; how can you say, "Show us the Father?" Do you not believe that I am in the Father and the Father in me? The words that I say to you I do not speak on my own authority; but the Father who dwells in me does his works. Believe me that I am in the Father and the Father in me; or else believe me for the sake of the works themselves.

Truly, truly, I say to you, he who believes in me will also do the works that I do; and greater works than these will he do, because I go to the Father. Whatever you ask in my name, I will do it, that the Father may be glorified in the Son; if you ask anything in my name, I will do it.

* The Promise of the Holy Spirit (Jn 14:15–31); F1–243; F8–692

Jesus: If you love me, you will keep my commandments. And I will pray the Father, and he will give you another Counselor, to be with you forever, even the Spirit of truth, whom the world cannot receive, because it neither sees him nor knows him; you know him, for he dwells with you, and will be in you.

I will not leave you desolate; I will come to you. Yet a little while, and the world will see me no more, but you will see me; because I live, you will live also. In that day you will know that I am in my Father, and you in me, and I in you. He who has my commandments and keeps them, he it is who loves me; and he who loves me will be loved by my Father, and I will love him and manifest myself to him.

St. John: Judas (not Iscariot) said to him,

Jude Thaddeus: Lord, how is it that you will manifest yourself to us, and not to the world?

St. John: Jesus answered him,

Jesus: If a man loves me, he will keep my word, and my Father will love him, and we will come to him and make our home with him. He who does not love me does not keep my words; and the word which you hear is not mine but the Father's who sent me.

These things I have spoken to you, while I am still with you. But the Counselor, the Holy Spirit, whom the Father will send in my name, he will teach you all things, and bring to your remembrance all that I have said to you.

Peace I leave with you; my peace I give to you; not as the world gives do I give to you. Let not your hearts be troubled, neither let them be afraid. You heard me say to you, "I go away, and I will come to you." If you loved me, you would have rejoiced, because I go to the Father; for the Father is greater than I.

And now I have told you before it takes place, so that when it does take place, you may believe. I will no longer talk much with you, for the ruler of this world is coming. He has no power over me; but I do as the Father has commanded me, so that the world may know that I love the Father. Rise, let us go hence.

John Chapter 15

* Jesus the True Vine (Jn 15:1–17); F1–308; F9–859

Jesus: I am the true vine, and my Father is the vinedresser. Every branch of mine that bears no fruit, he takes away, and every branch that does bear fruit he prunes, that it may bear more fruit. You are already made clean by the word which I have spoken to you.

Abide in me, and I in you. As the branch cannot bear fruit by itself, unless it abides in the vine, neither can you, unless you abide in me. I am the vine, you are the branches. He who abides in me, and I in him, he it is that bears much fruit, for apart from me you can do nothing.

If a man does not abide in me, he is cast forth as a branch and withers; and the branches are gathered, thrown into the fire and burned. If you abide in me, and my words abide in you, ask whatever you will, and it shall be done for you. By this my Father is glorified, that you bear much fruit, and so prove to be my disciples.

Jesus 2: As the Father has loved me, so have I loved you; abide in my love. If you keep my commandments, you will abide in my love, just as I have kept my Father's commandments and abide in his love. These things I have spoken to you, that my joy may be in you, and that your joy may be full.

Jesus 3: This is my commandment, that you love one another as I have loved you. Greater love has no man than this, that a man lay down his life for his friends. You are my friends if you do what I command you.

No longer do I call you servants, for the servant does not know what his master is doing; but I have called you friends, for all that I have heard from my Father I have made known to you.

Jesus 4: You did not choose me, but I chose you and appointed you that you should go and bear fruit and that your fruit should abide; so that whatever you ask the Father in my name, he may give it to you. This I command you, to love one another.

* The World's Hatred (Jn 15:18–16:4); F8–719; S4–1433

Jesus 4: If the world hates you, know that it has hated me before it hated you. If you were of the world, the world would love its own; but because you are not of the world, but I chose you out of the world, therefore the world hates you.

Jesus 5: Remember the word that I said to you, "A servant is not greater than his master." If they persecuted me, they will persecute you; if they kept my word, they will keep yours also. But all this they will do to you on my account, because they do not know him who sent me.

If I had not come and spoken to them, they would not have sin; but now they have no excuse for their sin. He who hates me hates my Father also.

If I had not done among them the works which no one else did, they would not have sin; but now they have seen and hated both me and my Father. It is to fulfill the word that is written in their law, "They hated me without a cause."

But when the Counselor comes, whom I shall send to you from the Father, even the Spirit of truth, who proceeds from the Father, he will bear witness to me; and you also are witnesses, because you have been with me from the beginning.

John Chapter 16

Jesus: I have said all this to you to keep you from falling away. They will put you out of the synagogues; indeed, the hour is coming when whoever kills you will think he is offering service to God. And they will do this because they have not known the Father, nor me.

But I have said these things to you, that when their hour comes you may remember that I told you of them.

* The Work of the Spirit (Jn 16:5–15); PF2–91; C8–2466

Jesus: I did not say these things to you from the beginning, because I was with you. But now I am going to him who sent me; yet none of you asks me, "Where are you going?"

But because I have said these things to you, sorrow has filled your hearts. Nevertheless I tell you the truth: it is to your advantage that I go away, for if I do not go away, the Counselor will not come to you; but if I go, I will send him to you.

Jesus 2: And when he comes, he will convince the world concerning sin and righteousness and judgment: concerning sin, because they do not believe in me; concerning righteousness, because I go to the Father, and you will see me no more; concerning judgment, because the ruler of this world is judged.

Jesus 3: I have yet many things to say to you, but you cannot bear them now. When the Spirit of truth comes, he will guide you into all the truth; for he will not speak on his own authority, but whatever he hears he will speak, and he will declare to you the things that are to come. He will glorify me, for he will take what is mine and declare it to you.

All that the Father has is mine; therefore I said that he will take what is mine and declare it to you.

* Sorrow Will Turn Into Joy (Jn 16:16–24); P–2615; LP1–2815

Jesus: A little while, and you will see me no more; again a little while, and you will see me.

St. John: Some of his disciples said to one another,

Some disciples: What is this that he says to us, "A little while, and you will not see me, and again a little while, and you will see me;" and, "because I go to the Father?"

St. John: They said,

Some disciples: What does he mean by "a little while?" We do not know what he means.

St. John: Jesus knew that they wanted to ask him; so he said to them,

Jesus: Is this what you are asking yourselves, what I meant by saying, "A little while, and you will not see me, and again a little while, and you will see me?" Truly, truly, I say to you, you will weep and lament, but the world will rejoice; you will be sorrowful, but your sorrow will turn into joy.

When a woman is in travail she has sorrow, because her hour has come; but when she is delivered of the child, she no longer remembers the anguish, for joy that a child is born into the world. So you have sorrow now, but I will see you again and your hearts will rejoice, and no one will take your joy from you.

In that day you will ask nothing of me. Truly, truly, I say to you, if you ask anything of the Father, he will give it to you in my name. Hitherto you have asked nothing in my name; ask, and you will receive, that your joy may be full.

* Peace for the Disciples (Jn 16:25–33); F6–661; LP1–2795

Jesus 2: I have said this to you in figures; the hour is coming when I shall no longer speak to you in figures but tell you plainly of the Father. In that day you will ask in my name; and I do not say to you that I shall pray the Father for you; for the Father himself loves you, because you have loved me and have believed that I came from the Father. I came from the Father and have come into the world; again, I am leaving the world and going to the Father.

St. John: His disciples said,

Disciples: Ah, now you are speaking plainly, not in any figure! Now we know that you know all things, and need none to question you; by this we believe that you came from God.

St. John: Jesus answered them,

Jesus 2: Do you now believe? The hour is coming, indeed it has come, when you will be scattered, every man to his home, and will leave me alone; yet I am not alone, for the Father is with me. I have said this to you, that in me you may have peace. In the world you have tribulation; but be of good cheer, I have overcome the world.

John Chapter 17

* Jesus Prays for the Church (Jn 17:1-26); LP1-2815; LP6–2849

St. John: When Jesus had spoken these words, he lifted up his eyes to heaven and said,

Jesus: Father, the hour has come; glorify your Son that the Son may glorify you, since you have given him power over all flesh, to give eternal life to all whom you have given him. And this is eternal life, that they know you the only true God, and Jesus Christ whom you have sent. I glorified you on earth, having accomplished the work which you gave me to do; and now, Father, glorify me in your own presence with the glory which I had with you before the world was made.

Jesus 2: I have manifested your name to the men whom you gave me out of the world; they were yours, and you gave them to me, and they have kept your word. Now they know that everything that you have given me is from you; for I have given them the words which you gave me, and they have received them and know in truth that I came from you; and they have believed that you did send me.

I am praying for them; I am not praying for the world but for those whom you have given me, for they are yours; all mine are yours, and yours are mine, and I am glorified in them. And now I am no more in the world, but they are in the world, and I am coming to you. Holy Father, keep them in your name, which you have given me, that they may be one, even as we are one.

While I was with them, I kept them in your name, which you have given me; I have guarded them, and none of them is lost but the son of perdition, that the Scripture might be fulfilled. But now I am coming to you; and these things I speak in the world, that they may have my joy fulfilled in themselves.

Jesus 3: I have given them your word; and the world has hated them because they are not of the world, even as I am not of the world. I do not pray that you should take them out of the world, but that you should keep them from the evil one. They are not of the world, even as I am not of the world. Sanctify them in the truth; your word is truth.

As you did send me into the world, so I have sent them into the world. And for their sake I consecrate myself, that they also may be consecrated in truth.

Jesus 4: I do not pray for these only, but also for those who believe in me through their word, that they may all be one; even as you, Father, are in me, and I in you, that they also may be in us, so that the world may believe that you have sent me.

The glory which you have given me I have given to them, that they may be one even as we are one, I in them and you in me, that they may become perfectly one, so that the world may know that you have sent me and have loved them even as you have loved me.

Jesus 5: Father, I desire that they also, whom you have given me, may be with me where I am, to behold my glory which you have given me in your love for me before the foundation of the world.

O righteous Father, the world has not known you, but I have known you; and these know that you have sent me. I made known to them your name, and I will make it known, that the love with which you have loved me may be in them, and I in them.

John Chapter 18

The Arrest of Jesus (Jn 18:1–11); F4–619; F4–607

St. John: When Jesus had spoken these words, he went forth with his disciples across the Kidron valley, where there was a garden, which he and his disciples entered. Now Judas, who betrayed him, also knew the place; for Jesus often met there with his disciples.

So Judas, procuring a band of soldiers and some officers from the chief priests and the Pharisees, went there with lanterns and torches and weapons. Then Jesus, knowing all that was to befall him, came forward and said to them,

Jesus: Whom do you seek?

St. John: They answered him,

Soldiers and officers: Jesus of Nazareth.

St. John: Jesus said to them,

Jesus: I am he.

St. John: Judas, who betrayed him, was standing with them. When he said to them, "I am he," they drew back and fell to the ground. Again he asked them,

Jesus: Whom do you seek?

St. John: And they said,

Soldiers and officers: Jesus of Nazareth.

St. John: Jesus answered,

Jesus: I told you that I am he; so, if you seek me, let these men go.

St. John: This was to fulfill the word which he had spoken, "Of those whom you gave me I lost not one." Then Simon Peter, having a sword, drew it and struck the high priest's slave and cut off his right ear. The slave's name was Malchus. Jesus said to Peter,

Jesus: Put your sword into its sheath; shall I not drink the chalise which the Father has given me?

Jesus Before the High Priest (Jn 18:12–14) F4–575

St. John: So the band of soldiers and their captain and the officers of the Jews seized Jesus and bound him. First they led him to Annas; for he was the father-in-law of Caiaphas, who was high priest that year. It was Caiaphas who had given counsel to the Jews that it was expedient that one man should die for the people.

~ Peter Denies Jesus (Jn 18:15–18)

St. John: Simon Peter followed Jesus, and so did another disciple. As this disciple was known to the high priest, he entered the court of the high priest along with Jesus, while Peter stood outside at the door. So the other disciple, who was known to the high priest, went out and spoke to the maid who kept the door, and brought Peter in. The maid who kept the door said to Peter,

Maid: Are not you also one of this man's disciples?

St. John: He said,

Peter: I am not.

St. John: Now the servants and officers had made a charcoal fire, because it was cold, and they were standing and warming themselves; Peter also was with them, standing and warming himself.

The High Priest Questions Jesus (Jn 18:19–24); F4–586

St. John: The high priest then questioned Jesus about his disciples and his teaching. Jesus answered him,

Jesus: I have spoken openly to the world; I have always taught in synagogues and in the temple, where all Jews come together; I have said nothing secretly. Why do you ask me? Ask those who have heard me, what I said to them; they know what I said.

St. John: When he had said this, one of the officers standing by struck Jesus with his hand, saying,

Officer: Is that how you answer the high priest?

St. John: Jesus answered him,

Jesus: If I have spoken wrongly, bear witness to the wrong; but if I have spoken rightly, why do you strike me?

St. John: Annas then sent him bound to Caiaphas the high priest.

~ Peter Denies Jesus Again (Jn 18:25–27)

St. John: Now Simon Peter was standing and warming himself. They said to him,

Bystanders: Are not you also one of his disciples?

St. John: He denied it and said,

Peter: I am not.

St. John: One of the servants of the high priest, a kinsman of the man whose ear Peter had cut off, asked,

Servant of the high priest: Did I not see you in the garden with him?

St. John: Peter again denied it; and at once the cock crowed.

Jesus Before Pilate (Jn 18:28–32); F4–596

St. John: Then they led Jesus from the house of Caiaphas to the praetorium. It was early. They themselves did not enter the praetorium, so that they might not be defiled, but might eat the Passover. So Pilate went out to them and said,

Pilate: What accusation do you bring against this man?

St. John: They answered him,

Jews: If this man were not an evildoer, we would not have handed him over.

St. John: Pilate said to them,

Pilate: Take him yourselves and judge him by your own law.

St. John: The Jews said to him,

Jews: It is not lawful for us to put any man to death.

St. John: This was to fulfill the word which Jesus had spoken to show by what death he was to die.

* Jesus Sentenced to Death (Jn 18:33–Jn 19:16); F3–559; C8–2471

St. John: Pilate entered the praetorium again and called Jesus, and said to him,

Pilate: Are you the King of the Jews?

St. John: Jesus answered,

Jesus: Do you say this of your own accord, or did others say it to you about me?

St. John: Pilate answered,

Pilate: Am I a Jew? Your own nation and the chief priests have handed you over to me; what have you done?

St. John: Jesus answered,

Jesus: My kingship is not of this world; if my kingship were of this world, my servants would fight, that I might not be handed over to the Jews; but my kingship is not from the world.

St. John: Pilate said to him,

Pilate: So you are a king?

St. John: Jesus answered,

Jesus: You say that I am a king. For this I was born, and for this I have come into the world, to bear witness to the truth. Everyone who is of the truth hears my voice.

St. John: Pilate said to him,

Pilate: What is truth?

St. John: After he had said this, he went out to the Jews again, and told them,

Pilate: I find no crime in him. But you have a custom that I should release one man for you at the Passover; will you have me release for you the King of the Jews?

St. John: They cried out again,

Jews: Not this man, but Barabbas!

St. John: Now Barabbas was a robber.

John Chapter 19

St. John: Then Pilate took Jesus and scourged him. And the soldiers plaited a crown of thorns, and put it on his head, and arrayed him in a purple robe; they came up to him, saying,

Soldiers: Hail, King of the Jews!

St. John: And struck him with their hands.

St. John: Pilate went out again, and said to them,

Pilate: See, I am bringing him out to you, that you may know that I find no crime in him.

St. John: So Jesus came out, wearing the crown of thorns and the purple robe. Pilate said to them,

Pilate: Behold the man!

St. John: When the chief priests and the officers saw him, they cried out,

Chief priests and officers: Crucify him, crucify him!

St. John: Pilate said to them,

Pilate: Take him yourselves and crucify him, for I find no crime in him.

St. John: The Jews answered him,

Jews: We have a law, and by that law he ought to die, because he has made himself the Son of God.

St. John: When Pilate heard these words, he was the more afraid; he entered the praetorium again and said to Jesus,

Pilate: Where are you from?

St. John: But Jesus gave no answer. Pilate therefore said to him,

Pilate: You will not speak to me? Do you not know that I have power to release you, and power to crucify you?

St. John: Jesus answered him,

Jesus: You would have no power over me unless it had been given you from above; therefore he who delivered me to you has the greater sin.

St. John: Upon this Pilate sought to release him, but the Jews cried out,

Jews: If you release this man, you are not Caesar's friend; everyone who makes himself a king sets himself against Caesar.

St. John: When Pilate heard these words, he brought Jesus out and sat down on the judgment seat at a place called The Pavement, and in Hebrew, Gabbatha. Now it was the day of Preparation of the Passover; it was about the sixth hour. He said to the Jews,

Pilate: Behold your King!

St. John: They cried out,

Jews: Away with him, away with him, crucify him!

St. John: Pilate said to them,

Pilate: Shall I crucify your King?

St. John: The chief priests answered,

Chief priests: We have no king but Caesar.

St. John: Then he handed him over to them to be crucified.

* The Crucifixion (Jn 19:17–30); F4–607; P–2561

St. John: So they took Jesus, and he went out, bearing his own cross, to the place called the place of a skull, which is called in Hebrew Golgotha. There they crucified him, and with him two others, one on either side, and Jesus between them. Pilate also wrote a title and put it on the cross; it read, "Jesus of Nazareth, the King of the Jews." Many of the Jews read this title, for the place where Jesus was crucified was near the city; and it was written in Hebrew, in Latin, and in Greek. The chief priests of the Jews then said to Pilate,

Chief priests: Do not write, "The King of the Jews," but, "This man said, 'I am King of the Jews.'"

St. John: Pilate answered,

Pilate: What I have written I have written.

St. John: When the soldiers had crucified Jesus they took his garments and made four parts, one for each soldier; also his tunic. But the tunic was without seam, woven from top to bottom; so they said to one another,

Soldiers: Let us not tear it, but cast lots for it to see whose it shall be.

St. John: This was to fulfill the Scripture, "They parted my garments among them, and for my clothing they cast lots." So the soldiers did this.

St. John: But standing by the cross of Jesus were his mother, and his mother's sister, Mary the wife of Clopas, and Mary Magdalene. When Jesus saw his mother, and the disciple whom he loved standing near, he said to his mother,

Jesus: Woman, behold, your son!

St. John: Then he said to the disciple,

Jesus: Behold, your mother!

St. John: And from that hour the disciple took her to his own home.

St. John: After this Jesus, knowing that all was now finished, said (to fulfill the Scripture),

Jesus: I thirst.

St. John: A bowl full of vinegar stood there; so they put a sponge full of the vinegar on hyssop and held it to his mouth. When Jesus had received the vinegar, he said,

Jesus: It is finished;

St. John: And he bowed his head and gave up his spirit.

* Jesus' Side is Pierced (Jn 19:31–37); F8–694; S1–1225

St. John: Since it was the day of Preparation, in order to prevent the bodies from remaining on the cross on the sabbath (for that sabbath was a high day), the Jews asked Pilate that their legs might be broken, and that they might be taken away.

So the soldiers came and broke the legs of the first, and of the other who had been crucified with him; but when they came to Jesus and saw that he was already dead, they did not break his legs. But one of the soldiers pierced his side with a spear, and at once there came out blood and water.

He who saw it has borne witness—his testimony is true, and he knows that he tells the truth—that you also may believe. For these things took place that the Scripture might be fulfilled, "Not a bone of him shall be broken." And again another Scripture says, "They shall look on him whom they have pierced."

* The Burial of Jesus (Jn 19:38–42); F4–624; F5–641

St. John 2: After this Joseph of Arimathea, who was a disciple of Jesus, but secretly, for fear of the Jews, asked Pilate that he might take away the body of Jesus, and Pilate gave him leave. So he came and took away his body.

St. John 3: Nicodemus also, who had at first come to him by night, came bringing a mixture of myrrh and aloes, about a hundred pounds' weight. They took the body of Jesus, and bound it in linen cloths with the spices, as is the burial custom of the Jews.

St. John 4: Now in the place where he was crucified there was a garden, and in the garden a new tomb where no one had ever been laid. So because of the Jewish day of Preparation, as the tomb was close at hand, they laid Jesus there.

John Chapter 20

* The Resurrection of Jesus (Jn 20:1–10); C3–2174; F5–640

St. John: Now on the first day of the week Mary Magdalene came to the tomb early, while it was still dark, and saw that the stone had been taken away from the tomb. So she ran, and went to Simon Peter and the other disciple, the one whom Jesus loved, and said to them,

Mary Magdalene: They have taken the Lord out of the tomb, and we do not know where they have laid him.

St. John: Peter then came out with the other disciple, and they went toward the tomb. They both ran, but the other disciple outran Peter and reached the tomb first; and stooping to look in, he saw the linen cloths lying there, but he did not go in.

Then Simon Peter came, following him, and went into the tomb; he saw the linen cloths lying, and the napkin, which had been on his head, not lying with the linen cloths but rolled up in a place by itself.

Then the other disciple, who reached the tomb first, also went in, and he saw and believed; for as yet they did not know the Scripture, that he must rise from the dead.

Then the disciples went back to their homes.

* Jesus Appears to Mary Magdalene (Jn 20:11–18); F5–645; LP1–2795

St. John: But Mary stood weeping outside the tomb, and as she wept she stooped to look into the tomb; and she saw two angels in white, sitting where the body of Jesus had lain, one at the head and one at the feet. They said to her,

Two angels: Woman, why are you weeping?

St. John: She said to them,

Mary Magdalene: Because they have taken away my Lord, and I do not know where they have laid him.

St. John: Saying this, she turned round and saw Jesus standing, but she did not know that it was Jesus. Jesus said to her,

Jesus: Woman, why are you weeping? Whom do you seek?

St. John: Supposing him to be the gardener, she said to him,

Mary Magdalene: Sir, if you have carried him away, tell me where you have laid him, and I will take him away.

St. John: Jesus said to her,

Jesus: Mary.

St. John: She turned and said to him in Hebrew,

Mary Magdalene: Rabboni!

St. John: (which means Teacher). Jesus said to her,

Jesus: Do not hold me, for I have not yet ascended to the Father; but go to my brethren and say to them, I am ascending to my Father and your Father, to my God and your God.

St. John: Mary Magdalene went and said to the disciples,

Mary Magdalene: I have seen the Lord;

St. John: And she told them that he had said these things to her.

* Jesus Gives the Disciples the Power to Forgive Sins (Jn 20:19–23); F10–976; S4–1485

St. John: On the evening of that day, the first day of the week, the doors being shut where the disciples were, for fear of the Jews, Jesus came and stood among them and said to them,

Jesus: Peace be with you.

St. John: When he had said this, he showed them his hands and his side. Then the disciples were glad when they saw the Lord. Jesus said to them again,

Jesus: Peace be with you. As the Father has sent me, even so I send you.

St. John: And when he had said this, he breathed on them, and said to them,

Jesus: Receive the Holy Spirit. If you forgive the sins of any, they are forgiven; if you retain the sins of any, they are retained.

* Jesus and Thomas (Jn 20:24–29); F5–645; F6–659

St. John: Now Thomas, one of the twelve, called the Twin, was not with them when Jesus came. So the other disciples told him,

Disciples: We have seen the Lord.

St. John: But he said to them,

Thomas: Unless I see in his hands the print of the nails, and place my finger in the mark of the nails, and place my hand in his side, I will not believe.

St. John: Eight days later, his disciples were again in the house, and Thomas was with them. The doors were shut, but Jesus came and stood among them, and said,

Jesus: Peace be with you.

St. John: Then he said to Thomas,

Jesus: Put your finger here, and see my hands; and put out your hand, and place it in my side; do not be faithless, but believing.

St. John: Thomas answered him,

Thomas: My Lord and my God!

St. John: Jesus said to him,

Jesus: Have you believed because you have seen me? Blessed are those who have not seen and yet believe.

The Purpose of This Book (Jn 20:30–31); F2–442; F3–514

St. John: Now Jesus did many other signs in the presence of the disciples, which are not written in this book; but these are written that you may believe that Jesus is the Christ, the Son of God, and that believing you may have life in his name.

John Chapter 21

* Jesus Appears to Disciples by the Sea of Tiberias (Jn 21:1–14); F5–645; F6–659

St. John: After this Jesus revealed himself again to the disciples by the Sea of Tiberias; and he revealed himself in this way. Simon Peter, Thomas called the Twin, Nathanael of Cana in Galilee, the sons of Zebedee, and two others of his disciples were together. Simon Peter said to them,

Peter: I am going fishing.

St. John: They said to him,

Other disciples: We will go with you.

St. John: They went out and got into the boat; but that night they caught nothing. Just as day was breaking, Jesus stood on the beach; yet the disciples did not know that it was Jesus. Jesus said to them,

Jesus: Children, have you any fish?

St. John: They answered him,

Disciples: No.

St. John: He said to them,

Jesus: Cast the net on the right side of the boat, and you will find some.

St. John: So they cast it, and now they were not able to haul it in, for the quantity of fish. That disciple whom Jesus loved said to Peter,

Disciple whom Jesus loved: It is the Lord!

St. John: When Simon Peter heard that it was the Lord, he put on his clothes, for he was stripped for work, and sprang into the sea.

But the other disciples came in the boat, dragging the net full of fish, for they were not far from the land, but about a hundred yards off.

When they got out on land, they saw a charcoal fire there, with fish lying on it, and bread. Jesus said to them,

Jesus: Bring some of the fish that you have just caught.

St. John: So Simon Peter went aboard and hauled the net ashore, full of large fish, a hundred and fifty-three of them; and although there were so many, the net was not torn. Jesus said to them,

Jesus: Come and have breakfast.

St. John: Now none of the disciples dared ask him, "Who are you?" They knew it was the Lord. Jesus came and took the bread and gave it to them, and so with the fish. This was now the third time that Jesus was revealed to the disciples after he was raised from the dead.

* Peter is Given a Command (Jn 21:15–19); S4–1429; S6-1551

St. John: When they had finished breakfast, Jesus said to Simon Peter,

Jesus: Simon, son of John, do you love me more than these?

St. John: He said to him,

Peter: Yes, Lord; you know that I love you.

St. John: He said to him,

Jesus: Feed my lambs.

St. John: A second time he said to him,

Jesus: Simon, son of John, do you love me?

St. John: He said to him,

Peter: Yes, Lord; you know that I love you.

St. John: He said to him,

Jesus: Tend my sheep.

St. John: He said to him the third time,

Jesus: Simon, son of John, do you love me?

St. John: Peter was grieved because he said to him the third time, "Do you love me?" And he said to him,

Peter: Lord, you know everything; you know that I love you.

St. John: Jesus said to him,

Jesus: Feed my sheep. Truly, truly, I say to you, when you were young, you girded yourself and walked where you would; but when you are old, you will stretch out your hands, and another will gird you and carry you where you do not wish to go.

St. John: (This he said to show by what death he was to glorify God.) And after this he said to him,

Jesus: Follow me.

Jesus and the Beloved Disciple (Jn 21:20–25); F9–878; F3–515

St. John: Peter turned and saw following them the disciple whom Jesus loved, who had lain close to his breast at the supper and had said, "Lord, who is it that is going to betray you?" When Peter saw him, he said to Jesus,

Peter: Lord, what about this man?

St. John: Jesus said to him,

Jesus: If it is my will that he remain until I come, what is that to you? Follow me!

St. John: The saying spread abroad among the brethren that this disciple was not to die; yet Jesus did not say to him that he was not to die, but, "If it is my will that he remain until I come, what is that to you?" This is the disciple who is bearing witness to these things, and who has written these things; and we know that his testimony is true.

All Readers: But there are also many other things which Jesus did; were every one of them to be written, I suppose that the world itself could not contain the books that would be written.

The Acts of the Apostles

Acts Chapter 1

* The Promise of the Holy Spirit (Acts 1:1–5); F3–512; F6–659

St. Luke: In the first book, O Theophilus, I have dealt with all that Jesus began to do and teach, until the day when he was taken up, after he had given commandment through the Holy Spirit to the apostles whom he had chosen. To them he presented himself alive after his passion by many proofs, appearing to them during forty days, and speaking of the kingdom of God. And while staying with them he charged them not to depart from Jerusalem, but to wait for the promise of the Father,

St. Luke: which, he said,

Jesus: you heard from me, for John baptized with water, but before many days you shall be baptized with the Holy Spirit.

The Ascension of Jesus (Acts 1:6–11); F6–659; F8–697

St. Luke: So when they had come together, they asked him,

Apostles: Lord, will you at this time restore the kingdom to Israel?

St. Luke: He said to them,

Jesus: It is not for you to know times or seasons which the Father has fixed by his own authority. But you shall receive power when the Holy Spirit has come upon you; and you shall be my witnesses in Jerusalem and in all Judea and Samaria and to the end of the earth.

St. Luke: And when he had said this, as they were looking on, he was lifted up, and a cloud took him out of their sight. And while they were gazing into heaven as he went, behold, two men stood by them in white robes, and said,

Two men: Men of Galilee, why do you stand looking into heaven? This Jesus, who was taken up from you into heaven, will come in the same way as you saw him go into heaven.

* Matthias is Chosen to Replace Judas (Acts 1:12–26); F8–726; S2–1310

St. Luke: Then they returned to Jerusalem from the mount called Olivet, which is near Jerusalem, a sabbath day's journey away; and when they had entered, they went up to the upper room, where they were staying, Peter and John and James and Andrew, Philip and Thomas, Bartholomew and Matthew, James the son of Alphaeus and Simon the Zealot and Judas the son of James. All these with one accord devoted themselves to prayer, together with the women and Mary the mother of Jesus, and with his brethren.

St. Luke: In those days Peter stood up among the brethren (the company of persons was in all about a hundred and twenty), and said,

Peter: Brethren, the Scripture had to be fulfilled, which the Holy Spirit spoke beforehand by the mouth of David, concerning Judas who was guide to those who arrested Jesus. For he was numbered among us, and was allotted his share in this ministry.

(Now this man bought a field with the reward of his wickedness; and falling headlong he burst open in the middle and all his bowels gushed out. And it became known to all the inhabitants of Jerusalem, so that the field was called in their language Akeldama, that is, Field of Blood.)

For it is written in the book of Psalms, "Let his habitation become desolate, and let there be no one to live in it"; and "His office let another take."

So one of the men who have accompanied us during all the time that the Lord Jesus went in and out among us, beginning from the baptism of John until the day when he was taken up from us—one of these men must become with us a witness to his resurrection.

St. Luke: And they put forward two, Joseph called Barsabbas, who was surnamed Justus, and Matthias. And they prayed and said,

Apostles: Lord, you know the hearts of all men, show which one of these two you have chosen to take the place in this ministry and apostleship from which Judas turned aside, to go to his own place.

St. Luke: And they cast lots for them, and the lot fell on Matthias; and he was enrolled with the eleven apostles.

Acts Chapter 2

* The Coming of the Holy Spirit (Acts 2:1-13); S2-1287; F8-696

St. Luke: When the day of Pentecost had come, they were all together in one place. And suddenly a sound came from heaven like the rush of a mighty wind, and it filled all the house where they were sitting.

And there appeared to them tongues as of fire, distributed and resting on each one of them. And they were all filled with the Holy Spirit and began to speak in other tongues, as the Spirit gave them utterance.

Now there were dwelling in Jerusalem Jews, devout men from every nation under heaven. And at this sound the multitude came together, and they were bewildered, because each one heard them speaking in his own language.

And they were amazed and wondered, saying,

Multitude: Are not all these who are speaking Galileans? And how is it that we hear, each of us in his own native language?

Parthians and Medes and Elamites and residents of Mesopotamia, Judea and Cappadocia, Pontus and Asia, Phrygia and Pamphylia, Egypt and the parts of Libya belonging to Cyrene, and visitors from Rome, both Jews and proselytes, Cretans and Arabians, we hear them telling in our own tongues the mighty works of God.

St. Luke: And all were amazed and perplexed, saying to one another,

All: What does this mean?

St. Luke: But others mocking said,

Others: They are filled with new wine.

* Peter Addresses the Crowd (Acts 2:14-36); F6-659; F9-788

St. Luke: But Peter, standing with the eleven, lifted up his voice and addressed them,

Peter: Men of Judea and all who dwell in Jerusalem, let this be known to you, and give ear to my words. For these men are not drunk, as you suppose, since it is only the third hour of the day; but this is what was spoken by the prophet Joel:

Joel: And in the last days it shall be, God declares, that I will pour out my Spirit upon all flesh, and your sons and your daughters shall prophesy, and your young men shall see visions, and your old men shall dream dreams; yes, and on my menservants and my maidservants in those days I will pour out my Spirit; and they shall prophesy.

And I will show wonders in the heaven above and signs on the earth beneath, blood, and fire, and vapor of smoke; the sun shall be turned into darkness and the moon into blood, before the day of the Lord comes, the great and manifest day.

And it shall be that whoever calls on the name of the Lord shall be saved.

Peter: Men of Israel, hear these words: Jesus of Nazareth, a man attested to you by God with mighty works and wonders and signs which God did through him in your midst, as you yourselves know—this Jesus, delivered up according to the definite plan and foreknowledge of God, you crucified and killed by the hands of lawless men.

But God raised him up, having loosed the pangs of death, because it was not possible for him to be held by it. For David says concerning him,

David: I saw the Lord always before me, for he is at my right hand that I may not be shaken; therefore my heart was glad, and my tongue rejoiced; moreover my flesh will dwell in hope.

For you will not abandon my soul to Hades, nor let your Holy One see corruption. You have made known to me the ways of life; you will make me full of gladness with your presence.

Peter: Brethren, I may say to you confidently of the patriarch David that he both died and was buried, and his tomb is with us to this day.

Being therefore a prophet, and knowing that God had sworn with an oath to him that he would set one of his descendants upon his throne, he foresaw and spoke of the resurrection of the Christ, that he was not abandoned to Hades, nor did his flesh see corruption.

This Jesus God raised up, and of that we all are witnesses. Being therefore exalted at the right hand of God, and having received from the Father the promise of the Holy Spirit, he has poured out this which you see and hear.

For David did not ascend into the heavens; but he himself says,

David: The Lord said to my Lord, Sit at my right hand, till I make your enemies a stool for your feet.

Peter: Let all the house of Israel therefore know assuredly that God has made him both Lord and Christ, this Jesus whom you crucified.

* The First Converts (Acts 2:37–42); PLG–3; S3–1329

St. Luke: Now when they heard this they were cut to the heart, and said to Peter and the rest of the apostles,

Multitude: Brethren, what shall we do?

St. Luke: And Peter said to them,

Peter: Repent, and be baptized every one of you in the name of Jesus Christ for the forgiveness of your sins; and you shall receive the gift of the Holy Spirit. For the promise is to you and to your children and to all that are far off, everyone whom the Lord our God calls to him.

St. Luke: And he testified with many other words and exhorted them, saying,

Peter: Save yourselves from this crooked generation.

St. Luke: So those who received his word were baptized, and there were added that day about three thousand souls. And they devoted themselves to the apostles' teaching and fellowship, to the breaking of bread and the prayers.

* Life among the Believers (Acts 2:43–47); F4–584; S3–1342

St. Luke: And fear came upon every soul; and many wonders and signs were done through the apostles. And all who believed were together and had all things in common; and they sold their possessions and goods and distributed them to all, as any had need.

And day by day, attending the temple together and breaking bread in their homes, they partook of food with glad and generous hearts, praising God and having favor with all the people. And the Lord added to their number day by day those who were being saved.

Acts Chapter 3

Peter Heals a Lame Beggar (Acts 3:1–10); F4–584; P–2640

St. Luke: Now Peter and John were going up to the temple at the hour of prayer, the ninth hour. And a man lame from birth was being carried, whom they laid daily at that gate of the temple which is called Beautiful to ask alms of those who entered the temple. Seeing Peter and John about to go into the temple, he asked for alms. And Peter directed his gaze at him, with John, and said,

Peter: Look at us.

St. Luke: And he fixed his attention upon them, expecting to receive something from them. But Peter said,

Peter: I have no silver and gold, but I give you what I have; in the name of Jesus Christ of Nazareth, walk.

St. Luke: And he took him by the right hand and raised him up; and immediately his feet and ankles were made strong. And leaping up he stood and walked and entered the temple with them, walking and leaping and praising God.

And all the people saw him walking and praising God, and recognized him as the one who sat for alms at the Beautiful Gate of the temple; and they were filled with wonder and amazement at what had happened to him.

* Peter Addresses the People in Solomon's Portico (Acts 3:11–26); F5–632; F5–635

St. Luke: While he clung to Peter and John, all the people ran together to them in the portico called Solomon's, astounded. And when Peter saw it he addressed the people,

Peter: Men of Israel, why do you wonder at this, or why do you stare at us, as though by our own power or piety we had made him walk?

The God of Abraham and of Isaac and of Jacob, the God of our fathers, glorified his servant Jesus, whom you delivered up and denied in the presence of Pilate, when he had decided to release him.

But you denied the Holy and Righteous One, and asked for a murderer to be granted to you, and killed the Author of life, whom God raised from the dead. To this we are witnesses.

And his name, by faith in his name, has made this man strong whom you see and know; and the faith which is through Jesus has given the man this perfect health in the presence of you all.

And now, brethren, I know that you acted in ignorance, as did also your rulers. But what God foretold by the mouth of all the prophets, that his Christ should suffer, he thus fulfilled.

Repent therefore, and turn again, that your sins may be blotted out, that times of refreshing may come from the presence of the Lord, and that he may send the Christ appointed for you, Jesus, whom heaven must receive until the time for establishing all that God spoke by the mouth of his holy prophets from of old.

Moses said,

Moses: The Lord God will raise up for you a prophet from your brethren as he raised me up. You shall listen to him in whatever he tells you. And it shall be that every soul that does not listen to that prophet shall be destroyed from the people.

Peter: And all the prophets who have spoken, from Samuel and those who came afterwards, also proclaimed these days. You are the sons of the prophets and of the covenant which God gave to your fathers, saying to Abraham,

God: And in your posterity shall all the families of the earth be blessed.

Peter: God, having raised up his servant, sent him to you first, to bless you in turning every one of you from your wickedness.

Acts Chapter 4

* Peter and John Before the Council (Acts 4:1–22); F2–432; S5–1507

St. Luke: And as they were speaking to the people, the priests and the captain of the temple and the Sadducees came upon them, annoyed because they were teaching the people and proclaiming in Jesus the resurrection from the dead.

And they arrested them and put them in custody until the morrow, for it was already evening. But many of those who heard the word believed; and the number of the men came to about five thousand.

On the morrow their rulers and elders and scribes were gathered together in Jerusalem, with Annas the high priest and Caiaphas and John and Alexander, and all who were of the high-priestly family. And when they had set them in the midst, they inquired,

Elders and scribes: By what power or by what name did you do this?

St. Luke: Then Peter, filled with the Holy Spirit, said to them,

Peter: Rulers of the people and elders, if we are being examined today concerning a good deed done to a cripple, by what means this man has been healed, be it known to you all, and to all the people of Israel, that by the name of Jesus Christ of Nazareth, whom you crucified, whom God raised from the dead, by him this man is standing before you well.

This is the stone which was rejected by you builders, but which has become the cornerstone. And there is salvation in no one else, for there is no other name under heaven given among men by which we must be saved.

St. Luke: Now when they saw the boldness of Peter and John, and perceived that they were uneducated, common men, they wondered; and they recognized that they had been with Jesus. But seeing the man that had been healed standing beside them, they had nothing to say in opposition. But when they had commanded them to go aside out of the council, they conferred with one another, saying,

Elders and scribes: What shall we do with these men? For that a notable sign has been performed through them is manifest to all the inhabitants of Jerusalem, and we cannot deny it. But in order that it may spread no further among the people, let us warn them to speak no more to any one in this name.

St. Luke: So they called them and charged them not to speak or teach at all in the name of Jesus. But Peter and John answered them,

Peter and John: Whether it is right in the sight of God to listen to you rather than to God, you must judge; for we cannot but speak of what we have seen and heard.

St. Luke: And when they had further threatened them, they let them go, finding no way to punish them, because of the people; for all men praised God for what had happened. For the man on whom this sign of healing was performed was more than forty years old.

The Believers Pray for Boldness (Acts 4:23-31); F2-436; F4-600

St. Luke: When they were released they went to their friends and reported what the chief priests and the elders had said to them. And when they heard it, they lifted their voices together to God and said,

Friends of the Apostles: Sovereign Lord, who did make the heaven and the earth and the sea and everything in them, who by the mouth of our father David, your servant, did say by the Holy Spirit, "Why did the Gentiles rage, and the peoples imagine vain things? The kings of the earth set themselves in array, and the rulers were gathered together, against the Lord and against his Anointed"—

For truly in this city there were gathered together against your holy servant Jesus, whom you did anoint, both Herod and Pontius Pilate, with the Gentiles and the peoples of Israel, to do whatever your hand and your plan had predestined to take place.

And now, Lord, look upon their threats, and grant to your servants to speak your word with all boldness, while you stretch out your hand to heal, and signs and wonders are performed through the name of your holy servant Jesus.

St. Luke: And when they had prayed, the place in which they were gathered together was shaken; and they were all filled with the Holy Spirit and spoke the word of God with boldness.

* The Believers Share Their Possessions (Acts 4:32–37); F9–952; LP1–2790

St. Luke: Now the company of those who believed were of one heart and soul, and no one said that any of the things which he possessed was his own, but they had everything in common.

And with great power the apostles gave their testimony to the resurrection of the Lord Jesus, and great grace was upon them all. There was not a needy person among them, for as many as were possessors of lands or houses sold them, and brought the proceeds of what was sold and laid it at the apostles' feet; and distribution was made to each as any had need.

Thus Joseph who was surnamed by the apostles Barnabas (which means, Son of encouragement), a Levite, a native of Cyprus, sold a field which belonged to him, and brought the money and laid it at the apostles' feet.

Acts Chapter 5

~ Ananias and Sapphira (Acts 5:1–11)

St. Luke: But a man named Ananias with his wife Sapphira sold a piece of property, and with his wife's knowledge he kept back some of the proceeds, and brought only a part and laid it at the apostles' feet. But Peter said,

Peter: Ananias, why has Satan filled your heart to lie to the Holy Spirit and to keep back part of the proceeds of the land? While it remained unsold, did it not remain your own? And after it was sold, was it not at your disposal? How is it that you have contrived this deed in your heart? You have not lied to men but to God.

St. Luke: When Ananias heard these words, he fell down and died. And great fear came upon all who heard of it. The young men rose and wrapped him up and carried him out and buried him. After an interval of about three hours his wife came in, not knowing what had happened. And Peter said to her,

Peter: Tell me whether you sold the land for so much.

St. Luke: And she said,

Sapphira: Yes, for so much.

St. Luke: But Peter said to her,

Peter: How is it that you have agreed together to tempt the Spirit of the Lord? Hark, the feet of those that have buried your husband are at the door, and they will carry you out.

St. Luke: Immediately she fell down at his feet and died. When the young men came in they found her dead, and they carried her out and buried her beside her husband. And great fear came upon the whole Church, and upon all who heard of these things.

The Apostles Heal Many (Acts 5:12–16); F8–699

St. Luke: Now many signs and wonders were done among the people by the hands of the apostles. And they were all together in Solomon's Portico. None of the rest dared join them, but the people held them in high honor. And more than ever believers were added to the Lord, multitudes both of men and women, so that they even carried out the sick into the streets, and laid them on beds and pallets, that as Peter came by at least his shadow might fall on some of them. The people also gathered from the towns around Jerusalem, bringing the sick and those afflicted with unclean spirits, and they were all healed.

* The Apostles are Imprisoned and Brought Before the Council (Acts 5:17–42); F2–450; C4–2242

St. Luke: But the high priest rose up and all who were with him, that is, the party of the Sadducees, and filled with jealousy they arrested the apostles and put them in the common prison. But at night an angel of the Lord opened the prison doors and brought them out and said,

Angel of the Lord: Go and stand in the temple and speak to the people all the words of this Life.

St. Luke: And when they heard this, they entered the temple at daybreak and taught. Now the high priest came and those who were with him and called together the council and all the senate of Israel, and sent to the prison to have them brought. But when the officers came, they did not find them in the prison, and they returned and reported,

Officers: We found the prison securely locked and the sentries standing at the doors, but when we opened it we found no one inside.

St. Luke: Now when the captain of the temple and the chief priests heard these words, they were much perplexed about them, wondering what this would come to. And someone came and told them,

Someone: The men whom you put in prison are standing in the temple and teaching the people.

St. Luke: Then the captain with the officers went and brought them, but without violence, for they were afraid of being stoned by the people. And when they had brought them, they set them before the council. And the high priest questioned them, saying,

High priest: We strictly charged you not to teach in this name, yet here you have filled Jerusalem with your teaching and you intend to bring this man's blood upon us.

St. Luke: But Peter and the apostles answered,

Peter and the Apostles: We must obey God rather than men. The God of our fathers raised Jesus whom you killed by hanging him on a tree. God exalted him at his right hand as Leader and Savior, to give repentance to Israel and forgiveness of sins. And we are witnesses to these things, and so is the Holy Spirit whom God has given to those who obey him.

St. Luke: When they heard this they were enraged and wanted to kill them. But a Pharisee in the council named Gamaliel, a teacher of the law, held in honor by all the people, stood up and ordered the men to be put outside for a while. And he said to them,

Gamaliel: Men of Israel, take care what you do with these men. For before these days Theudas arose, giving himself out to be somebody, and a number of men, about four hundred, joined him; but he was slain and all who followed him were dispersed and came to nothing.

After him Judas the Galilean arose in the days of the census and drew away some of the people after him; he also perished, and all who followed him were scattered.

So in the present case I tell you, keep away from these men and let them alone; for if this plan or this undertaking is of men, it will fail; but if it is of God, you will not be able to overthrow them. You might even be found opposing God!

St. Luke: So they took his advice, and when they had called in the apostles, they beat them and charged them not to speak in the name of Jesus, and let them go. Then they left the presence of the council, rejoicing that they were counted worthy to suffer dishonor for the name. And every day in the temple and at home they did not cease teaching and preaching Jesus as the Christ.

Acts Chapter 6

Seven Chosen to Serve (Acts 6:1–7); P–2632; F4–595

St. Luke: Now in these days when the disciples were increasing in number, the Hellenists murmured against the Hebrews because their widows were neglected in the daily distribution. And the twelve summoned the body of the disciples and said,

Apostles: It is not right that we should give up preaching the word of God to serve tables. Therefore, brethren, pick out from among you seven men of good repute, full of the Spirit and of wisdom, whom we may appoint to this duty. But we will devote ourselves to prayer and to the ministry of the word.

St. Luke: And what they said pleased the whole multitude, and they chose Stephen, a man full of faith and of the Holy Spirit, and Philip, and Prochorus, and Nicanor, and Timon, and Parmenas, and Nicolaus, a proselyte of Antioch. These they set before the apostles, and they prayed and laid their hands upon them. And the word of God increased; and the number of the disciples multiplied greatly in Jerusalem, and a great many of the priests were obedient to the faith.

~ The Arrest of Stephen (Acts 6:8–15)

St. Luke: And Stephen, full of grace and power, did great wonders and signs among the people. Then some of those who belonged to the synagogue of the Freedmen (as it was called), and of the Cyrenians, and of the Alexandrians, and of those from Cilicia and Asia, arose and disputed with Stephen. But they could not withstand the wisdom and the Spirit with which he spoke. Then they secretly instigated men, who said,

False accusers: We have heard him speak blasphemous words against Moses and God.

St. Luke: And they stirred up the people and the elders and the scribes, and they came upon him and seized him and brought him before the council, and set up false witnesses who said,

False witnesses: This man never ceases to speak words against this holy place and the law; for we have heard him say that this Jesus of Nazareth will destroy this place, and will change the customs which Moses delivered to us.

St. Luke: And gazing at him, all who sat in the council saw that his face was like the face of an angel.

Acts Chapter 7

* Stephen's Speech to the Council (Acts 7:1–53); F4–597; F4–601

St. Luke: And the high priest said,

High priest: Is this so?

St. Luke: And Stephen said:

Stephen: Brethren and fathers, hear me. The God of glory appeared to our father Abraham, when he was in Mesopotamia, before he lived in Haran, and said to him,

God: Depart from your land and from your kindred and go into the land which I will show you.

Stephen: Then he departed from the land of the Chaldeans, and lived in Haran. And after his father died, God removed him from there into this land in which you are now living; yet he gave him no inheritance in it, not even a foot's length, but promised to give it to him in possession and to his posterity after him, though he had no child.

And God spoke to this effect, that his posterity would be aliens in a land belonging to others, who would enslave them and ill-treat them four hundred years.

God: But I will judge the nation which they serve;

Stephen: said God,

God: And after that they shall come out and worship me in this place.

Stephen: And he gave him the covenant of circumcision. And so Abraham became the father of Isaac, and circumcised him on the eighth day; and Isaac became the father of Jacob, and Jacob of the twelve patriarchs.

And the patriarchs, jealous of Joseph, sold him into Egypt; but God was with him, and rescued him out of all his afflictions, and gave him favor and wisdom before Pharaoh, king of Egypt, who made him governor over Egypt and over all his household.

Stephen 1: Now there came a famine throughout all Egypt and Canaan, and great affliction, and our fathers could find no food. But when Jacob heard that there was grain in Egypt, he sent forth our fathers the first time.

Stephen 2: And at the second visit Joseph made himself known to his brothers, and Joseph's family became known to Pharaoh. And Joseph sent and called to him Jacob his father and all his kindred, seventy-five souls; and Jacob went down into Egypt. And he died, himself and our fathers, and they were carried back to Shechem and laid in the tomb that Abraham had bought for a sum of silver from the sons of Hamor in Shechem.

Stephen 3: But as the time of the promise drew near, which God had granted to Abraham, the people grew and multiplied in Egypt till there arose over Egypt another king who had not known Joseph. He dealt craftily with our race and forced our fathers to expose their infants, that they might not be kept alive.

Stephen 4: At this time Moses was born, and was beautiful before God. And he was brought up for three months in his father's house; and when he was exposed, Pharaoh's daughter adopted him and brought him up as her own son.

And Moses was instructed in all the wisdom of the Egyptians, and he was mighty in his words and deeds. When he was forty years old, it came into his heart to visit his brethren, the sons of Israel.

And seeing one of them being wronged, he defended the oppressed man and avenged him by striking the Egyptian. He supposed that his brethren understood that God was giving them deliverance by his hand, but they did not understand.

And on the following day he appeared to them as they were quarreling and would have reconciled them, saying,

Moses: Men, you are brethren, why do you wrong each other?

Stephen 4: But the man who was wronging his neighbor thrust him aside, saying,

Man who was wronging neighbor: Who made you a ruler and a judge over us? Do you want to kill me as you killed the Egyptian yesterday?

Stephen 4: At this retort Moses fled, and became an exile in the land of Midian, where he became the father of two sons. Now when forty years had passed, an angel appeared to him in the wilderness of Mount Sinai, in a flame of fire in a bush. When Moses saw it he wondered at the sight; and as he drew near to look, the voice of the Lord came,

God: I am the God of your fathers, the God of Abraham and of Isaac and of Jacob.

Stephen 4: And Moses trembled and did not dare to look. And the Lord said to him,

God: Take off the shoes from your feet, for the place where you are standing is holy ground. I have surely seen the ill-treatment of my people that are in Egypt and heard their groaning, and I have come down to deliver them. And now come, I will send you to Egypt.

Stephen 5: This Moses whom they refused, saying,

Israelites: Who made you a ruler and a judge?

Stephen 5: God sent as both ruler and deliverer by the hand of the angel that appeared to him in the bush. He led them out, having performed wonders and signs in Egypt and at the Red Sea, and in the wilderness for forty years. This is the Moses who said to the Israelites,

Moses: God will raise up for you a prophet from your brethren as he raised me up.

Stephen 6: This is he who was in the congregation in the wilderness with the angel who spoke to him at Mount Sinai, and with our fathers; and he received living oracles to give to us. Our fathers refused to obey him, but thrust him aside, and in their hearts they turned to Egypt, saying to Aaron,

Israelites: Make for us gods to go before us; as for this Moses who led us out from the land of Egypt, we do not know what has become of him.

Stephen 6: And they made a calf in those days, and offered a sacrifice to the idol and rejoiced in the works of their hands. But God turned and gave them over to worship the host of heaven, as it is written in the book of the prophets:

God: Did you offer to me slain beasts and sacrifices, forty years in the wilderness, O house of Israel? And you took up the tent of Moloch, and the star of the god Rephan, the figures which you made to worship; and I will remove you beyond Babylon.

Stephen 6: Our fathers had the tent of witness in the wilderness, even as he who spoke to Moses directed him to make it, according to the pattern that he had seen.

Our fathers in turn brought it in with Joshua when they dispossessed the nations which God thrust out before our fathers. So it was until the days of David, who found favor in the sight of God and asked leave to find a habitation for the God of Jacob. But it was Solomon who built a house for him. Yet the Most High does not dwell in houses made with hands; as the prophet says,

Prophet: Heaven is my throne, and earth my footstool. What house will you build for me, says the Lord, or what is the place of my rest? Did not my hand make all these things?

Stephen 7: You stiff-necked people, uncircumcised in heart and ears, you always resist the Holy Spirit. As your fathers did, so do you. Which of the prophets did not your fathers persecute? And they killed those who announced beforehand the coming of the Righteous One, whom you have now betrayed and murdered, you who received the law as delivered by angels and did not keep it.

* The Stoning of Stephen (Acts 7:54–8:1); F6–659; P–2635

St. Luke: Now when they heard these things they were enraged, and they ground their teeth against him. But he, full of the Holy Spirit, gazed into heaven and saw the glory of God, and Jesus standing at the right hand of God; and he said,

Stephen: Behold, I see the heavens opened, and the Son of man standing at the right hand of God.

St. Luke: But they cried out with a loud voice and stopped their ears and rushed together upon him. Then they cast him out of the city and stoned him; and the witnesses laid down their garments at the feet of a young man named Saul. And as they were stoning Stephen, he prayed,

Stephen: Lord Jesus, receive my spirit.

St. Luke: And he knelt down and cried with a loud voice,

Stephen: Lord, do not hold this sin against them.

St. Luke: And when he had said this, he fell asleep.

Acts Chapter 8

St. Luke: And Saul was consenting to his death.

~ Saul Persecutes the Church (Acts 8:2–3)

St. Luke: And on that day a great persecution arose against the church in Jerusalem; and they were all scattered throughout the region of Judea and Samaria, except the apostles. Devout men buried Stephen, and made great lamentation over him. But Saul laid waste the church, and entering house after house, he dragged off men and women and committed them to prison.

~ Philip Preaches in Samaria (Acts 8:4–8)

St. Luke: Now those who were scattered went about preaching the word. Philip went down to a city of Samaria, and proclaimed to them the Christ. And the multitudes with one accord gave heed to what was said by Philip, when they heard him and saw the signs which he did. For unclean spirits came out of many who were possessed, crying with a loud voice; and many who were paralyzed or lame were healed. So there was much joy in that city.

* Simon the Magician (Acts 8:9–25); S1–1226; C1–2121

St. Luke: But there was a man named Simon who had previously practiced magic in the city and amazed the nation of Samaria, saying that he himself was somebody great. They all gave heed to him, from the least to the greatest, saying,

Samaritans: This man is that power of God which is called great.

St. Luke: And they gave heed to him, because for a long time he had amazed them with his magic. But when they believed Philip as he preached good news about the kingdom of God and the name of Jesus Christ, they were baptized, both men and women.

Even Simon himself believed, and after being baptized he continued with Philip. And seeing signs and great miracles performed, he was amazed.

Now when the apostles at Jerusalem heard that Samaria had received the word of God, they sent to them Peter and John, who came down and prayed for them that they might receive the Holy Spirit; for it had not yet fallen on any of them, but they had only been baptized in the name of the Lord Jesus. Then they laid their hands on them and they received the Holy Spirit.

Now when Simon saw that the Spirit was given through the laying on of the apostles' hands, he offered them money, saying,

Simon: Give me also this power, that any one on whom I lay my hands may receive the Holy Spirit.

St. Luke: But Peter said to him,

Peter: Your silver perish with you, because you thought you could obtain the gift of God with money!

You have neither part nor lot in this matter, for your heart is not right before God. Repent therefore of this wickedness of yours, and pray to the Lord that, if possible, the intent of your heart may be forgiven you. For I see that you are in the gall of bitterness and in the bond of iniquity.

St. Luke: And Simon answered,

Simon: Pray for me to the Lord, that nothing of what you have said may come upon me.

St. Luke: Now when they had testified and spoken the word of the Lord, they returned to Jerusalem, preaching the gospel to many villages of the Samaritans.

* Philip and the Ethiopian Eunuch (Acts 8:26–40); F1–334; F2–454

St. Luke: But an angel of the Lord said to Philip,

Angel of the Lord: Rise and go toward the south to the road that goes down from Jerusalem to Gaza.

St. Luke: This is a desert road. And he rose and went. And behold, an Ethiopian, a eunuch, a minister of Candace, the queen of the Ethiopians, in charge of all her treasure, had come to Jerusalem to worship and was returning; seated in his chariot, he was reading the prophet Isaiah. And the Spirit said to Philip,

Holy Spirit: Go up and join this chariot.

St. Luke: So Philip ran to him, and heard him reading Isaiah the prophet, and asked,

Philip: Do you understand what you are reading?

St. Luke: And he said,

Ethiopian: How can I, unless someone guides me?

St. Luke: And he invited Philip to come up and sit with him. Now the passage of the Scripture which he was reading was this:

Isaiah: As a sheep led to the slaughter or a lamb before its shearer is mute, so he opens not his mouth. In his humiliation justice was denied him. Who can describe his generation? For his life is taken up from the earth.

St. Luke: And the eunuch said to Philip,

Ethiopian: About whom, pray, does the prophet say this, about himself or about someone else?

St. Luke: Then Philip opened his mouth, and beginning with this Scripture he told him the good news of Jesus. And as they went along the road they came to some water, and the eunuch said,

Ethiopian: See, here is water! What is to prevent my being baptized?

St. Luke: And he commanded the chariot to stop, and they both went down into the water, Philip and the eunuch, and he baptized him. And when they came up out of the water, the Spirit of the Lord caught up Philip; and the eunuch saw him no more, and went on his way rejoicing.

But Philip was found at Azotus, and passing on he preached the gospel to all the towns till he came to Caesarea.

Acts Chapter 9

* The Conversion of Saul (Acts 9:1–19); F5–639; F2–442

St. Luke: But Saul, still breathing threats and murder against the disciples of the Lord, went to the high priest and asked him for letters to the synagogues at Damascus, so that if he found any belonging to the Way, men or women, he might bring them bound to Jerusalem. Now as he journeyed he approached Damascus, and suddenly a light from heaven flashed about him. And he fell to the ground and heard a voice saying to him,

Jesus: Saul, Saul, why do you persecute me?

St. Luke: And he said,

Saul: Who are you, Lord?

St. Luke: And he said,

Jesus: I am Jesus, whom you are persecuting; but rise and enter the city, and you will be told what you are to do.

St. Luke: The men who were traveling with him stood speechless, hearing the voice but seeing no one. Saul arose from the ground; and when his eyes were opened, he could see nothing; so they led him by the hand and brought him into Damascus.

And for three days he was without sight, and neither ate nor drank.

St. Luke : Now there was a disciple at Damascus named Ananias. The Lord said to him in a vision,

Jesus: Ananias.

St. Luke : And he said,

Ananias: Here I am, Lord.

St. Luke : And the Lord said to him,

Jesus: Rise and go to the street called Straight, and inquire in the house of Judas for a man of Tarsus named Saul; for behold, he is praying, and he has seen a man named Ananias come in and lay his hands on him so that he might regain his sight.

St. Luke : But Ananias answered,

Ananias: Lord, I have heard from many about this man, how much evil he has done to your saints at Jerusalem; and here he has authority from the chief priests to bind all who call upon your name.

St. Luke : But the Lord said to him,

Jesus: Go, for he is a chosen instrument of mine to carry my name before the Gentiles and kings and the sons of Israel; for I will show him how much he must suffer for the sake of my name.

St. Luke : So Ananias departed and entered the house. And laying his hands on him he said,

Ananias: Brother Saul, the Lord Jesus who appeared to you on the road by which you came, has sent me that you may regain your sight and be filled with the Holy Spirit.

St. Luke: And immediately something like scales fell from his eyes and he regained his sight. Then he rose and was baptized, and took food and was strengthened.

Saul Preaches in Damascus (Acts 9:20–22); F2–442

St. Luke: For several days he was with the disciples at Damascus. And in the synagogues immediately he proclaimed Jesus, saying,

Saul: He is the Son of God.

St. Luke: And all who heard him were amazed, and said,

All who heard him: Is not this the man who made havoc in Jerusalem of those who called on this name? And he has come here for this purpose, to bring them bound before the chief priests.

St. Luke: But Saul increased all the more in strength, and confounded the Jews who lived in Damascus by proving that Jesus was the Christ.

~ Saul Escapes from the Jews (Acts 9:23–25)

St. Luke: When many days had passed, the Jews plotted to kill him, but their plot became known to Saul. They were watching the gates day and night, to kill him; but his disciples took him by night and let him down over the wall, lowering him in a basket.

~ Saul in Jerusalem (Acts 9:26–31)

St. Luke: And when he had come to Jerusalem he attempted to join the disciples; and they were all afraid of him, for they did not believe that he was a disciple. But Barnabas took him, and brought him to the apostles, and declared to them how on the road he had seen the Lord, who spoke to him, and how at Damascus he had preached boldly in the name of Jesus. So he went in and out among them at Jerusalem, preaching boldly in the name of the Lord. And he spoke and disputed against the Hellenists; but they were seeking to kill him. And when the brethren knew it, they brought him down to Caesarea, and sent him off to Tarsus. So the church throughout all Judea and Galilee and Samaria had peace and was built up; and walking in the fear of the Lord and in the comfort of the Holy Spirit it was multiplied.

Peter Heals Aeneas in Lydda (Acts 9:32–35); S5–1507

St. Luke: Now as Peter went here and there among them all, he came down also to the saints that lived at Lydda. There he found a man named Aeneas, who had been bedridden for eight years and was paralyzed. And Peter said to him,

Peter: Aeneas, Jesus Christ heals you; rise and make your bed.

St. Luke: And immediately he rose. And all the residents of Lydda and Sharon saw him, and they turned to the Lord.

~ Peter in Joppa (Acts 9:36–43)

St. Luke: Now there was at Joppa a disciple named Tabitha, which means Dorcas or Gazelle. She was full of good works and acts of charity. In those days she fell sick and died; and when they had washed her, they laid her in an upper room. Since Lydda was near Joppa, the disciples, hearing that Peter was there, sent two men to him entreating him,

Residents of Joppa: Please come to us without delay.

St. Luke: So Peter rose and went with them. And when he had come, they took him to the upper room. All the widows stood beside him weeping, and showing tunics and other garments which Dorcas made while she was with them. But Peter put them all outside and knelt down and prayed; then turning to the body he said,

Peter: Tabitha, rise.

St. Luke: And she opened her eyes, and when she saw Peter she sat up. And he gave her his hand and lifted her up. Then calling the saints and widows he presented her alive. And it became known throughout all Joppa, and many believed in the Lord. And he stayed in Joppa for many days with one Simon, a tanner.

Acts Chapter 10

Peter and Cornelius (Acts 10:1–33); F1–334

St. Luke: At Caesarea there was a man named Cornelius, a centurion of what was known as the Italian Cohort, a devout man who feared God with all his household, gave alms liberally to the people, and prayed constantly to God. About the ninth hour of the day he saw clearly in a vision an angel of God coming in and saying to him,

Angel of God: Cornelius.

St. Luke: And he stared at him in terror, and said,

Cornelius: What is it, Lord?

St. Luke: And he said to him,

Angel of God: Your prayers and your alms have ascended as a memorial before God. And now send men to Joppa, and bring one Simon who is called Peter; he is lodging with Simon, a tanner, whose house is by the seaside.

St. Luke: When the angel who spoke to him had departed, he called two of his servants and a devout soldier from among those that waited on him, and having related everything to them, he sent them to Joppa.

Peter Has a Vision

St. Luke: The next day, as they were on their journey and coming near the city, Peter went up on the housetop to pray, about the sixth hour. And he became hungry and desired something to eat; but while they were preparing it, he fell into a trance and saw the heaven opened, and something descending, like a great sheet, let down by four corners upon the earth. In it were all kinds of animals and reptiles and birds of the air. And there came a voice to him,

Voice: Rise, Peter; kill and eat.

St. Luke: But Peter said,

Peter: No, Lord; for I have never eaten anything that is common or unclean.

St. Luke: And the voice came to him again a second time,

Voice: What God has cleansed, you must not call common.

St. Luke: This happened three times, and the thing was taken up at once to heaven. Now while Peter was inwardly perplexed as to what the vision which he had seen might mean, behold, the men that were sent by Cornelius, having made inquiry for Simon's house, stood before the gate and called out to ask whether Simon who was called Peter was lodging there. And while Peter was pondering the vision, the Spirit said to him,

Holy Spirit: Behold, three men are looking for you. Rise and go down, and accompany them without hesitation; for I have sent them.

St. Luke: And Peter went down to the men and said,

Peter: I am the one you are looking for; what is the reason for your coming?

St. Luke: And they said,

Three men: Cornelius, a centurion, an upright and God-fearing man, who is well spoken of by the whole Jewish nation, was directed by a holy angel to send for you to come to his house, and to hear what you have to say.

St. Luke: So he called them in to be his guests. The next day he rose and went off with them, and some of the brethren from Joppa accompanied him. And on the following day they entered Caesarea. Cornelius was expecting them and had called together his kinsmen and close friends. When Peter entered, Cornelius met him and fell down at his feet and worshiped him. But Peter lifted him up, saying,

Peter: Stand up; I too am a man.

St. Luke: And as he talked with him, he went in and found many persons gathered; and he said to them,

Peter: You yourselves know how unlawful it is for a Jew to associate with or to visit any one of another nation; but God has shown me that I should not call any man common or unclean. So when I was sent for, I came without objection. I ask then why you sent for me.

St. Luke: And Cornelius said,

Cornelius: Four days ago, about this hour, I was keeping the ninth hour of prayer in my house; and behold, a man stood before me in bright apparel, saying,

Angel of God: Cornelius, your prayer has been heard and your alms have been remembered before God. Send therefore to Joppa and ask for Simon who is called Peter; he is lodging in the house of Simon, a tanner, by the seaside.

Cornelius: So I sent to you at once, and you have been kind enough to come. Now therefore we are all here present in the sight of God, to hear all that you have been commanded by the Lord.

* Gentiles Hear the Good News (Acts 10:34–43); F2–438; S2–1289

St. Luke: And Peter opened his mouth and said:

Peter: Truly I perceive that God shows no partiality, but in every nation any one who fears him and does what is right is acceptable to him. You know the word which he sent to Israel, preaching good news of peace by Jesus Christ (he is Lord of all), the word which was proclaimed throughout all

Judea, beginning from Galilee after the baptism which John preached: how God anointed Jesus of Nazareth with the Holy Spirit and with power; how he went about doing good and healing all that were oppressed by the devil, for God was with him.

And we are witnesses to all that he did both in the country of the Jews and in Jerusalem. They put him to death by hanging him on a tree; but God raised him on the third day and made him manifest; not to all the people but to us who were chosen by God as witnesses, who ate and drank with him after he rose from the dead.

And he commanded us to preach to the people, and to testify that he is the one ordained by God to be judge of the living and the dead. To him all the prophets bear witness that everyone who believes in him receives forgiveness of sins through his name.

The Gentiles Receive the Holy Spirit (Acts 10:44–48); S1–1226

St. Luke: While Peter was still saying this, the Holy Spirit fell on all who heard the word. And the believers from among the circumcised who came with Peter were amazed, because the gift of the Holy Spirit had been poured out even on the Gentiles. For they heard them speaking in tongues and extolling God. Then Peter declared,

Peter: Can any one forbid water for baptizing these people who have received the Holy Spirit just as we have?

St. Luke: And he commanded them to be baptized in the name of Jesus Christ. Then they asked him to remain for some days.

Acts Chapter 11

Peter Reports to the Church at Jerusalem (Acts 11:1–18); S7–1655

St. Luke: Now the apostles and the brethren who were in Judea heard that the Gentiles also had received the word of God. So when Peter went up to Jerusalem, the circumcision party criticized him, saying,

Brethren: Why did you go to uncircumcised men and eat with them?

St. Luke: But Peter began and explained to them in order:

Peter: I was in the city of Joppa praying; and in a trance I saw a vision, something descending, like a great sheet, let down from heaven by four corners; and it came down to me. Looking at it closely I observed animals and beasts of prey and reptiles and birds of the air. And I heard a voice saying to me,

Voice: Rise, Peter; kill and eat.

Peter: But I said, "No, Lord; for nothing common or unclean has ever entered my mouth." But the voice answered a second time from heaven,

Voice: What God has cleansed you must not call common.

Peter: This happened three times, and all was drawn up again into heaven. At that very moment three men arrived at the house in which we were, sent to me from Caesarea. And the Spirit told me to go with them, making no distinction. These six brethren also accompanied me, and we entered the man's house. And he told us how he had seen the angel standing in his house and saying,

Angel: Send to Joppa and bring Simon called Peter; he will declare to you a message by which you will be saved, you and all your household.

Peter: As I began to speak, the Holy Spirit fell on them just as on us at the beginning. And I remembered the word of the Lord, how he said,

Jesus: John baptized with water, but you shall be baptized with the Holy Spirit.

Peter: If then God gave the same gift to them as he gave to us when we believed in the Lord Jesus Christ, who was I that I could withstand God?

St. Luke: When they heard this they were silenced. And they glorified God, saying,

Brethren: Then to the Gentiles also God has granted repentance unto life.

~ The Church in Antioch (Acts 11:19–30)

St. Luke: Now those who were scattered because of the persecution that arose over Stephen traveled as far as Phoenicia and Cyprus and Antioch, speaking the word to none except Jews. But there were some of them, men of Cyprus and Cyrene, who on coming to Antioch spoke to the Greeks also, preaching the Lord Jesus. And the hand of the Lord was with them, and a great number that believed turned to the Lord.

St. Luke 1: News of this came to the ears of the church in Jerusalem, and they sent Barnabas to Antioch. When he came and saw the grace of God, he was glad; and he exhorted them all to remain faithful to the Lord with steadfast purpose; for he was a good man, full of the Holy Spirit and of faith. And a large company was added to the Lord.

St. Luke 2: So Barnabas went to Tarsus to look for Saul; and when he had found him, he brought him to Antioch. For a whole year they met with the church, and taught a large company of people; and in Antioch the disciples were for the first time called Christians.

St. Luke 3: Now in these days prophets came down from Jerusalem to Antioch. And one of them named Agabus stood up and foretold by the Spirit that there would be a great famine over all the world; and this took place in the days of Claudius. And the disciples determined, every one according to his ability, to send relief to the brethren who lived in Judea; and they did so, sending it to the elders by the hand of Barnabas and Saul.

Acts Chapter 12

James Killed and Peter Imprisoned by Herod (Acts 12:1–5); P–2636

St. Luke: About that time Herod the king laid violent hands upon some who belonged to the church. He killed James the brother of John with the sword; and when he saw that it pleased the Jews, he proceeded to arrest Peter also.

This was during the days of Unleavened Bread. And when he had seized him, he put him in prison, and delivered him to four squads of soldiers to guard him, intending after the Passover to bring him out to the people. So Peter was kept in prison; but earnest prayer for him was made to God by the church.

An Angel Rescues Peter from Prison (Acts 12:6–19); F1–334

St. Luke: The very night when Herod was about to bring him out, Peter was sleeping between two soldiers, bound with two chains, and sentries before the door were guarding the prison; and behold, an angel of the Lord appeared, and a light shone in the cell; and he struck Peter on the side and woke him, saying,

Angel: Get up quickly.

St. Luke: And the chains fell off his hands. And the angel said to him,

Angel: Dress yourself and put on your sandals.

St. Luke: And he did so. And he said to him,

Angel: Wrap your cloak around you and follow me.

St. Luke: And he went out and followed him; he did not know that what was done by the angel was real, but thought he was seeing a vision. When they had passed the first and the second guard, they came to the iron gate leading into the city. It opened to them of its own accord, and they went out and passed on through one street; and immediately the angel left him. And Peter came to himself, and said,

Peter: Now I am sure that the Lord has sent his angel and rescued me from the hand of Herod and from all that the Jewish people were expecting.

St. Luke: When he realized this, he went to the house of Mary, the mother of John whose other name was Mark, where many were gathered together and were praying. And when he knocked at the door of the gateway, a maid named Rhoda came to answer. Recognizing Peter's voice, in her joy she did not open the gate but ran in and told that Peter was standing at the gate. They said to her,

Disciples: You are mad.

St. Luke: But she insisted that it was so. They said,

Disciples: It is his angel!

St. Luke: But Peter continued knocking; and when they opened, they saw him and were amazed. But motioning to them with his hand to be silent, he described to them how the Lord had brought him out of the prison. And he said,

Peter: Tell this to James and to the brethren.

St. Luke: Then he departed and went to another place. Now when day came, there was no small stir among the soldiers over what had become of Peter. And when Herod had sought for him and could not find him, he examined the sentries and ordered that they should be put to death. Then he went down from Judea to Caesarea, and remained there.

~ The Death of Herod (Acts 12:20–25)

St. Luke: Now Herod was angry with the people of Tyre and Sidon; and they came to him in a body, and having persuaded Blastus, the king's chamberlain, they asked for peace, because their country depended on the king's country for food. On an appointed day Herod put on his royal robes, took his seat upon the throne, and made an oration to them. And the people shouted,

People: The voice of a god, and not of man!

St. Luke: Immediately an angel of the Lord smote him, because he did not give God the glory; and he was eaten by worms and died. But the word of God grew and multiplied. And Barnabas and Saul returned from Jerusalem when they had fulfilled their mission, bringing with them John whose other name was Mark.

Acts Chapter 13

* Barnabas and Saul Commissioned (Acts 13:1–3); F8–699; P–2632

St. Luke: Now in the church at Antioch there were prophets and teachers, Barnabas, Simeon who was called Niger, Lucius of Cyrene, Manaen a member of the court of Herod the tetrarch, and Saul. While they were worshiping the Lord and fasting, the Holy Spirit said,

Holy Spirit: Set apart for me Barnabas and Saul for the work to which I have called them.

St. Luke: Then after fasting and praying they laid their hands on them and sent them off.

~ The Apostles Preach in Cyprus (Acts 13:4–12)

St. Luke: So, being sent out by the Holy Spirit, they went down to Seleucia; and from there they sailed to Cyprus. When they arrived at Salamis, they proclaimed the word of God in the synagogues of the Jews. And they had John to assist them.

When they had gone through the whole island as far as Paphos, they came upon a certain magician, a Jewish false prophet, named Bar-Jesus. He was with the proconsul, Sergius Paulus, a man of intelligence, who summoned Barnabas and Saul and sought to hear the word of God. But Elymas the magician (for that is the meaning of his name) withstood them, seeking to turn away the proconsul from the faith. But Saul, who is also called Paul, filled with the Holy Spirit, looked intently at him and said,

Paul: You son of the devil, you enemy of all righteousness, full of all deceit and villainy, will you not stop making crooked the straight paths of the Lord? And now, behold, the hand of the Lord is upon you, and you shall be blind and unable to see the sun for a time.

St. Luke: Immediately mist and darkness fell upon him and he went about seeking people to lead him by the hand. Then the proconsul believed, when he saw what had occurred, for he was astonished at the teaching of the Lord.

* Paul and Barnabas in Antioch of Pisidia (Acts 13:13–52); F5–647; P–2606

St. Luke: Now Paul and his company set sail from Paphos, and came to Perga in Pamphylia.

And John left them and returned to Jerusalem; but they passed on from Perga and came to Antioch of Pisidia. And on the sabbath day they went into the synagogue and sat down. After the reading of the law and the prophets, the rulers of the synagogue sent to them, saying,

Synagogue rulers: Brethren, if you have any word of exhortation for the people, say it.

St. Luke: So Paul stood up, and motioning with his hand said:

Paul: Men of Israel, and you that fear God, listen. The God of this people Israel chose our fathers and made the people great during their stay in the land of Egypt, and with uplifted arm he led them out of it. And for about forty years he bore with them in the wilderness. And when he had destroyed seven nations in the land of Canaan, he gave them their land as an inheritance, for about four hundred and fifty years. And after that he gave them judges until Samuel the prophet. Then they asked for a king; and God gave them Saul the son of Kish, a man of the tribe of Benjamin, for forty years. And when he had removed him, he raised up David to be their king; of whom he testified and said,

God: I have found in David the son of Jesse a man after my heart, who will do all my will.

Paul: Of this man's posterity God has brought to Israel a Savior, Jesus, as he promised. Before his coming John had preached a baptism of repentance to all the people of Israel. And as John was finishing his course, he said,

John the Baptist: What do you suppose that I am? I am not he. No, but after me one is coming, the sandals of whose feet I am not worthy to untie.

Paul: Brethren, sons of the family of Abraham, and those among you that fear God, to us has been sent the message of this salvation. For those who live in Jerusalem and their rulers, because they did not recognize him nor understand the utterances of the prophets which are read every sabbath, fulfilled these by condemning him. Though they could charge him with nothing deserving death, yet they asked Pilate to have him killed. And when they had fulfilled all that was written of him, they took him down from the tree, and laid him in a tomb.

But God raised him from the dead; and for many days he appeared to those who came up with him from Galilee to Jerusalem, who are now his witnesses to the people. And we bring you the good news that what God promised to the fathers, this he has fulfilled to us their children by raising Jesus; as also it is written in the second psalm,

God: You are my Son, today I have begotten you.

Paul: And as for the fact that he raised him from the dead, no more to return to corruption, he spoke in this way,

God: I will give you the holy and sure blessings of David.

Paul: Therefore he says also in another psalm,

God: You will not let your Holy One see corruption.

Paul: For David, after he had served the counsel of God in his own generation, fell asleep, and was laid with his fathers, and saw corruption; but he whom God raised up saw no corruption.

Let it be known to you therefore, brethren, that through this man forgiveness of sins is proclaimed to you, and by him every one that believes is freed from everything from which you could not be freed by the law of Moses. Beware, therefore, lest there come upon you what is said in the prophets:

God: Behold, you scoffers, and wonder, and perish; for I do a deed in your days, a deed you will never believe, if one declares it to you.

St. Luke: As they went out, the people begged that these things might be told them the next sabbath. And when the meeting of the synagogue broke up, many Jews and devout converts to Judaism followed Paul and Barnabas, who spoke to them and urged them to continue in the grace of God.

The next sabbath almost the whole city gathered together to hear the word of God. But when the Jews saw the multitudes, they were filled with jealousy, and contradicted what was spoken by Paul, and reviled him. And Paul and Barnabas spoke out boldly, saying,

Paul: It was necessary that the word of God should be spoken first to you. Since you thrust it from you, and judge yourselves unworthy of eternal life, behold, we turn to the Gentiles. For so the Lord has commanded us, saying,

Lord: I have set you to be a light for the Gentiles, that you may bring salvation to the uttermost parts of the earth.

St. Luke: And when the Gentiles heard this, they were glad and glorified the word of God; and as many as were ordained to eternal life believed. And the word of the Lord spread throughout all the region.

But the Jews incited the devout women of high standing and the leading men of the city, and stirred up persecution against Paul and Barnabas, and drove them out of their district. But they shook off the dust from their feet against them, and went to Iconium. And the disciples were filled with joy and with the Holy Spirit.

Acts Chapter 14

Paul and Barnabas in Iconium (Acts 14:1–7); F8–699; S5-1507

St. Luke: Now at Iconium they entered together into the Jewish synagogue, and so spoke that a great company believed, both of Jews and of Greeks. But the unbelieving Jews stirred up the Gentiles and poisoned their minds against the brethren. So they remained for a long time, speaking boldly for the Lord, who bore witness to the word of his grace, granting signs and wonders to be done by their hands.

But the people of the city were divided; some sided with the Jews, and some with the apostles. When an attempt was made by both Gentiles and Jews, with their rulers, to molest them and to stone them, they learned of it and fled to Lystra and Derbe, cities of Lycaonia, and to the surrounding country; and there they preached the gospel.

* Paul and Barnabas in Lystra and Derbe (Acts 14:8–23); PF1–32; LT–1147

St. Luke 2: Now at Lystra there was a man sitting, who could not use his feet; he was a cripple from birth, who had never walked. He listened to Paul speaking; and Paul, looking intently at him and seeing that he had faith to be made well, said in a loud voice,

Paul: Stand upright on your feet.

St. Luke 2: And he sprang up and walked. And when the crowds saw what Paul had done, they lifted up their voices, saying in Lycaonian,

Crowds: The gods have come down to us in the likeness of men!

St. Luke 2: Barnabas they called Zeus, and Paul, because he was the chief speaker, they called Hermes. And the priest of Zeus, whose temple was in front of the city, brought oxen and garlands to the gates and wanted to offer sacrifice with the people. But when the apostles Barnabas and Paul heard of it, they tore their garments and rushed out among the multitude, crying,

Barnabas and Paul: Men, why are you doing this? We also are men, of like nature with you, and bring you good news, that you should turn from these vain things to a living God who made the heaven and the earth and the sea and all that is in them.

In past generations he allowed all the nations to walk in their own ways; yet he did not leave himself without witness, for he did good and gave you from heaven rains and fruitful seasons, satisfying your hearts with food and gladness.

St. Luke 2: With these words they scarcely restrained the people from offering sacrifice to them. But Jews came there from Antioch and Iconium; and having persuaded the people, they stoned Paul and dragged him out of the city, supposing that he was dead. But when the disciples gathered about him, he rose up and entered the city; and on the next day he went on with Barnabas to Derbe.

St. Luke: When they had preached the gospel to that city and had made many disciples, they returned to Lystra and to Iconium and to Antioch, strengthening the souls of the disciples, exhorting them to continue in the faith, and saying that through many tribulations we must enter the kingdom of God.

St. Luke 2: And when they had appointed elders for them in every church, with prayer and fasting they committed them to the Lord in whom they believed.

~ The Return to Antioch in Syria (Acts 14:24–28)

St. Luke 3: Then they passed through Pisidia, and came to Pamphylia. And when they had spoken the word in Perga, they went down to Attalia; and from there they sailed to Antioch, where they had been commended to the grace of God for the work which they had fulfilled. And when they arrived, they gathered the church together and declared all that God had done with them, and how he had opened a door of faith to the Gentiles. And they remained no little time with the disciples.

Acts Chapter 15

The Council at Jerusalem (Acts 15:1–21); F4–595; F4–578

St. Luke: But some men came down from Judea and were teaching the brethren,

Some men: Unless you are circumcised according to the custom of Moses, you cannot be saved.

St. Luke: And when Paul and Barnabas had no small dissension and debate with them, Paul and Barnabas and some of the others were appointed to go up to Jerusalem to the apostles and the elders about this question.

So, being sent on their way by the church, they passed through both Phoenicia and Samaria, reporting the conversion of the Gentiles, and they gave great joy to all the brethren. When they came to Jerusalem, they were welcomed by the church and the apostles and the elders, and they declared all that God had done with them. But some believers who belonged to the party of the Pharisees rose up, and said,

Some Pharisees: It is necessary to circumcise them, and to charge them to keep the law of Moses.

St. Luke: The apostles and the elders were gathered together to consider this matter. And after there had been much debate, Peter rose and said to them,

Peter: Brethren, you know that in the early days God made choice among you, that by my mouth the Gentiles should hear the word of the gospel and believe. And God who knows the heart bore witness to them, giving them the Holy Spirit just as he did to us; and he made no distinction between us and them, but cleansed their hearts by faith.

Now therefore why do you make trial of God by putting a yoke upon the neck of the disciples which neither our fathers nor we have been able to bear? But we believe that we shall be saved through the grace of the Lord Jesus, just as they will.

St. Luke: And all the assembly kept silence; and they listened to Barnabas and Paul as they related what signs and wonders God had done through them among the Gentiles. After they finished speaking, James replied,

James: Brethren, listen to me. Simon has related how God first visited the Gentiles, to take out of them a people for his name. And with this the words of the prophets agree, as it is written,

God: After this I will return, and I will rebuild the dwelling of David, which has fallen; I will rebuild its ruins, and I will set it up, that the rest of men may seek the Lord, and all the Gentiles who are called by my name, says the Lord, who has made these things known from of old.

James: Therefore my judgment is that we should not trouble those of the Gentiles who turn to God, but should write to them to abstain from the pollutions of idols and from unchastity and from what is strangled and from blood. For from early generations Moses has had in every city those who preach him, for he is read every sabbath in the synagogues.

~ The Council's Letter to the Gentile Believers (Acts 15:22–35)

St. Luke: Then it seemed good to the apostles and the elders, with the whole church, to choose men from among them and send them to Antioch with Paul and Barnabas. They sent Judas called Barsabbas, and Silas, leading men among the brethren, with the following letter:

Barsabbas and Silas: The brethren, both the apostles and the elders, to the brethren who are of the Gentiles in Antioch and Syria and Cilicia, greeting.

Since we have heard that some persons from us have troubled you with words, unsettling your minds, although we gave them no instructions, it has seemed good to us, having come to one accord, to choose men and send them to you with our beloved Barnabas and Paul, men who have risked their lives for the sake of our Lord Jesus Christ.

We have therefore sent Judas and Silas, who themselves will tell you the same things by word of mouth. For it has seemed good to the Holy Spirit and to us to lay upon you no greater burden than these necessary things: that you abstain from what has been sacrificed to idols and from blood and from what is strangled and from unchastity. If you keep yourselves from these, you will do well. Farewell.

St. Luke 2: So when they were sent off, they went down to Antioch; and having gathered the congregation together, they delivered the letter. And when they read it, they rejoiced at the exhortation. And Judas and Silas, who were themselves prophets, exhorted the brethren with many words and strengthened them. And after they had spent some time, they were sent off in peace by the brethren to those who had sent them. But Paul and Barnabas remained in Antioch, teaching and preaching the word of the Lord, with many others also.

~ Paul and Barnabas Separate (Acts 15:36–41)

St. Luke 2: And after some days Paul said to Barnabas,

Paul: Come, let us return and visit the brethren in every city where we proclaimed the word of the Lord, and see how they are.

St. Luke 2: And Barnabas wanted to take with them John called Mark. But Paul thought best not to take with them one who had withdrawn from them in Pamphylia, and had not gone with them to the work. And there arose a sharp contention, so that they separated from each other; Barnabas took Mark with him and sailed away to Cyprus, but Paul chose Silas and departed, being commended by the brethren to the grace of the Lord. And he went through Syria and Cilicia, strengthening the churches.

Acts Chapter 16

~ Timothy Accompanies Paul and Silas (Acts 16:1–5)

St. Luke: And he came also to Derbe and to Lystra. A disciple was there, named Timothy, the son of a Jewish woman who was a believer; but his father was a Greek. He was well spoken of by the brethren at Lystra and Iconium. Paul wanted Timothy to accompany him; and he took him and circumcised him because of the Jews that were in those places, for they all knew that his father was a Greek.

As they went on their way through the cities, they delivered to them for observance the decisions which had been reached by the apostles and elders who were at Jerusalem. So the churches were strengthened in the faith, and they increased in numbers daily.

~ Paul's Vision of the Man of Macedonia (Acts 16:6–10)

St. Luke: And they went through the region of Phrygia and Galatia, having been forbidden by the Holy Spirit to speak the word in Asia. And when they had come opposite Mysia, they attempted to go into Bithynia, but the Spirit of Jesus did not allow them; so, passing by Mysia, they went down to Troas. And a vision appeared to Paul in the night: a man of Macedonia was standing beseeching him and saying,

Man of Macedonia: Come over to Macedonia and help us.

St. Luke: And when he had seen the vision, immediately we sought to go on into Macedonia, concluding that God had called us to preach the gospel to them.

The Conversion of Lydia and Her Household (Acts 16:11–15); S1–1226; S1–1252

St. Luke: Setting sail therefore from Troas, we made a direct voyage to Samothrace, and the following day to Neapolis, and from there to Philippi, which is the leading city of the district of Macedonia, and a Roman colony. We remained in this city some days; and on the sabbath day we went outside the gate to the riverside, where we supposed there was a place of prayer; and we sat down and spoke to the women who had come together.

One who heard us was a woman named Lydia, from the city of Thyatira, a seller of purple goods, who was a worshiper of God. The Lord opened her heart to give heed to what was said by Paul. And when she was baptized, with her household, she besought us, saying,

Lydia: If you have judged me to be faithful to the Lord, come to my house and stay.

St. Luke: And she prevailed upon us.

* Paul and Silas Beaten and Imprisoned (Acts 16:16–40); F2–434; S1–1252

St. Luke: As we were going to the place of prayer, we were met by a slave girl who had a spirit of divination and brought her owners much gain by soothsaying. She followed Paul and us, crying,

Slave girl: These men are servants of the Most High God, who proclaim to you the way of salvation.

St. Luke: And this she did for many days. But Paul was annoyed, and turned and said to the spirit,

Paul: I charge you in the name of Jesus Christ to come out of her.

St. Luke: And it came out that very hour. But when her owners saw that their hope of gain was gone, they seized Paul and Silas and dragged them into the marketplace before the rulers; and when they had brought them to the magistrates they said,

Slave owners: These men are Jews and they are disturbing our city. They advocate customs which it is not lawful for us Romans to accept or practice.

St. Luke: The crowd joined in attacking them; and the magistrates tore the garments off them and gave orders to beat them with rods. And when they had inflicted many blows upon them, they threw them into prison, charging the jailer to keep them safely. Having received this charge, he put them into the inner prison and fastened their feet in the stocks.

But about midnight Paul and Silas were praying and singing hymns to God, and the prisoners were listening to them, and suddenly there was a great earthquake, so that the foundations of the prison were shaken; and immediately all the doors were opened and every one's fetters were unfastened.

When the jailer woke and saw that the prison doors were open, he drew his sword and was about to kill himself, supposing that the prisoners had escaped. But Paul cried with a loud voice,

Paul: Do not harm yourself, for we are all here.

St. Luke: And he called for lights and rushed in, and trembling with fear he fell down before Paul and Silas, and brought them out and said,

Jailer: Men, what must I do to be saved?

St. Luke: And they said,

Paul and Silas: Believe in the Lord Jesus, and you will be saved, you and your household.

St. Luke: And they spoke the word of the Lord to him and to all that were in his house. And he took them the same hour of the night, and washed their wounds, and he was baptized at once, with all his family.

Then he brought them up into his house, and set food before them; and he rejoiced with all his household that he had believed in God. But when it was day, the magistrates sent the police, saying,

Police: Let those men go.

St. Luke: And the jailer reported the words to Paul, saying,

Jailer: The magistrates have sent to let you go; now therefore come out and go in peace.

St. Luke: But Paul said to them,

Paul: They have beaten us publicly, uncondemned men who are Roman citizens, and have thrown us into prison; and do they now cast us out secretly? No! Let them come themselves and take us out.

St. Luke: The police reported these words to the magistrates, and they were afraid when they heard that they were Roman citizens; so they came and apologized to them. And they took them out and asked them to leave the city. So they went out of the prison, and visited Lydia; and when they had seen the brethren, they exhorted them and departed.

Acts Chapter 17

~ The Uproar in Thessalonica (Acts 17:1–9)

St. Luke: Now when they had passed through Amphipolis and Apollonia, they came to Thessalonica, where there was a synagogue of the Jews. And Paul went in, as was his custom, and for three weeks he argued with them from the Scriptures, explaining and proving that it was necessary for the Christ to suffer and to rise from the dead, and saying,

Paul: This Jesus, whom I proclaim to you, is the Christ.

St. Luke: And some of them were persuaded, and joined Paul and Silas; as did a great many of the devout Greeks and not a few of the leading women. But the Jews were jealous, and taking some wicked fellows of the rabble, they gathered a crowd, set the city in an uproar, and attacked the house of Jason, seeking to bring them out to the people. And when they could not find them, they dragged Jason and some of the brethren before the city authorities, crying,

Jealous Jews: These men who have turned the world upside down have come here also, and Jason has received them; and they are all acting against the decrees of Caesar, saying that there is another king, Jesus.

St. Luke: And the people and the city authorities were disturbed when they heard this. And when they had taken security from Jason and the rest, they let them go.

~ Paul and Silas in Beroea (Acts 17:10–15)

St. Luke: The brethren immediately sent Paul and Silas away by night to Beroea; and when they arrived they went into the Jewish synagogue. Now these Jews were more noble than those in Thessalonica, for they received the word with all eagerness, examining the Scriptures daily to see if these things were so. Many of them therefore believed, with not a few Greek women of high standing as well as men.

But when the Jews of Thessalonica learned that the word of God was proclaimed by Paul at Beroea also, they came there too, stirring up and inciting the crowds. Then the brethren immediately sent Paul off on his way to the sea, but Silas and Timothy remained there. Those who conducted Paul brought him as far as Athens; and receiving a command for Silas and Timothy to come to him as soon as possible, they departed.

* Paul in Athens (Acts 17:16–34); PF1–28; PF2–57

St. Luke: Now while Paul was waiting for them at Athens, his spirit was provoked within him as he saw that the city was full of idols. So he argued in the synagogue with the Jews and the devout persons, and in the market place every day with those who chanced to be there. Some also of the Epicurean and Stoic philosophers met him. And some said,

Philosophers: What would this babbler say?

St. Luke: Others said,

Others: He seems to be a preacher of foreign divinities.

St. Luke: —because he preached Jesus and the resurrection. And they took hold of him and brought him to the Areopagus, saying,

Athenians: May we know what this new teaching is which you present? For you bring some strange things to our ears; we wish to know therefore what these things mean.

St. Luke: Now all the Athenians and the foreigners who lived there spent their time in nothing except telling or hearing something new.

St. Luke: So Paul, standing in the middle of the Areopagus, said:

Paul: Men of Athens, I perceive that in every way you are very religious. For as I passed along, and observed the objects of your worship, I found also an altar with this inscription, "To an unknown god." What therefore you worship as unknown, this I proclaim to you.

The God who made the world and everything in it, being Lord of heaven and earth, does not live in shrines made by man, nor is he served by human hands, as though he needed anything, since he himself gives to all men life and breath and everything. And he made from one every nation of men to live on all the face of the earth, having determined allotted periods and the boundaries of their habitation, that they should seek God, in the hope that they might feel after him and find him. Yet he is not far from each one of us, for "In him we live and move and have our being"; as even some of your poets have said.

For we are indeed his offspring. Being then God's offspring, we ought not to think that the Deity is like gold, or silver, or stone, a representation by the art and imagination of man. The times of ignorance God overlooked, but now he commands all men everywhere to repent, because he has fixed a day on which he will judge the world in righteousness by a man whom he has appointed, and of this he has given assurance to all men by raising him from the dead.

St. Luke: Now when they heard of the resurrection of the dead, some mocked; but others said,

Others: We will hear you again about this.

St. Luke: So Paul went out from among them. But some men joined him and believed, among them Dionysius the Areopagite and a woman named Damaris and others with them.

Acts Chapter 18

* Paul in Corinth (Acts 18:1–17); S1–1252; S7–1655

St. Luke: After this he left Athens and went to Corinth. And he found a Jew named Aquila, a native of Pontus, lately come from Italy with his wife Priscilla, because Claudius had commanded all the Jews to leave Rome. And he went to see them; and because he was of the same trade he stayed with them, and they worked, for by trade they were tentmakers. And he argued in the synagogue every sabbath, and persuaded Jews and Greeks.

When Silas and Timothy arrived from Macedonia, Paul was occupied with preaching, testifying to the Jews that the Christ was Jesus. And when they opposed and reviled him, he shook out his garments and said to them,

Paul: Your blood be upon your heads! I am innocent. From now on I will go to the Gentiles.

St. Luke: And he left there and went to the house of a man named Titius Justus, a worshiper of God; his house was next door to the synagogue. Crispus, the ruler of the synagogue, believed in the Lord, together with all his household; and many of the Corinthians hearing Paul believed and were baptized. And the Lord said to Paul one night in a vision,

Lord: Do not be afraid, but speak and do not be silent; for I am with you, and no man shall attack you to harm you; for I have many people in this city.

St. Luke: And he stayed a year and six months, teaching the word of God among them. But when Gallio was proconsul of Achaia, the Jews made a united attack upon Paul and brought him before the tribunal, saying,

Jews: This man is persuading men to worship God contrary to the law.

St. Luke: But when Paul was about to open his mouth, Gallio said to the Jews,

Gallio: If it were a matter of wrongdoing or vicious crime, I should have reason to bear with you, O Jews; but since it is a matter of questions about words and names and your own law, see to it yourselves; I refuse to be a judge of these things.

St. Luke: And he drove them from the tribunal. And they all seized Sosthenes, the ruler of the synagogue, and beat him in front of the tribunal. But Gallio paid no attention to this.

Paul's Return to Antioch (Acts 18:18–23); C1–2102

St. Luke: After this Paul stayed many days longer, and then took leave of the brethren and sailed for Syria, and with him Priscilla and Aquila.

At Cenchreae he cut his hair, for he had a vow. And they came to Ephesus, and he left them there; but he himself went into the synagogue and argued with the Jews. When they asked him to stay for a longer period, he declined; but on taking leave of them he said,

Paul: I will return to you if God wills.

St. Luke: And he set sail from Ephesus. When he had landed at Caesarea, he went up and greeted the church, and then went down to Antioch. After spending some time there he departed and went from place to place through the region of Galatia and Phrygia, strengthening all the disciples.

~ Ministry of Apollos (Acts 18:24–28)

St. Luke: Now a Jew named Apollos, a native of Alexandria, came to Ephesus. He was an eloquent man, well versed in the Scriptures. He had been instructed in the way of the Lord; and being fervent in spirit, he spoke and taught accurately the things concerning Jesus, though he knew only the baptism of John. He began to speak boldly in the synagogue; but when Priscilla and Aquila heard him, they took him and expounded to him the way of God more accurately. And when he wished to cross to Achaia, the brethren encouraged him, and wrote to the disciples to receive him. When he arrived, he greatly helped those who through grace had believed, for he powerfully confuted the Jews in public, showing by the Scriptures that the Christ was Jesus.

Acts Chapter 19

Paul in Ephesus (Acts 19:1–10); S2–1288; F8–699

St. Luke: While Apollos was at Corinth, Paul passed through the upper country and came to Ephesus. There he found some disciples. And he said to them,

Paul: Did you receive the Holy Spirit when you believed?

St. Luke: And they said,

Some disciples: No, we have never even heard that there is a Holy Spirit.

St. Luke: And he said,

Paul: Into what then were you baptized?

St. Luke: They said,

Some disciples: Into John's baptism.

St. Luke: And Paul said,

Paul: John baptized with the baptism of repentance, telling the people to believe in the one who was to come after him, that is, Jesus.

St. Luke: On hearing this, they were baptized in the name of the Lord Jesus. And when Paul had laid his hands upon them, the Holy Spirit came on them; and they spoke with tongues and prophesied. There were about twelve of them in all.

And he entered the synagogue and for three months spoke boldly, arguing and pleading about the kingdom of God; but when some were stubborn and disbelieved, speaking evil of the Way before the congregation, he withdrew from them, taking the disciples with him, and argued daily in the hall of Tyrannus. This continued for two years, so that all the residents of Asia heard the word of the Lord, both Jews and Greeks.

The Sons of Sceva (Acts 19:11–20); F2–434

St. Luke: And God did extraordinary miracles by the hands of Paul, so that handkerchiefs or aprons were carried away from his body to the sick, and diseases left them and the evil spirits came out of them. Then some of the itinerant Jewish exorcists undertook to pronounce the name of the Lord Jesus over those who had evil spirits, saying,

Itinerant Jewish exorcists: I adjure you by the Jesus whom Paul preaches.

St. Luke: Seven sons of a Jewish high priest named Sceva were doing this. But the evil spirit answered them,

Evil spirit: Jesus I know, and Paul I know; but who are you?

St. Luke: And the man in whom the evil spirit was leaped on them, mastered all of them, and overpowered them, so that they fled out of that house naked and wounded.

And this became known to all residents of Ephesus, both Jews and Greeks; and fear fell upon them all; and the name of the Lord Jesus was extolled.

Many also of those who were now believers came, confessing and divulging their practices. And a number of those who practiced magic arts brought their books together and burned them in the sight of all; and they counted the value of them and found it came to fifty thousand pieces of silver. So the word of the Lord grew and prevailed mightily.

The Riot in Ephesus (Acts 19:21–41); F9–751

St. Luke: Now after these events Paul resolved in the Spirit to pass through Macedonia and Achaia and go to Jerusalem, saying,

Paul: After I have been there, I must also see Rome.

St. Luke: And having sent into Macedonia two of his helpers, Timothy and Erastus, he himself stayed in Asia for a while. About that time there arose no little stir concerning the Way. For a man named Demetrius, a silversmith, who made silver shrines of Artemis, brought no little business to the craftsmen. These he gathered together, with the workmen of like occupation, and said,

Demetrius: Men, you know that from this business we have our wealth. And you see and hear that not only at Ephesus but almost throughout all Asia this Paul has persuaded and turned away a considerable company of people, saying that gods made with hands are not gods. And there is danger not only that this trade of ours may come into disrepute but also that the temple of the great goddess Artemis may count for nothing, and that she may even be deposed from her magnificence, she whom all Asia and the world worship.

St. Luke: When they heard this they were enraged, and cried out,

Craftsmen: Great is Artemis of the Ephesians!

St. Luke: So the city was filled with the confusion; and they rushed together into the theater, dragging with them Gaius and Aristarchus, Macedonians who were Paul's companions in travel.

Paul wished to go in among the crowd, but the disciples would not let him; some of the Asiarchs also, who were friends of his, sent to him and begged him not to venture into the theater.

Now some cried one thing, some another; for the assembly was in confusion, and most of them did not know why they had come together. Some of the crowd prompted Alexander, whom the Jews had put forward. And Alexander motioned with his hand, wishing to make a defense to the people. But when they recognized that he was a Jew, for about two hours they all with one voice cried out,

Crowd: Great is Artemis of the Ephesians!

St. Luke: And when the town clerk had quieted the crowd, he said,

Town clerk: Men of Ephesus, what man is there who does not know that the city of the Ephesians is temple keeper of the great Artemis, and of the sacred stone that fell from the sky?

Seeing then that these things cannot be contradicted, you ought to be quiet and do nothing rash. For you have brought these men here who are neither sacrilegious nor blasphemers of our goddess. If therefore Demetrius and the craftsmen with him have a complaint against any one, the courts are open, and there are proconsuls; let them bring charges against one another. But if you seek anything further, it shall be settled in the regular assembly. For we are in danger of being charged with rioting today, there being no cause that we can give to justify this commotion.

St. Luke: And when he had said this, he dismissed the assembly.

Acts Chapter 20

~ Paul Goes to Macedonia and Greece (Acts 20:1–6)

St. Luke: After the uproar ceased, Paul sent for the disciples and having exhorted them took leave of them and departed for Macedonia. When he had gone through these parts and had given them much encouragement, he came to Greece. There he spent three months, and when a plot was made against him by the Jews as he was about to set sail for Syria, he determined to return through Macedonia.

Sopater of Beroea, the son of Pyrrhus, accompanied him; and of the Thessalonians, Aristarchus and Secundus; and Gaius of Derbe, and Timothy; and the Asians, Tychicus and Trophimus. These went on and were waiting for us at Troas, but we sailed away from Philippi after the days of Unleavened Bread, and in five days we came to them at Troas, where we stayed for seven days.

Paul Preaches and Heals Eutychus in Troas (Acts 20:7–16); S3–1329; S3–1343

St. Luke: On the first day of the week, when we were gathered together to break bread, Paul talked with them, intending to depart on the morrow; and he prolonged his speech until midnight. There were many lights in the upper chamber where we were gathered. And a young man named Eutychus was sitting in the window. He sank into a deep sleep as Paul talked still longer; and being overcome by sleep, he fell down from the third story and was taken up dead. But Paul went down and bent over him, and embracing him said,

Paul: Do not be alarmed, for his life is in him.

St. Luke 2: And when Paul had gone up and had broken bread and eaten, he conversed with them a long while, until daybreak, and so departed. And they took the lad away alive, and were not a little comforted.

But going ahead to the ship, we set sail for Assos, intending to take Paul aboard there; for so he had arranged, intending himself to go by land. And when he met us at Assos, we took him on board and came to Mitylene. And sailing from there we came the following day opposite Chios; the next day we touched at Samos; and the day after that we came to Miletus.

For Paul had decided to sail past Ephesus, so that he might not have to spend time in Asia; for he was hastening to be at Jerusalem, if possible, on the day of Pentecost.

Paul Speaks to the Elders of Ephesus (Acts 20:17–38); F9–798; P–2636

St. Luke: And from Miletus he sent to Ephesus and called to him the elders of the church. And when they came to him, he said to them:

Paul: You yourselves know how I lived among you all the time from the first day that I set foot in Asia, serving the Lord with all humility and with tears and with trials which befell me through the plots of the Jews; how I did not shrink from declaring to you anything that was profitable, and teaching you in public and from house to house, testifying both to Jews and to Greeks of repentance to God and of faith in our Lord Jesus Christ.

And now, behold, I am going to Jerusalem, bound in the Spirit, not knowing what shall befall me there; except that the Holy Spirit testifies to me in every city that imprisonment and afflictions await me. But I do not account my life of any value nor as precious to myself, if only I may accomplish my course and the ministry which I received from the Lord Jesus, to testify to the gospel of the grace of God.

And now, behold, I know that all you among whom I have gone preaching the kingdom will see my face no more. Therefore I testify to you this day that I am innocent of the blood of all of you, for I did not shrink from declaring to you the whole counsel of God.

Take heed to yourselves and to all the flock, in which the Holy Spirit has made you overseers, to care for the church of the Lord which he obtained with his own blood. I know that after my departure fierce wolves will come in among you, not sparing the flock; and from among your own selves will arise men speaking perverse things, to draw away the disciples after them.

Paul 2: Therefore be alert, remembering that for three years I did not cease night or day to admonish every one with tears. And now I commend you to God and to the word of his grace, which is able to build you up and to give you the inheritance among all those who are sanctified. I coveted no one's silver or gold or apparel. You yourselves know that these hands ministered to my necessities, and to those who were with me. In all things I have shown you that by so toiling one must help the weak, remembering the words of the Lord Jesus, how he said,

Jesus: It is more blessed to give than to receive.

St. Luke: And when he had spoken thus, he knelt down and prayed with them all. And they all wept and embraced Paul and kissed him, sorrowing most of all because of the word he had spoken, that they should see his face no more. And they brought him to the ship.

Acts Chapter 21

Paul's Journey to Jerusalem (Acts 21:1–16); P–2636

St. Luke: And when we had parted from them and set sail, we came by a straight course to Cos, and the next day to Rhodes, and from there to Patara. And having found a ship crossing to Phoenicia, we went aboard, and set sail. When we had come in sight of Cyprus, leaving it on the left we sailed to Syria, and landed at Tyre; for there the ship was to unload its cargo.

And having sought out the disciples, we stayed there for seven days. Through the Spirit they told Paul not to go on to Jerusalem. And when our days there were ended, we departed and went on our journey; and they all, with wives and children, brought us on our way till we were outside the city; and kneeling down on the beach we prayed and bade one another farewell. Then we went on board the ship, and they returned home.

When we had finished the voyage from Tyre, we arrived at Ptolemais; and we greeted the brethren and stayed with them for one day. On the morrow we departed and came to Caesarea; and we entered the house of Philip the evangelist, who was one of the seven, and stayed with him. And he had four unmarried daughters, who prophesied. While we were staying for some days, a prophet named Agabus came down from Judea. And coming to us he took Paul's belt and bound his own feet and hands, and said,

Agabus: Thus says the Holy Spirit,

Holy Spirit: So shall the Jews at Jerusalem bind the man who owns this belt and deliver him into the hands of the Gentiles.

St. Luke: When we heard this, we and the people there begged him not to go up to Jerusalem. Then Paul answered,

Paul: What are you doing, weeping and breaking my heart? For I am ready not only to be imprisoned but even to die at Jerusalem for the name of the Lord Jesus.

St. Luke: And when he would not be persuaded, we ceased and said,

Disciples: The will of the Lord be done.

St. Luke: After these days we made ready and went up to Jerusalem. And some of the disciples from Caesarea went with us, bringing us to the house of Mnason of Cyprus, an early disciple, with whom we should lodge.

Paul Visits James at Jerusalem (Acts 21:17–26); F4–595; C1–2102

St. Luke: When we had come to Jerusalem, the brethren received us gladly. On the following day Paul went in with us to James; and all the elders were present. After greeting them, he related one by one the things that God had done among the Gentiles through his ministry. And when they heard it, they glorified God. And they said to him,

James and the elders: You see, brother, how many thousands there are among the Jews of those who have believed; they are all zealous for the law, and they have been told about you that you teach all the Jews who are among the Gentiles to forsake Moses, telling them not to circumcise their children or observe the customs.

What then is to be done? They will certainly hear that you have come. Do therefore what we tell you. We have four men who are under a vow; take these men and purify yourself along with them and pay their expenses, so that they may shave their heads. Thus all will know that there is nothing in what they have been told about you but that you yourself live in observance of the law.

But as for the Gentiles who have believed, we have sent a letter with our judgment that they should abstain from what has been sacrificed to idols and from blood and from what is strangled and from unchastity.

St. Luke: Then Paul took the men, and the next day he purified himself with them and went into the temple, to give notice when the days of purification would be fulfilled and the offering presented for every one of them.

~ Paul Arrested in the Temple (Acts 21:27–36)

St. Luke: When the seven days were almost completed, the Jews from Asia, who had seen him in the temple, stirred up all the crowd, and laid hands on him, crying out,

Jews from Asia: Men of Israel, help! This is the man who is teaching men everywhere against the people and the law and this place; moreover he also brought Greeks into the temple, and he has defiled this holy place.

St. Luke: For they had previously seen Trophimus the Ephesian with him in the city, and they supposed that Paul had brought him into the temple. Then all the city was aroused, and the people ran together; they seized Paul and dragged him out of the temple, and at once the gates were shut. And as they were trying to kill him, word came to the tribune of the cohort that all Jerusalem was in confusion.

He at once took soldiers and centurions, and ran down to them; and when they saw the tribune and the soldiers, they stopped beating Paul. Then the tribune came up and arrested him, and ordered him to be bound with two chains. He inquired who he was and what he had done. Some in the crowd shouted one thing, some another; and as he could not learn the facts because of the uproar, he ordered him to be brought into the barracks. And when he came to the steps, he was actually carried by the soldiers because of the violence of the crowd; for the mob of the people followed, crying,

Mob of people: Away with him!

~ Paul Defends Himself (Acts 21:37–22:5)

St. Luke: As Paul was about to be brought into the barracks, he said to the tribune,

Paul: May I say something to you?

St. Luke: And he said,

Tribune: Do you know Greek? Are you not the Egyptian, then, who recently stirred up a revolt and led the four thousand men of the Assassins out into the wilderness?

St. Luke: Paul replied,

Paul: I am a Jew, from Tarsus in Cilicia, a citizen of no mean city; I beg you, let me speak to the people.

St. Luke: And when he had given him leave, Paul, standing on the steps, motioned with his hand to the people; and when there was a great hush, he spoke to them in the Hebrew language, saying:

Acts Chapter 22

Paul: Brethren and fathers, hear the defense which I now make before you.

St. Luke: And when they heard that he addressed them in the Hebrew language, they were the more quiet. And he said:

Paul: I am a Jew, born at Tarsus in Cilicia, but brought up in this city at the feet of Gamaliel, educated according to the strict manner of the law of our fathers, being zealous for God as you all are this day. I persecuted this Way to the death, binding and delivering to prison both men and women, as the high priest and the whole council of elders bear me witness.

From them I received letters to the brethren, and I journeyed to Damascus to take those also who were there and bring them in bonds to Jerusalem to be punished.

~ Paul Tells of His Conversion (Acts 22:6–16)

St. Luke: As I made my journey and drew near to Damascus, about noon a great light from heaven suddenly shone about me. And I fell to the ground and heard a voice saying to me,

Jesus: Saul, Saul, why do you persecute me?

Paul: And I answered, Who are you, Lord? And he said to me,

Jesus: I am Jesus of Nazareth whom you are persecuting.

Paul: Now those who were with me saw the light but did not hear the voice of the one who was speaking to me. And I said, "What shall I do, Lord?" And the Lord said to me,

Jesus: Rise, and go into Damascus, and there you will be told all that is appointed for you to do.

Paul: And when I could not see because of the brightness of that light, I was led by the hand by those who were with me, and came into Damascus. And one Ananias, a devout man according to the law, well spoken of by all the Jews who lived there, came to me, and standing by me said to me,

Ananias: Brother Saul, receive your sight.

Paul: And in that very hour I received my sight and saw him. And he said,

Ananias: The God of our fathers appointed you to know his will, to see the Just One and to hear a voice from his mouth; for you will be a witness for him to all men of what you have seen and heard. And now why do you wait? Rise and be baptized, and wash away your sins, calling on his name.

~ Paul Tells How He Was Sent to the Gentiles (Acts 22:17–29)

Paul: When I had returned to Jerusalem and was praying in the temple, I fell into a trance and saw him saying to me,

Jesus: Make haste and get quickly out of Jerusalem, because they will not accept your testimony about me.

Paul: And I said, "Lord, they themselves know that in every synagogue I imprisoned and beat those who believed in you. And when the blood of Stephen your witness was shed, I also was standing by and approving, and keeping the garments of those who killed him." And he said to me,

Jesus: Depart; for I will send you far away to the Gentiles.

~ Paul and the Roman Tribune (Acts 22:22–29)

St. Luke: Up to this word they listened to him; then they lifted up their voices and said,

Mob of people: Away with such a fellow from the earth! For he ought not to live.

St. Luke: And as they cried out and waved their garments and threw dust into the air, the tribune commanded him to be brought into the barracks, and ordered him to be examined by scourging, to find out why they shouted thus against him. But when they had tied him up with the thongs, Paul said to the centurion who was standing by,

Paul: Is it lawful for you to scourge a man who is a Roman citizen, and uncondemned?

St. Luke: When the centurion heard that, he went to the tribune and said to him,

Centurion: What are you about to do? For this man is a Roman citizen.

St. Luke: So the tribune came and said to him,

Tribune: Tell me, are you a Roman citizen?

St. Luke: And he said,

Paul: Yes.

St. Luke: The tribune answered,

Tribune: I bought this citizenship for a large sum.

St. Luke: Paul said,

Paul: But I was born a citizen.

St. Luke: So those who were about to examine him withdrew from him instantly; and the tribune also was afraid, for he realized that Paul was a Roman citizen and that he had bound him.

Paul Before the Chief Priests and the Council (Acts 22:30–23:11); F11–993

St. Luke: But on the next day, desiring to know the real reason why the Jews accused him, he unbound him, and commanded the chief priests and all the council to meet, and he brought Paul down and set him before them.

Acts Chapter 23

St. Luke: And Paul, looking intently at the council, said,

Paul: Brethren, I have lived before God in all good conscience up to this day.

St. Luke: And the high priest Ananias commanded those who stood by him to strike him on the mouth. Then Paul said to him,

Paul: God shall strike you, you whitewashed wall! Are you sitting to judge me according to the law, and yet contrary to the law you order me to be struck?

St. Luke: Those who stood by said,

Bystanders: Would you revile God's high priest?

St. Luke: And Paul said,

Paul: I did not know, brethren, that he was the high priest; for it is written, "You shall not speak evil of a ruler of your people."

St. Luke: But when Paul perceived that one part were Sadducees and the other Pharisees, he cried out in the council,

Paul: Brethren, I am a Pharisee, a son of Pharisees; with respect to the hope and the resurrection of the dead I am on trial.

St. Luke: And when he had said this, a dissension arose between the Pharisees and the Sadducees; and the assembly was divided. For the Sadducees say that there is no resurrection, nor angel, nor spirit; but the Pharisees acknowledge them all. Then a great clamor arose; and some of the scribes of the Pharisees' party stood up and contended,

Scribes: We find nothing wrong in this man. What if a spirit or an angel spoke to him?

St. Luke: And when the dissension became violent, the tribune, afraid that Paul would be torn in pieces by them, commanded the soldiers to go down and take him by force from among them and bring him into the barracks. The following night the Lord stood by him and said,

Jesus: Take courage, for as you have testified about me at Jerusalem, so you must bear witness also at Rome.

~ The Plot to Kill Paul (Acts 23:12–22)

St. Luke: When it was day, the Jews made a plot and bound themselves by an oath neither to eat nor drink till they had killed Paul. There were more than forty who made this conspiracy. And they went to the chief priests and elders, and said,

Several Jews: We have strictly bound ourselves by an oath to taste no food till we have killed Paul. You therefore, along with the council, give notice now to the tribune to bring him down to you, as though you were going to determine his case more exactly. And we are ready to kill him before he comes near.

St. Luke: Now the son of Paul's sister heard of their ambush; so he went and entered the barracks and told Paul. And Paul called one of the centurions and said,

Paul: Take this young man to the tribune; for he has something to tell him.

St. Luke: So he took him and brought him to the tribune and said,

Centurion: Paul the prisoner called me and asked me to bring this young man to you, as he has something to say to you.

St. Luke: The tribune took him by the hand, and going aside asked him privately,

Tribune: What is it that you have to tell me?

St. Luke: And he said,

Paul's nephew: The Jews have agreed to ask you to bring Paul down to the council tomorrow, as though they were going to inquire somewhat more closely about him. But do not yield to them; for more than forty of their men lie in ambush for him, having bound themselves by an oath neither to eat nor drink till they have killed him; and now they are ready, waiting for the promise from you.

St. Luke: So the tribune dismissed the young man, charging him,

Tribune: Tell no one that you have informed me of this.

~ Paul is Brought to Felix the Governor (Acts 23:23–35)

St. Luke: Then he called two of the centurions and said,

Tribune: At the third hour of the night get ready two hundred soldiers with seventy horsemen and two hundred spearmen to go as far as Caesarea. Also provide mounts for Paul to ride, and bring him safely to Felix the governor.

St. Luke: And he wrote a letter to this effect:

Tribune: Claudius Lysias to his Excellency the governor Felix, greeting. This man was seized by the Jews, and was about to be killed by them, when I came upon them with the soldiers and rescued him, having learned that he was a Roman citizen. And desiring to know the charge on which they accused him, I brought him down to their council. I found that he was accused about questions of their law, but charged with nothing deserving death or imprisonment. And when it was disclosed to me that there would be a plot against the man, I sent him to you at once, ordering his accusers also to state before you what they have against him.

St. Luke: So the soldiers, according to their instructions, took Paul and brought him by night to Antipatris. And on the morrow they returned to the barracks, leaving the horsemen to go on with him. When they came to Caesarea and delivered the letter to the governor, they presented Paul also before him. On reading the letter, he asked to what province he belonged. When he learned that he was from Cilicia he said,

Felix: I will hear you when your accusers arrive.

St. Luke: And he commanded him to be guarded in Herod's praetorium.

Acts Chapter 24

~ Paul before Felix at Caesarea (Acts 24:1–9)

St. Luke: And after five days the high priest Ananias came down with some elders and a spokesman, one Tertullus. They laid before the governor their case against Paul; and when he was called, Tertullus began to accuse him, saying:

Tertullus: Since through you we enjoy much peace, and since by your provision, most excellent Felix, reforms are introduced on behalf of this nation, in every way and everywhere we accept this with all gratitude. But, to detain you no further, I beg you in your kindness to hear us briefly.

For we have found this man a pestilent fellow, an agitator among all the Jews throughout the world, and a ringleader of the sect of the Nazarenes. He even tried to profane the temple, but we seized him. By examining him yourself you will be able to learn from him about everything of which we accuse him.

St. Luke: The Jews also joined in the charge, affirming that all this was so.

* Paul's Defense Before Felix (Acts 24:10–23); LC–1794; C8–2471

St. Luke: And when the governor had motioned to him to speak, Paul replied:

Paul: Realizing that for many years you have been judge over this nation, I cheerfully make my defense. As you may ascertain, it is not more than twelve days since I went up to worship at Jerusalem; and they did not find me disputing with any one or stirring up a crowd, either in the temple or in the synagogues, or in the city. Neither can they prove to you what they now bring up against me.

But this I admit to you, that according to the Way, which they call a sect, I worship the God of our fathers, believing everything laid down by the law or written in the prophets, having a hope in God which these themselves accept, that there will be a resurrection of both the just and the unjust. So I always take pains to have a clear conscience toward God and toward men.

Now after some years I came to bring to my nation alms and offerings. As I was doing this, they found me purified in the temple, without any crowd or tumult. But some Jews from Asia—they ought to be here before you and to make an accusation, if they have anything against me. Or else let these men themselves say what wrongdoing they found when I stood before the council, except this one thing which I cried out while standing among them, "With respect to the resurrection of the dead I am on trial before you this day."

St. Luke: But Felix, having a rather accurate knowledge of the Way, put them off, saying,

Felix: When Lysias the tribune comes down, I will decide your case.

St. Luke: Then he gave orders to the centurion that he should be kept in custody but should have some liberty, and that none of his friends should be prevented from attending to his needs.

~ Paul Held in Custody (Acts 24:24–27)

St. Luke: After some days Felix came with his wife Drusilla, who was a Jewess; and he sent for Paul and heard him speak upon faith in Christ Jesus. And as he argued about justice and self-control and future judgment, Felix was alarmed and said,

Felix: Go away for the present; when I have an opportunity I will summon you.

St. Luke: At the same time he hoped that money would be given him by Paul. So he sent for him often and conversed with him. But when two years had elapsed, Felix was succeeded by Porcius Festus; and desiring to do the Jews a favor, Felix left Paul in prison.

Acts Chapter 25

~ Paul Appeals to Caesar (Acts 25:1–12)

St. Luke: Now when Festus had come into his province, after three days he went up to Jerusalem from Caesarea. And the chief priests and the principal men of the Jews informed him against Paul; and they urged him, asking as a favor to have the man sent to Jerusalem, planning an ambush to kill him on the way. Festus replied that Paul was being kept at Caesarea, and that he himself intended to go there shortly. So, said he,

Festus: Let the men of authority among you go down with me, and if there is anything wrong about the man, let them accuse him.

St. Luke: When he had stayed among them not more than eight or ten days, he went down to Caesarea; and the next day he took his seat on the tribunal and ordered Paul to be brought. And when he had come, the Jews who had gone down from Jerusalem stood about him, bringing against him many serious charges which they could not prove. Paul said in his defense,

Paul: Neither against the law of the Jews, nor against the temple, nor against Caesar have I offended at all.

St. Luke: But Festus, wishing to do the Jews a favor, said to Paul,

Festus: Do you wish to go up to Jerusalem, and there be tried on these charges before me?

St. Luke: But Paul said,

Paul: I am standing before Caesar's tribunal, where I ought to be tried; to the Jews I have done no wrong, as you know very well. If then I am a wrongdoer, and have committed anything for which I deserve to die, I do not seek to escape death; but if there is nothing in their charges against me, no one can give me up to them. I appeal to Caesar.

St. Luke: Then Festus, when he had conferred with his council, answered,

Festus: You have appealed to Caesar; to Caesar you shall go.

~ Festus Consults King Agrippa (Acts 25:13–22)

St. Luke: Now when some days had passed, Agrippa the king and Bernice arrived at Caesarea to welcome Festus. And as they stayed there many days, Festus laid Paul's case before the king, saying,

Festus: There is a man left prisoner by Felix; and when I was at Jerusalem, the chief priests and the elders of the Jews gave information about him, asking for sentence against him. I answered them that it was not the custom of the Romans to give up any one before the accused met the accusers face to face, and had opportunity to make his defense concerning the charge laid against him.

When therefore they came together here, I made no delay, but on the next day took my seat on the tribunal and ordered the man to be brought in. When the accusers stood up, they brought no charge in his case of such evils as I supposed; but they had certain points of dispute with him about their own superstition and about one Jesus, who was dead, but whom Paul asserted to be alive. Being at a loss how to investigate these questions, I asked whether he wished to go to Jerusalem and be tried there regarding them. But when Paul had appealed to be kept in custody for the decision of the emperor, I commanded him to be held until I could send him to Caesar.

St. Luke: And Agrippa said to Festus,

King Agrippa: I should like to hear the man myself.

Festus: Tomorrow,

St. Luke: said he,

Festus: You shall hear him.

~ Paul is Brought Before Agrippa (Acts 25:23–37)

St. Luke: So on the next day Agrippa and Bernice came with great pomp, and they entered the audience hall with the military tribunes and the prominent men of the city. Then by command of Festus Paul was brought in. And Festus said,

Festus: King Agrippa and all who are present with us, you see this man about whom the whole Jewish people petitioned me, both at Jerusalem and here, shouting that he ought not to live any longer. But I found that he had done nothing deserving death; and as he himself appealed to the emperor, I decided to send him. But I have nothing definite to write to my lord about him. Therefore I have brought him before you, and, especially before you, King Agrippa, that, after we have examined him, I may have something to write. For it seems to me unreasonable, in sending a prisoner, not to indicate the charges against him.

Acts Chapter 26

~ Paul Makes His Defense Before Agrippa (Acts 26:1–11)

St. Luke: Agrippa said to Paul,

King Agrippa: You have permission to speak for yourself.

St. Luke: Then Paul stretched out his hand and made his defense:

Paul: I think myself fortunate that it is before you, King Agrippa, I am to make my defense today against all the accusations of the Jews, because you are especially familiar with all customs and controversies of the Jews; therefore I beg you to listen to me patiently.

My manner of life from my youth, spent from the beginning among my own nation and at Jerusalem, is known by all the Jews. They have known for a long time, if they are willing to testify, that according to the strictest party of our religion I have lived as a Pharisee. And now I stand here on trial for hope in the promise made by God to our fathers, to which our twelve tribes hope to attain, as they earnestly worship night and day. And for this hope I am accused by Jews, O king! Why is it thought incredible by any of you that God raises the dead?

I myself was convinced that I ought to do many things in opposing the name of Jesus of Nazareth. And I did so in Jerusalem; I not only shut up many of the saints in prison, by authority from the chief priests, but when they were put to death I cast my vote against them. And I punished them often in all the synagogues and tried to make them blaspheme; and in raging fury against them, I persecuted them even to foreign cities.

~ Paul Tells of His Conversion (Acts 26:12–18)

St. Luke: Thus I journeyed to Damascus with the authority and commission of the chief priests. At midday, O king, I saw on the way a light from heaven, brighter than the sun, shining round me and those who journeyed with me. And when we had all fallen to the ground, I heard a voice saying to me in the Hebrew language,

Jesus: Saul, Saul, why do you persecute me? It hurts you to kick against the goads.

Paul: And I said, "Who are you, Lord?" And the Lord said,

Jesus: I am Jesus whom you are persecuting. But rise and stand upon your feet; for I have appeared to you for this purpose, to appoint you to serve and bear witness to the things in which you have seen me and to those in which I will appear to you, delivering you from the people and from the Gentiles—to whom I send you to open their eyes, that they may turn from darkness to light and from the power of Satan to God, that they may receive forgiveness of sins and a place among those who are sanctified by faith in me.

Paul Tells of His Preaching (Acts 26:19–23); F4–601

Paul: Wherefore, O King Agrippa, I was not disobedient to the heavenly vision, but declared first to those at Damascus, then at Jerusalem and throughout all the country of Judea, and also to the Gentiles, that they should repent and turn to God and perform deeds worthy of their repentance.

For this reason the Jews seized me in the temple and tried to kill me. To this day I have had the help that comes from God, and so I stand here testifying both to small and great, saying nothing but what the prophets and Moses said would come to pass: that the Christ must suffer, and that, by being the first to rise from the dead, he would proclaim light both to the people and to the Gentiles.

~ Paul Appeals to Agrippa to Believe (Acts 26:24–32)

St. Luke: And as he thus made his defense, Festus said with a loud voice,

Festus: Paul, you are mad; your great learning is turning you mad.

St. Luke: But Paul said,

Paul: I am not mad, most excellent Festus, but I am speaking the sober truth. For the king knows about these things, and to him I speak freely; for I am persuaded that none of these things has escaped his notice, for this was not done in a corner. King Agrippa, do you believe the prophets? I know that you believe.

St. Luke: And Agrippa said to Paul,

King Agrippa: In a short time you think to make me a Christian!

St. Luke: And Paul said,

Paul: Whether short or long, I would to God that not only you but also all who hear me this day might become such as I am—except for these chains.

St. Luke: Then the king rose, and the governor and Bernice and those who were sitting with them; and when they had withdrawn, they said to one another,

King Agrippa, Bernice, and Festus: This man is doing nothing to deserve death or imprisonment.

St. Luke: And Agrippa said to Festus,

King Agrippa: This man could have been set free if he had not appealed to Caesar.

Acts Chapter 27

~ Paul Sails for Rome (Acts 27:1–12)

St. Luke: And when it was decided that we should sail for Italy, they delivered Paul and some other prisoners to a centurion of the Augustan Cohort, named Julius. And embarking in a ship of Adramyttium, which was about to sail to the ports along the coast of Asia, we put to sea, accompanied by Aristarchus, a Macedonian from Thessalonica.

The next day we put in at Sidon; and Julius treated Paul kindly, and gave him leave to go to his friends and be cared for. And putting to sea from there we sailed under the lee of Cyprus, because the winds were against us. And when we had sailed across the sea which is off Cilicia and Pamphylia, we came to Myra in Lycia.

There the centurion found a ship of Alexandria sailing for Italy, and put us on board. We sailed slowly for a number of days, and arrived with difficulty off Cnidus, and as the wind did not allow us to go on, we sailed under the lee of Crete off Salmone. Coasting along it with difficulty, we came to a place called Fair Havens, near which was the city of Lasea.

As much time had been lost, and the voyage was already dangerous because the fast had already gone by, Paul advised them, saying,

Paul: Sirs, I perceive that the voyage will be with injury and much loss, not only of the cargo and the ship, but also of our lives.

St. Luke: But the centurion paid more attention to the captain and to the owner of the ship than to what Paul said. And because the harbor was not suitable to winter in, the majority advised to put to sea from there, on the chance that somehow they could reach Phoenix, a harbor of Crete, looking northeast and southeast, and winter there.

The Storm at Sea (Acts 27:13–38); F1–334

St. Luke: And when the south wind blew gently, supposing that they had obtained their purpose, they weighed anchor and sailed along Crete, close inshore. But soon a tempestuous wind, called the northeaster, struck down from the land; and when the ship was caught and could not face the wind, we gave way to it and were driven.

And running under the lee of a small island called Cauda, we managed with difficulty to secure the boat; after hoisting it up, they took measures to undergird the ship; then, fearing that they should run on the Syrtis, they lowered the gear, and so were driven. As we were violently storm-tossed, they began next day to throw the cargo overboard; and the third day they cast out with their own hands the tackle of the ship.

And when neither sun nor stars appeared for many a day, and no small tempest lay on us, all hope of our being saved was at last abandoned. As they had been long without food, Paul then came forward among them and said,

Paul: Men, you should have listened to me, and should not have set sail from Crete and incurred this injury and loss. I now bid you take heart; for there will be no loss of life among you, but only of the ship. For this very night there stood by me an angel of the God to whom I belong and whom I worship, and he said,

Angel: Do not be afraid, Paul; you must stand before Caesar; and lo, God has granted you all those who sail with you.

Paul: So take heart, men, for I have faith in God that it will be exactly as I have been told. But we shall have to run on some island.

St. Luke: When the fourteenth night had come, as we were drifting across the sea of Adria, about midnight the sailors suspected that they were nearing land. So they sounded and found twenty fathoms; a little farther on they sounded again and found fifteen fathoms. And fearing that we might run on the rocks, they let out four anchors from the stern, and prayed for day to come.

And as the sailors were seeking to escape from the ship, and had lowered the boat into the sea, under pretense of laying out anchors from the bow, Paul said to the centurion and the soldiers,

Paul: Unless these men stay in the ship, you cannot be saved.

St. Luke: Then the soldiers cut away the ropes of the boat, and let it go. As day was about to dawn, Paul urged them all to take some food, saying,

Paul: Today is the fourteenth day that you have continued in suspense and without food, having taken nothing. Therefore I urge you to take some food; it will give you strength, since not a hair is to perish from the head of any of you.

St. Luke: And when he had said this, he took bread, and giving thanks to God in the presence of all he broke it and began to eat. Then they all were encouraged and ate some food themselves. (We were in all two hundred and seventy-six persons in the ship.) And when they had eaten enough, they lightened the ship, throwing out the wheat into the sea.

~ The Shipwreck (Acts 27:39–44)

St. Luke: Now when it was day, they did not recognize the land, but they noticed a bay with a beach, on which they planned if possible to bring the ship ashore. So they cast off the anchors and left them in the sea, at the same time loosening the ropes that tied the rudders; then hoisting the foresail to the wind they made for the beach. But striking a shoal they ran the vessel aground; the bow stuck and remained immovable, and the stern was broken up by the surf.

The soldiers' plan was to kill the prisoners, lest any should swim away and escape; but the centurion, wishing to save Paul, kept them from carrying out their purpose. He ordered those who could swim to throw themselves overboard first and make for the land, and the rest on planks or on pieces of the ship. And so it was that all escaped to land.

Acts Chapter 28

~ Paul on the Island of Malta (Acts 28:1–10)

St. Luke: After we had escaped, we then learned that the island was called Malta. And the natives showed us unusual kindness, for they kindled a fire and welcomed us all, because it had begun to rain and was cold. Paul had gathered a bundle of sticks and put them on the fire, when a viper came out because of the heat and fastened on his hand. When the natives saw the creature hanging from his hand, they said to one another,

Natives: No doubt this man is a murderer. Though he has escaped from the sea, justice has not allowed him to live.

St. Luke: He, however, shook off the creature into the fire and suffered no harm. They waited, expecting him to swell up or suddenly fall down dead; but when they had waited a long time and saw no misfortune come to him, they changed their minds and said that he was a god.

Now in the neighborhood of that place were lands belonging to the chief man of the island, named Publius, who received us and entertained us hospitably for three days. It happened that the father of Publius lay sick with fever and dysentery; and Paul visited him and prayed, and putting his hands on him healed him. And when this had taken place, the rest of the people on the island who had diseases also came and were cured. They presented many gifts to us; and when we sailed, they put on board whatever we needed.

~ Paul Comes to Rome (Acts 28:11–16)

St. Luke: After three months we set sail in a ship which had wintered in the island, a ship of Alexandria, with the Twin Brothers as figurehead. Putting in at Syracuse, we stayed there for three days. And from there we made a circuit and arrived at Rhegium; and after one day a south wind sprang up, and on the second day we came to Puteoli. There we found brethren, and were invited to stay with them for seven days. And so we came to Rome.

And the brethren there, when they heard of us, came as far as the Forum of Appius and Three Taverns to meet us. On seeing them Paul thanked God and took courage. And when we came into Rome, Paul was allowed to stay by himself, with the soldier that guarded him.

Paul and Jewish Leaders in Rome (Acts 28:17–22); F2–453

St. Luke: After three days he called together the local leaders of the Jews; and when they had gathered, he said to them,

Paul: Brethren, though I had done nothing against the people or the customs of our fathers, yet I was delivered prisoner from Jerusalem into the hands of the Romans. When they had examined me, they wished to set me at liberty, because there was no reason for the death penalty in my case. But when the Jews objected, I was compelled to appeal to Caesar—though I had no charge to bring against my nation. For this reason therefore I have asked to see you and speak with you, since it is because of the hope of Israel that I am bound with this chain.

St. Luke: And they said to him,

Jews of Rome: We have received no letters from Judea about you, and none of the brethren coming here has reported or spoken any evil about you. But we desire to hear from you what your views are; for with regard to this sect we know that everywhere it is spoken against.

~ Paul Preaches in Rome (Acts 28:23–31)

St. Luke: When they had appointed a day for him, they came to him at his lodging in great numbers. And he expounded the matter to them from morning till evening, testifying to the kingdom of God and trying to convince them about Jesus both from the law of Moses and from the prophets. And some were convinced by what he said, while others disbelieved.

So, as they disagreed among themselves, they departed, after Paul had made one statement:

Paul: The Holy Spirit was right in saying to your fathers through Isaiah the prophet:

Holy Spirit: Go to this people, and say, "You shall indeed hear but never understand, and you shall indeed see but never perceive. For this people's heart has grown dull, and their ears are heavy of hearing, and their eyes they have closed; lest they should perceive with their eyes, and hear with their ears, and understand with their heart, and turn for me to heal them."

Paul: Let it be known to you then that this salvation of God has been sent to the Gentiles; they will listen.

St. Luke: And he lived there two whole years at his own expense, and welcomed all who came to him, preaching the kingdom of God and teaching about the Lord Jesus Christ quite openly and unhindered.

REVELATION 11 AND 12

Revelation Chapter 11

~ The Two Witnesses (Rv 11:1–14)

St. John: Then I was given a measuring rod like a staff, and I was told:

Angel: Rise and measure the temple of God and the altar and those who worship there, but do not measure the court outside the temple; leave that out, for it is given over to the nations, and they will trample over the holy city for forty-two months. And I will grant my two witnesses power to prophesy for one thousand two hundred and sixty days, clothed in sackcloth.

St. John: These are the two olive trees and the two lampstands which stand before the Lord of the earth. And if any one would harm them, fire pours out from their mouth and consumes their foes; if any one would harm them, thus he is doomed to be killed. They have power to shut the sky, that no rain may fall during the days of their prophesying, and they have power over the waters to turn them into blood, and to smite the earth with every plague, as often as they desire.

St. John 2: And when they have finished their testimony, the beast that ascends from the bottomless pit will make war upon them and conquer them and kill them, and their dead bodies will lie in the street of the great city which is allegorically called Sodom and Egypt, where their Lord was crucified. For three days and a half men from the peoples and tribes and tongues and nations gaze at their dead bodies and refuse to let them be placed in a tomb, and those who dwell on the earth will rejoice over them and make merry and exchange presents, because these two prophets had been a torment to those who dwell on the earth.

St. John 3: But after the three and a half days a breath of life from God entered them, and they stood up on their feet, and great fear fell on those who saw them. Then they heard a loud voice from heaven saying to them,

Loud voice: Come up here!

St. John: And in the sight of their foes they went up to heaven in a cloud. And at that hour there was a great earthquake, and a tenth of the city fell; seven thousand people were killed in the earthquake, and the rest were terrified and gave glory to the God of heaven. The second woe has passed; behold, the third woe is soon to come. Then the seventh angel blew his trumpet, and there were loud voices in heaven, saying,

* The Seventh Trumpet (Rv 11:15–19); F2–450

Loud voice: The kingdom of the world has become the kingdom of our Lord and of his Christ, and he shall reign for ever and ever.

St. John 4: And the twenty-four elders who sit on their thrones before God fell on their faces and worshiped God, saying,

Elders: We give thanks to you, Lord God Almighty, who are and who were, that you have taken your great power and begun to reign. The nations raged, but your wrath came, and the time for the dead to be judged, for rewarding your servants, the prophets and saints, and those who fear your name, both small and great, and for destroying the destroyers of the earth.

St. John 4: Then God's temple in heaven was opened, and the ark of his covenant was seen within his temple; and there were flashes of lightning, loud noises, peals of thunder, an earthquake, and heavy hail.

Revelation Chapter 12

The Woman and the Dragon (Rv 12:1–6); LT–1138

St. John: And a great sign appeared in heaven, a woman clothed with the sun, with the moon under her feet, and on her head a crown of twelve stars; she was with child and she cried out in her pangs of birth, in anguish for delivery. And another sign appeared in heaven; behold, a great red dragon, with seven heads and ten horns, and seven diadems upon his heads. His tail swept down a third of the stars of heaven, and cast them to the earth. And the dragon stood before the woman who was about to bear a child, that he might devour her child when she brought it forth; she brought forth a male child, one who is to rule all the nations with a rod of iron,

St. John: but her child was caught up to God and to his throne, and the woman fled into the wilderness, where she has a place prepared by God, in which to be nourished for one thousand two hundred and sixty days.

* Michael Defeats the Dragon (Rv 12:7–12); F1–391; LP7–2852

St. John 2: Now war arose in heaven, Michael and his angels fighting
against the dragon; and the dragon and his angels fought, 8
but they were defeated and there was no longer any place
for them in heaven. And the great dragon was thrown down,
that ancient serpent, who is called the Devil and Satan, the
deceiver of the whole world—he was thrown down to the
earth, and his angels were thrown down with him. And I
heard a loud voice in heaven, saying,

Loud Voice: Now the salvation and the power and the kingdom of our God and the authority of his Christ have come, for the accuser of our brethren has been thrown down, who accuses them day and night before our God. And they have conquered him by the blood of the Lamb and by the word of their testimony, for they loved not their lives even unto death. Rejoice then, O heaven and you that dwell therein! But woe to you, O earth and sea, for the devil has come down to you in great wrath, because he knows that his time is short!

* The Dragon Makes War against the Woman's Offspring (Rv 12:13–17); F3–501; LP7–2853

St. John 3: And when the dragon saw that he had been thrown down to the earth, he pursued the woman who had borne the male child. But the woman was given the two wings of the great eagle that she might fly from the serpent into the wilderness, to the place where she is to be nourished for a time, and times, and half a time. The serpent poured water like a river out of his mouth after the woman, to sweep her away with the flood. But the earth came to the help of the woman, and the earth opened its mouth and swallowed the river which the dragon had poured from his mouth.

St. John 3: Then the dragon was angry with the woman, and went off to make war on the rest of her offspring, on those who keep the commandments of God and bear testimony to Jesus. And he stood on the sand of the sea.

Revelation Chapter 22

* River of the Water of Life (Rv 22:1–7); LT–1137; F12–1023

St. John: Then he showed me the river of the water of life, bright as crystal, flowing from the throne of God and of the Lamb through the middle of the street of the city; also, on either side of the river, the tree of life with its twelve kinds of fruit, yielding its fruit each month; and the leaves of the tree were for the healing of the nations. There shall no more be anything accursed, but the throne of God and of the Lamb shall be in it, and his servants shall worship him; they shall see his face, and his name shall be on their foreheads. And night shall be no more; they need no light of lamp or sun, for the Lord God will be their light, and they shall reign for ever and ever. And he said to me,

Angel: These words are trustworthy and true. And the Lord, the God of the spirits of the prophets, has sent his angel to show his servants what must soon take place.

Jesus: And behold, I am coming soon. Blessed is he who keeps the words of the prophecy of this book.

* Epilogue and Benediction (Rv 22:8–21); S3–1403; LP7–2853

St. John: I John am he who heard and saw these things. And when I heard and saw them, I fell down to worship at the feet of the angel who showed them to me; but he said to me,

Angel: You must not do that! I am a fellow servant with you and your brethren the prophets, and with those who keep the words of this book. Worship God.

St. John: And he said to me,

Angel: Do not seal up the words of the prophecy of this book, for the time is near. Let the evildoer still do evil, and the filthy still be filthy, and the righteous still do right, and the holy still be holy.

Jesus: Behold, I am coming soon, bringing my recompense, to repay every one for what he has done. I am the Alpha and the Omega, the first and the last, the beginning and the end. Blessed are those who wash their robes, that they may have the right to the tree of life and that they may enter the city by the gates. Outside are the dogs and sorcerers and fornicators and murderers and idolaters, and everyone who loves and practices falsehood. I Jesus have sent my angel to you with this testimony for the churches. I am the root and the offspring of David, the bright morning star.

St. John: The Spirit and the Bride say,

The Spirit and the Bride: Come.

St. John: And let him who hears say,

Him who hears: Come.

St. John: And let him who is thirsty come, let him who desires take the water of life without price. I warn everyone who hears the words of the prophecy of this book: if any one adds to them, God will add to him the plagues described in this book, and if any one takes away from the words of the book of this prophecy, God will take away his share in the tree of life and in the holy city, which are described in this book. He who testifies to these things says,

Jesus: Surely I am coming soon.

St. John: Amen. Come, Lord Jesus! The grace of the Lord Jesus be with all the saints. Amen.

Scriptures for the Rosary Mysteries

Joyful Mysteries	Some Related Scripture Verses
1 The Annunciation	Lk 1:26-38; Mt 1:18-25
2. The Visitation	Lk 1:39-56
3, The Birth of Our Lord Jesus Christ	Mt 2:1-11; Lk 2:1-20, Jn 1:1-14, Gal 4:4-7
4. The Presentation of Jesus in the Temple	Lk 2:22-39
5. The Finding of the Child Jesus in the Temple	Lk 2:41-52

Luminous Mysteries	Some Related Scripture Verses
1. The Baptism of Jesus	Mt 3:13-17; Mk 1:9-11; Lk 3:21-22; Jn 1:29-34
2. The Wedding Feast at Cana	Jn 2:1-12
3. The Proclamation of the Kingdom of God	Mt 10:1-42; Mk 1:15; Lk 7:47-48; Lk 9:1-6; Lk 10:1-24; Jn 3:1-36; Jn 18:33-37;
4. The Transfiguration	Mt 17:1-13; Mk 9:1-12; Lk 9:28-36; 2 Pt 1:16-21
5. The Institution of the Eucharist	Mt 26:26-29; Mk 14:22-25; Lk 22:14-20; Jn 6:22-70

Sorrowful Mysteries	Some Related Scripture Verses
1.The Agony in the Garden	Mt 26:36-55; Mk 14:32-52; Lk 22:39-53; Jn 18:1-11
2. The Scourging at the Pillar	Mt 27:26; Mk 15:15; Jn 19:1
3. The Crowning with Thorns	Mt 27:29; Mk 15:17; Jn 19:2
4. The Carrying of the Cross	Mt 27:31-32; Mk 15:20-22; Lk 23:26-32; Jn 19:17
5. The Crucifixion	Mt 27:35-50; Mk 15:24-37; Lk 23:33-46; Jn 19:18-30

Glorious Mysteries	Some Related Scripture Verses
1.The Resurrection of Jesus	Mt 28:1-15; Mk 16:1-18; Lk 24:1-49; Jn 20:1-23;
2. The Ascension of Jesus into Heaven	Mk 16:19-20; Lk 24:50-52; Acts 1:1-11
3. The Descent of the Holy Spirit	Jn 20:19-23; Acts 2:1-41; Acts 10:1-48, Acts 19:1-7
4. The Assumption of Mary	Lk 1:39-56; Rev 11*
5. The Crowning of Mary as Queen of Heaven and Earth	Lk 1:26-38;[1] Rev 12**

*The Assumption of Mary into Heaven is not in the Bible, but it may be foreshadowed in chapter 11 of the Book of Revelation which portrays the assumption of two figures thought to represent Enoch and Elijah who both according to Genesis 5:24 and 2 Kings 2:11 were taken up without dying. Revelation 11 concludes with St. John stating that, "God's temple in heaven was opened, and the ark of his covenant was seen within his temple."[13] Mary carried Jesus within her own body; St. Luke, in his account of the Visitation (cf. Lk 1:39–56), by paralleling an Old Testament scene regarding the Ark of the Covenant (cf. 2 Sm 6:10–14) infers that the Blessed Virgin Mary is the new Ark of the Covenant.

**The Crowning of Mary is not stated in the Bible, but Revelation 12 portrays the woman "clothed with the sun" pregnant with the child destined to "rule all the nations." crowned with twelve stars. Since Mary is the "Theotokos"–Mother of God—this may refer to the Crowning of Mary as Queen of Heaven and Earth.

www.gospel Theater.org

13. Rv 11:19.

www.ingramcontent.com/pod-product-compliance
Lightning Source LLC
LaVergne TN
LVHW010628110826
845149LV00014B/2805